INTRODUCING MACROECONOMIC ANALYSIS

INTRODUCING
MACROECONOMIC
ANALYSIS

ISSUES, QUESTIONS, AND COMPETING VIEWS

EDITED BY

Hassan Bougrine
Laurentian University

Mario Seccareccia
University of Ottawa

2010
Emond Montgomery Publications Limited
Toronto, Canada

Emond Montgomery Publications Limited
60 Shaftesbury Avenue
Toronto ON M4T 1A3
http://www.emp.ca/university

Printed in Canada on 100 percent recycled paper.

We acknowledge the financial support of the Government of Canada through the Book Publishing Industry Development Program (BPIDP) for our publishing activities.

Acquisitions and development editor: Mike Thompson
Marketing manager: Christine Davidson
Sales manager, higher education: Dave Stokaluk
Supervising editor: Jim Lyons
Copy editor: Sarah Gleadow
Proofreader: David Handelsman
Text designer and typesetter: Tara Wells
Indexer: Paula Pike
Cover designers: Stephen Cribbin & Simon Evers

Library and Archives Canada Cataloguing in Publication

Introducing macroeconomic analysis : issues, questions, and competing views / edited by Hassan Bougrine, Mario Seccareccia.

Includes index.
ISBN 978-1-55239-313-0

1. Macroeconomics—Textbooks. I. Bougrine, Hassan II. Seccareccia, Mario III. Title.

HB172.5.I568 2009   339   C2009-901423-8

Contents

III Macroeconomic Policies

IV International Economic Relations

Preface

Although economists agree on a lot more than the media generally suggest, there exist fundamental differences that at times seem completely intractable to the vast majority of students learning economics for the first time. Many introductory textbooks reinforce this problem by systematically neglecting to cover ideas that are not from the mainstream. These books often make little effort to present theoretical and methodological differences, even though the intellectual landscape of the discipline encompasses a true rainbow of perspectives. This is especially problematic in macroeconomics, where policy debates permeate practically all aspects of the subject matter. Yet textbooks frequently glaze over such differences, to the detriment of the student and to the disappointment of the excluded currents of thought, which sometimes describe this neglect as "autistic" behaviour that seeks to obfuscate rather than clarify student comprehension of what economics is all about. A different approach to introducing the discipline is desirable.

For a long time, we have felt the need for a book that would introduce the various perspectives at a level that would be accessible to the informed public, as well as to students at the introductory and intermediate levels of economics. Hence, when Emond Montgomery Publications invited us to put together a book that would systematically provide competing perspectives on all the broad areas of macroeconomics, we felt both the excitement that our wish might finally materialize, and the fear that the challenge might be insurmountable. With the support of the publisher, with the collaboration of the authors, and also, perhaps, with the help of the current global conjuncture that has brought to light the need to rethink the nature of our economic system, we are very pleased to say that we have achieved our goal.

The 26 contributions from the authors provide an updated analysis of all the major areas of introductory macroeconomics. The result is a book that can be used as a main text and that is also an ideal complement for students of economics who wish to push past the current limits of understanding delineated in most existing macroeconomic textbooks.

Acknowledgments

This book could not have come to fruition without the pregnant suggestion, support, and strong encouragement from Mike Thompson, acquisitions and development editor at Emond Montgomery Publications; for his efforts we are particularly grateful. We also wish to thank Sarah Gleadow, the copy editor, and Jim Lyons, the supervisor of Emond Montgomery's editorial and production team. We are also grateful to Ron Kneebone of the University of Calgary, Brian VanBlarcom of Acadia University, and Marianne Vigneault of Bishop's University for their thoughtful suggestions during the development of this project.

Most of all, we thank the authors, whose excellent contributions will be invaluable for the training of a new generation of students of economics, some of whom will continue to carry forward the conversation from where the book leaves off and make their own substantive contributions to a dynamic, evolving discipline.

About the Authors

David Andolfatto
Professor of Economics at Simon Fraser University

Eugene Beaulieu
Associate Professor of Economics at the University of Calgary

Manfred A. Bienefeld
Professor in the School of Public Policy and Administration at Carleton University

Ronald G. Bodkin
Professor Emeritus of Economics at the University of Ottawa

Hassan Bougrine
Professor of Economics at Laurentian University and Director of the International Economic Policy Institute

Thomas J. Courchene
Jarislowsky-Deutsch Professor of Economic and Financial Policy and Director of the Institute of Intergovernmental Relations at Queen's University

Gerald Epstein
Professor of Economics and Co-Director of the Political Economy Research Institute at the University of Massachusetts, Amherst

Pierre Fortin
Professor of Economics at the Université du Québec à Montréal

J.A. (Jack) Galbraith
Adjunct Research Professor of Economics at Carleton University

David Gray
Professor of Economics at the University of Ottawa

Ricardo Grinspun
Associate Professor of Economics at York University

Marc Lavoie
Professor of Economics at the University of Ottawa

Edwin Le Héron
Associate Professor of Economics at the Bordeaux Institute of Political Studies, France

Robert Prasch
Professor of Economics at Middlebury College, Vermont

Louis-Philippe Rochon
Associate Professor of Economics at Laurentian University

Nicholas Rowe
Associate Professor of Economics at Carleton University

Dominick Salvatore
Distinguished Professor of Economics and Director of the PhD Program in the Department of Economics at Fordham University

Eric Santor
Research Director, International Economic Analysis Department, Bank of Canada

William Scarth
Professor of Economics at McMaster University

Lawrence L. Schembri
Chief, International Economic Analysis Department, Bank of Canada

Carlos Schönerwald da Silva
Associate Professor of Economics at the University of the Sinos Valley (Unisinos), Brazil

Mario Seccareccia
Professor of Economics at the University of Ottawa and Editor of the International Journal of Political Economy

John Smithin
Professor in the Department of Economics and the Schulich School of Business at York University

Jim Stanford
Economist in the Research Department of the Canadian Auto Workers (CAW)

Niels Veldhuis
Director of Fiscal Studies at the Fraser Institute and Economics faculty member at Kwantlen Polytechnic University

Matías Vernengo
Associate Professor of Economics at the University of Utah

William Watson
Associate Professor and Chairman of the Economics Department at McGill University

L. Randall Wray
Professor of Economics at the University of Missouri—Kansas City

Key Figures in Economics

 Adam Smith
(1723–1790)

 Karl Marx
(1818–1883)

 Alfred Marshall
(1842–1924)

 Thorstein Veblen
(1857–1929)

 Irving Fisher
(1867–1947)

 John Maynard Keynes
(1883–1946)

 Friedrich von Hayek
(1899–1992)

 Joan Robinson
(1903–1983)

 Milton Friedman
(1912–2006)

 John Kenneth Galbraith
(1908–2006)

General Introduction

Hassan Bougrine and Mario Seccareccia

At the end of his most famous book, *The General Theory of Employment, Interest and Money* (1936)—which some would argue gave birth to modern macroeconomic analysis—John Maynard Keynes wrote: "The ideas of economists and political philosophers, both when they are right and when they are wrong, are more powerful than is commonly understood. Indeed, the world is ruled by little else."* We very much believe in the power of ideas to shape the world around us. Although the struggle over ideas can sometimes be a source of conflict that can be politically, socially, and economically destructive, in an open society differences in ideas are above all a source of intellectual enrichment and progress. It was the celebrated classical economist Adam Smith who long ago recognized the importance of the "marketplace of ideas" and pointed to how the powerful, instinctive desire of humans to persuade can be harnessed for socially productive purposes. By encouraging such a dialogue among economists, this book seeks the same end.

Instead of presenting a set of ready-made answers to economic problems, we have chosen to invite you to join a conversation among economists so as to understand better how the latter explain diverse macroeconomic phenomena that are traditionally discussed at both the introductory and the intermediate levels in macroeconomic theory. In the process, you will not only learn powerful new concepts in the various areas of macroeconomics, but will discover how economists have often made use of these concepts to defend competing policy perspectives.

The financial crisis that began in 2007 caused tremendous damage to the economy in terms of firms' closures and job losses, but seems to have made policy-makers much more pragmatic in their quest to lessen the impact of the crisis. In this context, even some very staunch mainstream economists who have traditionally opposed government intervention have, through *force majeure*, shown greater enthusiasm about the need for a stabilization policy. This represented a remarkable change in opinions and, some would argue, a welcome rapprochement between the various schools of thought. While it may be premature to conclude that a new consensus has emerged about issues that have divided economists in the past, the magnitude of the crisis has slowly but surely led to a new configuration of economic ideas.

---

* John Maynard Keynes, *The General Theory of Employment, Interest and Money* (London: Macmillan, 1936), 383.

Even Nobel laureates in economics—who have at times exhibited less inclination toward addressing what have sometimes been described as the "mundane" problems of public policy—have been showing greater willingness to put their theories to the test by proposing actual policies to deal with recessions, financial and banking crises, and other economic problems. One has only to look at how outspoken such distinguished economists as Robert Solow, Joseph Stiglitz, and—most recently—Paul Krugman (who received the Bank of Sweden Prize in Economics in Memory of Alfred Nobel in 1987, 2001, and 2008, respectively) have become. This greater openness to debate over public policy matters has made some mainstream economists more receptive to suggestions, and even criticism, from scholars whose views they do not necessarily share. The resulting dialogue has proven fruitful in the sense that it has prodded economists to generate new ideas and new ways to improve our understanding of the environment in which we live.

It is our belief that this dialogue must continue, and that discussion among competing views must be encouraged if we are serious about creating a healthy and creative environment for students and future generations of economists. Indeed, our personal experience has shown that students learn better—and, in fact, become more innovative—when they are presented with different interpretations and readings of the same facts. Our aim is to encourage students to develop inquisitive minds and critical thinking skills. In this respect, this book represents a clear methodological break from previous traditions in textbook writing, which produced texts that provide what is essentially a monistic view of economics. Unlike the biblical analogy of the Tower of Babel, methodological pluralism breathes life into the economics discourse and promotes progress if the channels of communication are opened to creative, reasoned thinking.

To create this text, we have selected 13 major topics in macroeconomics that generally coincide with chapter-by-chapter issues discussed in most textbooks and asked leading economists to debate them in a style that is accessible to students at the introductory and intermediate levels. The book is structured so that the first three parts deal mainly with domestic issues, with a clear focus on the role of government policies and how these affect the functioning of markets, consumption, investment, employment, taxing, spending, and the creation of money. The fourth part is devoted to international economic relations and includes debate on such topics as free trade, the movements of international money and exchange rates, and globalization and poverty. For each topic, we present the most recent thoughts and explanations from both the more established, orthodox perspective (usually the neoclassical approach) and the alternative, heterodox view (primarily the institutionalist, post-Keynesian, and Marxian approaches). It is our hope that this will generate a lively debate both inside and outside of the classroom.

The authors not only represent different perspectives in economic theory, but come from different parts of the world, bringing with them a rich international experience. Although the content of this book is directly relevant to Canadian readers, the essays are written in such a way as to allow readers to make comparisons and draw parallels with the experiences of other countries—particularly regarding economic policies affecting crucial issues such as unemployment, inflation, public finance, and globalization, among others. The lessons to be drawn from these policy conclusions are obviously relevant not only for students of economics both in Canada and abroad, but also for policy-makers around the world. The ultimate objective of this learning and exchange of ideas is to allow all participants to achieve a better understanding of how to make the world a better place to live for everyone.

PART I
The Whole Picture

The Market System and the Public Sector: What Role for the State?

COMPETING VIEWS

William Watson, " 'Let the Market Work!' The Market and the Public Sector"

Robert E. Prasch, "Markets, States, and Exchange: An Introduction to Economics"

Editors' Introduction

The debate over how societies should organize and manage their economic affairs has preoccupied philosophers, economists, and other social scientists for centuries. In societies where making a profit was not (or is not) the ultimate goal, the overriding concern has been how to ensure that the production of goods and services meets the needs of the members of the community. This has been true not only for ancient societies of hunter-gatherers but also for some modern, industrialized countries in which the overall production and distribution of wealth is centrally planned by the state.

In private-enterprise capitalist economies, production and distribution are highly decentralized and goods are rationed via the price mechanism. The state's primary involvement is in guaranteeing property rights and ensuring the enforcement of contracts. In such an economy, individuals who possess the capital goods would derive income in excess of what they could obtain purely from their labour, with the profit motive guiding single firms and the individuals managing them. Since the 18th century and beginning with Adam Smith, economists have celebrated the merits of the capitalist economy in successfully channelling private greed toward activities that ultimately maximize social output. However, macroeconomic experience—especially in recent years—would suggest that this might not necessarily generate socially desirable outcomes in terms of the so-called invisible hand of the market. For instance, some firms might resort to predatory behaviour, which has proven to be destructive to the lives of many people and quite disruptive to the entire system.

How should we manage our economy? Should we leave it all to the market, or should we require the government's involvement? According to supporters of the first option, a free market economy in which the government plays only a minimal role is the best way to achieve prosperity and well-being for everyone. This is largely the view defended in the contribution by William Watson. On the other hand, Robert Prasch argues for regulated markets, in which economic activity is carried out according to the government's rules and regulations, and adds the warning that these rules must still be questioned, since they often reflect the views and protect the interests of those who write them.

"Let the Market Work!" The Market and the Public Sector

William Watson

Introduction: Why Study Economics?

Some people who do economics do purely positive economics. "Positive" doesn't mean "uplifting" or "beneficial" or "optimistic," and its opposite isn't "negative." Rather, "positive" or "positivist" economics means "factual" or "descriptive" economics. People study economics to find out why or how things happen. Why does the world price of oil move up or down the way it does? What's the connection between the price of oil and the price of gasoline at the local pump? Why was Argentina one of the five richest nations in the world in the late 1800s but now ranks only 47th on the United Nations' ranking of countries by GDP (United Nations 2008, 229, Table 1)? In fact, this question—why some countries prosper and others don't—was the primary interest of Scottish philosopher Adam Smith when he wrote *An Inquiry into the Nature and Causes of the Wealth of Nations* (published in 1776, the same year as the American Declaration of Independence), a book that many people believe marked the beginning of modern economics.

"Positive economics" is both useful and fascinating. It is useful if you can figure out what's happening—or will happen—to prices in a market you are particularly interested in, perhaps because you run a business in that market or because you are thinking of investing in it. It is fascinating because it can lead to all sorts of conclusions—possibly peculiar at first glance—about why the world evolves as it does. The economic historian David Landes (1997, 46) argues that one of the most important inventions of the Middle Ages was the corrective lens, which effectively doubled the working life of many skilled artisans who otherwise would have lost their skills to bad eyesight. This invention encouraged the economic accumulation that eventually led to the Industrial Revolution. In his 2005 bestseller, *Freakonomics*, University of Chicago Professor Steven Levitt showed how a good understanding of simple economic incentives could help unravel otherwise puzzling examples of behaviour among people as diverse as Japanese Sumo wrestlers, Chicago real estate agents, and members of the Ku Klux Klan.[1] Positive economics is brimming with fascinating nuggets of insight—some perhaps obvious, others quite subtle—into why things happen the way they do.

But as rewarding and as interesting as positive economics can be, I have always been more interested in "normative economics," which studies how to make things work better. (In this context, the opposite of "positive" is "normative.") Applied normative economics deals in questions of public policy. What laws, rules, or incentives will get better results out of the economic system? And what do we mean by "better"? Better for everyone, or for some subset of people, or for this country at the expense of others? Better by what measures, exactly? By the effect on the total output of goods and services, or on people's willingness to pay for different goods and services, or according to some intuitive measure of the overall well-being of the people policy cares most about, such as the poorest members of society?

Good normative economics is built on good positive economics. If we use government policy to change a tax, price, or rule that affects production or consumption—such as outlawing incandescent light bulbs in order to slow down global warming—we need to know the effects this will have on people's behaviour. For example, if they merely double the number of energy-efficient bulbs they use in order to recreate the brighter, warmer lighting they were accustomed to from incandescent bulbs, the desired reduction in energy use may not occur and global warming will be unaffected, in spite of the righteous feeling the policy gives us. But although positive economics is an essential input into normative economics, the normative question, "How do we make something better happen?" is quite different from the positive question, "What happens and why?"

The Market Versus the Public Sector

Much of normative economics is about relatively small questions. For instance, if the government raises the legal minimum wage by 50 cents per hour, will the benefit to those who either keep their jobs and earn higher incomes or work fewer hours for the same income offset the loss to those who lose their jobs because some firms (perhaps even all firms) decide to shut down or to use less labour and more machines rather than pay more for labour? Answering that question with any confidence requires a lot of good positive economics (what will happen to employment, unemployment, workers' wages, and firms' profitability as a result of the forced wage change?) and some equally, maybe even more difficult, philosophical analysis: how do we weigh the financial gain to the winners against the employment loss to the losers?[2]

At a much more general level, however, the big question normative economics most commonly examines is whether it is better to use "the market" or "the public sector" to solve various social problems. Just after the fall of Soviet communism in the early 1990s, some rather silly commentary argued that this grand question had been answered decisively in favour of capitalism—the system that leaves most production in the hands of private interests. The "end of history" supposedly was at hand. But now, with the euphoria of the Cold War's ending having passed, it is clear that, even among the liberal democracies that are in geopolitical ascendance, there are many different ways of organizing economic activity. Some countries, such as Sweden and Denmark, have taxes of more than 48 percent of total economic output (as measured by GDP), while others have total taxation as low as just 28.3 percent of GDP (the United States), 27.9 percent (Japan), and 20.5 percent (Mexico) (OECD 2008, 19, table A). In the same way, some countries favour greater regulation of private economic activity while others prefer substantially less. Except in backwaters like North Korea, the Soviet communist idea that economies should be centrally planned is now utterly dead. History itself, however, is still very much alive. On an almost daily basis, countries find themselves having to decide whether to leave many activities to the market or have the public sector become involved in them. The exact division of responsibility differs from country to country and through time.[3]

The Virtues of the Market

Former British Prime Minister Margaret Thatcher is famous for, among many other things, having once said: "There is no such thing as society." Her political enemies accused her of believing social values either were or should not be important when governments made decisions. In fact, she was simply saying there is no organic, functional agent known as "society."[4] Rather, society is made up of many different actors—institutional, corporate, cooperative, and individual—and the term "society" is merely shorthand for the sum and results of their immensely complex interactions.

In much the same way and for essentially the same reason, it might be said that there is no such thing as "the market." True, some markets occupy a well-defined space; many stock markets operate (or operated, until trading became electronic) in a single, specific building, usually called "the stock exchange." Many small towns still have a farmer's "market" once or twice a week in a central square or common. But when economists talk about "the market," they are usually referring to an analytical concept rather than a real-world space. The market for potatoes, for instance, is made up of all potential buyers and sellers of potatoes. Many participants in that market may be actual buyers and sellers of potatoes—they do in fact exchange potatoes for money (or other things, if they prefer barter to cash). But many others would only engage in potato transactions if the price were much higher (if we are talking about sellers) or lower (if we have in mind the demanders of potatoes). If the price rises high enough, we may all become growers and sellers of potatoes; if it falls very low, even people who really don't like potatoes may end up consuming them.

The interaction of buyers and sellers in the potato market establishes both the price of potatoes and the amount produced and sold. If potatoes are in short supply—that is, if people want to buy more than are currently being sold—then their price will be bid up. If, on the other hand, there are more sellers than buyers, the price will fall. As prices move up and down, the quantity of potatoes produced and consumed will also change. When prices are high, potato growers will be tempted to grow more, and farmers who have been growing other crops may decide to plant potatoes instead. Over time, the new supply may bring prices back down. On the other hand, if in the meantime the demand for potatoes grows (meaning that the number people want at any given price rises), then perhaps the new supply can be accommodated without any decline in price. Economists refer to the price at which demand and supply are equal as the "equilibrium" price—a term that suggests the actual price will come to rest at this value. In fact, if consumers' demands—or, on the "supply side," the costs of producing potatoes—never settle down, the price may never settle down.

Man—and woman—does not live by potatoes alone, of course. People consume thousands and thousands of other goods and services. Not surprisingly, there are markets for almost all of them, with each defined analytically as all the potential buyers and sellers of whichever of these goods and services we are talking about. When economists talk about "the market," they're actually referring—Thatcher-style—to all the people, businesses, and institutions participating in these myriad different markets.[5]

A common catchphrase among economists is "leave it to the market." This is shorthand for saying that the complex interactions of tens of millions of buyers and sellers in the markets for all these thousands of goods and services may be the best way for "society" to make its economic decision about how much of each good or service will be produced and at what price. This may seem naïve, and perhaps it is, but it is based on the startling insight elaborated more than two centuries ago by Adam Smith—namely, that the self-interest of buyers and sellers may lead to potatoes (and almost everything else) making it to people's tables at the lowest possible prices, given the cost of producing them. As he wrote, "It is not from the benevolence of the butcher, the brewer or the baker that we expect our dinner, but from their regard for their own interest" (Smith 1776, chap. II). Suppliers have a strong interest in selling us good products at reasonable prices. They might prefer to sell shoddy products at inflated prices, but if they do, we will take our business elsewhere.[6]

To be slightly technical for a moment, another way of phrasing Smith's idea that "the market" produces the best possible combination of price and quantity is that the "equilibrium" is actually an "optimum." Where we are likely to end up is actually where we would like to end up. The mechanism that accomplishes this is the price of the good. Consumers consider the price of a product and decide whether buying it will leave them better off, given what they must pay for it. If they do decide to buy it, then presumably the increase in their well-being as a result of possessing it will be greater than the decrease in their well-being as a result of giving up the money necessary to buy it. People will never intentionally buy something unless they believe buying it will make them better off. Producers go through the same sort of calculation. They don't want to sell a good at a price lower than its cost of production. They may do so from time to time, but as a long-run strategy the practice is a recipe for going out of business. Producers will therefore aim to keep selling a good or service only if the price they can get for it exceeds its cost of production, an acceptable rate of profit included. They would obviously prefer to sell the good or service at a price that far exceeds its cost of production, but if there are many actual (or even potential) producers around, they will be undercut if they try. As a result, we can expect that consumers will buy all those products whose prices are less than the value they get from consuming them, while producers will produce all those products whose prices are greater than their cost of production. This means that all goods whose benefits to consumers exceed their cost of production will be produced, and no goods whose costs are greater than their benefits. As Martha Stewart would say: "That's a good thing!" And that's what we can expect "the market" to do. In a way, this is not surprising. If "the market" is simply the voluntary interaction of people, then "leaving things to the market" will produce all mutually profitable voluntary exchanges.

Producing all the goods whose benefits are greater than their costs is quite an achievement, but equally important is not producing those goods whose benefits are less than their costs. Producing goods that cost more than they are worth is a waste of time, energy, and other resources. This is why economists are usually suspicious of subsidies for the production of a particular good or service. A subsidy—that is, an extra payment by the government to the producer or consumer of the subsidized good—enables producers to sell it for less than it really cost to produce. But this means consumers value it at less than it cost to produce. They buy it only because the government picks up the difference. Producing things consumers value at less than their cost does not make good economic sense (though see the discussion of "externalities" that follows).

Market Failures

Economists do recognize that markets can fail. In some cases, markets for goods and services simply do not emerge, while in others markets do exist but the equilibrium they produce are not necessarily an optimum. As a result, government intervention can—at least in theory—improve on the voluntary interactions of producers and consumers.

Property Rights

One obvious requirement for a market system to thrive—maybe even for it to exist at all—is that there be well-defined property rights. If theft were legal—if what anyone produced were the property of everyone—there would be little incentive for people to produce things. Most societies have come to realize that the agreement of its members to be "governed" by rules outlawing murder, theft, and other crimes economizes on security costs and greatly increases people's potential output of goods and services. But being "governed" in this way means there is a "government," not just "the market"—even if it is not necessarily a big, complex government.

Income Distribution

In a market economy, people acquire purchasing power mainly by working or investing. Some people will possess skills "the market" values highly. People with these skills and the inclination to use them will make a lot of money. Others will not be very good at what the market values, or will be incapacitated in some way, or may simply prefer not to work and as a result will earn very little income. If the "distribution of income" that results from voluntary interactions in the "labour market" is too unequal, governments may decide that more levelling needs to be done than charity alone can accomplish, and may therefore decide to tax those with higher incomes or wealth and redistribute the proceeds to those with less.

Public Goods

If I eat a hamburger, I benefit and you don't.[7] But some goods do benefit more than one person. If I uncover the nature of a type of cancer and discover how it can be beaten, you can "consume" that knowledge, too; the fact that you understand it won't reduce my understanding it.[8] Knowing what you now know, however, you may decide not to invest in cancer research of your own but simply to "free-ride" off my research. In that way, you can reap the benefits of the research without having paid any of the costs. If I know you plan to free-ride, I may decide there is no point trying to earn a living or make a profit out of my cancer research—since you will simply appropriate any knowledge I acquire, I needn't bother. As a result, "society" may end up under-investing in cancer research.

Externalities

A similar situation occurs with externalities. In this case, people do not consume the same good simultaneously, but one person's consumption does affect another person in either a positive or a negative way. I am happy to buy gas from the local gas station, and the station owner is happy to sell it to me. But you may be very unhappy about the pollution my driving causes. Economists refer to your costs as "negative externalities." Externalities may also be positive. Education is widely believed to confer benefits even on those who do not themselves become educated. In general, the market may oversupply goods that produce negative externalities and undersupply those that produce positive externalities. In deciding how much to educate myself, for instance, I do not take into account your benefit from my learning and may therefore stop, even though our combined benefit from another year of my education would be greater than its costs to me.

Monopoly

As mentioned, the producers of a good or service would like to sell it for as high a price as they can get.[9] In a competitive market they cannot just charge any price they like, but in a market where competition is absent, a "monopolist" (the sole seller of a good or service) can raise prices well above costs. If the monopoly results from a temporary technological or entrepreneurial advantage, the harm it does may be limited. But if there are reasons to believe the monopoly will be permanent—that is, if it is a "natural monopoly," meaning the costs of production decline as output rises, so the monopolist will always have lower costs than any new competitor—then the government may decide to regulate the monopoly's prices, or even to take it over and run it as a publicly owned company charging competitive prices.

Asymmetric Information

With relatively simple goods—our humble potato, for instance—consumers can make informed judgments about how much their consumption will benefit them. When goods are complex, however, and consumers find it hard to evaluate their potential benefits, a situation of "asymmetric information" may result. But even if producers do know much more about their products than consumers do, "the market" may find ways around this difficulty. For example, prospective buyers of products, such as new cars, can read *Consumer Reports* or conduct their own investigations online to inform themselves about products they are thinking of buying. Or the medical profession can develop and enforce strict professional standards that discourage doctors from selling unnecessary operations to patients. But it's also possible, when problems of asymmetric information are severe, that governments may decide to regulate or even take over the production of particular goods.

Merit Goods

An extreme case of asymmetric information is what economists call "merit goods." The usual assumption is that consumers can judge for themselves what the benefits of consuming various goods are. But consumers may not always fully appreciate the dangers of, say, different kinds of drugs or other chemical substances. For this reason, governments may regulate these substances, making their consumption illegal without a doctor's prescription or, in some cases, outlawing them entirely. The consumer's judgment is simply overruled—for his or her own good.

Coordination Failures

The classic problem of "macroeconomics" (the study of inflation, unemployment, economic growth, and other phenomena that take place at the level of entire economies, and which are the subject of the rest of this book) is coordination failure. My income depends on your spending, but your income depends in turn on my spending. If I have reason to believe you're about to cut back your spending, I will anticipate a decline in my income and will cut back my spending. But that makes my fear self-fulfilling: my cut in spending reduces your income, so you spend less, which means my income does in fact decline. Coordination failures of this sort are a kind of market failure that makers of macroeconomic policy aim to avoid. Whether they can do so without actually making things worse—which most economists believe was the effect policy-makers had in the first years of the Great Depression—is an open question debated at length in this book.

Let the Market Work?

This above list of eight generic types of market failure by no means exhausts the possibilities. Since the Second World War, economic theorists have spent much of their time investigating ways in which markets may fail, and they have been extremely imaginative in doing so. Canadian philosopher Joseph Heath (2001) argues that market failure is in fact endemic, and that many of the government interventions that so bother small-government conservatives are attempts to correct for market failures. In his view, many of these interventions are successful, with the result that his native country comes about as close to economic "efficiency" as is humanly possible. In economists' (and Heath's) use of the word, "efficiency" means producing all things whose benefits are greater than their costs and none whose costs are greater than their benefits. Absent market failures, markets can be expected to do that. When market failures exist, however, markets can disappoint. They will produce too much pollution, not enough education, too many frauds, not enough national defence, too many drug addicts and obese people, not enough income at the bottom end of the distribution, and so on. Many types of government intervention will be necessary if "society" is to approach an optimal allocation of its resources.

Economist fans of the market were at first taken aback by this intellectual onslaught against "letting the market work," and market solutions fell out of favour in the 1950s and 1960s. But market supporters eventually counterattacked in a forceful, multipronged offensive.

Their first recourse was empirical: Can there really be so many serious market failures? Surely the critics of free markets had overstated the problem. In many instances, no doubt, markets do not work as perfectly as they do in textbooks, but, market enthusiasts suggested, most departures from optimality were likely not very substantial or serious.

Their second line of attack was more fundamental. Market failure is only a necessary condition for intervention to take place; it is not sufficient. There must also be a reasonable prospect that government will get the corrective intervention right. Markets may fail, yes, but governments can fail, too. Since addressing market failures takes time and resources, in many instances correcting them will not be worth the candle.

There are in turn at least two reasons to be skeptical about the idea that governments can bring societies to economic utopia by smoothly and efficiently correcting market failures.

The first is that getting the intervention right is not easy. Take pollution, for instance. Too much pollution is obviously a bad thing. But, strange to say, too little pollution can be a bad thing, too. How can there be "too little" pollution? Not all pollution is harmful. The first few million tons of carbon dioxide entering the atmosphere probably don't endanger the planet. On the other hand, preventing pollution is costly. Taxes or regulations could push cleanup efforts into ranges where less and less harmful pollution is being prevented at a greater and greater cost in economic activity. Most of the market failures described above do result in departures from the socially optimal amount of the activity in question. But in most instances, not just any intervention will do. In theory, too much intervention can do as much—maybe even more—harm as too little. Under a completely laissez-faire education system, too few people might go to university. But if everyone went, that might be too much education. Not everyone is suited to the demands of a university education. And if everyone did go, the financial return to a university education would be much lower than it was when having a degree was less common. After the fact, many people might think getting so much education had been a mistake. Unfortunately, in most cases the data we would need in order to make good decisions about "how much is enough" simply do not exist. In fact, it is the very nature of externalities that we don't really know the true cost of a negative externality or the benefit of a positive one. We may believe university-educated people generate positive externalities, but how would we calculate their value? And if we cannot calculate that, how do we decide how big a subsidy to give to prospective graduates? As a general point, correcting market failures is very tricky work. In most cases, it has to be done in an informational fog.

Then there's the problem of "unintended consequences." Many social interactions are very complex. Policy, by contrast, usually has to be simple. (In a famous phrase, the political scientist Charles Lindblom referred to governments as having "strong thumbs, no fingers.") It is therefore not surprising that many policies produce harmful side effects. The following are some examples:

- When apartment rents in big cities bubble skyward, a classic government intervention is to impose rent controls, the long-term effect of which is to reduce mobility sharply. People in rent-controlled apartments don't want to leave them.
- In the 1960s and 1970s in the United States, welfare systems that provided assistance to single mothers led to the breakdown of many African-American families. Because support went only to families without fathers, fathers had a strong financial incentive to leave.
- When at the beginning of the 21st century rich-country governments gave in to farm and environmental lobbies and paid generous subsidies for biofuels, this raised the world prices of corn and grain and brought hundreds of thousands of the world's poorest people to the brink of starvation.
- Donations of used clothing to Africa have helped clothe many Africans, but they have also undermined African clothing production by flooding the market for clothing and depressing prices.
- The United States subsidizes health insurance with big tax breaks for employer-sponsored health care. But a side effect of this policy is that many people won't quit their job, even when a better one comes along, for fear of losing their insurance. Labour mobility is high in the United States, but is lower than it would be if health care were subsidized in a different way.
- When in early 2009 the Obama administration limited the salaries of the executive officers of any financial institution that accepted emergency government bailout money, some banks that probably should have opted for a bailout decided not to.[10]

The world is a complicated place. People respond to the incentives that policies create, whether or not these incentives are intended. It is therefore extremely difficult to anticipate all the possible consequences of a policy intervention, and not surprising that in many cases policies may not be very effective. A recent *New Yorker* cartoon gives a hint of what those who would change people's behaviour are up against. Two business types in shirtsleeves and ties are sitting at a boardroom table, skimming through documents. One says to the other: "These new regulations will fundamentally change the way we get around them."

A second, even more serious reason to believe real-world governments won't get their interventions right is simply that they generally do not behave anything like textbook governments. Textbook governments are populated by highly trained economists dedicated to the single goal of maximizing social welfare. To achieve this, they carefully analyze market failures and devise the most efficient and precise intervention to remedy every such serious failure they encounter. Unlike textbook governments, real-world governments are populated by all kinds of people, including party leaders, Cabinet ministers, senior officials, mid-level bureaucrats, and clerks. The goals of these individuals are diverse, and range from maximizing their own electability or income, securing greater public largesse for the groups or regions they represent, achieving greater control (in the case of public officials or "bureaucrats") over their small corner of the government, or punishing those, such as "big business," who may be their political opponents. The effects of such complications can be perverse. Most civilized people presumably wish to ensure that poor children have enough to eat. Yet most industrialized countries—Canada included—pursue policies that deliberately raise the price of basic foodstuffs, such as milk, and make food more expensive.

If governments do not always aim to maximize social welfare, and if in many instances policy therefore does not even try to achieve economic efficiency (in the sense described above), then it should hardly be surprising that large-scale government intervention may not achieve that end. To paraphrase Winston Churchill's famous conclusion about democracy, "letting the market work" may be the worst possible way of running a "society"—except for all the others.

NOTES

1. Robert Frank does the same sort of thing in his 2007 book, *The Economic Naturalist*; see the list of suggested readings.
2. One way may be to ask whether the gainers gain enough to enable them to compensate the losers for their loss and still be better off. If so, then the benefits of the change are greater than its costs. But should we also insist that the payoff take place, so nobody is worse off and at least some workers are better off as a result of the new minimum wage? And should we not include employers in the calculation? Are they still as well off as they were before the increase in the minimum wage? Economists refer to changes that leave at least someone better off and no one worse off as "Pareto improvements," after Vilfredo Pareto, the early 20th-century Italian sociologist who developed the concept.
3. If anything, the public sector is enjoying a return to favour (in early 2009) as a result of the world financial crisis that began in August 2007, which many observers attributed to lax financial regulation. On the other hand, some analysts blame unwise decisions by government institutions such as the US Federal Reserve Board—which they allege seriously overinflated a bubble in house prices that eventually burst, with calamitous effects—and various changes in the rules about how financial institutions had to value their assets and acquire new capital in response to such changes. See Taylor (2009).
4. See Thatcher (1993, 626): "I expected great things from society in this sense because I believed that as economic wealth grew, individuals and voluntary groups should assume more responsibility for their neighbours' misfortunes. The error to which I was objecting was the confusion of society with the state as the helper of first resort."

5. All the markets put together constitute "the economy"—but if you believe there's no such a thing as "society," you probably also believe there's no such thing as "the economy."
6. Assuming, of course, that there *are* alternative suppliers (see the discussion of monopoly that follows).
7. Unless you are an unusually empathetic person and enjoy the "utility" I get from the hamburger. But you cannot actually consume the hamburger.
8. Though it may reduce the commercial value of that knowledge to me, since you have become a potential competitor in any attempt I might make to profit from it.
9. They will not always charge the highest price they can imagine, however. If they do, they may find they have no buyers at all.
10. Most of the above examples concern unintended consequences in the United States, not because US policy-makers are particularly prone to them, but because the United States is studied more than most countries.

DISCUSSION QUESTIONS

1. Which, if any, of the following goods or services would you think is subject to one or another kind of market failure? Which kind of market failure?
   (a) timber bought from the Brazilian rainforest
   (b) restaurant meals
   (c) family vacations
   (d) household appliances
   (e) milk
2. Can you think of a public policy where "government failure" seems to be evident?
3. What information would you need in order to do good positive economics about the likely effect of a tax on the import of goods from other countries (that is, a tariff)?

SUGGESTED READINGS AND ONLINE RESOURCES

Frank, Robert H. 2007. *The economic naturalist: Why economics explains just about everything.* New York: Basic Books.

Landes, David. 1997. *The wealth and poverty of nations: Why some are so rich and some so poor.* New York: W.W. Norton.

Levitt, Stephen D., and Stephen J. Dubner. 2005. *Freakonomics: A rogue economist studies the hidden side of everything.* New York: HarperCollins. http://freakonomicsbook.com.

Smith, Adam. 1776. *An inquiry into the nature and causes of the wealth of nations.* http://socserv.mcmaster.ca/econ/ugcm/3ll3/smith/wealth.

REFERENCES

Heath, Joseph. 2001. *The efficient society: Why Canada is as close to utopia as it gets.* Toronto: Penguin.

Landes, David. 1997. *The wealth and poverty of nations: Why some are so rich and some so poor.* New York: Norton.

Organisation for Economic Co-operation and Development (OECD). 2008. *Revenue statistics 1965–2007.* Paris: OECD.

Taylor, John B. 2009. *The financial crisis and the policy responses: An empirical analysis of what went wrong.* NBER Working Paper 14631. New York: National Bureau of Economic Research.

Thatcher, Margaret. 1993. *The Downing Street years.* New York: HarperCollins.

United Nations. 2008. *Human development report 2007/8.* New York: United Nations.

Markets, States, and Exchange: An Introduction to Economics

Robert E. Prasch

> In all disciplines theory plays a double role: it is both a lens and a blinder. As a lens, it focuses the mind upon specified problems, enabling conditional statements to be made about causal relations for a well-defined but limited set of phenomena. But as a blinder, theory narrows the field of vision. Questions that are meaningful in the world are often nonsense questions within a theory. (Minsky 1986, 99)

Introduction: The Simple Exchange Story

For at least 50 years it has been conventional for economics textbooks to begin with a highly stylized parable. The "simple exchange story" usually takes the form of a "folksy" narrative such as the following:

> Sophie has a large supply of chocolate chip cookies. Her sister Alison has a large supply of milk. Since their parents are not watching, each of them could consume their own cookies or milk. However, if they were to trade with one another, their pleasures are certain to be individually and collectively enhanced, as each of them would be able to enjoy a satisfying combination of cookies and milk. Clearly, both of them "win" if they enter into a free exchange. This example affirms the general proposition that freely negotiated market exchanges leave everyone better off.

Within a few paragraphs, the textbook will then intimate—if not state outright—that the principles of this simple exchange story hold for international trade agreements, financial transactions, labour markets, and seemingly everything else. Some students will ask questions or raise objections, but class is soon over and there is a new assignment for next week. In this way the simple exchange story is established as a powerful conceptual anchor for many of the ideas that will be developed before the end of the term. Indeed, it is usually positioned as the core idea and ideal of contemporary economic thought and pedagogy.

If questioned on the veracity of parables such as the one above, defenders will inevitably protest that "it is just a simple analogy whose only purpose is to provide some intuition." But what, exactly, is the content of the "intuition" being conveyed? What is its deeper meaning or—dare I say it—metaphysics? Is this elementary story of exchange really a simplification? Or is it simplistic, even an obfuscation? Happily, a review of these issues also presents us with an opportunity to formulate an alternative, and more substantive, understanding of how markets work (Prasch 2008).

The Elements of Exchange: Property and Contract

In modern economies, such as those of Canada and the United States, property is traded under a set of rules known as contract law. While some economists have, over the last few decades, considered the origin and importance of property and contract law, little of this effort has filtered into the introductory textbooks of the profession.[1] The following quotation (Commons 1893, 59) suggests that while this has been a mistake, it is one with a long heritage:

> The English economists have taken the laws of private property for granted, assuming that they are fixed and immutable in the nature of things, and therefore needed no investigation. But such laws are changeable—they differ for different peoples and places, and they have profound influence upon the production and distribution of wealth.

Property Law

Under the common law of England, Canada, and the United States, property is "the right of exclusive disposal." That is to say, when I have established a property right over some object, service, or privilege, I may legally exclude other people from its use. Should they fail to respect this right, I may call upon the state to enforce my claim. Consequences may include a court injunction, a suit for damages, or even a criminal charge. In this relatively trivial sense, the state's role is both fundamental and indispensable. Modern states explicitly forbid my hiring of a muscle-bound enforcer to travel to someone else's home or place of business to force restitution. But this is far from the state's only task. Rather, the state has three fundamental roles in the definition and management of property:

1. The state defines property rights, including the range of objects, services, and privileges (hereafter "goods"), that can be legitimately claimed as property. It also determines who may own property and which goods may constitute property. For example, most nations now forbid the ownership of people or heavy weapons, and many forbid a select variety of recreational intoxicants. Additionally, the state sets rules regarding who is eligible to own certain varieties of property; children, felons, and persons declared to be legally incompetent face a variety of restrictions. All of these prohibitions, distinctions, and restrictions have evolved over time, and will likely continue to do so in the future.
2. The state limits the range of activities to which individuals may apply their property. For example, it would be difficult to open or operate a

23

recycling centre, a rifle range, or an establishment featuring nude dancing in a suburban location. Likewise, while the law recognizes that individuals are the owners of their bodies, it is generally not legal for people to kill themselves or "rent" their bodies to another person for sexual purposes.
3. The state is the final adjudicator of all property and contract disputes. Although states have increasingly allowed binding arbitration to emerge as a mode of resolving disputes, in only a few narrowly defined circumstances may force be used to protect or resolve disputes between rivals over property rights.

Contract Law

A contract is "an offer and an acceptance." While every jurisdiction may have its own set of conditions, exceptions, and exemptions, the broader rules of contract are fairly constant. First, both parties must positively indicate their intention to be bound by the terms of the contract—usually with a signature or token payment. Second, any contract agreed to under coercion is invalid (of course, reasonable people—including judges and juries—can and have disagreed over what exactly constitutes "coercion"). Third, all contracts must be consistent with the law of the land. So, for example, courts will be unlikely to uphold an agreement to exchange illegal drugs or stolen goods. Only in the event that these core conditions are met will the state, through its courts, uphold and enforce a privately negotiated contract.

This brief summary of property and contract law supports the conclusion that all contracts—and for that reason all exchanges—necessarily involve three parties: the buyer, the seller, and the state (Commons 1924). As the state is an (implicit) party to all contracts, it is evident that the simple exchange story is woefully incomplete and perhaps even misleading. Moreover, markets, even those that we might wish to call "free markets," can neither exist nor operate outside of the rule-making and enforcement capacities of the state.

Additional Flaws in the Simple Exchange Story

An important, but hidden, element of the simple exchange story that opened this essay is that it ignored several considerations that are formative to the shape and outcome of exchanges. These include (1) the relative position of each party to the exchange, (2) whether it is a "spot" or "relational" contract, and (3) whether the item exchanged is an "inspection" or "experience" good. Each of these considerations will be addressed in turn.

Inequality and Bargaining Power

In the cookies-for-milk exchange depicted above, both parties *wanted* rather than *needed* to make the exchange. In the event that they failed to consummate an exchange for cookies, milk, or a close substitute, their ability to constitute them-selves as persons, citizens, or labourers would not have been in any way undermined (Prasch 1999). Why, however, should this be a consideration?

Perhaps it is obvious, but, to function in a realm where all property is owned, one must have something of value to exchange. Those persons without valuable goods or savings can, of course, trade their labour. But what are we to make of a situation wherein a substantial number of people have neither exchangeable goods nor savings *and* there is a dearth of employment at wages sufficient to maintain "life and limb"? From the above discussion of the law of property, it should be evident that people with few or no goods, savings, or current income will experience the world as a place of multiple, decentralized prohibitions. Everywhere they turn, goods are potentially available, but without access to means of payment, the poor lack any means to legally acquire the things they need to survive, much less prosper. Persons facing such conditions may be *formally* "free to choose," but this right will have little *substantive* meaning.

By contrast, let us consider the situation of a select number of people who have many valuable, exchangeable goods or a great deal of savings and who live in a society marked by tremendous inequalities of wealth, income, and opportunity. Let us also suppose that the "have-nots" of that society are often unemployed, or are employed at wages too low to sustain a socially approved standard of living. In such a case, our favoured few will find that they can command a great deal from the have-nots. Indeed, absent any non-market checks, their "freedom to choose" might be so extensive as to enable them to command much more than mere bargains over goods. Instead, they would be in a position to make purchasing decisions with virtual life-or-death implications for their impoverished counterparties. Rather than "liberty," such bargaining power would come to constitute a form of "licence" with important and troubling consequences for non-market concerns such as human dignity, social and political equality, and—ultimately—the political order.

To offset or forestall such outcomes, virtually every nation with a democratic polity has enacted policies designed to place a floor under individual incomes, and thereby a limit on bargaining power. Typically, this takes the form of a widely accepted understanding that the government is obliged to ensure that the economy consistently provide more or less full employment at some minimum wage. Not surprisingly, what specifically constitutes "full employment" or "a minimum wage" are politically sensitive issues.

To maintain a high level of employment, economists have advanced numerous—sometimes conflicting—proposals. Classical and neoclassical economists have argued that with enough time the "invisible hand" will bring about a rough approximation of full employment. By contrast, Keynesians have argued that the government should act as an "employer of last resort" by guaranteeing a job at a decent wage to everyone willing to work (Minsky 1986, chap. 13; Wray 1999;

Harvey 1989; see also Chapter 9 in this volume). Others have argued that it would be best to provide everyone with a "guaranteed income" as a substitute for both a jobs program and much of the welfare state (Van Parijs 2000). In practice, most modern democracies have relied on a mix of fiscal and monetary policies in conjunction with welfare-state expenditures to provide employment and income security during economic downturns.

"Spot" Versus "Relational" Contracts

The simple exchange story invites us to believe that all markets can and should be thought of as spot markets featuring highly—even perfectly—informed and knowledgeable participants. While it is true that most of the exchanges we enter into are *spot* exchanges, from the perspective of total value these exchanges represent only a modest proportion of our overall expenditures. Our most important exchanges—mortgages, car loans, college tuition, and so on—take the form of *relational* contracts.

What, then, are the characteristics of a "spot" market? A spot market is one wherein exchanges are typically negotiated and settled at one and the same time. An example would be an outdoor market for tourist trinkets. The tourist haggles over the price, settles the exchange with a cash payment, and walks away with the item in hand. A crucial characteristic of this exchange is that neither party needs much information concerning their counterparty. Questions of identity and creditworthiness, even trust and business reputation, are largely immaterial. A long-standing error—one that has plagued too many textbooks and, to be blunt, too much of advanced economic theory—is to suppose that spot exchanges are representative of modern capitalism.

Consider, again, the exchange of a trinket for cash described above. The information that each party to the exchange needs to know from the other can be readily ascertained. Does the tourist have cash? Well, payment is due immediately and in full, so this consideration has been verified. On the other side, the tourist can usually acquire enough information from a visual examination of the trinket to form a reasonably informed decision as to its underlying merits. If he has failed to notice in his assessment that the item is somewhat shoddy, however, his life and livelihood are not at stake; the percentage of the tourist's wealth or income presented in payment is generally trivial. The implication is that any error in assessing the underlying quality of the trinket will be inconsequential.

By contrast, a *relational* contract is one in which the parties agree to participate in an ongoing business relationship. Landlord–tenant, employer–employee, management–labour union, and creditor–debtor are all examples of relational contracts. These contracts differ from spot contracts in that each of the parties is necessarily concerned with the specific qualities and character of those with whom they are dealing. Consequently they will want to know more about their counter-parties, and will consider what they learn in the course of negotiating the contract.

"Inspection" Versus "Experience" Goods

Spot markets, as we have seen, work well in instances where information is perfect or where the cost of error is trivial. But the fact remains that when we consider the markets for homes, high-tech electronic devices, fancy automobiles, and complex financial instruments, the reality that most buyers are imperfectly informed must be taken seriously. James K. Galbraith argues, correctly, that when we purchase an item we are actually purchasing *both the item and some assurance* that it will work the way that it should (Galbraith 2007). If the market for such items is to work at all well, uncertain and wary buyers must have ready access to reliable information concerning the quality of a given product.

By contrast to the above, goods whose core qualities can be ascertained through direct observation—perhaps observation supplemented by some knowledge that may be presumed to be widely available in the community—can be characterized as "inspection goods." In the simple exchange stories presented above (cookies for milk or cash for tourist trinkets), direct inspection and the verbal assurances of sellers usually represent the extent of buyers' knowledge of the product. Of course, the qualities of cookies and milk are widely understood and appreciated by most North American children, so a visual examination readily reveals the most critical information. Are there sufficient chocolate chips in each cookie? Is the glass of milk being offered large or small?[2]

By contrast, many of the most important goods we purchase can more ac-curately be categorized as "experience goods." The reason is that most of us only come to understand the core qualities of such goods some time after we have taken possession of them. An automobile, a vacation package, a corporate bond, and an insurance policy are examples of experience goods. At the time of negotiation we depend upon our own limited experience and whatever we can learn from inter-mediaries to assess the qualities of the item in question. But unless we are unusually trusting, we will remain conscious of our ignorance. It follows that purchasing an experience good requires either a "leap of faith" or some credible guarantee that the item in question has all, or at least many, of the qualities claimed by the seller. Knowing this, sellers have devised various stratagems to improve the volume of business through allaying buyers' concerns. Sellers depend upon what are called "signals" to assure customers of their commitment to quality or safety. For example, some companies have invested heavily in their brand image or in guarantees, which would be compromised in the eyes of the public in the event of poor quality or performance.[3] Firms have also allowed, and in some cases induced, states to pass laws mandating greater disclosure of product quality or stated minimum standards in order to promote their industry's reputation. Other companies have presented assurances in the form of testimonials by trusted public figures such as sports stars or doctors. All of these strategies enhance sales and the size of firms' markets if they succeed in getting the customer to trust the assurances of the seller, thereby making the former more amenable to purchasing the good in question.[4]

Markets Are Shaped by State Decisions and Actions, and for That Reason Are Inherently Political

According to ancient mythology, the goddess Venus was fully formed at her birth. This, it would appear, is the understanding that too many economists have of the origin of markets. Reading their work often leaves one with the impression that markets are fully formed independently of the state. Markets appear to emerge out of some primordial "state of nature."

But such a presentation is clearly unsatisfactory. The answers to the questions of who is empowered by the state to make what sort of property claims and what the rules and conditions for allowing these claims to be exchanged are, have tremendous implications for the distribution of wealth, income, and opportunity. In light of this fact, it is not surprising that self-interested persons, corporations, and their paid representatives work hard to arrange or rearrange the rules of property or contract in a manner favourable to their current circumstances (Baker 2006). Ideally, a democratic polity can resist or offset these efforts, but the record suggests that the reality is otherwise.

Additionally, new discoveries and inventions create unforeseen opportunities that inevitably induce conflicting claims and claimants. All of these contingencies must be adjudicated, and every society (ideally) has institutions in place to manage these disputes. Of course, these resolutions are not always satisfactory. The history of humanity presents us with a long list of disturbances, political struggles, and even outright battles over the rights to the goods or opportunities generated by new resources or technologies.

Conclusion: The Role of the State in the Market Economy

In light of the above observations on property and contract law and their implications for our understanding of market exchange, let us briefly consider the proper role of the state in a reasonably well-functioning market economy.

First, it is evident that regulation can play a positive and constructive role in the formation, extension, and legitimation of markets. As has been observed, many of our most important exchanges occur within relational contracts, and many may involve experience goods. For such markets to function well, buyers must have some assurance as to the underlying qualities of their counterparties and the goods that they are hoping to acquire. Without this, they are likely to lower the prices they are willing to offer or the quantities they are willing to buy. While a firm's reputation plays an important and irreplaceable role in such transactions, experience teaches that reputation alone is generally not enough—despite what the many theorists of laissez-faire would have us believe. Pointing to the many formerly reputable firms of the American financial sector is sufficient proof of this proposition.

In the absence of clear regulation, civil suits can present an important check on firms, as buyers generally retain the option of suing for damages. For large firms making large transactions, arbitration or lawsuits are viable alternatives to regulation. But for smaller entities, such as a family trying to buy healthy food or non-toxic medicines, these options are usually too uncertain and expensive to provide effective or timely protection. In such instances the state may emerge as the institution best positioned to test and supervise the underlying quality of goods. It can then use its regulatory capacity to mandate a minimum standard of product safety or greater disclosure (Law 2004).

What has been lost in the discourse of contemporary policy debate is the fact that well-conceived regulation is often in the interest of firms pursuing "best practice" methods (Galbraith 2008, 129–131). The state's threat that it will impose sanctions in the event of misbehaviour enables best practice firms to convey a "credible" message of reliability and quality to consumers. In this manner, regulation facilitates the efficiency of the market to the extent that it can effectively transform an experience good into something more akin to an inspection good. For example, I do not know enough about the process of designing and manufacturing an automobile to understand the relative qualities and performances of various modern airbag systems. I can, however, learn something about an automobile's comfort, colour, and price. To the extent that I have some assurance concerning its safety features—that is to say, the experience goods element of a vehicle, which I hope never to actually test—I can focus on the inspection goods aspect that I do understand and can readily evaluate.[5]

Second, in a world of ubiquitous private property and an extensive division of labour, few of us are self-sufficient in the sense that we can meet our basic needs out of our own skills or resources. Of course, this is not a pressing concern in the event that we have sufficient savings in reasonably safe and liquid assets. But many of us are in situations that meet neither of the above criteria. The implication is that in the event of sustained unemployment, or employment at wages below the social cost of labour (Prasch 2005), we must turn to transfers from private sources (family and friends), private charities, or the public—that is to say, the welfare state—if we are to survive adverse circumstances. If for no other reason than to maintain public order, all developed nations have devised a variety of market interventions, including laws governing minimum wages, maximum working hours, and child labour; unemployment insurance; and a variety of programs collectively termed the "welfare state."

Third and finally, every free society is committed to a variety of ends that cannot or should not be provided for through private expenditure in markets. Museums based on civic or educational themes, the naturalization of new citizens, defence, playgrounds for children, and the establishment and maintenance of public parks, historic buildings, national monuments, and so on are all valued by society for their ability to create and sustain identities, communities, and cultures. Some of the expenditure for these items can be (and often is) met through private donations. But such gifts are generally inadequate and unreliable, and for this reason public funds or other encouragements are periodically needed to maintain these public programs or places. Moreover, most citizens believe that these expenditures should be met by public funds, even in the event that private funds are available.

The basis of this last conclusion is the widespread belief of most thinking people and political philosophers that some activities are part of the "core functions" of a state; the judiciary, safe water, acceptable schools, and fighting foreign wars can be found on almost everyone's list. With the hegemony of free market thinking over these past several decades, many of these tasks have been quietly outsourced to private firms. The numerous scandals that have followed in the wake of this ill-considered trend have given us cause to relearn what was once obvious to almost every citizen without a direct or indirect stake in the privatization movement: that the state has a crucial role to play in the modern economy. Moreover, the economic record of neo-liberalism from the 1980s to the present (2009) has induced many of the world's citizens to rethink the hegemony of "free market" ideologies and return to the common sense of previous generations—the understanding that a viable market system requires an active, capable, and adequately funded state sector.

NOTES

1. Strictly speaking, economists have begun to *reconsider* these issues. Formally, it was an interest largely of concern to economists outside of the mainstream, including Richard Ely (1854–1943), Thorstein Veblen (1857–1929), and John Commons (1862–1945).
2. One might note that this example still features a number of "unobservables" of substantial importance, including the possibility that the milk might be adulterated. These concerns, combined with the desire of firms to expand their market, contributed to the development of early 20th-century state food and drug laws regulating processed food and drugs (Law 2004).

3. A fascinating aspect of the myopia of modern American capitalism is the willingness, almost eagerness, of established firms to run down the value of painstakingly established brands. One might expect such behaviour when a firm is under duress, but we find this behaviour exhibited increasingly across all phases of the business cycle. A plausible conjecture is that the increasing dependence of firms on relatively impatient sources of finance, such as the commercial paper market, has contributed to this trend. Another culprit might be the relatively recent trend of rewarding senior managers on the basis of the near-term performance of a company's stock.

4. It should be noted that labour markets have several characteristics that distinguish them from the "spot" markets of standard textbooks. Labour's needs, consciousness, and conscience—including a sense of right and wrong—are each and severally important considerations. However, in the interest of brevity, these issues will not be raised here (see Prasch 2008, chaps. 5–8).

5. It is perhaps trivial to observe that such concerns are rife in the financial sector and have contributed to the systemic instability that has long been understood to be its defining characteristic.

DISCUSSION QUESTIONS

1. What are the conditions of a binding contract?
2. Under what market conditions will the simple exchange model be an appropriate economic theory? When should we be most wary of it?
3. What, at a minimum, is the role of the state in market transactions?

SUGGESTED READINGS

Baker, Dean. 2006. *The conservative nanny state: How the wealthy use the government to stay rich and get richer.* Washington, DC: Center for Economic and Policy Research. http://www.conservativenannystate.org.

Commons, John R. 1924. *Legal foundations of capitalism.* New Brunswick, NJ: Transaction Publishers.

Galbraith, James K. 2008. *The predator state.* New York: Free Press.

Prasch, Robert E. 2008. *How markets work: Supply, demand and the "real world."* Northampton, MA: Edward Elgar.

REFERENCES

Baker, Dean. 2006. *The conservative nanny state: How the wealthy use the government to stay rich and get richer.* Washington, DC: Center for Economic and Policy Research. http://www.conservativenannystate.org.

Commons, John R. 1893. *The distribution of wealth.* New York: Kelley Reprints.

Commons, John R. 1924. *Legal foundations of capitalism.* New Brunswick, NJ: Transaction Publishers.

Galbraith, James K. 2007. Predation from Veblen til now. Remarks to the Veblen Sesquicentennial Conference, Vadres, Norway.

Galbraith, James K. 2008. *The predator state.* New York: Free Press.

Harvey, Philip L. 1989. *Securing the right to employment: Social welfare policy and the unemployed in the United States.* Princeton, NJ: Princeton University Press.

Law, Marc T. 2004. The origins of state pure food regulation. *Journal of Economic History* 63 (4): 1103–1130.

Minsky, Hyman. 1986. *Stabilizing an unstable economy.* New Haven, CT: Yale University Press.

Prasch, Robert E. 1999. Needs. In *Encyclopedia of political economy,* ed. Phillip O'Hara, 783–785. New York: Routledge.

Prasch, Robert E. 2005. The social cost of labor. *Journal of Economic Issues* 39 (2): 439–445.

Prasch, Robert E. 2008. *How markets work: Supply, demand and the "real world."* Northampton, MA: Edward Elgar.

Van Parijs, Philippe. 2000. A basic income for all. *Boston Review* (October/November). http://bostonreview.net/BR25.5/vanparijs.html.

Wray, L. Randall. 1999. *Understanding modern money: The key to full employment and price stability.* Northampton, MA: Edward Elgar.

2

What Is Money? How Is It Created and Destroyed?

COMPETING VIEWS

David Andolfatto, "The Theory of Money"

John Smithin, "The Importance of Money and Debt–Credit Relationships in the Enterprise Economy"

Editors' Introduction

The general public often reacts with some disbelief when told that there is in fact no single, generally accepted measure of the quantity of money. In much the same way, students are often surprised when they read that there are at least two broad views on the origin and role of money in an economy and that, moreover, these competing views have existed for over two millennia and persist in the contemporary world.

The first, more established view (represented principally in David Andolfatto's contribution), which can be traced back to the philosophers of antiquity, regards money as an object whose purpose is to facilitate exchange. Given the need to minimize transactions costs, someone must have discovered that it would be more efficient to engage in trade and acquire the benefits of the division of labour by relying on a generally accepted object that is divisible, durable, fungible, portable, sufficiently rare, and—above all—that could be easily used as a medium of exchange. Instead of pursuing cumbersome two-way barter exchange, the introduction of money would ensure that the gains from exchange are maximized.

According to this view, money was initially an actual commodity (for instance, gold), but it eventually became less costly for monetary exchange to involve the circulation of paper notes in lieu of commodity money. Sanctioned by the state, the issuing of currency came under the exclusive control of central banks by the 20th century. However, the lifting of the ultimate resource (precious metals) constraint on the amount of money in circulation was also seen as a source of potential instability, since an excessive emission of central-bank money could generate inflationary pressures. Within this broad tradition, represented by the quantity theory of money, banks were often perceived as pure financial intermediaries that would extend credit as a multiple of the amount of reserves of central-bank money set exogenously by the monetary authorities. Hence, it may be said that monetary expansion is looked upon primarily as supply-led, and could become a source of inflationary pressures when an increase in the quantity of money exceeds the growth of real output.

The second tradition (represented primarily by the contribution of John Smithin) begins from a somewhat different story regarding the origin of money. It emphasizes money's unit-of-account role rather than its function as a medium of exchange; in this tradition, then, money represents a debt–credit relation. Although there are many debt–credit relations in society, what sits at the top of the "pyramid" of debts that can serve as money is the state's own currency, which is generally accepted largely because it can be used ultimately for payment of taxes.

Hence, even in ancient societies, what set a commodity such as gold apart from other commodities was not so much its particular characteristic as a rare metal, but the fact that it was chosen and stamped as legal tender by the sovereign authority and could be used to discharge one's obligations vis-à-vis the state. It is through government expenditure that this state liability is issued to the public, and it is by raising tax revenues that the government can remove from circulation this state liability over time. The emergence of commercial banking historically merely extended this ability to create/destroy money to a second-tier group of agents—the commercial banks—via loan/deposit creation. A bank loan would increase the amount of bank money equivalent to the increase in the quantity of deposits in the banking system, while the reimbursement of a bank loan would destroy an equivalent amount of bank money. This view of the monetary system—according to which the quantity of money is the endogenous result of the net spending of various economic agents, beginning with the state—is sometimes referred to as "chartalism." These two views on the nature of money are broadly analyzed in the following two contributions.

The Theory of Money

David Andolfatto*

Introduction

What follows is a short essay on the theory of money. By a *theory* of money, I mean an explanation for *why* money is useful or necessary to facilitate trade. Having such a theory is useful because it helps us understand (or at least *interpret*) the apparent demand for money. And as the demand for any product or service is likely to generate a supply to satisfy it, the theory can also help us understand the business of money creation—and whether the regulation of this business is in any way desirable.

Before we can begin theorizing about money, however, we need to define the term. My preferred definition is as follows: money is an object that circulates widely as a *medium of exchange*. Throughout the course of human history, a wide variety of objects appear to have fit this definition, including beads, seashells, metallic coins, and even salt (from which we derive the word "salary"). In the 19th century, money predominantly took the form of paper notes issued by private banks. More recently, governments have legislated themselves control of the paper money supply, with banks retaining a prominent role in managing (creating and destroying) the economy's "electronic" money supply.

With these thoughts in mind, my essay begins by describing a theory of money demand (that is, the demand for a circulating medium of exchange). I turn next to describing a theory of the money supply. Because the supply of money is so intricately linked to the business of banking, I take some time to consider a theory of banking as well. And finally, because the subject of banking features so prominently in periods of financial crisis, I discuss two competing theories of what commentators describe as "bank runs."

The Demand for Money

Explanations for why money is useful or necessary typically centre on the difficulties associated with barter exchange. Barter exchange requires that there exist *bilateral gains to trade* (gains to trade between two parties); this is sometimes called a "double coincidence of wants."[1]

* I would like to thank, without implicating, Doug Allen, Ken Kasa, Fernando Martin, and Meera Nair for their comments.

If all the gains to trade in an economy can be exhausted through barter exchange, then there is obviously no need for a circulating medium. People would simply trade directly for the goods they want in exchange for the goods they have. However, it is frequently the case that the gains to trade are *multilateral* (rather than bilateral) in nature. The existence of multilateral gains to trade implies a *lack* of double coincidence of wants. To understand what I mean by this, it is useful to consider an example.

An ABC Economy

Imagine a world inhabited by three people: Adam, Betty, and Charlie (ABC). Adam likes to eat bread in the morning; Betty likes to eat bread in the afternoon; and Charlie likes to eat bread at night. Adam has the ability to produce bread at night; Betty has the ability to produce bread in the morning; and Charlie has the ability to produce bread in the afternoon. Assume that once it is produced, bread must be consumed immediately (it will otherwise spoil). Finally, assume that producing bread entails a cost (that is, it requires some effort).

In the ABC economy described above, Adam is hungry in the morning, and Betty has the ability to produce morning bread. Unfortunately, Betty does not value what Adam has to offer (night bread). In this meeting between Adam and Betty, there are no *bilateral* gains to trade. In fact, it should take no longer than a moment to realize that there are no bilateral gains to trade for *any* pairing of these people. In this economy, there is a complete lack of double coincidence of wants (no bilateral gains to trade).

At the same time, it should be obvious that the people in the above economy could be made better off by engaging in some form of trade (that is, there exist *multilateral* gains to trade). In fact, everyone would be better off if they were to follow these instructions: Betty produces bread in the morning for Adam, Charlie produces bread in the afternoon for Betty, and Adam produces bread at night for Charlie. In this way, everyone expends a little effort producing bread, and everyone is able to consume bread when they value it the most; see Figure 1.[2]

It is commonly asserted that a lack of double coincidence makes money necessary. And indeed, one could well imagine how money might be used in the economy described above. That is, if Adam is endowed with a dollar, then he could use the dollar to purchase his morning bread.[3] The dollar could then pass from Betty to Charlie, and then back to Adam. In this manner, the dollar might circulate as a medium of exchange over time.

There is, unfortunately, a significant defect in attempting to explain the role of money as a solution to the lack of double coincidence. The defect is that money does not appear to be necessary. In particular, what is to prevent Adam, Betty, and Charlie from simply following my earlier instructions to produce bread when they

FIGURE 1 Multilateral Gains to Trade and a Lack of Double Coincidence in the ABC Economy

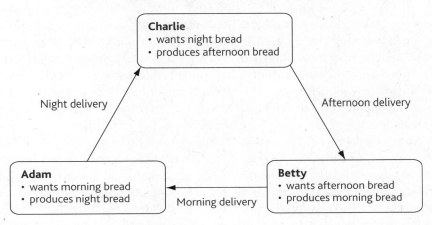

have the ability to do so and to consume it when they are hungry? I have described nothing in this economy that would prevent it from functioning as a communal gift-giving economy, with each producer making a "gift" of output that is to be reciprocated by some other member of the community at a later date.[4]

To develop a theory of money, we need to ask what prevents the world from operating along simple "communist" principles.[5] If money is a solution, then there must be some problem that it is solving. What is the problem? Evidently, the problem cannot simply be a lack of double coincidence, as is commonly asserted.

Information and Incentives

Society might function well enough as a communal gift-giving network if people could generally be relied upon to behave in a socially responsible manner. Our experience with human behaviour, however, suggests that this is not likely to happen—at least not as frequently as we might like. Individuals typically respond to real, private incentives, not idealistic social obligations.

If this is true, then the question becomes one of designing a system where people feel a private incentive to achieve the social good. What sort of arrangement might Adam, Betty, and Charlie adopt that gives each of them the private incentive to do what is best for the community (and by extension, for themselves)?

One arrangement that might work is for each of them to adopt a "tit-for-tat" strategy. That is, imagine that, in the morning of the first day, Betty produces bread for Adam. For every period following, imagine that each person produces bread for the person who desires it, but only in the event that the recipient has a record of having made a similar gift in the past. If everyone adopts this mode of behaviour, then each person should have a private incentive to do the right thing. In particular, while failing to produce when one has the opportunity to do so confers a short-term gain (a saving of work effort), at the same time it invites a future retaliatory response (foregone consumption). The threat of retaliation can be sufficiently strong to keep everyone working. If this is the case, then money is not necessary.

Social scientists frequently claim to observe tit-for-tat behaviour, interpreting it as a mechanism designed to induce cooperation among groups of people that are not intrinsically cooperative in nature.[6] The feasibility of a tit-for-tat system when there are multilateral gains to trade, however, relies on the public availability of information relating to personal trading histories. In practice, this type of information may not be easily observable, which might make it subject to manipulation.

Imagine then that our ABC model is afflicted with this type of information problem. In particular, imagine that it is impossible for society to monitor the trading histories of its members. So, for example, while Adam may personally know whether Betty has produced bread for him, assume that there is no way for Charlie to corroborate this fact. Likewise, while Betty may personally know whether Charlie has produced bread for her, assume that there is no way for Adam to observe this; and so on. Moreover, assume that there is no way to record information in the form of written records (that is, assume that these can be costlessly counterfeited, so that issuing personal receipts or IOUs is not feasible). If this is the case, then—absent any innovation—trade will not occur.[7]

Money as a Record-Keeping Device

Fortunately, the situation described above can be rescued with the innovation of monetary exchange. As I described earlier, Adam can now use a dollar to purchase his morning bread from Betty. Betty then approaches Charlie with the idea of acquiring bread in the afternoon. But how does Charlie know that Betty produced bread for Adam? The answer is simple: he can ask Betty to "show me the money." If counterfeiting or theft is not a problem in this economy, then the only way for Betty to have acquired her dollar is by having worked for it at some earlier time (that is, by having made a gift to society). Upon seeing her dollar, Charlie asks that she pay for her bread with it. The dollar in Charlie's hand now serves as evidence that *he* has made a gift to society; at night, the evidence will pass back into Adam's hands. Note that, in this scenario, the people are motivated to work hard for money in the same way that they were willing to work hard in the tit-for-tat economy to maintain their reputations. The inability to monitor individual trading histories makes money *necessary* for trade.

According to this theory, then, the economic function of money is to serve as a *record-keeping device*.[8] Specifically, the monetary object serves as a cost-efficient substitute for the information that might otherwise have been gathered and recorded by some public monitoring device. Money would be superfluous (even with a lack of double coincidence) if people could be trusted to commit to their promises or if their past actions were publicly observable at zero cost.[9]

The Money Supply

According to the theory outlined above, the purpose of money is to serve as a record-keeping device. The question concerning the supply of money might therefore be cast in terms of asking how society might best arrange this record-keeping service.

The idea of money as a record-keeping device implies that the role of money is to encode a certain type of information—in particular, information relating to individuals' past contributions to society. There are many ways to record such information. Physically, information can be encoded in either a tangible or intangible manner. Examples of *tangible* money include physical tokens, coins, or paper notes. Examples of *intangible* money include abstract book-entry items, such as the electronic digits that represent your bank account.

Another important distinction to be made in terms of monetary objects is whether they are *backed* or *unbacked*. A backed monetary instrument is a debt instrument (an IOU) that represents a claim against something of intrinsic value. An example of this would be a government operating under a "gold standard," with small denomination government paper notes representing claims against gold. Another example would be private banks issuing paper notes (banknotes) redeemable in specie (gold or silver coins) and representing senior claims against the bank's physical capital (land and buildings) in the event of bankruptcy. There have also been several historical episodes in which private companies have issued paper notes or coupons redeemable in store merchandise (much like Canadian Tire money or Air Miles reward miles). Finally, any form of commodity money is in a sense backed by the intrinsic value of the underlying commodity.

Unbacked money, as the name suggests, is a monetary object that does not represent a claim against anything of intrinsic value. I am unaware of any private agency ever having issued unbacked money—although the practice appears to be widespread among modern-day governments. Most of the world's currencies today (such as the US dollar, the euro, and the yen) are essentially unbacked; they derive their value primarily by government fiat, so that unbacked money is commonly referred to as "fiat money." In other words, governments around the world have typically legislated themselves monopoly control over the business of small denomination paper note issue, and these notes have value to the extent that people find making cash payments useful. At the same time, private agencies with government charters are allowed to create money in electronic form (although money in this form is typically required to be made redeemable for government cash).

Private Money

Although the business of money creation has almost always been subject to heavy government regulation (if not outright control), it is not immediately obvious why this should be the case. To see how private money-issue might work in theory, it will be useful to refer back to the ABC economy described above. In that model, I assumed that it was impossible to monitor the trading histories of all the members of society. I also assumed that Adam was endowed with a "dollar," without explaining where this money came from.

Let me now modify the information structure in this ABC economy. In particular, assume that Adam can be costlessly monitored—that is, that his actions are observable (and remembered) by all members of society. I continue to assume that Betty and Charlie *cannot* be monitored. It may be useful to think of Adam as some "famous" person (or agency) and everyone else as "anonymous" people.

Because Adam now has a public reputation, he can use it to his advantage. In particular, he is in a position to make promises that others might value.[10] Imagine that Adam issues a security (an IOU) that, if presented to him at night by any person, entitles that person to a loaf of bread. Note that Adam has an incentive to keep this promise, as failing to do so would destroy his reputation (no one would ever value his promises again).

It should be clear enough that Adam's IOU might serve as a medium of exchange. That is, while Betty does not value Adam's IOU directly, she should anticipate that it will be valued by someone (in particular, Charlie—who can redeem the IOU at night for bread). In this manner, Adam simply creates the money he needs, and the money is "destroyed" (taken out of circulation) whenever it is presented for redemption.

Well, this is the way that things might work in theory, at least. But is there any evidence to suggest that this has ever happened in history? The answer is, most certainly, yes. (See, for example, Champ (2007). Consider also Bodenhorn (1993, 812–813), who quotes an Italian general secretary of the Banco D'Italia explaining how, prior to 1874, "everyone was issuing notes, even individuals and commercial firms; the country was overrun with little notes of 50, 25, and 20 centimes issued by everyone who liked to do so." The author also notes that when state legislation banned US banks from issuing notes of less than $5, railroad companies, public houses, merchants, and even churches filled the void with their own notes.)

Government Money

There is a long tradition of government involvement in the business of money creation. In principle, the public provision of money poses no obvious theoretical obstacle. Indeed, a case could be made that the business of money creation is a sort of natural monopoly—that is, that a single uniform currency might naturally dominate a system with multiple currency issuers (a similar argument is used by advocates of common currency areas). In the context of the ABC model above, Adam's private IOU might easily be replaced by a government money that performs the same essential function.

In practice, the public provision of money has not always worked so smoothly. This is because there is frequently a great temptation on the part of the government to exploit its legislated monopoly position to extract seigniorage revenue from the population, especially during periods of fiscal crisis (as in periods of war). "Seigniorage" refers to the act of printing unbacked money to finance government expenditures. Inevitably, this process results in inflation—a systematic rise in the price of goods and services (or, equivalently, a systematic decline in the purchasing power of money). The resulting inflation acts like a tax on money holdings, and for this reason it is sometimes called an "inflation tax" (another name for seigniorage).

There are, of course, both economic and political limits associated with the government's ability to extract seigniorage revenue from the population. The economic limits are governed by the demand for money (people may not be willing to hold as much money during periods of high inflation—an effect that reduces the tax base) and the availability of currency substitutes (which the government may try very hard to suppress through legislation).[11] The political limits are those commonly associated with oppressive taxation.

Banking

There is probably no business that is less well understood than that of banking. The reason for this no doubt lies in the fact that the business of banking is in practice multifaceted and highly complicated. However, the basic principles of banking are easy to understand, even if the details are sometimes messy and confusing.

The first thing to keep in mind is that, while a bank is a financial intermediary, not all financial intermediaries are banks. Financial intermediaries are best thought of as *asset transformers*. For example, insurance companies transform their assets into insurance policies (state-contingent liabilities), pension funds transform their assets into pension plans (time-contingent liabilities), and banks transform their assets into demand-deposit liabilities (demandable liabilities).[12]

The liabilities created by most intermediaries are typically *illiquid*. For example, it is difficult to purchase your morning coffee by selling off a part of your insurance policy or pension plan. The distinguishing characteristic of banks vis-à-vis other financial intermediaries is that the demandable liabilities created by banks are commonly used as a form of money (which is to say, they are *liquid*). To put things another way, banks are financial intermediaries specialized in the

41

business of money creation. In days gone by, private banks regularly issued small denomination paper notes redeemable in specie. For example, in the US "free banking" era (1836–1863), there were literally hundreds of banks that issued their own currency (a practice that was abolished by both the Northern and Southern governments during the US Civil War).[13] The demand-deposit liabilities issued by chartered banks today no longer exist in paper form; instead, they exist in the form of electronic digits recorded in centralized accounts. Moreover, this modern "bank money" is redeemable not for specie, but for government cash. It is of interest to note that most of the "money supply" in any well-developed economy is created by the private sector.

THE ABCs OF BANKING

Let us again consider the ABC economy, but with the following modifications. First, assume that Adam, Betty, and Charlie cannot be publicly monitored, so that their personal IOUs are worthless as a circulating medium. Second, assume the existence of another agent (or agency) called "the bank." Unlike Adam, Betty, and Charlie, the bank has no ability to produce output. The bank's only advantage is that its reputation is publicly observable.

The situation now is as follows. Adam has an asset (his IOU), but no reputation that would support its value in the market. The bank, on the other hand, has a reputation, but no assets to exploit it. Adam and the bank each have something that the other values; perhaps they can strike a deal for their mutual benefit (and incidentally, for the benefit of society).

Imagine that Adam and the bank agree to the following "contract." Adam is required to "deposit" his IOU with the bank as collateral for a loan. The bank creates paper notes that are backed by the value of this collateral and lends them to Adam. Adam agrees to pay back the money loan at the end of the night (he might throw in a little extra bread as interest—after all, bankers have to eat, too).

Note that, while Adam's reputation (credit history) is not *publicly* observable, it is observable to the bank. Adam is therefore motivated to pay back his loan—at least if he wishes to maintain his future access to bank credit. To pay back his loan at night, Adam will have to produce night bread and sell it for banknotes (money). Hence, Charlie should be willing to produce bread in the afternoon in exchange for banknotes, and Betty to produce bread in the morning for banknotes. Of course, morning bread is precisely what Adam values; to acquire this bread, he will first have to agree to the loan contract described above.

The bank's reputation in this example is important for the purpose of maintaining the integrity of its money. As the value of the bank's money ultimately rests on the quality of its loan portfolio, the bank will have to ensure that its loan applicants have sound business plans. A bank that creates banknotes and lends them out in a haphazard manner will quickly see the value of its money (and hence, its business) fall to zero. This is why screening loan applicants, managing portfolio risk, and collecting on money loans are some of the important activities associated with the business of banking. At the end of the day, however, the essential function of banking is to transform illiquid assets (like Adam's IOU) into liquid liabilities (banknotes).

DEMANDABLE LIABILITIES

The example of banking described above, while accurate in some respects, is missing an important aspect of the way in which banks operate in reality. Most monetary systems are in fact what one might term "dual money regimes" in that there are usually two coexisting monetary objects, sometimes called "outside" money and "inside" money. Outside money supply—sometimes also called "base money"—is usually more liquid. Historically, base money took the form of specie (gold or silver coin); in modern times, it comes in the form of small denomination government paper notes and coin. Inside money supply is somewhat less liquid, and is typically issued by private banks and made convertible (on demand) for base money. Historically, these demandable liabilities took the form of private banknotes convertible into specie; in modern times, they take the form of electronic digits convertible into government cash.

The demandability property found in inside money is a peculiar financial innovation. The idea that you can convert your bank money into cash whenever you want is an attractive one, and is no doubt one reason why banks eager to attract business offer their clients this option. To put things another way, the demandability clause makes bank money more widely acceptable as a means of payment, allowing banks to better fulfill the economy's need for a supply of liquidity that responds rapidly to changing business conditions.

The demand for cash likely stems from the fact that (even in this age of electronic payments) it is a more economical method of payment for small purchases. Moreover, not all merchants are willing to accept cheques, and not all points of sale are hooked up to an electronic payments system.[14] For these reasons, banks will keep cash in reserve to meet the need for daily withdrawals. At the same time, these reserves are replenished by merchants making cash deposits out of their daily sales. The upshot of all this is that the balance sheet for a bank (or the consolidated banking sector) looks something like this:

Assets	*Liabilities*
Cash reserves: $10,000	Demandable liabilities: $100,000
Illiquid assets: $90,000	
Total assets: $100,000	Total liabilities: $100,000

According to the balance sheet above, the bank has $100,000 in "demand-deposit liabilities"—that is, the bank's clients have $100,000 credited to their accounts that they can convert into cash whenever they wish. Note that, although the bank's clients may believe that there is $100,000 in their bank, this is subject to an important qualification: while there is indeed $100,000 in the form of money, there is only $10,000 in the form of cash (the remainder is in the form of electronic digits). People are frequently shocked to discover this fact, but it is an essential property associated with the business of banking (the function of which is to convert the $90,000 of illiquid assets into a liquid form).

Financial Crises

As described above, the demandability clause built into bank liabilities enhances their use as a means of payment. But this peculiar property has a potential downside risk attached to it. Demandable liabilities are, by construction, *short-term* debt instruments—that is, they give people the right to cash out on very short notice. In contrast, the asset side of a bank's balance sheet consists predominantly of *long-term*, illiquid assets—for example, personal loans (like Adam's IOU), or a portfolio of individual mortgages. The illiquid nature of a bank's assets and the liquid nature of its liabilities is frequently referred to as "security mismatch."

Bank Runs

The potential problem with security mismatch is as follows: what happens if, for some reason, everyone wants to withdraw their money from the bank (or banking system) at the same time? In such an event, called a "bank run," the bank is clearly not in a position to honour all of its obligations—there is not enough cash in reserve to do so. The only way that the bank can acquire the cash that people want is to start selling off its assets. But a bank's assets are by nature illiquid, which means that the bank will either have to wait a long time before it finds someone who is willing to pay full value, or it will have to dispose of its assets at fire-sale prices. Alternatively, the bank may temporarily suspend withdrawals. Either act may potentially lead to bankruptcy proceedings.

The interesting theoretical possibility associated with security mismatch is the idea that a bank run may become a self-fulfilling prophecy.[15] That is, imagine that, for some unexplained reason, people become fearful that their bank is insolvent. The particular reason for this expectation does not matter (for example, it may simply be based on an unsubstantiated rumour). Nevertheless, conditional on the expectation, it will make sense for each individual depositor to "run" their bank—that is, to withdraw cash, even if they have no pressing need for it. But if all depositors act in this manner, the bank may have to dispose of its assets at fire-sale prices, which may then lead to insolvency—an event that would confirm the initial expectations. In other words, if everyone believes that their bank is insolvent, this belief may in the end come true, regardless of whether or not the bank was truly insolvent to begin with.

Lender of Last Resort

Most countries (or common currency areas) have a central bank that is responsible for managing the supply of base money.[16] The central bank (the "monetary authority") serves as a banking agent for the government (the "fiscal authority"), as well as for some commercial banks and other financial agencies. Chartered banks typically hold some cash reserves in their accounts with the central bank, and the government holds deposits at both the central bank and designated chartered banks.

One important function of the central bank is to serve as a "lender of last resort" for chartered banks. The idea here is the central bank may be in a position to avoid a banking panic if it stands ready to lend cash to banks that are subject to a bank run. Normally, such emergency lending is performed through a "discount window" facility—that is, the central bank "injects" cash reserves into a troubled bank in exchange for the bank's high-grade assets (typically, government bonds). In other words, this is a form of collateralized lending.

In periods of unusual financial stress, such as that experienced during the financial crisis of 2008, a central bank may expand the list of eligible securities that it will accept as collateral (such as prime-grade mortgages) for short-term cash loans. The securities in question are typically illiquid (otherwise, a troubled bank could raise the required cash by disposing of them on the open market). The whole idea behind a bank run, however, is that illiquid securities can only be disposed of quickly in the market at a huge discount. Rather than bear the cost of a fire sale on its assets, a troubled bank can offer them to the central bank at a much more "reasonable" discount. Once the crisis passes, a (formerly) troubled bank will be able to pay off its debt (and reacquire the illiquid assets it put up as collateral). At least, this is the way things are supposed to work in theory.

Bank Runs: An Alternative Interpretation

Not everyone agrees that security mismatch exposes banks to self-fulfilling bank runs. Of course, no one doubts the fact that banks sometimes fail, or that many fail during economic crises. The point of disagreement is with regard to what precipitates bank failure. The popular view is that a sudden loss of confidence can become a self-fulfilling prophecy. But an alternative interpretation is that the loss of confidence is merely a symptom—not the cause—of a financial crisis. After all, even non-bank firms are known to fail, and there are typically many such failures during an economic crisis. The crisis is likely caused by bets (risky investments) that turn out badly, leading to a *fundamental* decline in the value of assets throughout the economy (or the firm in question).

At issue, then, between these two very different interpretations, is the direction of causality. The popular view is that a loss of confidence can ultimately lead to a deterioration of economic fundamentals (justifying the initial loss of confidence). The alternative view is that deteriorating fundamentals are normal occurrences in the process of economic development, and that a loss of confidence is symptomatic of these events.[17]

Empirically, it is very difficult to discriminate between these two competing views. This is unfortunate, because the two views have very different policy implications. The self-fulfilling view generally justifies the use of government policies to "stabilize" the banking sector. The fundamental view, in contrast, suggests that many "stabilizing" policies are likely to be counterproductive. In particular, lender-of-last-resort facilities and federal deposit insurance programs may induce banks to finance riskier bets than they might otherwise undertake in the absence of such policies.

NOTES

1. Barter may involve a quid pro quo exchange of goods or services (for example, "I'll scratch your back if you'll scratch mine"); a credit arrangement (for example, "I'll scratch your back today if you'll scratch my back tomorrow"); or an insurance arrangement (for example, "Let's agree to scratch each other's backs whenever we feel an itch").
2. Figure 1 depicts a version of the famous "Wicksellian triangle," named after Swedish economist Knut Wicksell (1851–1926).
3. Historically, the term "dollar" (derived from the German "thaler") referred to a specific quantity of silver. But for this example, you can think of a dollar as taking any form, such as a shell or a token coin. For this dollar to possess exchange value, it must necessarily be difficult or impossible to counterfeit.
4. In fact, many primitive economies appear to have functioned precisely in this manner. Even today, exchange is commonly organized in this manner among small groups of people (for example, in families or clubs).
5. In his 1875 *Critique of the Gotha Program*, Karl Marx wrote a phrase that is considered by many to be a defining principle of a communist system: "From each according to his ability, to each according to his needs."
6. See, for example, http://en.wikipedia.org/wiki/Live_and_let_live_(World_War_I).
7. These assumptions are admittedly extreme. But the logic of the argument that follows will continue to hold as long as there are some people who are difficult to monitor.
8. Ostroy (1973) appears to be the first to make this idea explicit; see also Kocherlakota (1998). Alternatively, money is sometimes said to be a communication device, as its possession communicates information concerning a personal trading history; see, for example, Townsend (1987).

9. Kiyotaki and Moore (2002) suggest that the inability to keep promises is an "evil," and that therefore, "evil is the root of all money" (the title of their paper, and a reversal of Timothy 6:10, which states: "For the love of money is the root of all evil").

10. The promises of anonymous people are not likely to count for anything, as they can always deny having made them.

11. Governments sometimes prevent their citizens from using foreign currency or opening foreign currency accounts, for example.

12. "Demandable liabilities" are securities that can be redeemed for cash on demand (for example, when you choose to withdraw cash from a bank machine). Note that by "cash," I mean a tangible monetary object. Today, this would be primarily in the form of small denomination government paper, but historically was found in the form of specie.

13. Rolnick and Weber (1985) dispel some commonly held myths concerning this famous episode in the history of banking.

14. The underground economy, whose participants are not eager to leave records of their transactions, is also a major source of the demand for cash.

15. This idea was first formalized by Diamond and Dybvig (1983). See also Diamond (2007).

16. Rolnick, Smith, and Weber (2000) examine an interesting historical episode of a private central bank.

17. See, for example, Allen and Gale (1998).

DISCUSSION QUESTIONS

1. Should anyone who wishes to create his or her own money be allowed to do so? Why or why not?

2. Imagine that you wish to start a business. You will need to borrow money to buy or rent premises and to pay for labour. Although you may try to raise funds by issuing shares or bonds in the financial market, explain why, as a small business owner, you are likely to find cheaper financing by taking out a bank loan. What does this tell you about the social value of a banking system?

3. Some people argue that government insurance of bank deposits leads banks to take excessive risks, and that such programs "privatize gains, while socializing losses." Explain the rationale that underlies this view and what might be done in the way of banking regulations to mitigate this potential problem.

SUGGESTED READINGS

Bryan, Michael F., and Bruce Champ. 2002. Fear and loathing of central banks in America. *Economic Commentary* (Federal Reserve Bank of Cleveland) (June). http://www.clevelandfed.org/Research/commentary/2002/0602.pdf.

Goldberg, Dror. 2005. Famous myths of fiat money. *Journal of Money, Credit and Banking* 37 (5): 957–967.

Smith, Vera C. 1936. *The rationale of central banking.* Westminster: P.S. King and Son.

ONLINE RESOURCES

Davies, Roy. 2005. Origins of money and of banking. http://projects.exeter.ac.uk/
RDavies/arian/origins.html.
Wikipedia. 2009. History of Money. http://en.wikipedia.org/wiki/History_of_money.
Wikipedia. 2009. History of Banking. http://en.wikipedia.org/wiki/History_of_banking.

REFERENCES

Allen, Franklin, and Doug Gale. 1998. Optimal financial crises. *Journal of Finance*
53: 1245–1284.
Bodenhorn, Howard. 1993. Small-denomination banknotes in antebellum America.
Journal of Money, Credit and Banking 25 (4): 812–827.
Champ, Bruce. 2007. Private money in our past, present, and future. *Economic
Commentary* (Federal Reserve Bank of Cleveland) (January 1). http://www
.clevelandfed.org/research/commentary/2007/0101.pdf.
Diamond, Doug. 2007. Banks and liquidity creation: A simple exposition of the
Diamond-Dybvig model. *Economic Quarterly* (Federal Reserve Bank of
Richmond) 93 (2): 189–200.
Diamond, Doug, and Philip Dybvig. 1983. Bank runs, deposit insurance, and
liquidity. *Journal of Political Economy* 91 (5): 401–419.
Kiyotaki, Nobuhiro, and John Moore. 2002. Evil is the root of all money. *American
Economic Review* 92 (2): 62–66.
Kocherlakota, Narayana. 1998. The technological role of fiat money. *Federal Reserve
Bank of Minneapolis Quarterly Review* 22 (3): 2–10.
Ostroy, Joseph. 1973. The informational efficiency of monetary exchange. *American
Economic Review* 63: 597–610.
Rolnick, Arthur J., and Warren E. Weber. 1985. Banking instability and regulation
in the US free banking era. *Federal Reserve Bank of Minneapolis Quarterly
Review* 9 (3). http://www.minneapolisfed.org/research/QR/QR931.pdf.
Rolnick, Arthur J., Bruce D. Smith, and Warren E. Weber. 2000. The Suffolk Bank
and the panic of 1837. *Federal Reserve Bank of Minneapolis Quarterly Review*
24 (2): 3–13. http://www.minneapolisfed.org/research/QR/QR2421.pdf.
Townsend, Robert M. 1987. Economic organization with limited communication.
American Economic Review 77 (5): 954–971.

The Importance of Money and Debt–Credit Relationships in the Enterprise Economy

John Smithin

Introduction

From a commonsense point of view, the economy is all about money (Smithin 2000, 1). Yet many of the social science and business disciplines involved in studying economic activity pay less attention to this "most important institution in capitalist society" (Ingham 2004, 195) than it deserves. There are theories about what money *does*: economic theories about money and inflation, political theories about money and power, and sociological theories about money's cultural significance. What is missing, however, is a detailed discussion of the *ontology* of money (Searle 2005, 1)—what money is, how it comes into being, and what its nature is. In disciplines like accounting and finance, it is taken for granted that sums of money are subjects for discussion, without much further inquiry. In economics, one of the most influential approaches teaches that money itself is not important and that what is really going on when economic activity occurs is a barter exchange of goods and services.

Is Money a Commodity?

For many centuries, well into the modern era, the value of money was thought to derive from its worth as a commodity, as it was made from precious metals like gold and silver in coins or ingots. Such things were believed to be money because market forces had made one of them the most acceptable or "exchange worthy" item in trade in a given society.[1] This gave rise to the concept of the "medium of exchange," which still appears prominently in textbooks but is misleading because it implies that the most characteristic transaction is a simple "spot" exchange of goods for money (Hicks 1989, 41). This is not so in reality, and, particularly for the more important transactions, some sort of agreement (a formal or informal "contract") is required before trade takes place. It is not possible to be dogmatic about timing. The contract comes first, but sometimes the buyer must pay "in advance"—before delivery of the item—while at other times payment is made later. Spot payment is only a special case of one of three types of contract (Hicks

1989, 42). In all three cases, it is implicit that money, the thing offered in payment, is in a different *category* from the particular goods and services being sold. Otherwise, when trading an apple for an orange, why not call either of *them* the medium of exchange?

A major weakness of traditional economic thinking was that the only attempt made to understand the trading process was the assumption that market forces select one, or a limited number, of actual physical objects to serve as money. Even when money was obviously *not* a substantial object (for instance, when it was a piece of paper or a book entry), it was held to be "symbolic" of the more intrinsically valuable commodity. The idea that the value of money could be guaranteed in this way (for example, by a gold standard) was always dubious (Innes 2004, 15); today, when the physical form of money may be nothing more than electronic impulses in a computer, it is impossible to sustain. The numbers on the screen are symbolic only of a general claim to a part share of total goods and services—what is usually called "purchasing power"—and this is subject to continual fluctuation as prices change. It should be noted, though, that (however physically insubstantial modern money may be) the advent of computers and the Internet has *not* led to the disappearance of money, as was frequently claimed would happen around the end of the 20th century. Money retains the same importance in social life that it has always had, and current financial problems are discussed in much the same terms as they were throughout the 18th, 19th, and 20th centuries.

What Is Money?

What, then, *is* money? The main alternative to a commodity theory is a "credit" or "claim" theory of money (Ingham 2004, 6). This is sometimes expressed by stating that "all money is credit" or "all money is debt," but credit and debt are just mirror images of each other. If a bank extends a loan to an individual or a firm, that is *credit*, and the loan is an earning asset to the bank.[2] If someone makes a deposit *in* a bank, from the bank's point of view that is a *debt* or *liability*. Confusion can arise because, by definition, assets equal liabilities in a balance sheet. When a bank extends credit, its asset portfolio increases, but the liabilities side of the balance sheet must also increase. In the simplest case, the person or firm receiving the loan deposits the funds with the same bank, but—even if they pay away the funds to another institution—assets and liabilities of the system *as a whole* rise to the same extent. There is both "credit creation" and "money creation" at the same time, and when the loans are paid back it amounts to the "destruction" of money and credit. Which side of the balance sheet, however, contains the entries that are actually the *money*? The correct answer is that the funds on the liabilities side are money, to the extent that they can be transferred from one party to another and used to pay off other debt. This corresponds to the definition of money given by Hicks (1989, 42): "Money is paid for a discharge of debt when that debt has been expressed in terms of money." This also covers the historical, special case of precious metal coins. The issuer or guarantor of coins had to accept them back in payment of obligations to itself, but it was the acceptability that was the key, not the physical properties of the coins themselves (Ingham 2004, 198).

As debts are "expressed in terms of money," this introduces the notion of a "money of account," which Keynes (1971, 3) said was "the primary concept of a theory of money." Modern textbooks also list one of the functions of money as the "unit of account" (meaning the abstract concept of a "dollar," a "yen," and so on) in which prices are expressed, accounts are recorded, and profit is calculated. Unlike Keynes, however, textbook writers apparently do not think that this function is important. But this is a mistake; if there were no such function, it would be impossible to conduct business on a rational basis—quoting prices, keeping accounts, and obtaining finance. It is true that the notion of a unit of account, by itself, is not enough to establish a monetary economy. There must also be a *means of payment* recognized as actually constituting so many units of account when transferred. Keynes explained that money of account was the "*description* [of the thing]" and money itself "the *thing* that answers to the description" (1971, 3). It has already been stressed that the means of payment need not be a physical object, but can easily be a book entry or computer transfer, as seen every day. All that is necessary is that what is transferred "counts as" the required sum. There is therefore no real mystery in understanding why deposits in banks and other financial institutions can play this role.

A number of the textbook "functions of money" have already been mentioned. Sometimes, it is said that money is "a unit of account, a *medium of exchange*, and store of value," while in other treatments money is described as "a unit of account, a *means of payment*, and store of value." We have also seen that "medium of exchange" and "means of payment" are *not* the same thing (though the terms are often used interchangeably), and that the latter concept is more useful. What, though, of money as a "store of value"? In academic theories of "portfolio choice" or the "demand for money," this is treated as important, but again the emphasis seems wrong. If money is to constitute purchasing power, it must retain value to a certain extent from one period to the next, but money is not the only—or necessarily the best—store of value. A diamond ring or a painting by a famous artist can serve the same purpose, sometimes much better. Also, historically, money has frequently continued to perform the unit-of-account/means-of-payment functions long after inflation rates have reached very high levels, showing that these are what really seem to matter (Hicks 1989, 42). This is not to deny that money might be more "useful" in capitalism if its real value could be kept more stable; however, as will be argued later, this does not necessarily mean that the inflation rate itself must be zero.

Money as a Social Relation

It sometimes bothers people to learn that money is "created" when financial institutions make loans and "destroyed" when loans are called in. The idea that all is done "with the stroke of a pen" (today, more likely a keystroke) is somehow disquieting. Just because something is not defined by its physical properties, however, does *not* mean that it is not "real" or cannot have causal effects in the physical world. This is a characteristic property of all social institutions, social relations, or social facts (Ingham 2005; Searle 2005)—they are in a different category from "brute facts" (physical facts), and money is a prime example. A social fact is what it is, not by the laws of nature, but because it is accepted as such by convention. It will involve such things as collective intentionality, the assignment of status function (Searle 2005, 19), and the adherence to rules and norms of behaviour. A classic example would be a "line drawn in the sand" (Smithin 2009, 51) as a boundary between two warring factions, or even between two quarrelsome individuals on a beach. If both parties respect the boundary, it keeps the peace, not by virtue of its physical properties (nothing prevents anyone from stepping over the line) but because it is respected as such. It nonetheless can be *effective*, and has an impact in the world, as long as its conditions of existence are in place. From this can be drawn obvious parallels with many important economic institutions, including money itself, private property, firms, banks, mortgages, and pension plans. All these rely on the same sorts of conditions of existence, and can be just as real and "binding" on the individuals participating in them. The example of the line also illustrates how easily social consensus can evaporate. The boundary may seem at one moment to represent a solid institution and an unbreakable taboo. At the next, if someone steps over it and no retaliation follows, it simply crumbles. There is a clear correspondence between this and a typical sequence of events in the financial world.

The Hierarchy of Money

Bell (2005, 505) reminds us that, as money is a social relation involving indebtedness, there must be a hierarchy of money, depending on the issuer. Debts are of different quality from the point of view of the creditor (Hicks 1989, 48), and some types of money are more acceptable than others. This point is often obscured in textbooks, making it difficult for readers to understand such things as why central banks can conduct monetary policy by manipulating interest rates, or what happens in a financial crisis.

Any individual or institution can issue promises to pay (IOUs) in the unit of account, and Bell (2005, 505–508) envisages a four-tier "debt pyramid" in ascending order of acceptability, with households at the bottom, firms on the third tier, banks on the second, and the state or government at the top. A promise to pay by a household or a firm is not necessarily accepted at face value because it may not be reliable. To deliver the required number of units of account, a firm would have to make profits correctly denominated in the units and in an acceptable form, a household would have to make wages, and so on. One way of making lower-tier IOUs acceptable might be a promise of conversion into the debt of an entity higher in the pyramid. Alternatively, the lower-tier securities may trade at discount, or offer a higher rate of interest as a "risk premium" (Bell 2005, 506). Obligations of banks in the second tier frequently *will* be acceptable at face value, because they are in principle convertible into higher-level obligations—those of the state central bank. Finally, the liabilities of the central bank itself, consisting of currency in the hands of the public plus bank reserves,[3] are at the top of the pyramid and do not need to be converted into anything else. The most plausible explanation for this is given by the "chartalist" school (Knapp 1973; Wray 1998), which argues that the state has the power to levy taxes but must also accept its own liabilities in tax payment. If the general principle is that the most acceptable form of payment rests on the collective agreement or belief that it is so, the chartalists add that the specific social relation decisive in practice is the power of the state. The state will also accept the liabilities of certain second-tier financial institutions directly in tax payment (Bell 2005, 506–507). This, then, validates such obligations as money over and above any convertibility feature. In any actual economy, therefore, the *money supply* consists mostly of some subset of the total deposit liabilities of second-tier financial institutions, such as commercial banks, and the liabilities of the state central bank serve as the *monetary base*. Using a variety of financial techniques, the central bank directly controls the interest rate on loans of base money. This has different names in different countries ("federal funds rate" in the United States, "overnight rate" in Canada, and so on); in general, we refer to it as the "policy rate." In turn, changes in the policy rate also affect interest rates both charged and received by the commercial banks. Commercial banks need central bank base money to settle claims among themselves, and no individual bank can afford to get too far out of step with its rivals in the composition of its portfolio. *Reductions* in the policy rate are therefore intended to reduce interest rates in general, increase commercial bank lending, and *increase* the money supply, whereas *increases* in the policy rate are intended to have the opposite effect.

Money and Capitalism

If orthodox economists have been confused about the notion of money, much the same is true about the concept of an "economy." The usual idea is that this term refers to different methods of obtaining provisions. Therefore, the fictional character Robinson Crusoe, alone on a deserted island, is as much engaged in economic activity as anyone else. This is nonsense as social science, however, as the decisions Crusoe makes are not relevant to anyone but himself.

Once we move beyond the isolated individual and make "provision" for more than one person, there are only three basic frameworks for achieving this (Heilbroner 1992, 10). The first is the "traditional economy," of which there are many practical variations, such as hunting and gathering or traditional agriculture. The main principle is that the work that gets done, by whom, and how the proceeds are shared is settled by tradition. The second is a "command" economy, where someone gives orders about what should be done and how the produce should be divided, and others obey. This also covers many variants—it is the method of an army, but also of slavery and state socialism. The third method, as defined by the sociologist Max Weber, is "the provision of human needs by the method of enterprise, which is to say by private businesses seeking profit" (Collins 1986, 21–22). Moreover, this is evidently the main or underlying principle of contemporary "capitalist" economies (although in the real world there are also substantial command elements, such as government bureaucracy, the police, and nationalized industries).[4] Two issues arise in considering the method of "enterprise." First, that economic analysis as a specialized field really applies only in this case (Heilbroner 1992, 10–16). There is no need for any expertise in "economics" to understand the other methods (or the problem of an isolated individual). It is therefore the method of enterprise that economists *should* be studying, rather than general mathematical theories of resource allocation. Second, and crucially, what is this "profit" that provides the incentive for private firms to act? Most obviously, it is a sum of money—bringing us back to the point that the system could not function in the absence of money, and ruling out the possibility of achieving the same results through barter.

Karl Marx described what was later called the "monetary circuit" (Parguez and Seccareccia 2000, 101) in the following way:[5]

$$M - C - C' - M'$$

The entrepreneurs acquire money, M (for instance, by borrowing or issuing shares), with which they then acquire commodities, C, that are used in a production process to make more commodities, C'. The newly produced commodities are finally sold for more money, M'. The difference between M' and M is the money profit, without which there would be no incentive for production to take place.

A key question to ask in attempting to understand how the system works is how it is actually *possible* for M' to be greater than M (written $M' > M$) in the aggregate, and thereby for profits to exist. There can only be one answer: during the circuit, money and credit creation must have taken place. The orthodox economic concept of an increase in the velocity of circulation (of a fixed amount of money) is not relevant here. A $20 bill may pass from hand to hand and, in doing so, appear to generate as much as $100, $200, or $300 of business. However, nobody can end up with more than $20 in his or her pocket. For a more concrete example, imagine a world with initially only one entrepreneur, who wants to make money manufacturing "widgets." The entrepreneur goes to a bank and takes out a loan of $100,000 to spend on wages and raw materials, which also creates $100,000 worth of money in bank deposits. Suppose furthermore that nothing else occurs on the financial side, and that in the meantime the widgets are produced and offered for sale. It is actually *impossible* for the entrepreneur to make a profit, as there is only $100,000 in existence. Even if widget workers and sellers of raw materials are willing to spend *all* their incomes on widgets (unlikely), there is not enough money to pay interest to the bank, let alone make a profit. How can the situation be resolved? The answer is that someone else must be willing to go into debt, for profits accrue to the first mover. There are basically only three possibilities. First, other entrepreneurs might be willing to take the same sort of chance. If a maker of "super widgets" also borrows $100,000 but the new product takes longer to produce, when the original widgets come on the market there will be a total of $200,000 in existence. It will then be *possible* for the widget-maker to make profits and repay interest and principal, if enough people decide to buy widgets. Note, however, that the money supply declines when the loans are paid off, meaning that the "super widgets"-maker will now need somebody else to become indebted, in turn, to make a profit. There has to be, for example, a manufacturer of "extra-super widgets" also willing to borrow, and so on. This is why Keynes (1964, 161) said that there would be trouble if the "animal spirits" of entrepreneurs faltered. The second possibility is that consumers themselves (domestic or foreign) might be willing to become indebted in terms of domestic currency to buy widgets. In this case, there is an issue of how a consumer-led boom can keep going if consumers have trouble paying their debts. Third, the state itself could go into debt; it could run a budget deficit and create monetary demand in that way. This was important historically in the actual genesis of capitalism, and there is no question of the state going bankrupt, as it is the issuer of the money. There could be problems, however, because of the reactions of politicians who *are* concerned about this and who therefore call for a budget surplus or "fiscal responsibility," thereby threatening to shut everything down. Those who already have money could also point to the opposite danger: that the budget deficit could be too large, too *much* money might be created, and existing wealth would be devalued through inflation.

This brings up the general point that for profits to be "real" (not inflationary), $M' > M$ must stimulate production, $C' > C$, to the same extent. If the quantity of commodities, C, stays constant, then $M' > M$ will only mean a rise in prices. This is what those who complain about excessive credit creation or propose to strictly limit the quantity of money are thinking about. This is misguided, though—restrictions will actually tend to lead to economic problems because there is no incentive for production unless there *are* money profits to be made. Rather, the goal of policy should be to allow enough credit creation to make $M' > M$ roughly correspond to $C' > C$, though this is easier said than done.

Monetary Policy

Because of the complex relationship between the state's power to levy taxes and the phenomena of money and credit creation, the main control that the central bank has over monetary policy is over the policy rate of interest (and thereby, in-directly, over interest rates in general). What matters is the "real," rather than the "nominal," policy rate. The nominal policy rate is the number quoted in the financial press—say, 1 percent, 3.25 percent, or 5.5 percent. The real rate is the nominal rate *less* expected inflation. (In the examples above, if expected inflation is 2 percent, the real policy rates would be -1.0 percent, 1.25 percent, and 3.5 percent respectively.) The real policy rate is the true cost of borrowing base money (and the same logic applies to other rates in the system). A high real policy rate will tend to reduce bank lending, reduce the money supply, reduce inflation, and may also cause an economic downturn. A low real rate will encourage lending, increase the money supply, and help stimulate the economy, but may also cause the inflation rate to increase. If the real rate becomes negative, this also "encourages borrowing," but may now lead to outright inflationary instability. In this case there is an unlimited incentive to borrow, and those currently holding money are getting a negative return and will try to spend their money as soon as possible. Smithin (2007, 114) has therefore argued that the safest monetary policy would be to stabilize the real policy rate at a "low but still positive" level. A low real rate provides stimulus for credit creation and productive economic activity, and, as long as it does not fall negative, financial holdings retain their real value and money performs the store-of-value function as well as can be expected. Note that stabilizing a *real* interest rate would still require relatively frequent changes to the *nominal* interest rate, whenever expected inflation changes. Therefore, the practical conduct of monetary policy under a real rate rule might not at first sight seem very different than when the authorities are pursuing other objectives. It would, however, avoid the excessive swings in real rates that occur under other regimes.

An alternative policy of keeping the nominal rate itself at a constant level (no matter how high or low) would lead to instability as soon as there was any change in inflation expectations. If the nominal interest rate is constant and something causes inflation (from either the demand or cost side), then the real rate must fall. This will encourage more borrowing and more inflation, and the real rate will eventually become negative. If a deflationary tendency (falling prices) sets in with the nominal rate constant, the real rate rises, causing further deflationary pressure. What is arguably the worst-case scenario will occur if the nominal interest rate is already zero and then deflation sets in. The real rate will be rising, and the result will be a recession. In such circumstances, monetary policy relying on interest rate changes becomes impotent, in an updated example of Keynes's (1964, 207) "liquidity trap." It would be necessary to cut real interest rates in such a situation, but this cannot be done since the nominal policy rate cannot go below zero. The only alternative is expansionary fiscal policy. The government must increase spending, cut taxes, or both, if it wants to boost the economy.

International Relations

Up to now the discussion has assumed the existence of a self-contained monetary network arranged in a hierarchical manner, dominated by a single central bank whose liabilities represent the money of account and ultimate means of payment. In reality, however, there is more than one such network in the world, and the international economy can be seen as the interaction of the competing monetary networks (which are often, but not necessarily, identified with the boundaries of political nation-states). The exchange rate between the different currencies can be floating or fixed. In the first case, the *nominal* exchange rate between two currencies (the foreign currency price of one unit of domestic currency) changes every day on the international markets. In the case of a fixed exchange rate, central banks themselves intervene directly in financial markets (buying and selling their own currencies) to keep the nominal exchange rate at a certain level. Although many people think that this is desirable in order to stabilize international trade, it must be recognized that the nominal exchange rate is only one of many factors determining international competitiveness. To assess the competitive position, it is necessary also to consider price levels in different countries and work out a *real effective* exchange rate.

A hierarchical debt pyramid, based now on the acceptability of different national currencies, can emerge in the international arena, in a way that is similar to what happens domestically within a given monetary network (Bougrine and Seccareccia 2008, 5–7). The currency of one particular issuer may become the international "reserve currency" at a certain point in history, as happened with the British pound in the 19th century and the US dollar in the 20th. This gives a degree of hegemonic power to the nation concerned, and its financial policies influence the whole world economy. As there is no world government, there is no clearcut explanation (as there was with national money) as to *why* a particular currency emerges as the most powerful. It is a question of global politics and history. However, if the system *does* have an inherent tendency to concentrate financial power, in the international sphere—where questions of political legitimacy are difficult to resolve—it would seem sensible to diffuse that power as much as possible (Smithin 2003, 206). This is an argument in favour of a flexible-exchange-rate system, which would allow the policy-makers in each country to pursue an independent course. It is an argument against fixed exchange rates, "dollarization," currency boards, or a common currency.

Conclusion

Money is a social relation or social institution, but is entirely "real" and has important causal effects in our lives. Orthodox economics makes a major error by ignoring this, treating economic activity mainly as a question of barter exchange. Specifically, the real interest rate and the real exchange rate are important *monetary* variables.

As a result of its nature, in practice money is likely to be a "creature of the state" (Lerner 2005, 467). To say this, however, is not necessarily to favour government control of the economy, or socialism; it is just to recognize (social) reality. Rather, the possibilities of success for the market economy/capitalism seem to depend on the judicious use of those monetary and fiscal policy instruments that *are* available to government.

NOTES

1. There is a fallacy/circularity in this reasoning because, apparently, we can have a sufficiently extensive market in place to be able to determine which money will be chosen *even before* one of the main preconditions of real-world market exchange—namely, money itself—has been invented.
2. The same applies when the bank purchases another type of security, such as a bond or an equity.
3. In the United States, the widely used term "federal funds" is revealing.
4. Sometimes, the phrase "mixed economy" is used to describe this.
5. However, like the classical economists, Marx himself arguably did not grasp the full implications of the fact that money must be involved (Ingham 2004, 61).

DISCUSSION QUESTIONS

1. Why is credit creation necessary for both money and profit to exist?
2. What is the modern version of Keynes's concept of the "liquidity trap"?
3. What is the difference between a "means of payment" and a "medium of exchange"?
4. How does the state central bank usually conduct monetary policy?
5. Why might national governments find it advantageous to allow the exchange rate to float?
6. How does the method of "enterprise" differ from an economy conducted by barter exchange?

SUGGESTED READINGS

Hicks, John. 1989. *A market theory of money.* Oxford: Oxford University Press.
Ingham, Geoffrey. 2004. *The nature of money.* Cambridge: Polity Press.
Smithin, John. 2009. *Money, enterprise and income distribution: Towards a macro-economic theory of capitalism.* London: Routledge.
Wray, L. Randall. 1998. *Understanding modern money: The key to price stability and full employment.* Cheltenham: Edward Elgar.

ONLINE RESOURCES

Bank of Canada: http://www.bank-banque-canada.ca.
Board of Governors of the Federal Reserve System: http://www.federalreserve.gov.
Davies, Glyn, and Roy Davies. 2002. A comparative chronology of money: Monetary history from ancient times to the present day. http://projects.exeter.ac.uk/RDavies/arian/amser/chrono.html.
International Monetary Fund: http://www.imf.org/external/index.htm.

REFERENCES

Bell, Stephanie. 2005. The role of the state and the hierarchy of money. In *Concepts of money: Interdisciplinary perspectives from economics, sociology and political science,* ed. Geoffrey Ingham, 496–510. Cheltenham: Edward Elgar.
Bougrine, Hassan, and Mario Seccareccia. 2008. Financing development: Removing the external constraint. Paper presented at an international conference "Financing Development: Where Do We Find the Money?" Laurentian University, Ontario, October 17–18.
Collins, Randall. 1986. *Weberian sociological theory.* London: Routledge.
Heilbroner, Robert. 1992. *Twenty-first century capitalism: The Massey lectures 1992.* Toronto: House of Anansi Press.
Hicks, John. 1989. *A market theory of money.* Oxford: Oxford University Press.
Ingham, Geoffrey. 2004. *The nature of money.* Cambridge: Polity Press.
Ingham, Geoffrey. 2005. Money is a social relation. In *Concepts of money: Interdisciplinary perspectives from economics, sociology and political science,* ed. Geoffrey Ingham, 221–244. Cheltenham: Edward Elgar.
Innes, A. Mitchell. 2004. What is money? In *Credit and state theories of money,* ed. L. Randall Wray, 14–49. Cheltenham: Edward Elgar. First published May 1913 in *Banking Law Journal.*
Keynes, John Maynard. 1964. *The general theory of employment, interest and money.* London: Harcourt Brace. First published 1936 by Macmillan.
Keynes, John Maynard. 1971. *A treatise on money: The pure theory of money.* Vol. V of *The collected writings of John Maynard Keynes,* ed. Donald Moggridge. Cambridge: Cambridge University Press. First published 1930 by Macmillan.
Knapp, Georg Friedrich. 1973. *The state theory of money.* Clifton, NJ: Augustus M. Kelley. First published 1924 by Macmillan.

Lerner, Abba P. 2005. Money as a creature of the state. In *Concepts of money: Interdisciplinary perspectives from economics, sociology and political science*, ed. Geoffrey Ingham, 467–472. Cheltenham: Edward Elgar. First published May 1947 in *American Economic Review*.

Parguez, Alain, and Mario Seccareccia. 2000. The credit theory of money: The monetary circuit approach. In *What is money?*, ed. John Smithin, 101–123. London: Routledge.

Searle, John. 2005. What is an institution? *Journal of Institutional Economics* 1: 1–22.

Smithin, John. 2000. What is money? In *What is money?*, ed. John Smithin, 1–15. London: Routledge.

Smithin, John. 2003. *Controversies in monetary economics*. Rev. ed. Cheltenham: Edward Elgar.

Smithin, John. 2007. A real interest rate rule for monetary policy? *Journal of Post Keynesian Economics* 30: 101–118.

Smithin, John. 2009. *Money, enterprise and income distribution: Towards a macro-economic theory of capitalism*. London: Routledge.

Wray, L. Randall. 1998. *Understanding modern money: The key to price stability and full employment.* Cheltenham: Edward Elgar.

PART II

The Behaviour of Key Macroeconomic Variables

Consumption and Saving: Should We Spend or Be Thrifty?

COMPETINGVIEWS

Ronald G. Bodkin, "Consumption Theory to the Turn of the Millennium (and Shortly Beyond)"

Mario Seccareccia, "The Determinants of Consumption and Saving from a Heterodox Perspective"

Editors' Introduction

Consumption is a key component of overall spending in the economy, constituting over 60 percent of GDP. While in the final analysis all would agree that consumption is the ultimate purpose of production, economists are somewhat ambivalent regarding its role. Keynesians, as well as other non-mainstream economists, emphasize the positive role of consumption in determining human welfare, but also point to its critical importance in determining macroeconomic performance. Although they largely agree on the welfare-enhancing implications of consumption, traditional neoclassical economists emphasize that an economy ultimately faces a trade-off between consumption and long-run capital accumulation, and that the latter is determined by saving, not consumption. In this view, what is needed for long-run growth is saving, or the act of abstaining from consumption.

As if this disagreement is not enough, there is even further discord regarding what is behind consumption spending. Mainstream economists point to an individual's underlying wealth position as being the ultimate driving force behind consumption. Hence, what matters in explaining long-run consumption behaviour is the long-term stream of current and future incomes (or one's "permanent income"). Ronald Bodkin discusses this view in his contribution and provides a useful review of the pertinent literature. Heterodox economists direct their analysis instead to the role played by household heterogeneity, consumption group norms, and income distribution in the determination of both the short-run and long-run patterns of consumption—as discussed in the contribution by Mario Seccareccia. But what is behind consumption? Is it the conduct of consumers, who maximize their utility subject to their long-run wealth constraint? Or is it more their sociological behaviour as consumers who tend to emulate pattern-setters even as their own real incomes and wealth positions persistently deteriorate?

There was a time when, in answering this question, there was genuine confidence among a majority of economists in asserting that it was the level of real wealth achieved by the community that played the single most important role. However, the last two decades have presented a challenge, as the extraordinary growth in consumption spending cannot be accounted for easily by the long-term growth in real income and wealth. The movement of the aggregate saving rate out of personal disposable income tending toward zero (or even negative rates)—as has been experienced in Canada and the United States—has encouraged economists to consider explanations that had not previously found favour in the profession.

Consumption Theory to the Turn of the Millennium (and Shortly Beyond)

Ronald G. Bodkin*

Introduction

Sir Isaac Newton is reported to have said, "If I have seen further it is by standing on the shoulders of giants." This sentiment would appear to be particularly apt in consumption theory. In this essay we shall meet, among others, four titans who have contributed mightily to the development of macroeconomic consumption theory. They are (in alphabetical order): Milton Friedman (1912–2006), John Maynard Keynes (1883–1946), Franco Modigliani (1918–2004), and James Tobin (1918–2002). These men stood at the top of the economics profession; Friedman, Modigliani, and Tobin all won (at different times) the Bank of Sweden's Nobel Memorial Prize in economics, while many would consider Keynes the greatest economist of the first half of the 20th century. Moreover, their work on consumption theory was certainly a central part of their research efforts.[1] It was my privilege and pleasure to have known (except for Keynes) each of these scholars personally and to have been able to learn from them.[2]

Before we look at specific theories and substantive results—that is, both the dominant theories (as these emerged historically during the years immediately following the Second World War) and the more recent evidence (which seems at times to substantiate the mainstream point of view)—I would like to say something about methodology. We shall follow the dominant paradigm, in which behaviour is modelled at the level of the individual or individual household, and then the individual behavioural relationships are aggregated to an economy-wide relationship. (Sometimes the process is abridged by the useful if doubtful procedure of assuming a representative individual consumer.) However, as Francis Green (1991) points out, there is an alternative approach, namely, to begin directly with the

* Without implicating them in any errors of fact or interpretation, I would like to thank James S. Duesenberry and Mario Seccareccia for their helpful comments and the latter for his encouragement.

relationships among the aggregative variables. This would be the approach of methodological globalism, as contrasted to *methodological individualism*. In dealing with relationships among aggregate variables, it is a debatable issue whether one of these two approaches is more fruitful than its rival, although mainstream economists have almost universally preferred methodological individualism.

Keynes and the Absolute Income Hypothesis: An Example

It is well known that Keynes (1936) postulated that real (price-deflated) consumption (C) was a function of real income (Y), namely:

$$C = f(Y_d) \tag{1},$$

where Y_d is price-deflated disposable income.[3] If we linearize this relationship, it becomes:

$$C = a + bY_d \tag{2},$$

where the parameter b is the marginal propensity to consume, which is supposed to lie strictly between the values of zero and unity. Keynes termed this relationship a "fundamental psychological law" (1936, 96). If the parameter a is strictly positive, then the proportion of disposable income consumed will decrease as income increases, though Keynes was less sure about this possibility. In some treatments, the parameter a has been interpreted as the subsistence level of consumption—that is, the amount of consumption that is absolutely necessary for survival, even if disposable income is zero. We may note that the two panels of Figure 1 are consistent with a marginal propensity to consume less than unity, and we shall see that in some recent studies there has been some empirical support for both of these views of the consumption function.

For the moment, let us turn to Figure 2, where the consumption level (in 1965 Canadian dollars) is plotted against disposable income, also in 1965 Canadian dollars, for one consumer unit—the author. The sample period is 1957–2001, except that only the last seven months of 1957 are represented (following the receipt of my undergraduate degree) and only the first six months (pre-retirement) of 2001 appear. (The source of these data is income tax records and private accounts, and disposable income includes estimated pension saving, including my share of the University of Ottawa's defined benefit pension plan.) It will be seen immediately that consumption appears to follow disposable income rather well until the end of the 1980s, when disposable income soars but consumption appears anchored to the levels of the 1980s. I shall comment further on this phenomenon, but for

FIGURE 1   Two Possible Consumption Functions

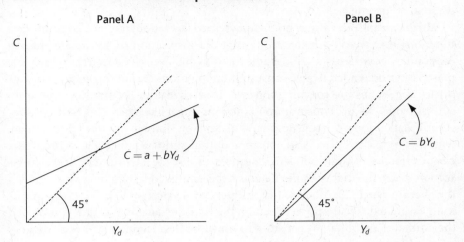

Panel A   Panel B

FIGURE 2   Disposable Income (Y_d) and Consumption (C), in Constant (1965 Cdn) Dollars, RGB, 1957-II Through 2001-I

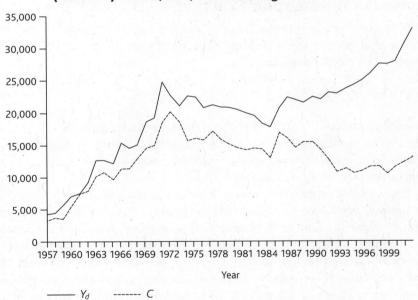

the moment one can conclude that there is more to real consumption than real disposable income.[4]

In the meantime, we may note some stylized facts about the early consumption functions that were estimated, following the inspiration of Keynesian macroeconomic theory. Cross-section studies of individual households in the immediate postwar period tended to give consumption functions resembling panel A of Figure 1 (namely, positive consumption even at a zero income level), while time series studies tended to give consumption functions much like panel B of Figure 1, suggesting that the long-run consumption function was simply a ray through the origin, with a marginal propensity to consume only slightly less than one. Moreover, a curious result was found with cross-section studies: the later the date of the cross-section study, the higher in the field was the estimated level of consumption (in the relevant range). In other words, the greater the constant term, *a*, of the empirically estimated consumption function, the later the date of the study—provided the estimated marginal propensities to consume (the parameter *b*) were roughly equivalent, which, in general, they were.

James Tobin's Modification of the Standard Consumption Function

In the mid-20th century James Tobin (1951) pointed out that the stylized facts mentioned at the end of the previous section could be accounted for by a consumption function of the form

$$C = a + bY_d + dNW \tag{3},$$

where the variables C and Y_d and the parameter b retain their previous meanings, while the symbol NW is the price-level-adjusted value of net worth (for either individual or aggregate consumption functions) and the symbol d represents the propensity to spend out of household wealth.[5]

Tobin's introduction of this new variable was certainly neat, because there was now an easy explanation for the difference between the cyclical (or cross-section) and the secular (or time series) consumption functions (see Figure 3). Because wealth increases with economic growth, over time the cyclical or short-term consumption function will drift upward. Thus a judicious cross-cut of these shifting, short-run consumption functions can reproduce the results found by such famous economists as Simon Kuznets and Raymond Goldsmith in the long run for the US economy—namely, that of a ray (through the origin) with a steep slope just below unity. This possibility is diagrammed in Figure 3.[6]

Important early postwar studies of the consumption function were conducted by James Duesenberry (1948, 1949) and T. Merritt Brown (1952). Although a

FIGURE 3 Long-Run Consumption Function as a Cross-Cut of Short-Run Consumption Functions

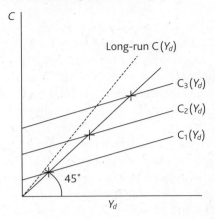

discussion of these analyses is beyond the scope of this essay, readers can find a detailed presentation in Bodkin (1977).

Franco Modigliani and the Life Cycle Theory of Saving

Franco Modigliani and his junior collaborators, Richard E. Brumberg and Albert Ando, built a theory of aggregate consumption based on the simple insight that most saving in a modern, developed economy is retirement saving—namely, saving through financial institutions, such as life insurance companies, designed to finance retirement consumption (Modigliani and Brumberg 1954; Ando and Modigliani 1963). It is posited that during one's working life the representative individual will save enough to finance consumption *at the same level* during the retirement years. Hence dissaving during the retirement years is an integral part of this theory of consumption and saving. If one adds the simplifying assumptions of a known lifespan, a zero rate of interest, and (most critically) an absence of estate motivation, one can easily calculate the intended consumption pattern of the representative household unit, either in the working or in the retirement years.[7] In particular, it follows that the typical consumer unit will adjust its consumption to average income expected over the remainder of its lifetime. Moreover, if this representative consumer unit receives a positive or negative windfall (such as winning the lottery or suffering a business loss), then the unit will increase or decrease its consumption by only a small fraction of the change in economic circumstances, because the changed plan will spread the unexpected gain or loss over all of the remaining years of life.

69

What are the implications of this theory for an aggregate consumption function? Ando and Modigliani (1963) show that, with some additional aggregation assumptions, they can derive an aggregate consumption function in which consumption depends on current labour income, expected future labour income, and the initial stock of wealth. Moreover, the expected value of the constant term of this long-run consumption function is, theoretically, zero. Also, the coefficient of current labour income and initial wealth will be small (say, between 0.02 and 0.06), and it is expected future labour income that will carry the freight for consumption; this is because, for the typical working individual, labour income is expected to persist many years into the future.

A very interesting corollary follows from this theory, namely, a proposition that M.J. Farrell (1959) termed the "rate of growth hypothesis." In particular, it is clear that, under the life cycle hypothesis, a static society (one with neither population growth nor growth in income per capita) will generate no net saving, as the saving of the economically active will be just offset by the dissaving of the retired members of the community. Now let the society enjoy either population growth or growth of income per head (or both). In this case, the dissaving of the retired will be inferior to the saving of the economically active population, because either there are proportionately more of the economically active persons or the current workers are earning more than their aged counterparts did during their economically active years (or both). Using the consumption function elaborated in the preceding paragraph, it can be shown that there will be a long-run growth equilibrium in which income, saving, and wealth are all growing at the same rate; moreover, the rate of saving is strictly proportional to this common rate of growth.

Milton Friedman and the Permanent Income Hypothesis

As this will be my third pass at summarizing the late Milton Friedman's major contribution to consumption theory (see Bodkin 1977 or 1993), I shall be relatively brief. First, it should be remarked that, in a world of absolute certainty, there would be no appreciable difference between Modigliani's and Friedman's theories (except, perhaps, for the issue of estate motivation). In principle, the household's total wealth is just the discounted value of all current and future receipts of income, and permanent income is simply the periodic flow that represents an assumed rate of return on this wealth. (Thus, permanent income can be interpreted as simply the level of consumption that the unit can make, period after period, without impairing its wealth.) It is assumed that the representative unit will optimize its consumption flow over the present period and all future periods, as suggested by a stable utility function. Presumably, the typical, rational consumer unit would opt for a steady stream of consumption over time, or else a slightly rising stream of real consumption, according to its tastes. So far, this is simply an extended life cycle theory, as presented, for instance, in Somermeyer and Bannink (1973).

Because we don't live in a certain world, however, the theory has to be modified considerably. Friedman divides both income and consumption into permanent and transitory components, with the permanent components being the systematic variables of the system. The transitory components are said formally to exhaust their effects within the time horizon (estimated by Friedman to be three years for American households in the first half of the 20th century), but they can be assumed to be essentially random disturbances. In particular, the permanent and transitory components of both income and consumption are uncorrelated with each other, and (critically) the transitory components of income and of consumption are uncorrelated (and hence independent of each other, if each follows a normal probability distribution). Finally, we note that permanent (systematic) consumption is strictly proportional to permanent income,[8] and incidentally, that the term "horizon" is somewhat misleading in this context because the permanent factors are those whose effects are not exhausted within the time horizon. Hence, Friedman's permanent income hypothesis (PIH) requires the representative unit to look beyond the horizon.

Some consequences follow from these assumptions. First, and most controversially, note that this strict version of the PIH implies that the marginal propensity to consume transitory income is strictly zero. After all, where could a positive transitory income shock go? It cannot influence permanent consumption, because transitory income is uncorrelated with permanent income and hence is uncorrelated with permanent consumption, which is strictly proportional to permanent income. However, this positive transitory income shock cannot affect transitory consumption either, as these two components are postulated to be uncorrelated (or even independent). Much work has gone into testing this implication of the theory, often with negative results. (For example, Bird and Bodkin (1965) found that the marginal propensity to consume transitory income was definitely less than the marginal propensity to consume permanent income, but probably greater than zero.) We shall review some recent tests of this proposition in the concluding section.

The cyclical and secular aggregative consumption functions are well explained by the PIH. Subject to aggregation, the long-run consumption function is simply the proportionality relationship between permanent consumption and permanent income. Friedman (1957) found that this factor of proportionality was roughly 0.9 in the United States in the mid-20th century, which agrees with the earlier empirical work of Kuznets and Goldsmith.

Friedman (1957) briefly applied his model to issues of macroeconomic stabilization policy. He argued that the Keynesian multiplier would be considerably weaker than traditional Keynesians would expect, again due to the contaminating influence of transitory income. In particular, he felt that temporary tax cuts were of limited efficacy in attempting to stimulate an economy about to go into recession, because consumers would take the temporary nature of the cuts into account and hence not engage heavily in additional spending. It has to be admitted that the American experience during the second half of the 20th century has largely confirmed Friedman on this point.

Some Recent Studies and Conclusions

During the last few decades a number of important studies have supported the life cycle theory/PIH to varying degrees. These studies—notably, the work of Robert E. Hall (1978) and Campbell and Mankiw (1989, 1990)—emphasize the importance of wealth in the determination of consumption behaviour. In this section we will examine five recent studies, all conducted around the turn of the millennium, which offer rather mixed support for the mainstream hypothesis.

Nicholas S. Souleles (1999) devised an ingenious test of the implication that the marginal propensity to spend transitory income is zero, under the strict PIH. Souleles looked at income tax refunds, which, as they are based on events in the prior calendar year, should be quite predictable to individual households. Consequently, the life cycle theory/PIH should predict no response from the actual receipt of the refund—but that is not what Souleles found. Rather, using some sophisticated empirical techniques, he found that the month of the receipt of the refund was generally associated with greater expenditures. Souleles's conclusion, therefore, was that there was significant evidence of excess sensitivity in the response of households' consumption to their income tax refunds. Indeed, he calculated that the marginal propensity to spend within the calendar quarter out of income tax refunds could be as little as 0.35 or as high as 0.6.

A related test of the strict PIH/life cycle theory was carried out by Jonathan A. Parker (1999) and published in the same issue of the *American Economic Review* as the Souleles study. Parker used the fact that there is an income cap on Social Security contributions (taxes) in the United States; consequently, medium- and high-income earners will see greater disposable income in the months toward the end of the calendar year, after their Social Security taxes will have been paid in full. The Keynesian absolute income hypothesis would predict that consumption would rise in these latter months, while the life cycle theory/PIH would predict a smooth pattern of consumption throughout the calendar year. Parker uses a variant of Hall's (1978) statistical approach to test this proposition. He finds overwhelming evidence that "[c]onsumers do not perfectly smooth their demand for goods at quarterly frequencies across expected income changes" (Parker 1999, 969). Instead, consumption tends to be higher in those quarters in which disposable income is higher due to the taxation procedures of the Social Security legislation. Parker also adduces some evidence that his results may reflect "bounded rationality"—namely, that the calculations necessary for perfect optimization across the calendar year may be so complicated that the reward is not proportional to the effort involved.

Social Security payments (not taxes) are the centre of the analysis in Stephens's (2003) study. Melvin Stephens Jr. uses the institutional fact that Social Security payments to retirees arrive on the third day of the month to ask whether patterns of consumption are affected by this institutional datum. Using a sophisticated empirical technique, Stephens concludes that consumption is quite sensitive to the timing of Social Security receipts, particularly for households for whom this payment is a primary source of household income. The magnitude of the resulting spending increases for the week following the Social Security receipt ranges from 7 to 20 percent of average expenditures, with considerable increases found on the day of the receipt and the day immediately following. Obviously, this is rather strong evidence against the strict PIH/life cycle theory; if households cannot smooth within the month, how can they possibly do so over a lifetime?

Matthew D. Shapiro and Joel Slemrod (2003) used a survey of US households to gauge the effects of the 2001 tax rebate program of former president George W. Bush. They found that only 22 percent of households surveyed reported that they used the tax rebate primarily to increase spending; the others said they used it primarily for savings or to pay off debts (apparently the popular mind does not consider debt repayment as saving). The results are surprising on either point of view about consumption theory, as the tax reductions were supposed to be in place for at least ten years. Of course, the result could be explained by the notion that a current tax cut means a higher future tax bill, at least if government expenditure is not reduced (this highly orthodox view is sometimes termed the "Ricardo-Barro equivalence proposition"). Some might interpret these results as reflecting the unreliability of asking individuals what they are going to do in the future. In any case, Milton Friedman would no doubt consider these results as confirming his skepticism about tax cuts as an effective instrument of macroeconomic stabilization.

By contrast, the final study reviewed contradicts the results of Souleles, Parker, and Stephens. Chang-Tai Hsieh (2003) examined a sample of Alaska residents, all of whom received relatively large payments from the Alaska Permanent Fund, which distributes (partially) Alaskan oil revenues to permanent residents of Alaska. (These amounts are not small; as Hsieh points out, a family of four would have received a distribution of US\$6,164 in 1998.) The amounts have always been paid out in the fourth quarter of the year, which facilitates the testing procedure. Hsieh compares consumption in the fourth quarter of the year with that in the third quarter, using a Hall-type statistical method for which the Alaska distribution variable is one of the explanatory variables. This variable is always statistically insignificant and, moreover, its sign is often perverse. Hence, in this instance, the PIH/life cycle theory is clearly confirmed. Hsieh believes that the difference between his results and those of the studies reviewed earlier may be due to the large size of the Alaska Permanent Fund distributions; their great magnitude may make the calculations to smooth consumption (and its associated marginal utility) worthwhile.

Conclusion

It is time to sum up. Consumption expenditures seem difficult to explain, both at the level of the individual consumer and in the aggregate. One reason for this was suggested by the Campbell and Mankiw studies cited above (1989, 1990). In particular, these results may reflect consumer heterogeneity, as some of the consumer units may be life cycle consumers while others may be Keynesian consumers. George A. Akerloff (2007) has suggested that consumption theory should give much more attention to mental accounting or "norms." According to him, some income (for example, wages and salaries) is meant to be consumed and some is meant to be saved. Akerloff believes that "[a] major determinant of consumption is what people think they *should* consume" (2007, 15; italics in the original). His emphasis on psychological factors recalls the earlier work of Keynes (1936), who described a value of the marginal propensity to consume lying between zero and unity as a "fundamental psychological law." It also recalls the work of George Katona (1960), who argued that economists tend to underestimate greatly the importance of psychological factors influencing consumption. In any case, if these psychological factors are important, then individual households will differ—sometimes greatly—in their consumption behaviour and in their reactions to external changes. Hence aggregation over such a diverse set of consumers is likely to muddy the waters, leaving the poor macro theorist with no clear result.[9]

NOTES

1. Friedman (1993, 186) has stated that his 1957 volume on consumption was his favourite research publication.
2. However, three other distinguished scholars should be mentioned explicitly. James Duesenberry (b. 1918), the only survivor of the previous generation of consumption theorists, developed an interesting approach to consumption theory (relative income at the micro level, morphing into the previous peak income hypothesis at the macro level), which—because of space considerations and because it is discussed in the following essay by Mario Seccareccia—will not be discussed here. T. Merritt Brown, who was my colleague at the University of Western Ontario from 1967 until his untimely death in 1973, introduced the level of the preceding period's consumption as an additional explanatory variable. Finally, I wish to acknowledge an intellectual debt to the late Irwin Friend (1915–1987), an active participant in these debates and controversies.

Professor Friend, my MA thesis adviser, generously gave me his National Service Life Insurance dividend project in the late 1950s, thus providing me with an immediate entrance into these fascinating debates (see Bodkin 1959).

3. Keynes (1936) preferred to deflate nominal magnitudes by the wage rate (a wage index) rather than by a price index. Most later macroeconomists have treated this as a secondary matter, largely reflecting the underdevelopment of index theory in Keynes's day.

4. Keynes (1936) made this point explicitly in his chapters on the consumption function; however, he thought that the empirical importance of these additional factors was limited.

5. The estimated values of the parameter d are much lower and fall generally in the range of 0.02 to 0.06. At times, wealth effects can be quite important; in some interpretations, the boom of 2002–2007 in the United States was fuelled by wealth effects emanating from the bubble in housing values. Note also that the parameter a can still be interpreted as a subsistence level of income, as it is the predicted level of consumption with zero income and zero net worth.

6. Smithies, Livingston, and Mosak (1945) interpreted the upward drift in the short-run consumption functions as reflecting a developing taste for new luxury goods as economic growth proceeds. Note that this interpretation is incompatible with the postulate of stable utility functions, which remain unchanged over time.

7. Somermeyer and Bannink (1973) have generalized the Modigliani–Brumberg–Ando framework to include family formation and estate motivation. Wim Somermeyer once remarked to the author that the formulation of the life cycle theory by Modigliani and his co-authors was essentially a "bachelor's" theory!

8. Well, not precisely constant! The parameter k (the ratio of permanent consumption to permanent income) can depend, in Friedman's theoretical formulation, on several additional variables, such as the rate of interest, demographic factors, and the proportion of total wealth that comes from property (non-human) sources. The point is that this proportion, in Friedman's formulation, is strictly independent of the level of permanent income.

9. To return to Figure 2, one interpretation of these data is that the author was a Keynesian consumer until the end of the 1980s but a life cycle consumer (saver) for the last decade or so prior to his retirement. Two factors explain the divergence between consumption and disposable income during the decade of the 1990s. First, the rise in income was largely fuelled by hefty returns on the University of Ottawa's pension plan, and it certainly would have been unwise to borrow against these for a consumption binge. (As Akerloff (2007) says, some income is for spending and some for saving.) Second, in 1990, the Supreme Court of Canada ruled (in *McKinney v. University of Guelph*) that mandatory retirement, while it was indeed age discrimination, was socially justifiable and hence permitted. This meant that I could count on little more than a decade of a senior professional salary income and

would have to save at a much greater pace if I wanted to continue to enjoy the standard of living to which I had become accustomed. Thus the same individuals may change their approach to income and consumption over the life cycle, further complicating the issue of formulating a satisfactory aggregate consumption function.

DISCUSSION QUESTIONS

1. How important are community standards in determining an individual consumer's division of disposable income between consumption and saving?
2. Do many individuals switch from current-income to life cycle consumers (or savers), or is the author's experience somewhat unusual?

SUGGESTED READINGS

Bodkin, Ronald G. 1959. Windfall income and consumption. *American Economic Review* 49 (September): 602–614.

Brown, T.M. 1952. Habit persistence and lags in consumer behaviour. *Econometrica* 20 (July): 207–233.

Duesenberry, James S. 1948. Income–consumption relations and their implications. In *Income, employment and public policy: Essays in honor of Alvin Hansen*, 54–81. New York: Norton.

Keynes, John Maynard. 1936. *The general theory of employment, interest and money*, chaps. 8–10. New York: Harcourt, Brace.

REFERENCES

Akerloff, George A. 2007. The missing motivation in macroeconomics. *American Economic Review* 97 (March): 5–36.

Ando, Albert, and Franco Modigliani. 1963. The "life-cycle" hypothesis of saving: Aggregate implications and tests. *American Economic Review* 53 (March): 55–84.

Bird, Roger C., and Ronald G. Bodkin. 1965. The national service life insurance dividend of 1950 and consumption: A further test of the strict permanent income hypothesis. *Journal of Political Economy* 73 (October): 499–515.

Bodkin, Ronald G. 1959. Windfall income and consumption. *American Economic Review* 49 (September): 602–614.

Bodkin, Ronald G. 1977. Keynesian econometric concepts: Consumption functions, investment functions, and the multiplier. In *Modern economic thought*, ed. Sidney Weintraub, 67–92. Philadelphia: University of Pennsylvania Press.

Bodkin, Ronald G. 1993. La théorie du revenu permanent et consommation de Milton Friedman [Milton Friedman's theory of permanent income and consumption]. In *Milton Friedman et son oeuvre* [Milton Friedman and His Works], ed. Marc Lavoie and Mario Seccareccia, 101–110. Montreal: Les Presses de l'Université de Montréal.

Brown, T.M. 1952. Habit persistence and lags in consumer behaviour. *Econometrica* 20 (July): 207–233.

Campbell, John Y., and Gregory N. Mankiw. 1989. Consumption, income and interest rates: Reinterpreting the time series evidence. In *NBER macroeconomics annual*, ed. Olivier Jean Blanchard and Stanley Fischer, 185–216. Cambridge, MA: MIT Press.

Campbell, John Y., and Gregory N. Mankiw. 1990. Permanent income, current income, and consumption. *Journal of Business and Economic Statistics* 18 (July): 265–279.

Duesenberry, James S. 1948. Income–consumption relations and their implications. In *Income, employment and public policy: Essays in honor of Alvin Hansen*, 54–81. New York: Norton.

Duesenberry, James S. 1949. *Income, saving, and the theory of consumer behavior.* Cambridge, MA: Harvard University Press.

Farrell, M.J. 1959. The new theories of the consumption function. *Economic Journal* 69 (December): 678–696.

Friedman, Milton. 1957. *A theory of the consumption function.* Princeton, NJ: Princeton University Press.

Friedman, Milton. 1993. Postface [Epilogue]. In *Milton Friedman et son oeuvre*, ed. Marc Lavoie and Mario Seccareccia, 185–190. Montreal: Les presses de l'Université de Montréal.

Green, Francis. 1991. Institutional and other unconventional theories of saving. *Journal of Economic Issues* 25 (March): 93–113.

Hall, Robert E. 1978. Stochastic implications of the life cycle-permanent income hypothesis: Theory and evidence. *Journal of Political Economy* 86 (December): 971–986.

Hsieh, Chang-Tai. 2003. Do consumers react to anticipated income changes? Evidence from the Alaska Permanent Fund. *American Economic Review* 93 (March): 397–405.

Katona, George. 1960. *The powerful consumer.* New York: McGraw-Hill.

Keynes, John Maynard. 1936. *The general theory of employment, interest and money.* New York: Harcourt, Brace.

McKinney v. University of Guelph. 1990. [1990] 3 SCR 229.

Modigliani, Franco, and Richard E. Brumberg. 1954. Utility analysis and the consumption function: An interpretation of cross-section data. In *Post-Keynesian economics*, ed. Kenneth K. Kurihara, 398–436. New Brunswick, NJ: Rutgers University Press.

Parker, Jonathan A. 1999. The response of household consumption to predictable changes in social security taxes. *American Economic Review* 89 (September): 959–973.

Shapiro, Matthew D., and Joel Slemrod. 2003. Consumer response to tax rebates. *American Economic Review* 93 (March): 381–396.

Smithies, Arthur, Morris Livingston, and Jacob L. Mosak. 1945. Forecasting postwar demand: I, II, and III. *Econometrica* 13 (January): 1–37.

Somermeyer, W.H., and R. Bannink. 1973. *A consumption–savings model and its applications.* New York: Elsevier.

Souleles, Nicholas S. 1999. The response of household consumption to income tax refunds. *American Economic Review* 89 (September): 947–958.

Stephens, Melvin, Jr. 2003. "3rd of tha [sic] Month": Do social security recipients smooth consumption between checks? *American Economic Review* 93 (March): 406–422.

Tobin, James. 1951. Relative income, absolute income and saving. In *Money, trade, and economic growth: Essays in honor of John Henry Williams,* 135–156. New York: Macmillan.

The Determinants of Consumption and Saving from a Heterodox Perspective

Mario Seccareccia

Introduction: The Keynesian Notion of the Aggregate Consumption Function

Numerous social philosophers since antiquity have recognized that the ultimate goal of production is consumption, and that consumption depends on income generated from productive activity. The formal recognition of a fundamental bi-causal relationship between consumption and income can be traced as far back as some 18th-century French economic writings (see Cochrane 1970). Indeed, these early French economists had discovered the multiplier effect—that is, they had theorized that an initial change in some autonomous spending could have a magnified effect on overall income through successive second-round, or feedback, effects on consumption expenditures.

The modern concept of a consumption function, however, finds its origin in the work of John Maynard Keynes—more precisely, in his *General Theory of Employment, Interest and Money*, published in 1936. Keynes labelled the relationship between consumption and income the "consumption function" and argued that it was a stable relationship resting on a "fundamental psychological law" conditioned by habits and institutions. This fact ensured that changes in current real disposable income would trigger proportional changes in consumption spending. Keynes's theory can be depicted in functional form as: $C = f(Y_d)$, where C is real consumption expenditures, Y_d is real disposable income, and f is usually depicted as a linear non-homogeneous function. In addition to these stable, underlying "subjective" factors, Keynes referred to a series of other factors—including windfall gains/losses (say, in the stock market) and the relationship between current and expected future income—that could affect the overall propensity to consume. However, he did not think that variables other than the current level of real income played a very significant role, thus suggesting a fairly stable aggregate consumption relationship for policy consideration. Indeed, he supposed that the slope of the consumption function (the so-called marginal propensity to consume, or the first derivative, f') did not change much within a reasonably short time horizon, while the ratio of consumption to income (the average propensity to consume) might well decline as real income trended upward over the long term.

Competing Conceptions of Aggregate Consumer Behaviour

The Mainstream View

In the 1950s, mainstream (neoclassical) as well as non-mainstream (heterodox) economists challenged this Keynesian aggregate consumption function. Traditional economists, who subscribe to an individualist methodology and prefer to model consumer behaviour based on the so-called representative agent, did not find much fault with Keynes's aggregate function. The latter was a relationship, for instance, that did not differentiate household consumption behaviour according to income classes. What was deemed by the mainstream to be somewhat problematic was Keynes's reliance on current income as the single most important determinant of consumption spending. This is because it defied the well-established neoclassical view of consumer behaviour that, at the micro level of the representative household, individual households are assumed to carry out their spending not only on the basis of their current real disposable income but, above all, on the basis of the wealth that they command (their overall budget constraint).

Even more importantly, however, the policy implications of a stable consumption function raised problems for those traditional economists who were ideologically predisposed against government policy intervention. A consumption function that rests exclusively on current real disposable income would predict stronger output/ employment multiplier effects from an increase in, say, government expenditures than a consumption function that included wealth as an independent variable, or what Milton Friedman dubbed "permanent income." This is because, if consumption depends primarily on wealth rather than on current income, any change in disposable income (arising from either a temporary tax cut or an increase in government spending) could only make a minor dent on overall household wealth (or the so-called permanent income), thereby inducing limited second-round cumulative consumption effects. For those strong, pro-market theorists—such as Milton Friedman—who were engaged in an ideological battle against postwar Keynesian economists advocating government fiscal intervention in the economy, it was convenient to argue in favour of a model of consumer behaviour that could not readily be used to justify activist fiscal policy. The suggested powerful positive impact of government expenditures on output and employment that had earlier been emphasized by Keynes would thus seemingly be purged of its usefulness in stabilizing economic activity.

Heterodox Perspectives

For heterodox economists, the problem was not whether it is wealth or income that determines consumption. Instead, it was primarily the aggregative nature of Keynes's original analysis, based on the representative consumer, which caused some concern. Hence, while accepting Keynes's theory that consumption depends primarily on real disposable income, heterodox economists distinguished propensities to consume according to income class affiliations. In sum, for the sake of greater realism, low-income workers were postulated to have a high propensity to consume (a low propensity to save), while high-income earners were assumed to have a low propensity to consume (a high propensity to save).

Indeed, one of the most famous of these postulated consumption/saving functions is sometimes referred to as the classical savings function based on a simplified, two-income class model of the economy; the function is normally associated with the names Michal Kalecki, Nicholas Kaldor, and Luigi Pasinetti (see Green 1991, 104 et seq.). Instead of assuming an economy-wide consumption function, these economists postulated that savings out of wage income would be very low or approximately zero—with workers accumulating little assets (other than, perhaps, saving enough to own their own homes)—while the saving propensity out of property income would be high, thereby ensuring that the owners of the firms (the capitalists) would continue to accumulate assets. In this case, the policy implications of, for instance, a government fiscal stimulus would be very different. A change in autonomous spending could have a high (or low) multiplier effect on income and employment depending on whether income is distributed more (or less) evenly in an economy, that is to say, depending on whether the change in autonomous expenditures goes toward raising the income primarily of the poor (or the rich) in a community. Indeed, would the second-round effects not be potentially more powerful if, for instance, a billion dollars of government funds could be spent on expanding government transfers to the unemployed (whose propensity to consume would be very high) instead of on safeguarding the financial assets and sustaining the incomes of some wealthy financiers (whose propensity to save would be high)—as seems to have occurred with many of the financial bailouts internationally in 2008?

Heterodox economists also pointed to alternative models of consumer behaviour that were not depicted in either Keynes's original conceptualization of the consumption function or the mainstream models of consumption by wealth holders. In fact, in his original model of consumer behaviour, Keynes did point to habits and institutions, and recognized "ostentation" and "extravagance" as determinants of the aggregate consumption function (Mason 2000, 556). However, having been trained in the Marshallian neoclassical tradition, he never made much of this. Following Keynes, others offered what economists often identify as "sociological" explanations of consumer behaviour. One such explanation, which originated in the early works of the famous heterodox economist Thorstein Veblen and was popularized by some economists in the wake of the Second World War (such as Harvard economists James Duesenberry and Harvey Leibenstein), was based on the emulative behaviour of households—which in recent times has been recognized, even by some well-established mainstream economists, as an important "missing motivation" in macroeconomics (Akerlof 2007).

Contrary to the mainstream view, emulation is seen as a powerful motive shaping consumption spending. Individual choice is not made in a vacuum; rather it is a byproduct of an individual's upbringing and the institutions that have moulded his or her preferences, which are often connected with a household's social-class affiliation. Individuals, therefore, compare their consumption with that of other groups and engage in a process of emulation. The poor have a higher propensity to consume than the wealthy, not only because they must spend most of their income for reasons of necessity (that is, just to remain alive, as emphasized by early 19th-century classical economists) but also because the higher ostentatious spending of certain households ignites aspirations that even low-income earners seek to meet. This could explain in part why, even if real income remains unchanged for a group over a considerable period of time—thereby suggesting a low growth in "permanent income"—the propensity to consume may change, contrary to the predictions of traditional neoclassical theories based on the Friedman variety. In other words, consumption and household indebtedness might in fact grow significantly over time because of emulation, regardless of the trend in real income.

Which Approach Can Better Explain the Evolution of Consumption over Time?

If one looks at the evolution of consumption and disposable income since the 1970s, as Frank (2005) points out, models based on consumer emulation can explain—and even outperform—those mainstream models based on the significance of wealth in explaining patterns of consumption. For instance, while the relationship between real consumption and real disposable income is indeed very close regardless of the time period analyzed, the actual relationship between the average propensity to consume/average propensity to save and the evolution of real income seems to be moving in a direction that may not be as supportive of the mainstream hypothesis. For instance, if we look at Figure 1, which depicts the statistical behaviour of the saving rate and the rate of change of real personal disposable income in Canada and the United States since 1980, we observe that these two variables show a very weak, albeit *positive*, correlation. That is to say, as the rate of growth of real per capita disposable income declined (and actually turned

FIGURE 1 **Evolution of Personal Saving Rate and Rate of Change of Real Per Capita Personal Disposable Income in Percentage Terms, Canada and the United States, 1980–2007, Annual Observations**

Panel A: Canada

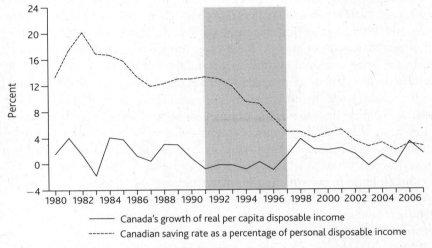

Source: Statistics Canada, CANSIM II series V3860248, V508765, V508766, V691782, V691783.

Panel B: United States

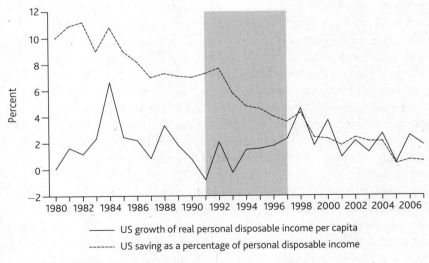

Source: US Department of Commerce, Bureau of Economic Analysis.

negative), as during the 1990s, the saving rate plummeted. This is most obvious during the post-1980 slow growth period, which was characterized by an average growth rate of approximately 2.1 percent for the years 1980–1989, down to a 0.5 percent average for 1990–1999, and then finally to 1.4 percent average growth of real per capita disposable income for 2000–2007. Indeed, in the case of Canada, the average growth rate was actually negative for over half a decade during the early to mid-1990s. Yet, during that same period of negative growth in real per capita personal disposable income, the average propensity to consume rose dramatically (see shaded areas for both Canada and the United States in Figure 1). A temporary decline in real income, leading to a higher ratio of consumption to income, is consistent with the mainstream "permanent income" hypothesis. This is because consuming households are assumed to look at their long-term wealth position rather than their current income status when making decisions regarding consumption, thereby maintaining their consumption in the face of a fall in real income. However, when growth did return during the late 1990s, albeit at a significantly lower long-term growth rate, the saving rate continued to decline somewhat. This latter evidence would *not* be consistent with the mainstream hypothesis.

The heterodox perspective on aggregate consumption behaviour, on the other hand, points to two separate factors that would explain not only the initial decline arising from a slump such as occurred during the early 1980s and the first half of the 1990s in Canada, but also the persistence of the decline in the saving rate throughout most of that era. Firstly, the peak income hypothesis, originally put forth by James Duesenberry during the late 1940s, argues that, when income falls, consumption would be maintained because of habit formation and emulation—in which case the ratio of saving to disposable income would inevitably decline during recessions (as seen, for instance, in the case of Canada during the early 1990s). Moreover, consumer emulation and endogenous preference formation would explain the persistence of household spending and why consumption could continue to rise regardless of whether disposable income rises or declines. In this case, consumer expenditures could actually follow a somewhat autonomous pattern.

Secondly, as discussed earlier, heterodox economists place great emphasis on the role of income distribution in explaining the behaviour of aggregate consumption spending. Because of long-term tendencies resulting from labour market factors and the effects of globalization, in both Canada and the United States the distribution of income has become ever more uneven since the 1980s, with a falling share of total income accruing to low-income groups and a rising share to high-income groups (Korty 2008). Given the importance of peer group comparison and emulation in expenditures, the effect has been to increase spending at the bottom end of the income ladder as a result of rising consumption and financial norms (Cynamon and Fazzari 2008). Indeed, during the post-1980 slow growth era, this is what was happening on the consumption side, as the saving rates of low-income groups not only declined but became progressively more negative—especially as household debt became much more socially acceptable and financial institutions began to apply less stringent criteria for advancing credit for consumer purposes (Seccareccia 2005). The effect of this post-1980 decline in the saving rate was to push household debt ratios to record high levels.

Table 1 provides some interesting data that corroborate the heterodox view of the significance of income distribution in explaining household saving propensities. The evidence supports the view, previously described, that high-income groups have a much higher propensity to consume than low-income groups. While the overall saving rate declined significantly in Canada from 1986 to 2006 (which is consistent with the national accounting data also displayed in Figure 1), the data for each income quintile suggest that there was a clear evolution in the pattern of household spending by income quintile. While the higher-income quintiles were actually raising their saving rates, not only did middle- and low-income groups see their saving rates decline sharply, but the low-income groups were actually falling deeper into debt just to attain the rising consumption norms. Students will undoubtedly be familiar with the growing incidence of student debt used to pay for studies at colleges and universities nowadays; this was neither socially as acceptable nor even an option for a lot of young people as recently as the 1960s and 1970s. However, the most spectacular occurrence in recent years is what happened with the subprime mortgage market in the United States in 2007–2008, when numerous American households defaulted on their mortgage payments and faced foreclosure. Low-income groups were lured into going into debt to achieve the North American dream of buying one's own home, but these poorer households did not have sufficient income support to ensure that they would be able to service their mortgages over time. This triggered a financial crisis internationally in 2008–2009 of a magnitude not witnessed since the Great Depression of the 1930s. This crisis, perhaps more than any other example, drives home the importance of consumer emulation in determining macroeconomic outcome that would be difficult to explain on the basis of the mainstream wealth hypothesis.

Is High Consumption Good or Bad for Long-Term Growth?

Now that we have described some essential elements of the heterodox explanation of aggregate consumption, let us briefly try to address the question of whether high consumption is good for long-term macroeconomic performance. The chronic rise in the average propensity to consume—hovering ever closer to 100 percent of personal disposable income at the time of writing (early 2009)—and the explosion of household debt in North America have been the focus of much criticism from certain economists.

TABLE 1   Evolution of the Saving Rate in Canada, Total and by Income Quintile, 1986–2006

Year	Total personal saving rate (national accounting basis)	Lowest quintile	Second quintile	Third quintile	Fourth quintile	Highest quintile
1986	13.4	−12.1	−1.6	5.4	11.2	22.0
1996	7.0	−17.1	0.9	11.1	17.0	28.3
2006	3.1	−37.5	−6.4	4.9	14.4	29.7

Sources: Statistics Canada, *National Income and Expenditures Accounts*, CANSIM II series V691783; Statistics Canada, *Family Expenditure in Canada*; Statistics Canada, *Survey of Household Spending* (calculated from micro data made available from the Income Statistics Division of Statistics Canada).

Mainstream neoclassical economists who subscribe to some variant of what is often described as the "loanable funds" theory of capital formation begin from the premise that savers·are critical to the investment process. It is ultimately the supply of savings that finances investment. If consumption were high and, therefore, saving low, there would be fewer funds made available in the financial capital markets, which would result in high interest rates that would restrain long-term growth because of lower business investment. Hence what is needed for the long-term rise of private investment is a policy that encourages households to increase their supply of savings over time, for instance, by increased tax incentives, such as improved registered retirement savings plans (RRSPs), and so on.

Keynesian economists reject the causality stipulated above and essentially stand the neoclassical argument on its head. For such economists, it is not saving that determines investment but investment that determines saving. There is no predetermined level of saving that finances investment, since the latter could be financed *ex nihilo* by bank credit in a modern monetary economy. Hence investment, regardless of how it is financed, determines saving residually once income is generated from the initial investment via the multiplier. Indeed, contrary to the loanable funds theory, *lower* saving may actually *accelerate* the rate of investment, since the higher consumer demand would ultimately encourage firms to increase their productive capacity. With increased cash flow to business enterprises and higher rates of capacity utilization, declining household saving could thus have positive, stimulating effects on the rate of capital accumulation in the long run.

The sustained growth of both the Canadian and US economies, at least until 2007, would largely confirm the Keynesian view that very low rates of household saving are not in and of themselves inimical to growth. However, there are some within the Keynesian camp who, along with followers of the famous heterodox economist Hyman P. Minsky, did perceive some possible negative consequences of a long-term fall in the household saving rate and the concomitant rise in the debt-to-income ratio of consumers. Since the drop in the saving rate has been accompanied by a general increase in household debt ratios, difficulties of long-run financial sustainability can ensue (Cynamon and Fazzari 2008). The concern of these heterodox Keynesians, however, has nothing to do with the neoclassical analytics about the relevance of the savings constraint on capital accumulation. Instead, it has to do largely with the macroeconomic implications of the highly leveraged household sector's financial ability to sustain consumer demand in the long term.

The international financial crisis that had its origin in the US subprime mortgage crisis of 2007 does point to the dangers of an excessively leveraged household sector. However, the problem was not the consumption spending that somehow contained the seeds of its own collapse. Rather, it was primarily the insufficiently regulated financial sector and the string of financial innovations (which made leveraging ever easier) that led to the end of a long period of consumption-led growth on the North American continent. At the time of writing, there are fears that we may repeat some of the experience of the Great Depression with regard to the behaviour of consumption. Just as many feared (correctly) that the inordinate expansion of household debt ratios in the 1920s would lead to an implosion of consumption spending, as overly leveraged households sought to allot a sharply increased proportion of their disposable income for debt repayment during the years immediately following the Great Crash of 1929, so some now fear that a similar scenario might unfold in the aftermath of the 2007–2008 financial meltdown and the ensuing credit freeze.

It is noteworthy that, while governments have been busy providing liquidity to the financial system and packaging fiscal stimulus packages internationally, there is no one who is advising the traditional neoclassical prescription that we should increase the rate of household saving so as to stimulate investment and long-term growth (with the possible exception of policy-makers in the developing world, where, paradoxically, the International Monetary Fund and the World Bank continue to sing the old tune about the need to increase saving rates). Policy-makers in the industrialized countries most afflicted by the financial crisis have understood that such a prescription would be folly and would merely compromise long-term economic performance. Unless household consumption—albeit an environmentally friendlier type—is once again set in motion, the North American economies will be staring into the face of stagnation, much as Japan's did during the 1990s and the Western economies did during the 1930s.

DISCUSSION QUESTIONS

1. Explain why emulation might be a powerful driving force behind consumption spending and why, in the short run, household spending may be constrained more by credit finance than the growth of real personal disposable income.

2. Would an understanding of different propensities to consume by policy-makers be helpful in the implementation of an appropriate fiscal policy stimulus in a recession?
3. Discuss why high consumption could actually stimulate investment rather than slow it down.

SUGGESTED READINGS AND ONLINE RESOURCES

Chawla, Raj K. 2007. Spending patterns in Canada and the US. *Perspectives on Labour and Income* (Statistics Canada) (September): 18–27. http://www.statcan.gc.ca/pub/75-001-x/2007109/article/10351-eng.pdf.

Chawla, Raj K., and Ted Wannell. 2005. Spenders and savers. *Perspectives on Labour and Income* (Statistics Canada) (March): 5–13. http://www.statcan.gc.ca/pub/75-001-x/10305/7797-eng.pdf.

Fonseca, Golçalo L. History of economic thought website. http://homepage.newschool.edu/het (includes a discussion of competing schools of thought, with entries on John Maynard Keynes, Milton Friedman, and James Duesenberry, among others).

Statistics Canada. Summary tables on household spending and saving. http://www40.statcan.gc.ca/l01/ind01/l3_3868_2180-eng.htm?hili_famil10.

REFERENCES

Akerlof, George A. 2007. The missing motivation in macroeconomics. *American Economic Review* 97 (1): 5–36.

Cochrane, James L. 1970. *Macroeconomics before Keynes*. Glenview, IL: Scott Foresman.

Cynamon, Barry Z., and Steven M. Fazzari. 2008. Household debt in the consumer age: Source of growth—Risk of collapse. *Capitalism and Society* 3 (2): 1–30.

Frank, Robert H. 2005. The mysterious disappearance of James Duesenberry. *New York Times*, June 9. http://www.robert-h-frank.com/PDFs/ES.6.9.05.pdf.

Green, Francis. 1991. Institutional and other unconventional theories of saving. *Journal of Economic Issues* 25 (1): 93–113.

Korty, Doug. 2008. Comment on "Household debt in the consumer age: Source of growth—Risk of collapse" (by Barry Z. Cynamon and Steven M. Fazzari). *Capitalism and Society* 3 (3): 1–2.

Mason, Roger. 2000. The social significance of consumption: James Duesenberry's contribution to consumer theory. *Journal of Economic Issues* 34 (3): 553–572.

Seccareccia, Mario. 2005. Growing household indebtedness and the plummeting saving rate in Canada: An explanatory note. *Economic and Labour Relations Review* 16 (1): 133–151.

4 *What Drives Investment?*

COMPETING VIEWS

William Scarth, "What Drives Investment? An Orthodox Perspective"

Jim Stanford, "What Drives Investment? A Heterodox Perspective"

Editors' Introduction

Investment is an essential economic variable. Most economists would agree that it plays a major role in expanding the economy and in promoting growth, and that it remains the single most important factor in generating cyclical fluctuations. New investments often create new jobs and improve labour productivity when they bring in more sophisticated machinery and equipment. Higher productivity in turn often results in higher wages and better living standards for workers.

The question of what makes private firms decide to invest more or to cut back on their investment plans is a highly controversial one in economics. The more widely accepted, orthodox view—which is presented to a certain extent in the contribution by William Scarth—essentially argues that investment is ultimately driven by the amount and availability of savings. According to this view, industrially advanced countries have grown faster and reached their level of development because they have had higher propensities to save than developing countries. Consequently, orthodox economists conclude that in order for an economy to grow and be more prosperous, government authorities must adopt policies that encourage saving and discourage consumption spending. At the same time, since investors are assumed to borrow those savings made available by the community for investment purposes, the cost of financing the investment becomes a crucial factor. Hence, emphasis is placed on the relationship between the cost of financing (mainly the interest cost) and the expected return from the investment, with other factors playing a less critical role.

On the other hand, Jim Stanford, representing the heterodox perspective, argues that the act of investment actually precedes the act of saving in modern, monetary capitalist economies and therefore cannot be constrained by what is put aside. It is changes in the flow of investment, through its multiplicative effect on income, that generate additional flows of saving. Investment projects are financed through bank credit, whereby new money is created from scratch. Banks will lend money to investors only after they have assessed the creditworthiness of the latter and only if they believe that the projects will indeed be profitable. Profits and profit expectations are the main driving force behind investment decisions for firms and for those providing the financing (that is, the banks). Moreover, greater importance is placed on overall demand in the economy—or what are sometimes referred to as "accelerator" effects—as reflected in the degree to which productive capacity is being utilized, and less is placed on the additional cost of financing the purchase of new capital goods. Further insight will be gained through a comparison of the two essays in this chapter.

What Drives Investment? An Orthodox Perspective

William Scarth

Introduction

In discussion among non-economists, people speak of the purchase of a GIC or of some equities as "investing." Economists, however, call these purchases acts of household *saving*. Traditionally, we reserve the term "investment" to refer to the purchases made by firms on such things as new machines, equipment, or bigger factories—anything that adds to the firm's stock of man-made inputs that are used in the production process. The accumulated stock of such inputs is referred to as the firm's "capital." We find it helpful to use the terms in this way, since it highlights the fact that the decisions to save and invest are made quite independently within a non-centrally planned economy such as ours. Households decide to postpone spending—that is, decide not to consume some of the nation's output in a given year; in short, households make the savings decision. But it is firms that make the decision to acquire more capital—that is, to invest by purchasing some of the newly produced output that the households did not want. Firms and households do not consult each other directly when making these decisions. Thus, it is possible that households may wish to save more than firms wish to invest. If so, there will not be enough demand to buy up all of the nation's output. In such an environment, investment spending by firms will not be big enough to make up for the fact that households are not spending all of their income, so firms will be stuck with rising inventories; as a result, they will cut back operations and lay off some workers. In short, a recession will occur. Given these facts, if we want to investigate whether a recession may occur at any time, we need to direct our attention to the question of whether (and why) saving and investment may get temporarily out of alignment.

Our interest in saving and investment goes far beyond a concern about short-run cycles in economic activity. We are also much interested in having the economy function in such a way that we enjoy rising material living standards over a period of many years. Firms can afford to pay ever-rising wages only if workers are ever more productive. This in turn requires that workers have more and better machines and knowledge with which to work. In other words, workers need an ever-bigger stock of capital at their disposal. To be more precise, let us use I, K, and Δ to denote investment, the stock of capital, and "the change in," respectively. Since this year's investment is this year's increase in the capital stock, $I = \Delta K$. So if we want higher K, we need high I, and high I is possible only if households do not consume all of each year's output. In other words, an ongoing rise in living standards ultimately requires high saving.

With this background, we can list the important factors that drive investment. First, anything that stimulates more saving (such as tax policies that lead households to save and not spend) makes more investment possible. Second, anything that makes the firms' cost of buying machines lower (such as lower borrowing costs) increases capital accumulation. Third, since firms finance much of their investment spending by issuing new equities, the cost of investment is low when the new equities can be sold at high prices; thus, a boom in the stock market is another factor that drives investment. Fourth, recessions are a big disincentive for firms to invest—why should firms add to their capacity when they are not fully utilizing what they already have? Thus, a less volatile business cycle stimulates higher investment. Finally, other taxes—such as those levied on foreigners who allow their capital to be used within Canada—matter for investment. In the following sections, I will discuss each of the aforementioned investment drivers.

Consumption Taxes Versus Income Taxes

Since the early 1960s, our federal governments, whether conservative or liberal, have enacted a series of policies aimed at increasing household saving; indirectly, such policies are aimed at raising investment. In early 2009, tax-free savings accounts were instituted with the aim of encouraging households to save more by offering an increased return on savings. Another example is the registered retirement savings plan (RRSP) system, introduced in 1957, which generates an immediate tax break for the individual when each contribution is made; interest within the plan accumulates without tax until retirement. Thus, through the RRSP system, the government extends an interest-free loan to households over a period of many decades, which households can receive only if they save. When the GST was introduced in 1991, cuts were made to the personal income tax system, so that the tax substitution package was revenue-neutral. The idea behind this tax reform was that, while a sales tax can be avoided if people save, the same is not true of an income tax.

One final, pro-investment initiative of the last 25 years has been disinflation. Through contractionary monetary policy, the Bank of Canada decreased the annual inflation rate for the consumer price index (CPI) from 12 percent to 2 percent. This has stimulated people to save more, since our tax system taxes nominal—not real—interest rates. A simple numerical illustration can clarify this point. Suppose that households are willing to save when the following conditions are met: the nominal interest rate is 6 percent, they face a 50 percent tax rate on interest income, and there is 2 percent inflation. In this case, the after-tax interest yield is (6 %)(0.5) = 3% (nominal) and (3% − 2%) = 1% (real). Suppose that inflation rises 10 percentage points, to 12 percent, and nominal interest rates rise by the same amount (as they usually do), from 6 percent to 16 percent. In this scenario, it appears that savers will be compensated for the loss in money's purchasing power while they lend out their funds. But what has happened to the after-tax real yield? It has become (16%)(0.5) − 12% = −4%. Households do not save much when the effective real yield is negative. Thus, a primary purpose of the Bank of Canada's attempt to eliminate inflation was to remove this disincentive to save (the negative real yield on savings); in other words, the disinflation policy was an initiative designed to drive investment.

Borrowing Costs and Corporate Taxes

A core principle in microeconomics is that any activity should be expanded up to the point at which the *additional* benefits that are received from expanding that activity have been pushed down to the level of the additional costs of expanding that activity. One application of this reasoning is the "optimal hiring" rule for firms. In the case of hiring inputs for production, the rule is that each factor of production be hired up to the point that its marginal product (MP) equals the price the firm must pay to employ that input. In the case of labour (L), the rule is: expand employment until $MPL = wage$. It is because firms follow this rule that wages rise over time (because labour's productivity does).

Things are more complicated in the case of capital, since installation costs exist for machines that do not exist for workers. As a result, firms move slowly to close the gap between capital's marginal product (MPK) and the rental price of capital, or the interest that must be paid on the loan that is necessary to rent the machine (r). We summarize this gradual adjustment strategy in a simple equation: $I = f(MPK/r)$. Since we assume that the f function within this equation is a positive one, the equation states that investment rises whenever the marginal product of capital exceeds capital's rental price, and that investment falls whenever the marginal product of capital falls short of capital's relative price. As already noted, the rental price depends on the interest rate, since that yield on other assets represents the opportunity cost of capital—that is, it reflects what firms could earn if they bought those other assets instead of the machine. This relationship highlights one of the important drivers of investment: the (real) interest rate. The lower the interest rate is, the more willing firms are to incur the installation costs—and so the higher investment is. This is the reason why Canadian policy-makers want Canada to be perceived by individuals in the rest of the world as a safe place to put their savings. If we appear to be a country that is riddled with political uncertainties (for instance, due to the prospect of Quebec's separation or the inability of our government to control the growth of its indebtedness), foreign savers will demand that a "risk premium" be included in Canadian interest rates. When interest rates are pushed up by such a premium, we get lower investment and smaller growth in living standards.

How does the corporate tax system figure into this discussion? Does a corporate tax cut stimulate investment? The answer is "yes," but only to a modest extent. Such a tax cut brings both a benefit and a cost to the firm. The benefit is the obvious and direct effect: the portion of profits that flow from the investment that must be given to the government is smaller. The cost stems from the fact that the depreciation allowances that the tax system permits the firm to deduct when calculating its taxes are smaller as well. A numerical illustration can clarify this issue. Suppose the firm buys a small piece of capital—a computer that costs $1,000. The computer has a useful life of four years, so it is said that this capital wears out (or depreciates) at a rate of 25 percent per year. If the government knew this true depreciation rate, it would insist that the firm claim $250 in each year as expenses in the four years following the purchase. The firm, however, would like the government to believe that the computer wears out fully in one year, since the government would then let the firm claim the entire $1,000 expense in the first year. By allowing the firm to claim the entire expense early, the government would be extending an interest-free loan to the firm—and that's good for profits. Rather than argue about the true economic lifespan of every machine, the government has established arbitrary depreciation-rate allowance schedules that firms are obliged to follow. In the manufacturing and processing sector, that rule is that machines must be assumed to wear out by 50 percent of their value in each of the first two years. The present value of this schedule of depreciation allowances is almost unity. (The present value is $(0.5) + (0.5/(1 + r)) = 0.976$ if the interest rate is 5 percent.) This means that the indirect cost of a corporate tax cut to the firm (the value of the reduced depreciation allowances) is 97.6 percent of the value of the direct benefit of the corporate tax cut. Thus, while a lower tax rate is an investment driver in that it amounts to the equivalent of a small reduction in the effective borrowing rate, this effect is so small that such a policy of corporate tax cuts is a very inefficient way to stimulate investment. The government suffers a large loss in revenue to generate just a small increase in investment.

Such concerns are magnified if the firm is a subsidiary of a multinational corporation. In this case, the international tax agreements are important. These arrangements call for the "head office"—say, in the United States—to calculate its global profits (including those generated by the subsidiary in, say, Canada) and to apply the US corporate tax rate to that tax base to calculate its provisional tax obligation to the US government. Then, the company is allowed to deduct taxes already paid to foreign governments to arrive at its actual obligation to the US authorities. Thus, when the Canadian government grants a corporate tax cut here, this has no effect on multinationals based elsewhere. Tax dollars are simply transferred, one for one, from the Canadian government to the US government. Such a transfer is not an investment driver.

Stock Markets and the State of Business Confidence

John Maynard Keynes was probably the most influential economist of the 20th century. Given this fact, we would be remiss if we did not report on his writings concerning what drives investment. Keynes did not base his discussion on the classical economists' analysis of the optimal hiring rule (as we did in the previous section). Instead, he emphasized the following, more intuitive analysis that highlights the stock market. Keynes asked the question, When is the best time for a firm to issue more equities? The benefit of selling additional stock certificates is that the current owners receive funds that can be used to expand the business (that is, that can be invested). The cost of selling more equities is that the ownership of the company becomes diluted. With more stocks outstanding, the original owners receive a smaller portion of the profits each year when dividends are distributed. Keynes reasoned that the original owners should permit this expansion in the ownership group only if the amount that can be raised by selling the new equity claims on profits will permit the firm to expand by a greater proportion than the proportion by which ownership is diluted. If this condition is satisfied, the total profit will expand by more than the pool of individuals who had a claim on that total, and the dividend income of the original owners will go up. In short, if the buyers of new equities are prepared to pay more for the claims on capital than it costs the firm to buy the additional capital, there is something left over for the original owners. Thus, at such times—and only at such times—they should sell new equities and invest.

We can make this reasoning slightly more precise by focusing on how stock prices are determined. A stock gives the owner the right to receive a share of the firm's profits every year into the indefinite future. The present value of that income stream can be represented by the following equation:

$$PV = [profits\ year\ 1] + [profits\ year\ 2/(1 + r)] + [profits\ year\ 3/(1 + r)^2] + \ldots$$

For the sake of simplicity, let us assume that profits and interest rates are expected to stay constant. In this case, the present value becomes $PV = (annual\ profits)(sum)$, where $sum = 1 + b + b^2 + b^3 + \ldots = 1/(1 - b) = 1/r$ since $b = 1/(1 + r)$, so $PV = (profits)/r$. A common assumption that economists make about a firm's input–output relationship is that it involves constant returns to scale (that is, if all inputs are doubled, output doubles). In this case, production and sales (Y) must just equal $[(MPL)(L) + (MPK)(K)]$. Since profit equals sales minus wage bill, and since labour is paid its marginal product, profits must equal $(MPK)(K)$. Putting all this together, a stock entitles its owner to an income stream that has a present value equal to $[(MPK)(K)/r]$. Keynes assumed that, as long as stock market participants were reasonably well informed, this formula would provide the long-run anchor to equity values. He argued that stock prices fluctuate above and below this fundamental determinant of stock value as individuals go through "waves" of optimism and pessimism. He referred to these swings in mood as the "animal spirits" of the participants in the stock market.

As explained in the previous two paragraphs, Keynes focused on the ratio of the stock market's *evaluation* of the nation's capital stock to the capital stock's *actual value*, and he argued that investment would occur when this ratio exceeded unity. Defining this ratio as $q = (stock\ value)/(actual\ capital\ value) = [(MPK)(K)/r]/K$, and the investment relationship as $I = f(q)$, we see that the Keynesian investment theory and the classical investment theory, $I = f(MPK/r)$, amount to the same thing (since the expression for q simplifies to $(MPK)/r$). This equivalence should be reassuring, since it means that we do not need to choose between these alternative ways of thinking about what drives investment. The classical approach is appealing because it is consistent with optimal factor-demand theory, and Keynes's approach is appealing because it is consistent with our intuitive understanding of how stock markets work. The standard theory of investment allows us to embrace both interpretations.

One advantage of the Keynesian approach, however, is that it teaches us that the waves of optimism and pessimism that characterize the stock market can be expected to be major drivers of investment. Keeping this in mind helps us understand how the connection between saving and investment might break down. Figure 1 is a supply and demand diagram for loans. The interest rate is on the price axis, and saving and investment are measured along the quantity axis. The supply of loans summarizes household saving behaviour. The positive slope captures individuals' willingness to save more at higher interest rates. The important shift influences for this curve are the tax rates that households face and their moods. (Lower taxes on interest income and decreased confidence/optimism shift this schedule to the right.) The demand for loans summarizes the behaviour of firms wishing to invest in a larger stock of capital. The negative slope captures the proposition that more spending occurs when borrowing costs are lower. The shift influences for this curve are corporate tax rates and the level of confidence that firms have concerning the demand for their products. (Corporate tax increases and fears of limited product demand shift this schedule to the left.)

As just noted, all the investment drivers discussed in earlier sections can be interpreted as factors that shift either the supply or demand function for loans. Thus, as long as this loan market is functioning efficiently (that is, as long as the market outcome point is at the intersection of supply and demand), investment

FIGURE 1   Market for Loans

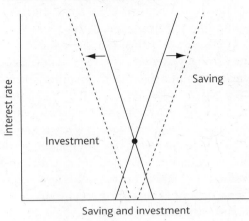

will increase when any of these drivers increase. There is another implication of assuming that the market observation point is always coincident with the supply–demand intersection—that is, there is no meaningful sense in which society can be saving "too much," so that the fear of having insufficient total demand to avoid a recession can be viewed as a non-issue. But, it could be the case that the market does not clear. For example, suppose that the supply and demand schedules are both fairly steep curves, as shown in Figure 1. If there is a dramatic wave of pessimism among both households and firms—so that supply shifts significantly to the right (as savings rise) and demand shifts significantly to the left (as investment is postponed)—then the two curves may no longer intersect at a positive interest rate. This outcome is illustrated by the dashed supply and demand curves in Figure 1. Thus, if both households and firms are afraid to spend, we may have a glut in saving, in which case there *is* a role for temporary government deficit spending—namely, to stimulate overall activity in an attempt to defeat the mood of pessimism. Readers will recognize this situation as a description of the challenge that faced many governments around the world at the time this book went to press (2009).

The Interdependence of Investment and Business Cycles

Our discussion thus far has been based on the notion that a firm's input demands depend on input prices. This approach presumes that it is physically possible for firms to substitute one input for another when producing a particular level of output. In some cases, such substitutability is limited; as a result, economists have developed an alternative approach, which we now consider. In this approach, it is assumed that there is a rigid input–output coefficient that represents the fixed amount of capital (K) that is needed to produce a particular level of output (Y). For simplicity, assuming that the firm expects this period's sales to equal last period's level, the desired stock of capital today (period t) will equal the fixed technology coefficient, a, times yesterday's (period $t-1$) sales: $K_t = aY_{t-1}$. Since investment is the increase in capital that the firm acquires during that period, investment is given by: $I_t = K_t - K_{t-1} = a(Y_{t-1} - Y_{t-2})$. This theory of investment is called the "accelerator." This is because investment falls whenever output growth slows. In aggregate, this lower investment makes aggregate demand fall, so a recession ensues. Then, as the recession reaches its trough and the output reductions begin to get smaller, the accelerator relationship indicates that investment will rise, so the recession ends simply because of this built-in momentum. In other words, the accelerator gives the economy a kind of perpetual-motion mechanism: output keeps going up and down because of the variations in investment, and those variations in investment occur simply because output is going up and down. So, simultaneously investment is one of the prime causes of business cycles and those cycles are in turn one of the primary drivers of investment.

You can explore this ongoing interaction using a simple spreadsheet. You can embed the investment function given in the previous paragraph into a simplified model economy by adding two more equations: $Y = C_t + I_t + G_t$ and $C_t = cY_{t-1}$, where c is the marginal propensity to consume. Combining the three equations yields a solution equation for GDP: $Y_t = (c+a)Y_{t-1} - aY_{t-2} + G_t$. Next, you can take the following illustrative parameter values ($c = 0.75$, $a = 1.0$) and initial conditions ($Y_{t-1} = Y_{t-2} = 1$ and $G_t = 0.25$), and then assume that G drops to 0.20 for just one period (and then returns to 0.25 forever). Your simulation will show that GDP fluctuates in an ongoing series of cycles (going 10 percent above and below its starting value) forever, even though there is no additional outside disturbance beyond the first period. Through the simulation, you can verify the perpetual-motion aspect of business cycles that can develop when investment adjusts according to the accelerator.

Taxes on Foreigners

To simplify the exposition, most of this essay has discussed the interaction of saving and investment as if the Canadian economy were disconnected from the rest of the world. Of course this is not the case, and a word or two about this is now appropriate. Firms operating in Canada can spend more on investment than Canadian households save, since they can rely on foreigners' willingness to save. Domestic firms can sell bonds to foreigners to finance the excess of their investment spending over domestic household saving. When they do so, Canadians acquire an international debt to service, but if the return on the investment is adequate we can service the foreign debt and still have something left over for ourselves. Many commentators, such as Mintz (2001), have argued that we should not discourage foreigners' willingness to place their savings in Canada if our goal is to reach a higher standard of living in this country. When a withholding tax on foreigners' interest earnings is levied, foreign savers react by withdrawing some of their funds. The result is a *one-time* reduction in our living standards, since there is a drop in the capital stock that Canadian employees have to work with. But Scarth (2008) shows that living standards may still be improved, despite this one-time loss in capital, if the government uses the revenue it collects from the foreign withholding tax to lower the personal income tax rate applied to domestic households on their interest income. The increased saving can increase the *growth rate* of living standards. In present-value terms, this improvement in the growth rate of living standards dominates the one-time reduction in living standards, so a withholding tax on foreign savers is supported after all. While additional discussion of this debate is beyond the scope of this essay, we can note that the extreme mobility of financial capital in today's globalized world does not appear to be as important a rationale for avoiding foreign withholding taxes as is often supposed.

Conclusions

We have explored the main drivers of investment as the term is traditionally interpreted (spending by firms to acquire more physical capital). But there are other forms of investment, making it appropriate to suggest a few references for further reading. Households invest in durables, such as housing, and firms invest in inventories. Mankiw and Scarth (2008, chap. 17) cover these and other topics. Furthermore, firms invest in knowledge, and it is becoming increasingly apparent that a significant portion of our rising living standards results from investments in this "human capital." Many believe that we must think much more broadly if we wish to understand the determinants of this kind of investment. For example, it is likely that different legal structures and institutions provide very different incentives for innovation and learning. An accessible introduction to this set of issues is Russell Roberts's interview with Paul Romer, a leading researcher in the human capital field. It is hoped that readers of the present essay, armed with the background that it has provided, will pursue this complementary set of issues by "listening" to their conversation (see Roberts 2007).

DISCUSSION QUESTIONS

1. Explain why a high savings rate may be desirable in the long run but undesirable in the short run.
2. Explain one argument in favour of replacing income taxes with sales taxes and one argument for rejecting this proposal.

3. Explain Keynes's theory of how firms' investment spending depends on stock prices, and discuss whether his approach is consistent with marginal-productivity theory.

SUGGESTED READINGS

Buchholtz, Todd. 2007. Chapter 9: Keynes; Bon vivant as savior. In *New ideas from dead economists*, 206–228. 2nd ed. New York: Plume.

Heilbroner, Robert. 1999. Chapter 9: The heresies of John Maynard Keynes. In *The worldly philosophers: The lives, times and ideas of the great economic thinkers*, 248–287. 7th ed. New York: Touchstone.

Mankiw, N.G., and W.M. Scarth. 2008. Chapter 17: Investment. In *Macroeconomics*, 536–562. 3rd Canadian ed. New York: Worth Publishers.

ONLINE RESOURCES

Government of Canada. 2008. Canadian economy online. http://www.canadianeconomy.gc.ca/english/economy.

Hassett, Kevin A. 2008. Investment. In *The concise encyclopedia of economics*, ed. David R. Henderson. 2nd ed. http://www.econlib.org/library/Enc/Investment.html.

Kotlikoff, Laurence J. 2008. Saving. In *The concise encyclopedia of economics*, ed. David R. Henderson. 2nd ed. http://www.econlib.org/library/Enc/Saving.html.

Romer, Paul M. 2008. Economic growth. In *The concise encyclopedia of economics*, ed. David R. Henderson. 2nd ed. http://www.econlib.org/library/Enc/EconomicGrowth.html.

REFERENCES

Mankiw, N.G., and W.M. Scarth. 2008. *Macroeconomics*. 3rd Canadian ed. New York: Worth Publishers.

Mintz, J. 2001. Most favoured nation: Building a framework for smart economic policy. Policy Study 36. Toronto: C.D. Howe Institute.

Roberts, R. 2007. An interview with Paul Romer on economic growth. Library of Economics and Liberty. http://www.econlib.org/library/Columns/y2007/Romergrowth.html.

Scarth, W.M. 2008. Taxing foreign-owned capital: An application of second-best analysis. Paper presented at the Conference on Small Open Economies in a Globalized World, Wilfrid Laurier University, June 14.

What Drives Investment? A Heterodox Perspective

Jim Stanford

Introduction

Business investment gets a lot of day-to-day public attention: in newspapers, from business leaders, and in debates among politicians. CEOs trumpet their latest investment plans, politicians jockey over how best to improve the investment "climate," and workers worry whether their employers are investing enough to keep their workplaces up to date and viable.

Perhaps surprisingly, however, investment gets rather less attention from most economists. Business executives, local economic development officers, and even ordinary workers have a commonsense awareness that investment decisions are crucial to prosperity and employment in their companies, industries, and communities. But in conventional (or "neoclassical") economics, ironically, investment doesn't really carry any special importance. Contrary to the proactive, often desperate efforts of local plant managers, communities, and even entire countries to attract and stimulate investment, economists exhibit a more lackadaisical attitude. They traditionally see investment as a passive, almost automatic outcome of social decisions to *save*. All a country must do if it really wants more investment is decide collectively to save more; automatic market mechanisms[1] then take care of the rest (ensuring not only that all savings are invested, but moreover that they are invested in their most productive uses).

This makes it all sound easy. Yet those local development officers know full well that investment is scarce, hard to come by, and incredibly important to the rise and fall of industries and communities. That's why they work so hard to try to attract it!

How do we reconcile these contrasting impressions: the real-world view that attracting business investment is very important and the theoretical conclusion in economics that investment is automatic, passive, and nothing to worry about? In an alternative approach to economics, which I broadly term "heterodox" (to distinguish it from conventional or "orthodox" market-clearing approaches[2]), investment plays a crucial leading role in determining production, employment, growth, and overall economic evolution. What's more, there is an independence and an agency to investment decisions: they are not the *passive* outcome of the clearing of a market for capital, but rather reflect the independent, *active* hopes, passions, and expectations of companies and entrepreneurs who dream of new products, new markets, and—above all—new profits. That makes investment a more complex, unpredictable, and fascinating object of study.

What Is Investment, Anyway?

To start with, there's even a lot of confusion about how to define investment. Many people equate "investment" with the acquisition of a financial asset of some kind (such as a stock, bond, or unit in a mutual fund). While these personal financial investments are important in household financial planning, they are quite different from how economists understand investment. In economics, investment is something *real*, not something *financial*. It refers to the allocation of a portion of current real output toward the expansion of future production (instead of using that real output for current consumption). In other words, an economy invests when it takes some of its current real production and uses that production in turn to facilitate additional production down the road. (In theory, financial investments are supposed to translate into real capital investments, but in practice it doesn't work that way—as will be discussed later in this essay.)

Investment, therefore, refers to real expenditure on buildings, machinery and equipment, and any other tangible "tools" that are subsequently used in production. (Tangible goods used in the production of other products are known as "real capital.") Investment in this sense exists in several different forms. Most important to overall economic performance is private business investment in *fixed* capital. The two major types of fixed capital are structures (such as buildings, factories, offices, and pipelines), and machinery and equipment (including machines and tools of all kinds, computers and software, telecommunications equipment, and transportation equipment). Businesses also invest smaller amounts in *inventories*, representing the raw materials, partly finished or unsold goods, and other tangible items that a business must keep on hand at any given time. It's not just businesses that invest: governments do, too—in broader public infrastructure (roads, bridges, power grids, and so on) and in specific capital assets used by public enterprises (like the buildings, structures, or equipment used in hospitals, utilities, schools, or police forces). Meanwhile, individuals can also undertake real *residential* investments in their own homes.[3] Of all these investment flows, business fixed investment is the largest; it also plays the most important and strategic role in influencing the rise and fall of the overall economy.

Every economy must constantly undertake a certain amount of investment just to offset the wear and tear of existing capital equipment. That deterioration in existing capital is called "depreciation." What economists call "gross investment" represents the total amount of spending on new physical capital. In contrast, "net investment" is what's left after deducting current depreciation from gross investment. In other words, net investment represents the net addition to an economy's overall capital stock (since, when net investment is positive, new capital is being added faster than old capital is wearing out). Needless to say, given the incredible variety in the kinds of capital assets, measuring and valuing capital, depreciation, and net investment is a very tricky task, dependent on many assumptions regarding the value and expected service life of different types of capital assets.[4]

In a modern, high-tech economy, investment can also encompass less tangible but still important forms of expenditure. For example, research and development activity represents an investment: the effort of researchers seeking to develop a new product, or a new way of doing things (from their employers' perspective, the investment is represented by the cost of paying those researchers while they are working). As with investment in physical capital, this is a process of dedicating current output (the work of the researchers) to the future expansion (in either quantity or quality) of future production, rather than using that output (work) for the sake of current consumption. From the perspective of an individual company, advertising and marketing can also represent an "investment" in the future profile and appeal of the company and its products. Similarly, for an individual, acquiring new education or skills is an investment: allocating current work effort not for immediate consumption, but to enhance that individual's long-run economic and earnings potential (that's why some economists refer to knowledge and skills as "human capital"). For the purposes of the present discussion, however, we will concentrate on the narrower conception of investment as representing additions to physical capital.[5] In particular, business investment in non-residential fixed capital plays a uniquely important role in the performance of the overall economy, and hence understanding its determinants is a crucial piece of economic knowledge.

Investment Under Capitalism

All economies require investment. Even a simple subsistence farming economy must invest: its farmers must set aside enough seeds from their current crop to plant the fields again next year (or they will starve). That's investment, and it's essential to survival, as well as to the historical development and improvement of any economy over time. Today, however, we live in a very particular economic system, called capitalism. This system has some key features that impart special importance to the process of investment:

1. In capitalism, most production (about 85 percent of GDP in Canada's case) is undertaken by private businesses that are trying to generate a profit from their activity. The decision by the owner of a private firm (the "capitalist," if you like) to invest in a new undertaking—by purchasing equipment and

raw materials, spending on research and advertising, paying the initial wages of workers, and so on—is the initial act that starts the whole economic ball rolling. It's like pushing the "start" button on capitalism: without investment, nothing else happens. Because of this dependence of the entire economy on profit-seeking private investment, expectations regarding the likelihood of profit are essential to whether or not investment occurs (and hence to the performance of the overall economy).

2. Capitalism has always been a *monetary* system: goods and services are bought and sold for money, and (crucially) profit is measured and paid out in money terms. The introduction and use of money (and, subsequently, of credit, which is the main source of *new* money today[6]) means that investment decisions take on further independence. In particular, because of the existence of credit and finance (broadly defined to include loans or other sources of finance, such as stocks and equities), a business owner can mobilize resources for a new investment solely on the basis of his or her conviction (backed by the confidence of his or her lenders) that the venture stands a good chance of being profitable. In this regard, investment is always "prior" to savings in a profit-driven, monetary capitalist economy.[7]

Real Investment and the "Paper" Economy

As noted, the existence of a sophisticated credit and financial system provides companies with an important degree of freedom in their investment activities. As long as they can convince lenders of the viability of their proposal, entrepreneurs can finance the real capital purchases required for their venture. In theory, this "lubricating" function is the raison d'être of the whole financial industry (including conventional banks, as well as related institutions such as stock markets, investment banks, and hedge funds).

Indeed, when the financial sector is optimistic and expansionary, it can demonstrate incredible vitality and exuberance in financing exciting new ventures— long before "savers" ever could set aside real resources to pay for those ventures. Examples of this vitality include the vibrant, rapid allocation of new finance to high-tech ventures (the so-called dot-com industry) in Silicon Valley and other key technology clusters during the late 1990s, and the overzealous provision of new finance for US real estate developments in the mid-2000s.

On the other hand, what goes up must come down, and each period of financial exuberance is typically followed by a predictable interlude of financial contraction. Stung by losses, financiers stop creating credit, leaving even worthy ventures starved of needed finance. This regular boom-and-bust cycle of private credit and finance (often called the "bankers' cycle") stems from deeply rooted aspects of the financial sector.[8] When their greed (for profits from new lending and new financial activities) overwhelms their fear (that borrowers may default), the private financial sector expands credit rapidly, leading to rapid real economic growth and/or rising inflation (in either consumer prices or asset prices). When the reverse occurs and fear overwhelms greed, the financial system withdraws credit even from trustworthy clients, and real investment (and hence overall economic growth) is constrained by the resulting "credit freeze."[9]

Even in more stable periods, however, the relationship between the hyperactive world of finance and the more mundane business of real investment in real capital is secondary and indirect. Most private businesses finance the vast majority of their real investment spending from retained earnings and internal cash flow (including from the allowances that they set aside for the depreciation of their existing capital). They turn to the private financial system for extra credit when needed, but that is surprisingly rarely. In recent years, in fact, global business on an aggregate basis has been investing substantially less in real capital than has been generated by internal corporate cash flows; the result has been a significant and secular decline in corporate indebtedness (as businesses pay off old debts and hoard excess cash).[10] By the same token, the vast majority of the buying and selling of financial, or "paper," assets that occurs in the financial system (in excess of 95 percent) represents the recycling of already issued securities, including corporate equities, bonds, derivatives, and others—a repetitive, speculative process that bears no direct relationship whatsoever to the supply of credit to finance new investment ventures.

At the best of times, therefore, the high-profile workings of the "paper" markets play an indirect, secondary role in the crucial economic process of real investment. At the worst of times, the booms and busts of the paper economy disrupt and undermine the process of real investment. It is therefore important to keep a strict distinction in mind between the important economic process of real business investment and the endless—but often pointless—wheelings and dealings of the financial industry.

The Macroeconomic Importance of Investment

For the overall economy, investment is a positive and hugely important economic force. Some of the broader economic benefits of strong investment include:

- **Growth.** Investment spending is the most important source of economic growth under capitalism. When investment is strong, economies grow more quickly, and so do incomes. The most significant episodes of rising living standards in recent history were all associated with very strong and sustained levels of investment (see Table 1). And statistical evidence suggests that business investment spending is the most important precursor to economic growth among all the components of national income.[11]

TABLE 1   Golden Ages of Investment and Prosperity

Era	Gross business investment (% of GDP)	Annual growth real wages (%)
Europe (1960s)	25%	4%
Japan (1960s and 1970s)	32%	5%
Korea (1990s)	35%	5%
Canada (1960s and 1970s)	23%	3%
Australia (1960–1975)	22%	3.5%
China (1990–present)	38%	5–10%?

Source: Stanford (2008, 141).

- **Employment.** Business investment is the first step in initiating production, and hence is essential to job creation and employment. But the jobs created directly by a company undertaking a new investment are just the beginning: by initiating a circular cycle of employment, production, consumption spending (as employed workers spend their earnings), and additional production, each investment produces a multiplied amount of total employment in the economic system.[12] It is true that, in some cases, advanced new capital equipment is intended to *replace* workers, rather than create new jobs—yet the level of *overall* growth and employment (at the macroeconomic level) nevertheless depends strongly on business investment.
- **Economic evolution.** Economies and companies don't just *expand*, they *change* over time, adapting to technology, consumer preferences, and social and environmental challenges. Structural and technological changes don't occur seamlessly, however. New technologies, products, and ways of working almost always need to be embodied in new capital (like equipment, buildings, and infrastructure), and ongoing investment is essential in order to allow the economy to incorporate these structural changes.[13]
- **Productivity.** Statistical studies have proven[14] that investment in new machinery and equipment is especially important to productivity growth—which in turn is an essential precondition for rising living standards over time.
- **Environment.** One way to reduce the environmental damage caused by the economy is through major investments in energy-efficient technologies and pollution abatement, such as high-tech heating and cooling systems, fuel-efficient vehicles, and cleaner power generation equipment. Building a more sustainable economy will require massive investments in these green technologies.

It is ironic, but because of all these positive "spinoffs" from investment spending, the broader economy may have more at stake in strong business investment than business itself does. In other words, the *social benefits* of investment spending are greater than the *private benefits* (that is, the benefits received internally by the private companies that do the actual investing). This is why governments regularly implement measures aimed at stimulating more business investment—not to mention why those local economic development officials expend so much energy "chasing smokestacks"!

The Determinants of the Amount of Investment

At a basic level, investment is motivated by the expectation that a business owner will earn back the original investment, plus an attractive profit margin. Investment is therefore a *forward-looking* decision, and for this reason investment spending is an inherently subjective, volatile, and hard-to-predict economic variable. Capitalists review current business conditions to judge whether an investment will be profitable in the future. But they always temper those judgments with additional information about how the business environment may change. After all, investment involves long-term, largely irreversible commitments, so business leaders will be inherently cautious about new projects, taking into account a wide and unpredictable range of influences and expectations.

The following specific factors tend to be the most important for companies in determining the amount of business investment spending:

- **Current business profits.** Current profits are important as an indication of future profits. As noted above, current profits also provide most of the funds for new business investment: when profits (or, more precisely, cash flow[15]) are strong, businesses can pay for a large amount of new investment without needing to tap banks or other institutions for incremental finance.
- **Capacity utilization.** Whether a company's existing facilities are being used to the utmost (what economists call "capacity utilization") is another crucial factor. Even if current profits are high, a company will not invest in new facilities if its existing capacity is still partly idle.
- **Growth.** We know that investment causes growth. But it is also true that growth causes investment. If an economy is growing quickly, then companies will expand investment, since they're more confident that they will be able to sell their output and it is less likely that they'll have any excess capacity. In general, investment and growth thus reinforce each other: more investment leads to more growth, which in turn leads to more investment. This positive feedback of growth on investment is called the "investment accelerator." On the other hand, strong investment can sometimes *undermine* future profits if it generates too much competition (especially from new companies entering an industry) or too much

supply. The links between investment, growth, and profits are therefore complex and unpredictable.

- **Cost of capital.** Interest rates (and financing costs more generally) also affect investment spending. When companies need to raise external funds to pay for a new investment (in cases where internal cash flow is insufficient), interest costs are a necessary deduction from revenues. Interest rates also indicate how much investors could earn by buying a purely financial asset, such as a bond. If investors can earn high profits on paper assets (say, 8–10 percent per year), they are much less likely to take on the extra risk and trouble of investing in a real business. On the other hand, if purely financial returns are low (say, 4–5 percent per year or even lower), then companies should be more willing to put their money into motion in the real economy, by making a real investment.

- **Institutional and political climate.** Finally, private investors will also take account of the broad political, economic, and legal climate before they commit funds for a new investment. They review regulatory, tax, or policy changes that might affect future profits, and monitor the overall economic and political stability of the country where they are investing (to ensure that it will remain a sufficiently business-friendly jurisdiction). If they worry about future "stability" (from their perspective), they will withhold investment—which in turn will make the economic and political situation even worse.

The Determinants of the Location of Investment

The preceding factors are all important in determining whether a company chooses to invest in a new project. But in many cases, the investing company then faces a second and largely separate decision: where should it make that investment? Some types of business (such as most service industries, as well as some kinds of perishable agriculture and manufacturing) must locate very near to their customers; these industries are called "non-tradeable" industries, because their products cannot be shipped great distances. Most goods-producing industries, however, and some service industries (including telecommunications and banking) *can* trade their output over great distances. In these cases, companies can freely choose an investment location that will maximize their profit (taking into account, of course, any legal or trade barriers that affect their businesses).

The following factors will be important considerations for companies in determining the location of new investment spending:

- **Production costs.** Companies will naturally favour locations with lower production costs (which allow for a larger profit margin once all the bills have been paid). Labour costs are important here. Low wages will be appealing, but must be considered relative to the level of productivity (companies actually care more about unit labour costs, which equals labour costs divided by productivity, than about low wages per se). Indeed, most low-wage countries are not at all attractive to investors, because those ultra-low wages are associated with very poor productivity, poverty, and instability. Other cost factors that enter the equation include the availability of reliable infrastructure (such as good electricity and telecommunications services); the costs of transporting supplies and finished goods; the level of taxes levied on company profits; and the availability of reliable, cost-competitive supplies of raw materials, parts, and supplies.

- **Access to markets.** Companies will locate their investments near to the countries or regions where they sell significant volumes of their output. This reduces transportation costs for finished output, avoids tariffs and other trade barriers, and keeps companies in touch with local consumer tastes. Trade policy (the use of tariffs and other levers to enhance local investment and production) can reinforce this "local market effect" by making it more attractive to produce goods locally rather than import them.
- **Institutional and political climate.** A stable, business-friendly environment is another critical determinant of investment location. Companies will not make expensive, long-term commitments in jurisdictions—even low-cost ones—where they fear for the long-run security of their businesses. Competing efforts by countries around the world to make themselves more "investor-friendly" in recent decades, by assuring investors of their stability and business-friendly attitudes, have been a crucial factor in changing patterns of foreign investment. Nationalization, and even expropriation, were real threats to investors in many parts of the world in the 1970s. Today (2009) this risk is rare; even left-wing governments are desperate to lay out the welcome mat to investors, in light of the importance of business investment to a country's overall growth and productivity.

A combination of technological changes (including dramatic improvements in communications, and reductions in transportation costs and barriers) and far-reaching policy and political changes (especially the advent of business-friendly "free trade agreements," a prime effect of which has been to make it easier and more secure for companies to invest in foreign lands) has dramatically heightened the global mobility of business investment. If a country can combine low wages, a disciplined and productive workforce, a decent infrastructure and supply network, and political stability, then it can expect to win a larger share of total global investment (although not necessarily with any impact on the overall global level of investment spending). The long-term migration of investment to lower-cost, pro-business jurisdictions (like China and Mexico) proves that pro-business policies can have a dramatic impact on investment location. At the same time, considerable pain and dislocation is experienced in those jurisdictions that have less business-favourable conditions and that lose investment as a result. And this intense global competition for investment may produce macroeconomic side effects (including a tendency to global wage deflation) that in fact undermine global growth and hence overall investment performance. In this regard, the competition for investment—while it affects the location of investment—may in fact damage *aggregate* investment.

Recent Trends in Business Investment

If investment depends on current and expected profits and on the existence of a stable, business-friendly political and legal climate, then one would think that global business would have stepped up its investment activity significantly in light of the substantial pro-business shifts in economic policy that occurred in most countries over the past quarter-century. Since the late 1970s, governments in most jurisdictions have emphasized controlling inflation at low levels, reducing government spending and taxes (especially income taxes and business taxes), liberalizing foreign trade and investment, privatizing and deregulating many industries (thereby creating more terrain for private investment), and shifting social policy and labour laws in favour of employers (for example, reducing upward wage pressures and producing a more insecure, compliant workforce). In the wake of these changes, business profits—whether measured as a share of output or as a proportion of invested capital—have grown in most countries. Curiously, however, despite these business-friendly shifts in laws and policies, and the consequent expansion in profits, business investment has remained surprisingly sluggish.

Figure 1 portrays net investment spending (after depreciation) in the leading capitalist economies, measured as a share of total output. Global investment was especially sluggish in the 1980s, as the system adjusted to the initial shock of this hard-nosed shift in economic policies (including much higher interest rates, cutbacks in government spending, and other "tough-love," market-friendly medicine). Even as the economy adapted to this new policy context, however, and profits and macroeconomic performance improved, business did not respond to the more favourable climate with a more vigorous investment effort. Net investment has remained weaker—despite bullish business attitudes and supposedly strong economic "fundamentals"—than it was during the crisis-ridden 1970s. Furthermore, the data in Figure 1 end before the onset of the global financial crisis and recession in 2008, which obviously damaged business investment spending quite badly.

New investment spending has not kept up with the growth of profits. As a result, companies have been paying off debt and accumulating idle cash. But economies

FIGURE 1   The Investment Slowdown, G7 Economies, 1970–2006

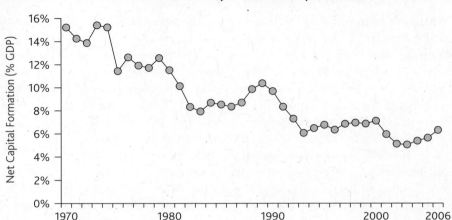

Note: Unweighted average.
Source: Stanford (2008, 149).

(including Canada's) are not getting the investment they need in order to take full advantage of new technology, boost productivity, and generate jobs. The reasons for this weak response of business investment to stronger profits and a more pro-business institutional climate are complex and uncertain. Certainly, the intense but pointless hyperactivity of financial markets has diverted attention from the task of undertaking and managing real investment. The rise of less capital-intensive service industries (like retail and hospitality services) may also be a factor explaining sluggish investment spending. Or it might just be that those policy changes, so painful for so many, were motivated more by a desire to *redistribute* economic output (in favour of businesses and the individuals who own them) than by a desire to genuinely enhance the *growth* of output.

It is also ironic that the investment effort has slowed so notably, even though the economic conditions for *saving* seem to have improved. With much lower inflation rates, favourable tax breaks on investment income, and greater access to a range of financial assets, the impulse to save (which, in the neoclassical model, ultimately drives the process of investment and capital accumulation) should have been enhanced. Yet investment rates (and correspondingly, personal saving rates, in most countries) have declined, not increased. This suggests that the negative impact of slow investment on overall economic growth, employment, and incomes has exerted a negative influence on personal saving that has been more important than the supposedly more favourable savings climate.

111

Conclusion

Whatever the reasons, it is clear that pro-business policy shifts and resulting strong profits have had a very weak impact on business investment. This seriously undermines the logic behind "trickle-down" economics: namely, the idea that enhancing business profits will stimulate more investment, more jobs, and rising incomes. It may be time to consider other ways of stimulating stronger investment spending in the future (especially in light of the global financial meltdown that began in 2008–2009, which so badly damaged both the confidence and the financial capacities of private companies). There may be more effective ways to elicit more spending from private companies than endlessly enhancing their profits and/or cutting their taxes—such as developing deliberate sector investment and development strategies, co-funded by state agencies, of the sort that have been so successful in Japan, Korea, and now China.[16] At the same time, our economy is also going to need an expansion of public investment in infrastructure, public programs, and environmental protection, in order to both meet pressing needs in these areas and to offset the weakness of private investment spending. The current crisis in private finance, and the resulting slowdown in conventionally motivated private business spending, may spark needed experiments with these alternative strategies for eliciting more investment spending.[17]

NOTES

1. Specifically, this model assumes that a market for "loanable funds," supplied with the autonomously determined savings of households, is cleared thanks to fluctuations in an interest rate that in turn reflects the assumed real productivity of invested capital. In this manner, savers are enticed to save by the interest attained on savings, which in turn depends on the real economic usefulness of the capital purchased with those savings. The neoclassical theory has been criticized on several grounds, including the nature of interest rate determination and logical problems in the theory of capital's "productivity"; see Rogers (1989) and Pollin (1997) for a complete description and critique of the neoclassical model.
2. More specifically, the treatment of business investment described in this essay is broadly compatible with several streams of heterodox economic analysis, including post-Keynesian, structuralist, and even Marxian. See Gordon (1994) for a more detailed consideration of the approaches to the analysis of business investment taken by these various heterodox schools.
3. In national economic statistics, residences are treated like "capital assets," not current consumption, because they are long lasting; hence new residential construction is considered an investment, not consumption.
4. Indeed, that measurement problem is at the root of the logical difficulties inherent in the aforementioned neoclassical theory of capital and investment:

in practice, it is impossible to value the aggregate stock of capital in the economy without knowing the rate of profit on capital investment, and hence it is impossible to explain the rate of profit on the basis of the amount of capital invested (and its supposed productivity); see Burmeister (2000) for a convenient summary of this problem and its associated debates.

5. At any rate, both the determinants and the economic effects of investments in research and development, skills, and other intangible "capital" are similar to those that apply to physical capital.

6. In modern, developed capitalist economies, printed currency accounts for less than 5 percent of the total stock of money in the economy; most money consists of deposits and accounts in the banking system, and banks' decisions to issue new loans are the most important source of *new* money created through that system.

7. Combined with the fact that capitalist economies are almost always demand-constrained (that is, limited by the amount of spending power rather than by the supply of available labour and other productive resources), this explains why—in the heterodox understanding—investment causes savings, rather than the other way around (as in the neoclassical model).

8. Minsky (1992) described well the tendency of private credit to exhibit patterns of overexpansion followed by overcontraction in a for-profit banking system, driven by the shifting balance between loan profits and default risk and reinforced by the interconnections and feedback effects that link the apparent value of lenders' assets (and hence their ability to issue new loans) with the rise and fall of broader financial conditions.

9. At the time of writing, in 2009, the global economy is entering a serious recession as a result of precisely that chain of events, originating with the collapse of speculative lending practices in the US real estate industry some years earlier.

10. Tomas (2006) documents this aggregate failure by corporations to reinvest the proceeds of their current operations.

11. See, for example, Stanford (1999, 85 and 104), reporting statistical causality tests that confirm both that business investment is a precursor to overall economic growth and that it is more closely associated with overall growth than any other component of output.

12. This circular process of employment, production, consumption spending, and subsequent additional production underpins what heterodox economists call the "investment multiplier." A given amount of investment spending generates a much larger (or "multiplied") amount of total output. Neoclassical economists reject the notion of the investment multiplier, since it is assumed that all resources (including labour) will be fully employed in any event, thanks to the operation of market-clearing mechanisms.

13. This is the concept of "transformational growth" enunciated by Nell (1995); in this theory, investment is crucial for incorporating both technological and social changes.

14. See De Long and Summers (1991) and Rao et al. (2008).
15. "Cash flow" equals profits adjusted for non-cash revenues and expenses. The largest non-cash expense is usually depreciation on existing capital assets, which provides an ongoing source of cash flow for companies to at least replenish their existing assets.
16. See Poon (2006) for a useful summary of those initiatives and their positive impact on investment in those countries.
17. Stanford (2008, chap. 26) proposes a set of policies aimed at developing a "high-investment, sustainable economy"—using a range of tax, financial, and macroeconomic levers to both elicit more investment spending and channel that spending in better directions.

DISCUSSION QUESTIONS

1. Why do local economic development officers and politicians expend so much energy trying to attract important investments to their respective communities? Is there any economic logic underpinning these efforts, and if so, what is it?
2. Mutual fund companies often advertise their services as converting the personal savings of their clients into concrete capital investments in promising, profitable companies—"picking winners," in other words. What is the connection, if any, between buying units in a mutual fund and actual investment in real capital? Do you believe that by purchasing units in a mutual fund, you are assisting the growth of dynamic, growing companies? Why or why not?

SUGGESTED READINGS

Coen, Robert M., Robert Eisner, Francesca Rondina, and Steven N. Durlauf. 2008. Investment (neoclassical). In *The new Palgrave dictionary of economics online*, ed. Steven N. Durlauf and Lawrence E. Blume. http://www.dictionaryofeconomics.com/dictionary.
Fazzari, Steven M. 1997. Investment. In *Business cycles and depressions: An encyclopedia*, ed. David Glasner, 336–339. New York: Garland.
Pollin, Robert, ed. 1997. *The macroeconomics of saving, finance, and investment.* Ann Arbor: University of Michigan Press.
Stanford, Jim. 2008. *Economics for everyone: A short guide to the economics of capitalism*, chaps. 10 and 12. London: Pluto Books.

ONLINE RESOURCES

United Nations Conference on Trade and Development (UNCTAD). *The world investment report.* http://www.unctad.org.
World Bank. *The world development report 2005: A better investment climate for everyone.* http://go.worldbank.org/4DP5PX4M30.

REFERENCES

Burmeister, Edwin. 2000. The capital theory controversy. In *Critical essays on Piero Sraffa's legacy in economics*, ed. Heinz D. Kurz, 305–314. Cambridge: Cambridge University Press.

De Long, J. Bradford, and Lawrence Summers. 1991. Equipment investment and economic growth. *Quarterly Journal of Economics* 106 (2): 445–502.

Gordon, David M. 1994. Putting heterodox macro to the test: Comparing post-Keynesian, Marxian, and social structuralist macroeconometric models of the post-war US economy. In *Competition, technology and money: Classical and post-Keynesian perspectives*, ed. Mark A. Glick, 143–185. Aldershot: Edward Elgar.

Minsky, Hyman. 1992. Financial instability hypothesis. The Jerome Levy Economics Institute of Bard College Working Paper 74. http://www.levy.org/pubs/wp74.pdf.

Nell, Edward J. 1995. *The general theory of transformational growth: Keynes after Sraffa*. Cambridge: Cambridge University Press.

Pollin, Robert, ed. 1997. *The macroeconomics of saving, finance, and investment*. Ann Arbor: University of Michigan Press.

Poon, Daniel. 2006. *Understanding East Asian industrial success*. Toronto: Canadian Auto Workers.

Rao, Someshwar, Jianmin Tang, and Wiemin Wang. 2008. What explains the Canada–US productivity gap? *Canadian Public Policy* 34 (2): 163–192.

Rogers, Colin. 1989. *Money, interest and capital: A study in the foundations of monetary theory*. Cambridge: Cambridge University Press.

Stanford, Jim. 1999. *Paper boom: Why real prosperity requires a new approach to Canada's economy*. Toronto: James Lorimer.

Stanford, Jim. 2008. *Economics for everyone: A short guide to the economics of capitalism*. London: Pluto Books.

Tomas, A. 2006. Recent trends in corporate finance. *Canadian Economic Observer* 19 (4): 3.22–3.31.

Why Is There Unemployment? Is Inflation the Ineluctable Consequence of High Employment?

Editors' Introduction

Unemployment is a statistical measure of the difference between the supply of labour (approximated by the number of workers in the labour force) and the demand for labour (reflected in the number of available jobs in an economy). This gap had been rising throughout most of the 1970s and 1980s in Canada. However, since the early 1990s, it had been falling steadily as a percentage of the labour force until it reached bottom during the 2008–9 financial crisis; it has since risen again. While economists in general would argue that changes in unemployment are the result of changes in both the supply and the demand for labour, mainstream neoclassical economists tend to emphasize the supply-side nature in explaining long-term unemployment. On the other hand, most heterodox economists place much greater emphasis on the demand side of the labour market—and especially on the overall level of demand—in explaining the evolution of unemployment over time.

In addition to referring to demographic characteristics of the labour force, broadly speaking, mainstream economists explain unemployment by pointing to the disincentive effects of social programs, such as employment insurance (EI), or to legislated minimum wages that prevent wages from falling. Much of this resulting unemployment is deemed "voluntary," either because workers choose not to take up available jobs (they may prefer collecting EI benefits or receiving provincial welfare support) or because of the collective choice on the part of government or trade unions not to permit wages to fall. The contribution by Pierre Fortin offers an eclectic analysis that recognizes both demand- and supply-side factors in explaining long-term unemployment, with a clear emphasis on factors pertaining to labour supply behaviour in explaining trend unemployment in Canada. Moreover, most established neoclassical economists would also argue that any attempt on the part of the government to reduce actual unemployment below this long-term level of unemployment (described by Milton Friedman as the "natural rate" of unemployment) would inevitably lead to accelerating inflation. Because of the possible inflationary consequences, they recommend that it is best not to intervene in the labour market through Keynesian demand-side policies, since the effect would be destabilizing.

As described by Marc Lavoie in his contribution, heterodox economists instead draw attention to the movement of aggregate demand in explaining the trend path of unemployment. While supply-side factors can play a role, heterodox economists regard unemployment as primarily involuntary in nature since the economic system is considered to be demand-constrained. Hence, if the labour market shows a trend rise in the unemployment rate, this is more likely due to declining long-term aggregate spending than to changing labour supply phenomena. In addition, since heterodox economists do not recognize the existence of a long-term "natural" rate of unemployment, a falling rate of unemployment (as seen in Canada from the early 1990s until 2008) need not necessarily be accompanied by rising inflation.

Unemployment in Canada

Pierre Fortin

Introduction: Unemployment Defined

Each month, Statistics Canada runs a sample survey of about 53,000 households across the country called the Labour Force Survey. Respondents are asked to answer two key questions:

1. Do you currently work at a job?
2. If you don't work at a job, have you done anything to find one?

Based on answers to these questions, Statistics Canada classifies every respondent aged 15 or older (called the "working-age population") into one—and only one— of three categories: employed, unemployed, or "not in the labour force." If you answer "yes" to the first question, you are employed. If you answer "no" to the first question but "yes" to the second, you are unemployed. And if you answer "no" to both questions, you are "not in the labour force."

Adding the first two categories gives the number of individuals who want to hold a job. If they are employed, they already have a job. If they are unemployed, they don't have one but are looking for one. These two groups both participate in the labour market. Together, they are said to form the "labour force."

Labour force = Employed + Unemployed

This explains why members of the third group—those who don't have a job and are not looking for one—are considered "not in the labour force." The "unemployment rate" in a society is defined as the percentage of the labour force that is unemployed. The unemployment rate is therefore a measure of the failure of individuals to have a job *when they want to have one*.

Unemployment rate = (Unemployed/Labour force) × 100

Table 1 shows the figures when survey responses are extrapolated for the entire Canadian working-age population (aged 15 and over) and the averages of monthly numbers are calculated for the year 2008.

The table shows that in 2008 there were 26.9 million Canadians at or above the minimum working age of 15. Of them, 17.1 million were employed and 1.1 million

TABLE 1   Labour Force Characteristics of the Total Working-Age Canadian Population, 2008

Category	Million people
Population in labour force	18.2
of which employed	17.1
of which unemployed	1.1
Population not in labour force	8.7
Total working-age population	26.9

Source: Statistics Canada, CANSIM table 282-0002.

were unemployed, forming a total labour force of 18.2 million. The remaining 8.7 million Canadians were not in the labour force.

Is 6 Percent a High Unemployment Rate?

According to these numbers, in 2008 Canada's unemployment rate was 1.1/18.2 = 6.1 percent. Is this a high or a low unemployment rate? By tracing the history of Canadian unemployment as far back as 1921, Figure 1 provides an answer. Several facts stand out. First, one must go back to 1974 to find an unemployment rate that was less than the 6 percent rates of 2007 and 2008; Canada's 2008 unemployment rate represents a 34-year low. Second, the unemployment rate was less than 6 percent for most of the preceding 34-year period (1941–1974) and for the entire decade of the 1920s. Third, the unemployment rate reached stratospheric levels during the Great Depression of the 1930s, with the highest level—19 percent—attained in 1933. (By the way, there was no employment insurance in those days.)

Fourth, since the end of the Second World War in 1945, Canada has suffered from three major recessions: from 1958 to 1960, 1981 to 1982, and 1990 to 1992. Peak unemployment rates occurred in 1961 (7.1 percent), 1983 (12 percent), and 1993 (11.4 percent). In contrast to the Great Depression, which resulted from an unwanted and unexpected collapse of the financial system, all three of these postwar recessions were *strategic* recessions: they were engineered by the Bank of Canada as weapons aimed at reducing inflation. The standard chain of causation (described in every macroeconomics textbook) in each case is that the central bank raised interest rates to induce firms and households to cut spending. The result was increased unemployment, which in turn cooled down wage growth and thus reduced price inflation.

A fifth observation is that the minimum unemployment rate attained at peaks of economic expansions is not necessarily the same from one cycle to the next. For example, Figure 1 indicates that minimum unemployment was on the rise (from

FIGURE 1   Unemployment Rate, Canada, 1921–2008

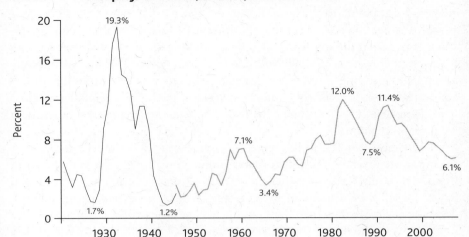

Note: There is a break in the series in 1946. Before this date, the armed forces are included in the labour force and employment, and the unemployment rate is the June figure. From 1946 on, the armed forces are excluded from the labour force and employment, and the employment rate is the average for the whole year.

Sources: Statistics Canada. 1983. *Historical statistics of Canada*. Catalogue no. 11-516, series D124-D133; Statistics Canada, CANSIM table 282-0002.

1.2 percent in 1944 to 3.4 percent in 1966, and 7.5 percent in 1979 and 1989) and then declined to 6.0 percent in 2007, before the onset of the 2009 recession. This is because aggregate demand-led economic expansions can be of varying strength and length, but also because labour markets undergo *structural* change over time. (To anticipate a bit, it will be argued later in this review of Canada's unemployment record that the decline in structural unemployment over the last 20 years can be attributed in part to such developments as the declining share of young workers in the labour force, the continuing progress of educational attainment, increased international and domestic competitive pressure on Canadian firms, and a string of restrictive amendments to the *Employment Insurance Act*.)

How Reliable Is Our Official Measure of Unemployment?

Although our official measure is in full conformity with the standard international definition, it does underestimate "true" unemployment somewhat. Not counted as unemployed are discouraged job searchers, those waiting for recall or replies, and involuntary part-timers. According to Statistics Canada, correcting the official

2008 figure of 6.1 percent for these misses would raise the unemployment rate by 2.7 percentage points, to 8.8 percent (Statistics Canada, CANSIM table 282-0086).

This is not the end of the story, however. Clearly, a number of survey respondents, even if they correctly say they are looking for work, do not search very intensively; they are accordingly classified as unemployed. This has the opposite effect of exaggerating "true" unemployment. The quantitative importance of this bias is unknown. The safe conclusion is that the official 2008 unemployment rate of 6.1 percent does underestimate "true" unemployment, but probably by less than 2.7 percentage points.

Differences in job search intensity also explain why the official measure of unemployment tends to produce lower numbers in the United States than in Canada. Basically, for a jobless person to be counted as unemployed in the United States, she must be *actively* involved in the search for a job. For example, if she does nothing more than read want ads, she will be categorized as unemployed in Canada but as "not in the labour force" in the United States. Statistics Canada has estimated that, if calculated according to the more stringent US rules, the official 2008 unemployment rate in Canada would have been 5.3 percent instead of 6.1 percent (Statistics Canada, CANSIM table 282-0086).

Another difference between the measures of unemployment in Canada and the United States concerns the prison population. This group has a high incidence of unemployment, but is excluded from labour force surveys in both countries. The problem is that, since the rate of incarceration is many times greater in the United States than in Canada, the exclusion rule could have the effect of reducing the official estimate of unemployment in the United States below that in Canada by an additional 0.3 percentage points.

Unemployment Is a Dynamic Phenomenon

Unemployment is not a static phenomenon, but a dynamic one. It is like running water, not a still lagoon. On average in North America, 40 percent of those who are classified as unemployed in any given month no longer belong to this category the following month (see Jones 1993). They are replaced by roughly the same number of newly unemployed individuals who were previously employed or outside of the labour force. This does *not* mean that unemployment is a benign problem. Despite the short duration of the majority of unemployment spells, the largest portion of the total time spent unemployed by various groups can be attributed to a certain minority of workers. In other words, unemployment is characterized by high turnover *and* by high concentration among a minority of disadvantaged workers.

What is true in North America is not necessarily true in Europe. While unemployment is mostly a high-frequency, short-duration phenomenon in North America, one usually finds the opposite in Europe. On average, unemployment there is a low-frequency, long-duration experience. This follows from the fact that the two continents have different labour market institutions. North America emphasizes employment flexibility, while Europe prefers employment protection. A corollary is that two countries that otherwise have the same national unemployment rate, such as Canada and Belgium, can be subject to entirely different underlying labour market dynamics.

Unemployment Is High in Winter, Low in Autumn

Dynamics aside, it is important to keep in mind that unemployment varies systematically by season, age and sex, educational attainment, and region.

There are systematic, within-year seasonal fluctuations in labour market activity even when the underlying strength of the economy remains unchanged. The low season is from January to March. The high season is from October to December, ending with Christmas. Unemployment is high in the winter, low in autumn.

How large are those within-year seasonal fluctuations? On average, Canada's unemployment rate is about 0.5 percentage points above trend in the winter and about 0.5 points below trend in the fall (Statistics Canada, CANSIM tables 282-0001 and 282-0087). The amplitude of this seasonal wave is obviously smaller in warm, southern British Columbia than in cold, northern Saskatchewan, and smaller in Ontario than in Quebec and Atlantic Canada. Most of the time, reported unemployment in any given month is "seasonally adjusted." This means that the purely seasonal component of the unemployment rate has been removed from the measure in order to make its underlying trend easier to recognize.

Unemployment Is Higher Among Young Workers and Among Men

The aggregate unemployment rate is not evenly distributed across age groups and genders. Table 2 shows that unemployment affects young workers more than mature workers, and men more than women. In 2008 the unemployment of young Canadians aged 15 to 24 was more than twice as high as that of mature workers aged 25 and over (11.6 percent against 5.1 percent). A high unemployment rate for the young is a universal characteristic of labour markets. Young adults are new entrants in the labour force. They often feel the need to experiment with various opportunities before settling into a job more permanently. They leave their current jobs and enter new jobs more frequently than experienced workers. This explains why their unemployment rate is higher.

Concerning gender, Table 2 shows that in 2008 the unemployment rate for all Canadian women (aged 15 and over) was 1 point *below* the rate for men (5.7 percent against 6.6 percent). This is a significant change from 30 years ago, when the unemployment rate for women was 2 points *above* men's rate (Statistics Canada,

TABLE 2 Unemployment Rates by Sex and Age Group in Canada, 2008 (Percentages)

Age group	Men	Women	Total
15 to 24	13.1	10.0	11.6
25 and over	5.3	4.8	5.1
Total	6.6	5.7	6.1

Source: Statistics Canada, CANSIM table 282-0002.

CANSIM table 282-0002). The fact that we now have a knowledge economy and that women have a higher level of educational attainment than men can go some way to explaining this development. For example, Statistics Canada (2006) reports that, among labour force participants, 17 percent of Canadian men but only 13 percent of Canadian women were without any degree in 2006. The obvious implication is that it must be easier for women than men to keep their current jobs or find new ones, as the need may be. Hence, women's unemployment rate is lower.

The fact that unemployment is much higher for young workers than mature workers implies that demographic change over the last 30 years has exerted downward pressure on the aggregate unemployment rate. To see what is involved, let us observe that the aggregate unemployment rate can be obtained as a weighted average of two group-specific unemployment rates: that of young workers aged 15 to 24 and that of mature workers aged 25 and over. The weights used in this calculation are the corresponding shares of these two groups in the labour force. Clearly, if the weight given to the age group with the higher unemployment rate (that is, the young workers) declines over time, the aggregate unemployment rate will decrease to that extent. This is exactly what has occurred since the mid-1970s in Canada. The share of young workers in the total labour force has declined sharply, from 28 percent in 1978 to 16 percent in 2008.[1] This has reduced the aggregate unemployment rate by 0.8 points. In other words, without this demographic change the aggregate unemployment rate in 2008 would have been 6.9 percent instead of 6.1 percent.

Dropping Out of High School Is Bad for Employment Prospects

Figure 2 shows that there is a strong negative correlation between unemployment and educational attainment. In 2006 the average unemployment rate was 4.5 percent for university graduates at one extreme and 11.1 percent for Canadians with no degree whatsoever at the other extreme. In every industrialized country in the past few decades, dropping out of high school has increasingly been a passport for labour market disaster. (Examples of famous high school dropouts that have had

FIGURE 2   Unemployment Rate According to Highest Degree Obtained, Canada, 2006

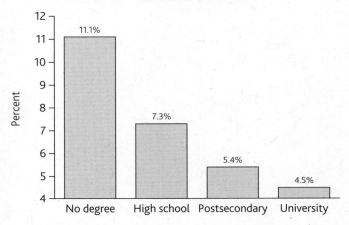

Note: "Postsecondary" combines apprenticeship or trades certificate, college or CEGEP degree, and university certificate below bachelor level.

Source: Statistics Canada. 2006. *Census of Canada 2006*. Catalogue no. 97-559.

very successful careers, such as Céline Dion, are relished by the media. But note that they are remarkable precisely because they are so exceptional.)

The general rise in the average level of schooling of the labour force over the last 30 years has exerted continuous downward pressure on Canadian unemployment. Fewer and fewer labour force participants hold no degree at all (those who do have found themselves subject to unemployment rates such as 11.1 percent in 2006), and more and more have postsecondary or university degrees, which reduces their unemployment rates to 4 or 5 percent. It is a bit adventurous to estimate what the aggregate unemployment rate would have been in 2006 had the educational achievement of the labour force remained at the 1976 level, but a reasonable guess is between 1 and 2 percentage points higher.

Unemployment Decreases from East to West

For decades it has been observed that unemployment varies systematically across Canadian regions, basically declining from East to West. Figure 3 gives the picture for 2008. The highest unemployment rates were found in Atlantic Canada and the lowest in Western Canada, with Quebec and Ontario standing in the middle. Climate and other seasonal factors, education levels, and the ups and downs of natural resources extraction all play a role in the uneven distribution of unemployment across the provinces. Extraction booms and busts come and go by definition, but differences in climate and educational attainment are more persistent.

FIGURE 3   Unemployment Rate by Province, Canada, 2008

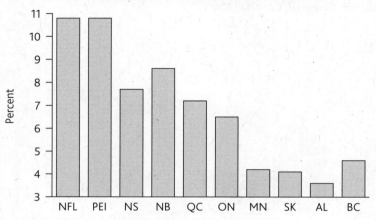

Source: Statistics Canada, CANSIM table 282-0002.

Due to Turnover and Search, There Is Always a Minimum Amount of Unemployment

By definition, the unemployment rate cannot be a negative number. It also cannot be zero. The reason for this is that economic activity always undergoes change. There are job separations (layoffs and quits) and new entries into the labour force all the time. These are initiated in part by firms that introduce technological and organizational change or react to shifts in market demand for their products, and result in part from decisions made by workers to look for a first job or search for a new job. There is always a minimal amount of turnover unemployment (also called "frictional"). In addition, the matching process between firms and workers is not instantaneous. It takes time for firms to find new workers and for workers to find new jobs, depending on the number, skills, and location of existing job vacancies and searching workers.

Initiatives such as greater investment by firms in onsite training and worker job satisfaction will not eliminate turnover unemployment, but they will make it less frequent. Likewise, timely information on available workers and vacancies, good manpower training policies, and reasonable support for worker mobility will not suppress search unemployment, but will make it shorter.

In the Last 20 Years, Unemployment in OECD Countries Has Fluctuated Between 1.6 Percent and 20 Percent

How much can unemployment be reduced? To answer this question, it is helpful to look at what countries have actually been able to achieve in the past. Table 3 summarizes the unemployment experience of the 30 member countries of the Organisation

TABLE 3 Descriptive Statistics of Unemployment Rates in OECD Countries, 1989–2008 (Percentages)

Country	Minimum	Maximum	Average	Variability
Australia	4.2	10.6	7.1	1.9
Austria	3.6	5.2	4.2	0.5
Belgium	6.4	9.8	8.1	1.1
Canada	6.0	11.4	8.2	1.7
Czech Republic	3.9	8.7	6.3	1.8
Denmark	3.5	9.5	5.8	1.7
Finland	3.1	16.8	9.9	3.9
France	7.8	11.6	9.6	1.2
Germany	4.2	10.6	8.3	1.5
Greece	6.3	12.0	9.2	1.6
Hungary	5.7	12.1	8.1	2.0
Iceland	2.0	5.3	3.3	1.0
Ireland	3.9	15.6	8.9	4.6
Italy	6.1	11.3	9.2	1.6
Japan	2.1	5.4	3.7	1.1
Korea	2.0	7.0	3.4	1.3
Luxembourg	1.6	5.0	3.0	1.1
Mexico	2.5	6.2	3.5	0.9
Netherlands	2.2	6.8	4.6	1.5
New Zealand	3.6	10.4	6.3	2.1
Norway	2.6	6.6	4.5	1.3
Poland	7.1	20.0	14.9	3.9
Portugal	4.0	8.1	5.9	1.4
Slovak Republic	9.7	19.3	14.8	3.2
Spain	8.3	19.5	13.2	3.5
Sweden	1.6	9.9	6.4	2.4
Switzerland	2.6	4.4	3.6	0.6
Turkey	6.5	10.5	8.6	1.4
United Kingdom	4.7	10.2	6.7	1.8
United States	4.0	7.5	5.4	0.9
Average	5.8	7.8	6.8	1.8

Note: National unemployment rates are "harmonized" by the OECD so as to conform to international standards. The first few years of data are missing for eight countries. For each country, the measure of variability is the standard deviation of its unemployment rate during the period.

Source: OECD. 2009. *OECD Economic Outlook* 85, annex tables.

for Economic Co-operation and Development (OECD) over the last 20 years (1989–2008)—a sample of several hundred annual observations. The first two columns give the minimum and maximum unemployment rates recorded in each individual country. On the minimum side, it can be seen that Iceland, Korea, Luxembourg, and Sweden have been able to post unemployment rates as low as 2 percent or less. Conversely, on the maximum side, Finland, Ireland, Poland, the Slovak Republic, and Spain have all suffered from unemployment rates in excess of 15 percent.

The last two columns of Table 3 indicate how high and variable unemployment has been on average in the 30 countries. Six of them have been able to maintain average unemployment rates of less than 4 percent over the period: Iceland, Japan, Korea, Luxembourg, Mexico, and Switzerland. Unemployment rates have been most stable in Austria, Iceland, Mexico, and the United States.

As Table 3 illustrates, Canada's performance over the past two decades has not been particularly impressive. Canadian unemployment has been high and variable. Only 10 of the 30 countries posted a higher average unemployment rate than Canada, and only 11 had a worse record on unemployment variability. The good news is that, if so many countries have done better than Canada, it must be possible for Canada to improve its performance in the future.

Europeans Emphasize Employment Protection

Can certain types of social policies increase unemployment? Yes—if they are pushed too far. For example, the emphasis on employment protection in Europe has often led to requirements, such as large severance payments, that make it costly for firms to lay off workers. Such interventions can be successful in reducing the frequency of unemployment.

But there is a downside. Firms that are subjected to the high cost of separations tend to become cautious in hiring new workers. As a result, jobs are harder to find, which increases the duration of unemployment. There is less firing, but also less hiring, which can be particularly harmful to new entrants into the labour force such as young workers. In the end, aggregate unemployment could even increase on net, although evidence of this outcome is not strong. Recognizing these problems, a number of European countries (such as Denmark, Finland, and the Netherlands) have recently modified their employment protection regulations significantly and made their labour markets more flexible.

Above a Certain Level, the Minimum Wage Destroys Jobs

In Canada, the social policies most widely discussed for their impact on unemployment are the minimum wage and employment insurance.

In jurisdictions where almost all workers are covered by minimum labour standards, an increase in the minimum wage could reduce the number of hours worked and increase unemployment for low-wage workers, most of whom are teenagers, young adults, and women. It is natural to think that, if this type of labour becomes more expensive to employ, firms will hire less of it. The important question is: how much less? Research done in the United States during the 1990s concluded that the impact of the minimum wage on employment was very small (see Card and Krueger 1995). This was not surprising, since in that decade the federal minimum wage as a fraction of the average hourly wage was low and falling, so that very few workers were paid at the minimum. Since 2000, however, an increasing number of states have set minimum wages above the federal minimum. In many states today, the local minimum wage is higher than 45 percent of local average wages.[2] With these new developments, the minimum wage could once again have a negative impact on employment. In fact, a 2009 study found that a 10 percent increase in state minimum wages would reduce youth employment by 2 percent (Keil, Robertson, and Symons 2009).

It seems reasonable to conclude that increases in the minimum wage do little harm to low-wage employment when the minimum wage is initially less than 40 percent of the average wage, but that the effect on jobs could be significant if the minimum is at or above 45 percent of the average wage. In Figure 4, we can see that in 2008 the minimum-to-average wage ratio was less than 45 percent in six provinces and was 45 percent or higher in Prince Edward Island, Quebec, Manitoba, and Saskatchewan. Minimum-wage regulations in the latter provinces would be on the edge of hurting low-wage employment seriously. However, because workers who are paid minimum wages usually represent less than 10 percent of the total labour force, the impact of minimum-wage increases on the *aggregate* unemployment rate is unlikely to be significant—it will rarely exceed a few tenths of a percentage point.

Employment Insurance Increases Both Employment and Unemployment

The impact of employment insurance on *aggregate* unemployment is potentially more important than that of the minimum wage. Suppose you are told that a minimum of 10 weeks of work will entitle you to a maximum of 42 weeks of employment insurance benefits worth 60 percent of your weekly wage. With this kind of deal, 10 weeks of actual work would entitle you to a total annual income worth 35.2 weeks of full-time salary (10 + 60 percent of 42 = 35.2). From 1977 to 1990, this was in essence what the federal *Unemployment Insurance Act* offered Canadian workers in those regions where the unemployment rate exceeded 11.5 percent. The basic objective of the Act was to entice hundreds of thousands of Canadians that were previously out of the labour force to enter the mainstream labour market, get jobs, and acquire greater financial independence.

This policy was successful—it did attract hundreds of thousands more Canadians into the labour force. However, many of these newcomers suffered from higher unemployment rates than the rest of the labour force. Consequently, the

FIGURE 4   Minimum Wage as a Percentage of Average Hourly Earnings of Hourly-Paid Employees in the Ten Canadian Provinces, 2008

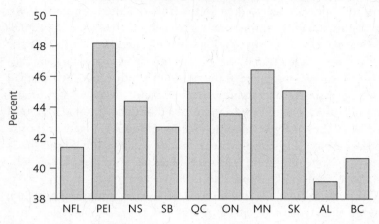

Sources: Human Resources and Social Development Canada. 2009. Hourly minimum wages in Canada for adult workers. http://srv116.services.gc.ca/dimt-wid/sm-mw/rpt2.aspx?dec=5; Statistics Canada, CANSIM table 281-0030.

national unemployment rate increased. By how much? The median estimate that can be drawn from the numerous studies of the effect of the Act on aggregate un- employment is 1.5 percentage points (see Fortin, Keil, and Symons 2001; this article reviews previous work and provides new estimates regarding the effect of the Act on unemployment).

From 1990 to 1996, successive amendments brought several restrictions to the Act (whose name was changed to the *Employment Insurance Act*), such as increases in the minimum number of weeks an individual was required to work in order to be eligible for benefits, reductions in the maximum duration of the benefit period, a smaller benefit-to-wage ratio, and penalties for repeat unemployment. This elim- inated much of the motivation for individuals to enter the labour force that the reform of unemployment insurance had originally sought to achieve in the 1970s. There is continuing debate over whether the amendments of the 1990s went too far in the opposite direction.

Globalization, Technological Change, the Size of Government, and Union Coverage Are Not Causes of Permanent Unemployment

Over time, the public debate has generated many explanations for high unemploy- ment. Although a detailed examination of each one is beyond the scope of this essay, four of them are so widespread—and so misguided—that they deserve some attention. They are: (1) globalization, (2) technological change, (3) the size of government, and (4) union coverage of the labour force. It is often said that foreign competition, technological progress, ubiquitous government, and powerful unions slow down job creation. The truth is that none of these factors qualifies as a systematic job killer.

Table 4 allows for a quick examination of the facts. The average unemployment rate, the degree of involvement in external trade ("openness"), the level of technology, the size of government, and the coverage of employees by labour union contracts are reported for 23 OECD countries. As can be seen, unemployment is not correlated with any of these four factors, whether taken individually or collectively. Among countries that have had low unemployment, one finds countries that are highly exposed to foreign competition (such as the Czech Republic and the Netherlands), are technologically advanced (such as Norway and the United States), have large government sectors (such as Denmark and Sweden), and have wide union coverage (such as Austria and the Netherlands). Conversely, among countries that have had high unemployment, one finds countries that have low exposure to foreign competition (such as France, Italy, and Spain), are not very advanced technologically (such as Hungary and Poland), have modest public sectors (such as Canada and Turkey), and have limited union coverage (again, Canada and Turkey).

On Net, NAFTA and the WTO Have Encouraged Job Creation in Canada

Should we be surprised by these results? No. The North American Free Trade Agreement between Canada, the United States, and Mexico (NAFTA), and freer trade with the 152 other members of the World Trade Organization (WTO) increased competitive pressure on Canadian firms sharply beginning in 1989. Remember that globalization has two faces: more foreign imports penetrate Canadian markets, but Canadian exports have freer access to growing international markets. On balance, many more jobs have been created by exports than destroyed by imports. In fact, from 1988 to 2008, export sales by Canadian firms increased by 137 percent in volume, while their domestic sales rose by just 40 percent (Statistics Canada, CANSIM table 380-0017).

In 200 Years of Technological Change, Unemployment Rates Have Not Increased

Technological innovation allows firms to produce more output per employee. In this process, some firms will lay off employees. But as the increased income generated by higher productivity is spent in the economy, aggregate demand will increase. This will allow the laid-off employees to find new jobs elsewhere. If technological

TABLE 4 **Unemployment Rate and Indicators of the Degree of Openness, the Level of Technology, the Size of Government, and Union Coverage in 23 OECD Countries (Percentages)**

Country	Unemployment	Openness	Technology	Government	Unions
Australia	7.1	22	83	31	83
Austria.	4.2	54	87	42	98
Belgium.	8.1	87	105	44	93
Canada.	8.2	35	81	33	32
Czech Republic.	6.3	75	46	36	33
Denmark.	5.8	51	82	49	83
Finland	9.9	42	82	43	93
France	9.6	28	101	44	93
Germany	8.3	43	95	36	68
Hungary	8.1	78	46	39	39
Italy	9.2	28	75	43	83
Korea	3.4	43	42	29	12
Netherlands.	4.6	70	102	38	83
New Zealand.	6.3	31	57	36	28
Norway	4.5	38	134	43	73
Poland	14.9	41	39	34	28
Portugal.	5.9	35	52	37	79
Spain	13.2	29	80	37	83
Sweden.	6.4	48	88	48	93
Switzerland	3.6	50	81	30	43
Turkey	8.6	33	41	24	24
United Kingdom.	6.7	31	85	37	33
United States.	5.4	14	100	28	14
Average	7.3	44	78	37	61
Correlation with unemployment.	1.00	−0.17	−0.23	0.04	0.07

Note: Seven OECD countries are omitted due to missing values for union coverage. "Unemployment" is the average annual unemployment rate over the 20-year period from 1989 to 2008, as in Table 3. "Openness" is the ratio of international trade (average of imports and exports) to GDP in 2006. "Level of technology" is GDP per hour worked in 2007 (index US = 100). "Size of government" is total government revenue as a percentage of GDP in 2007. "Union coverage" is the percentage of employees that were covered by labour union contracts according to calculations by the OECD and the International Labour Organization (ILO). None of the simple correlation coefficients that appear in the last line of the four right-hand columns can be said to be different from zero with any confidence. In a multiple regression of unemployment on the four explanatory variables together, the joint hypothesis that none of them has any explanatory power cannot be rejected at usual levels of significance (p-value = 0.38). When all of the above statistical experiments are repeated with the average unemployment rates for the 5-year period from 2004 to 2008 (instead of the 20-year period from 1989 to 2008), all conclusions remain the same.

Sources: OECD. 2009. *OECD Economic Outlook* 85, annex tables (data for unemployment); OECD.Stat databases, http://webnet.oecd.org/wbos/ (data for openness, level of technology, and size of government); Stephen Nickell. 2008. Is the US labor market truly exceptional? *Journal of Economic Literature* 46 (2): 384–395, table 1 (data for union coverage).

change were a net job killer, unemployment rates would be very high in those countries where technology is most advanced, such as the United States. But we know that this is not the case. Not only is the US unemployment rate no higher today than it was 200 years ago, but the United States is among the low-unemployment countries of the last 20 years (see Table 3).

What Matters Is What the Government Does, Not Its Size

The impact of government on employment and unemployment is not determined by its size, but by what it does to labour markets. What matters are the specific health, education, and welfare policies; labour market regulations; and tax policies that a government adopts. A frequently asked question is whether payroll taxes destroy jobs because they add to the cost of hiring labour. The answer is that it depends on how wages react. If an increase in payroll taxes is offset by a proportionate reduction in wages, then firms will not incur any increase in their labour costs and there will be no impact on jobs. The burden of the tax increase will be carried entirely by workers. Economic research has found that this is indeed largely the way things work.

The Impact of Unions on Unemployment Can Go in Either Direction

Are unions good or bad for employment? According to the evidence presented in Table 4, the answer is not a clear "yes" or "no." Again, it depends on what unions do, and what they do can vary according to the time and place.

In countries where union coverage of the labour force is wide (such as in most of Europe, but not in North America; see the right-hand column of Table 4), the union movement is a major player in the wage-setting process. Since wages are the largest contributor to unit costs, and therefore to prices, union behaviour has important macroeconomic consequences. First, very high wages can destroy jobs, particularly if foreign competition prevents domestic firms from increasing prices. Second, if accelerating wages raise the level of inflation to any extent, the anti-inflation fighter—the central bank—will enter the scene and raise interest rates. This will slow aggregate demand and (again) increase unemployment.

In this context, unions must choose between two possible courses of action: (1) pressing hard for higher wages at the risk of triggering higher inflation, interest rates, and unemployment, or (2) opting for wage moderation, low inflation, and plenty of jobs, but risking a decline in the share of national income going to their members. In the course of history, union policy has often shifted between these two options. For example, during the period from 1965 to 1980, a wage explosion accompanied by rising unemployment occurred in most European countries; this led unions in many countries to revise their policies during the 1980s. In a few instances, it even led to "tripartite agreements" that included wage moderation and protection of labour's share of national income as specific elements. Some of these agreements, including the famous Wassenaar Agreement in the Netherlands, continue to guide wage negotiations to this day.

This explains why wide union coverage of the labour force is not necessarily associated with persistently high unemployment. Austria, Denmark, the Netherlands, and Norway are good examples of countries that are highly unionized but are nevertheless near-fully employed most of the time. The statistical outcome (clear from Table 4) is that the correlation between unemployment and the extent of union coverage is near zero.

Currently, 32 percent of the Canadian labour force is covered by labour union contracts (Statistics Canada, CANSIM table 282-0078). This figure is lower than in many European countries. One implication is that centralized wage agreements are unlikely in Canada. Although our decentralized collective bargaining system gives some stability to the inflation-unemployment process, this is precisely what makes it more difficult to reduce unemployment to very low levels through aggregate demand management without triggering increases in inflation. Without the help of central coordination, the trade-off between inflation and unemployment is harder to improve. In Canada in recent years, it seemed that 6 percent was the lowest unemployment rate that could be sustained without causing inflation to rise. This number is usually called the "non-accelerating inflation rate of unemployment," or "NAIRU." In contrast, unemployment rates were 4 percent or less in highly unionized countries such as Austria, Denmark, the Netherlands, and Norway.

Much Unemployment Is Involuntary, Painful, and Costly

The final question (which should actually be the first) to be addressed is: why should we be concerned by unemployment at all? The answer is: because much of it is involuntary, painful, and costly.

Most Canadians who are involuntarily unemployed would have preferred to have kept their jobs rather than be laid off, or would like to find a new job today instead of six months from now. Most members of this group are ready to work at their customary—or even at a lower—wage. The basic explanation for their becoming and remaining unemployed involuntarily is well known: from time to time, aggregate demand declines, and the economic system is unable to absorb the slack that follows in labour and product markets on short notice.

Involuntary unemployment is a social scourge that entails considerable human costs. It deprives people of their natural social environment. It makes them feel useless, guilty, and undignified. It hinders personal development and the acquisition of experience on the job. It is the cause of multiple individual, family, and social pathologies. It falls on the working poor more often and for longer periods than on other workers. It is arguable that these human costs of involuntary joblessness hurt the unemployed more than the loss of income that is inflicted on them.

Conclusion: The Bottom Line

Because much unemployment is involuntary, painful, and costly, we should take every step to prevent inflation and recessions, and we should establish the kind of institutions that are most likely to minimize joblessness. This is a difficult—but most worthy—endeavour.

NOTES

1. The smart reader can readily get to this conclusion with the help of the data in Table 2; see Statistics Canada, CANSIM table 282-0002.
2. Minimum wages of US states can be found at the US Department of Labor's website at http://www.dol.gov/esa/minwage/america.htm.

DISCUSSION QUESTIONS

1. From time to time, Statistics Canada may report, for instance, that last month the number of employed Canadians increased by 15,000 over the previous month, but at the same time that the unemployment rate increased. How is this possible?
2. "In North America, people become unemployed often, but usually not for long. In Europe, they rarely become unemployed, but when they do, they tend to remain unemployed for extended periods." Discuss the reasons for this difference between the two continents.
3. "A province should set its minimum wage as high as possible, but not so high as to destroy jobs." Discuss the two assertions in this sentence.
4. Even at the height of the 2002–2008 employment boom, Canada's unemployment rate seemed stuck at around 6 percent. Why? What do you think could have been done to reduce the minimum unemployment rate to, say, 4 or 5 percent?
5. "The process of technological change consists of replacing people with machines. Therefore, technological change is actually a serious source of unemployment." Discuss.
6. What effect do unions have on unemployment? Why?

SUGGESTED READINGS

Bellemare, Diane, and Lise Poulin-Simon. 1991. The challenge of full employment. In *On the political economy of social democracy*, ed. A. Fenichel and S.H. Ingerman. Montreal and Kingston: McGill-Queen's University Press.

Broadfoot, Barry. 1997. *Ten lost years, 1929–1939*. Toronto: McClelland & Stewart.
Liebow, Elliot. 2003. *Tally's corner: A study of Negro streetcorner men*. 2nd ed.
    Lanham, MD: Rowman & Littlefield.

ONLINE RESOURCES

The most useful source of information on Canadian unemployment is Statistics
Canada's website at www.statcan.gc.ca. You can read current news by clicking on
"*The Daily*." If you click on "Publications" and then choose "Labour," you can
access a wealth of information and studies done by Statistics Canada's highly
competent personnel.

Internationally, the most useful website is that of the Organisation for Economic Co-operation and Development (OECD), at www.oecd.org. You can find
statistics and analysis by personnel of the OECD, whose membership includes 30
industrialized countries. On employment and unemployment, the most useful
source is the OECD *Employment Outlook*, which is published annually.

REFERENCES

Card, David, and Alan B. Krueger. 1995. *Myth and measurement: The new economics
    of the minimum wage*. Princeton, NJ: Princeton University Press.
Fortin, Pierre, Manfred Keil, and James Symons. 2001. The sources of unemployment
    in Canada, 1967–91: Evidence from a panel of regions and demographic
    groups. *Oxford Economic Papers* 53 (1): 67–93.
Jones, Stephen R.G. 1993. Cyclical and seasonal properties of Canadian gross flows
    of labour. *Canadian Public Policy* 19 (1): 1–17.
Keil, Manfred, Donald Robertson, and James Symons. 2009. Univariate regressions
    of employment on minimum wages in the panel of US states. Robert Day
    School of Economics and Finance Research Paper 2009-03.
Statistics Canada. 2006. *Census of Canada 2006*. Catalogue no. 97-559.

Two Views on Unemployment

Marc Lavoie

Introduction

There are two broad views about what causes unemployment. One view is that unemployment is voluntary and is essentially a supply-side phenomenon—there is unemployment when rigidities in the labour market (such as minimum-wage laws and imperfect information) discourage firms from offering jobs and workers from accepting them. The other view is that unemployment is involuntary and is mainly a demand-driven phenomenon. Unemployment, in this view, is essentially caused by an insufficient amount of aggregate demand for goods, which leads to an insufficient demand for labour. The first view is associated with the neoclassical or mainstream school of thought. The second view is linked to famed British economist John Maynard Keynes and his 1936 *General Theory of Employment, Interest and Money*. It is now endorsed mainly by heterodox economists, and is known as the "Keynesian" view.

The Keynesian view has not been very popular within academic circles over the last 40 years or so. However, it came back with a vengeance during the financial crisis that first hurt numerous banks in August 2007, and which then repeatedly hit the American economy in 2008, engulfing financial institutions, stock markets, indebted households, and firms all over the world. Many governments embarked on a Keynesian policy response, increasing public deficits and government expenditures—in particular, infrastructure expenditures—in an effort to raise aggregate demand and sustain employment and economic activity.

Many of the controversies that have arisen in macroeconomics have turned around the so-called Phillips curve, which says that there is a negative relationship between rates of inflation and rates of unemployment. The Phillips curve is a downward-sloping curve, with inflation on the vertical axis and the unemployment rate on the horizontal axis, thus indicating that there is a possible trade-off between inflation and unemployment. For example, there could be less unemployment, but this would be accompanied by higher inflation rates. The implications of such a relationship, and whether the downward slope is truly representative of all economies under all circumstances, have been the subject of intensive debates.

In this essay, I will first present the supply-side view of unemployment—that of neoclassical theory—which I will then contrast with the heterodox Keynesian view.

The Neoclassical View

The neoclassical view of unemployment is not fully homogeneous. It has many twists, but in the end it always comes down to the same thing: if there is unemployment, it is either because some people prefer not to work or because there are rigidities that stop the labour market from freely adjusting to the full-employment real wage.

The simplest neoclassical interpretation of the above statement is provided by the so-called new classical economists. In their view, the labour market is best represented as a market that is always in equilibrium, meaning that the demand for and the supply of labour are always equal to each other. It is assumed that firms' demand for labour diminishes when the workers' real wage rate—the nominal wage divided by the consumer price index—gets higher. And it is assumed that workers supply more labour when their real wage rises, either because they agree to work longer hours or because more workers enter the workforce. Supply equates to demand thanks to the flexibility of the real wage rate. If the demand for labour falls—for instance, because technology is not as efficient as it used to be (a so-called negative supply-side shock)—the real wage rate will adjust downward, and anybody willing to work at this new rate will be able to. Hence, if there is any reduction in employment, it will be attributed entirely to workers refusing to work at the new lower real wage, perhaps quitting their jobs in the hope of finding better-paying jobs elsewhere.

As was just pointed out, the ability of the economic system to secure full employment within this equilibrium view of the labour market depends very much on the realized value of the real wage. But workers, when they negotiate their nominal wage rate, do not know what the general price level, or the consumer price level, will be during the course of their wage agreement. Thus workers, when they decide whether or not to work at the offered wage rate, must rely on expectations about the future price level. They do not know what real wage they will get; they only know of an *expected* real wage, which is the nominal wage rate they are offered divided by the price level they anticipate on the basis of expected price inflation. Thus, when workers overestimate inflation, they are more likely to turn down job offers because the offered real wage will seem too low. For this reason, according to the most sophisticated new classical models, cyclical unemployment is essentially due to workers having overly high estimates of future prices and inflation. By contrast, when workers underestimate the rate of inflation, they will be fooled into accepting low actual real wages, which will induce firms to increase employment. Unemployment in this view is thus entirely voluntary, and dependent on the decisions of workers to work or not to work. For instance, new classical economists would argue that the unemployment rate rose in the course of the 2009 recession, which was induced by the financial crisis, because too many people turned down job offers or quit their jobs.

Such a theory looks absurd, especially considering that very few workers know or care about the rate of inflation. Furthermore, empirical studies have shown repeatedly that workers do not quit their jobs when unemployment rates are high or rising; instead, quit rates are high when unemployment rates are low or falling. During a recession, firms reduce the number of new employees hired, more workers are laid off, and fewer workers quit their jobs (Statistics Canada 1998). Statistical evidence thus suggests that unemployment is not a matter of choice, but is mainly involuntary. Astoundingly, the most sophisticated macroeconomic models used by central banks throughout the world assume that cyclical unemployment is determined entirely by the decisions of workers to accept or refuse employment based on their estimates of future inflation and interest rates. Thus it is not surprising that, in the fall of 2008, when financial markets all over the world were either freezing or collapsing, the vice-governors at the Bank of Canada were going merrily on, delivering speeches about the past usage of shells and beaver pelts as money and the desirability of having constant price level targets instead of zero-inflation targets.

The NAIRU and Neoclassical Economists

Neoclassical economists believe in the existence of a non-accelerating inflation rate of unemployment (the "NAIRU"). This is the rate of unemployment that keeps the rate of inflation at a steady level. It is the kingpin of neoclassical macroeconomics. If the actual rate of unemployment were kept at a level any lower than the NAIRU, the rate of inflation would rise continually; if it were to exceed the NAIRU, the rate of inflation would decrease. Some neoclassical economists believe that market forces ineluctably push the economy toward the NAIRU, while others think that the central bank must intervene to ensure that the economy is driven toward it, in order to keep the inflation rate from accelerating or decelerating. In any case, whether through pure market forces or discretionary monetary policies, the NAIRU is said to act as an attractor for the actual rate of unemployment. Since there is a single sustainable rate of unemployment—the NAIRU—the Phillips curve, defined in the introduction, is said to be vertical in the long run.

In a world devoid of rigidities, the NAIRU would be the "natural rate of unemployment," the term coined by the famous University of Chicago economist Milton Friedman. It would correspond to a frictional kind of unemployment that arises only when people are in a transition between jobs, as they attempt to improve their lot or as they respond to changes in the regional or industrial structure of employment. In a more realistic world, the NAIRU is believed to be higher than the natural rate of unemployment. Neoclassical economists tend to blame rigidities for this higher NAIRU: the more rigidities there are, the higher the NAIRU will be.

The link between labour market rigidities and unemployment is now often called the OECD view, because the Organisation for Economic Co-operation and

Development (OECD) has repeatedly attributed the high levels of unemployment in European countries to those countries' numerous labour market rigidities. What are these rigidities? We can classify them under the following five headings: minimum-wage laws, which push the real wage above its equilibrium level; overly strong labour unions, which also push real wages too high; employment insurance programs, which protect workers from the negative consequences of unemployment, thus leading them to bargain for overly high real wages; other laws favourable to workers, for instance, laws that make it difficult or costly for firms to lay off their employees, thus inducing firms not to hire new workers when economic activity is expanding; and finally, income taxes on wage income as well as payroll taxes, which drive a wedge between the real wage that firms must pay and the real wage ultimately obtained by workers, thus making it harder to strike a bargain between employers and employees. Overall, all these rigidities encourage workers to slack off at work or to decline job offers.

Surprisingly, despite the strong belief that labour rigidities cause unemployment, empirical evidence for this has been hard to come by (Howell et al. 2006). Statistical evidence supporting the conventional OECD wisdom has been unconvincing, though believers prefer not to acknowledge this. And even when some relationship has been found between rigidities and unemployment, it can always be questioned on the grounds of reverse causality. For instance, some researchers have found that high unemployment benefits are associated with higher rates of unemployment, leading them to conclude that generous unemployment benefits induce workers to turn down jobs and instead remain at home. However, causality is also likely to go the other way: governments tend to raise access to unemployment benefits and provide more generous benefits when economic conditions are poor and unemployment rates are high. This is indeed what various political parties recommended in the wake of the Canadian federal budget of January 2009.

The NAIRU theoretical construction has had substantial consequences for economic policy. With the advent of this construction in the 1970s, most governments gave up the goal of full employment, being content with containing inflation at low levels. The OECD pursued a NAIRU agenda, inducing its sponsoring governments to shift from *full employment* policies to *full employability* policies. In particular, this meant reductions in income support programs in an effort to minimize disincentives for individuals to enter the workforce, as well as an emphasis on retraining programs—some of them bordering on the workfare approach, whereby program beneficiaries are obliged to participate in order to keep their benefits—based on the assumption that high unemployment rates are the result of deficient individual working skills rather than systemic failure. The NAIRU agenda implies that decision-makers have little choice: the only way to reduce unemployment rates permanently, according to the dominant OECD view, is to pursue microeconomic policies aimed at reducing labour market rigidities. Macroeconomic policies, such as expansionary fiscal policies, will only have temporary effects, including a detrimental effect on inflation rates. Neoclassical economists express this view with the "TINA" acronym: There Is No Alternative!

In 2004 and 2006, following years of inconclusive statistical research, the OECD backed away from its previous position. OECD researchers now admit that employment protection legislation and high real wages (labour market rigidities) are unlikely to be the main cause of high unemployment rates, saying that the evidence supporting this view is mixed at best (Mitchell and Muysken 2008, chap. 5).

The Heterodox Keynesian View

One of the best-known claims of Keynes was that unemployment—in particular, the rates of unemployment of 20 percent or so that were observed during the Great Depression of the 1930s—is essentially involuntary.

Keynesian authors of heterodox persuasion view employment determination in a completely different light than neoclassical economists. Whereas neoclassical economists believe that unemployment arises because of some supply-side rigidity that occurs in the labour market, heterodox economists believe that unemployment arises from a lack of aggregate demand in the product markets. Because the latter view is precisely what Keynes argued in 1936, it seems appropriate to simply label these heterodox authors "Keynesians." They contend that when firms expect to sell more, they produce more, and to produce more they need to employ more workers. If the rate of unemployment is high, it is because there aren't enough expenditures in the economy. Under what circumstances might that be the case?

To find out, we must look at the components of aggregate demand, as given by the national accounts. Aggregate demand depends on consumption, residential and business investment, government expenditures, and net exports. A reduction in any of these components is likely to increase the rate of unemployment. If Canadians prefer to purchase goods produced abroad, this will likely reduce employment at home; similarly, if foreign markets forsake Canadian products, this will also cause employment to fall. Government policies, too, have an obvious effect on aggregate demand and employment. Monetary policies that set high interest rates will have a negative impact on investment by enterprises and on investment in the housing industry (that is, the purchase of new houses), as well as on consumption of durable goods, such as cars, refrigerators, or flat-screen TVs. When governments willingly reduce their expenditures and increase taxes in an effort to achieve budget surpluses, this will also have a negative effect on aggregate demand.

Obviously, consumption will depend on the propensity to consume, or the proportion of their income that households are willing to spend. Assuming all else is equal, the higher the overall propensity to consume is, the higher aggregate demand is—and hence the lower the rate of unemployment. But consumption will also depend—in a *positive* way—on real wages. This is because the overall propensity to consume depends on income distribution. Since firms save a large portion of their profits in the form of retained earnings, thus leaving less for households to spend, the propensity to consume out of profits is much smaller than the propensity to consume out of wages. As a result, any income redistribution toward wages and away from profits—as occurs when real wages rise with constant labour productivity—will have a positive impact on the overall propensity to consume, and hence on aggregate demand and employment. Thus, looking at the labour market from the aggregate demand perspective, we see that *higher* real wages generate *higher* employment. A negative impact may only arise if the higher real wages cut into the profit perspectives of firms, thus inducing them to reduce their investment expenditures. As long as the positive effects of higher real wages on consumption overcome their possible negative effect on investment, higher real wages will have a positive impact on aggregate demand and employment. This is in contrast to the neoclassical view, which claims that high real wages are detrimental to employment.

To conclude, from the Keynesian perspective, unemployment is the result of insufficient aggregate demand. If private aggregate demand is too weak, it becomes the responsibility of the public sector to generate enough aggregate demand through either monetary policy (by decreasing interest rates) or fiscal policy (by increasing government expenditures and going into budget deficits).

The NAIRU and the Keynesians

Still, the neoclassical NAIRU analysis that we discussed earlier says that active macroeconomic policies—and fiscal policies in particular—are useless in bringing down rates of unemployment permanently, and that the only useful tool is a policy that will bring down the NAIRU by dismantling labour rigidities. How do Keynesians respond to such claims?

Keynesians reject the NAIRU concept. They deny that there exists a unique rate of unemployment that can keep the rate of inflation steady. This rejection has taken two forms. First, the empirical evidence supporting a vertical Phillips curve—a NAIRU—has been flimsy at best. From very early on, Keynesian economists claimed that the NAIRU relied more on *a priori* doctoring than on sound empirical research. Some of the best econometricians have denied the existence of a long-run vertical Phillips curve, asserting that all their statistical tests systematically show the existence of a long-run downward-sloping Phillips curve, thus laying to rest the claim that a single unemployment rate is compatible with steady inflation. Instead, their empirical inquiries show that low rates of unemployment are quite compatible with steady inflation rates, even when long-term effects are taken into consideration.

Furthermore, empirical work over the last ten years or so has questioned the existence of a necessary trade-off between inflation and unemployment. It has been shown that over a relatively large range of unemployment rates, lower unemployment rates are *not* accompanied by higher inflation rates. Thus, as long as unemployment rates remain within the lower and upper bounds of this range, the rate of inflation can be kept constant despite higher aggregate economic activity (and hence despite lower rates of unemployment). On this basis, heterodox economists claim that there is room for a substantial amount of discretion in macroeconomic policy. For instance, if private aggregate demand brings the economy to high rates of unemployment corresponding to the upper bound, discretionary expansionary fiscal policy can bring the economy to lower rates of unemployment (near the lower bound) without fear that this will generate accelerating inflation. Choices *can* be made, contrary to the TINA slogan of neoclassical economics.

The second kind of critique of the NAIRU arose out of the admission by neoclassical economists that their NAIRU measures kept changing over time. They then proclaimed that while the NAIRU was unique at each point in time, it was varying *through* time. This argument came to be known as the "TV-NAIRU": the time-varying NAIRU. Heterodox Keynesian authors soon pointed out that the estimates of the NAIRU appeared to follow past realized rates of unemployment. Keynesians thus reasoned very early on that, while the NAIRU may act as an attractor for the actual rate of unemployment at any point in time, it is also highly plausible that the actual rate of unemployment will be a primary determinant of the NAIRU through time. This means that, if restrictive monetary policies are put in place to tame inflation, initially causing high rates of unemployment, these high rates of unemployment will have a feedback effect on the value of the NAIRU, driving it upward, toward previously realized rates of unemployment. Plenty of empirical research has demonstrated the likelihood of such a two-way effect, and theoretical explanations of such a mechanism have been provided. These range from unemployed workers being unable to keep their skills up to date and thus becoming unemployable, to unused machinery that induces entrepreneurs to forgo investment, thus leading to reduced productive capacity in the future—both of which will lead to higher sustainable rates of unemployment in the long run (higher NAIRUs).

Conclusion: The Demise of the NAIRU

The neoclassical response to these critiques has been that such a feedback effect of actual rates of unemployment on the NAIRU could only be of a *temporary*, not a permanent, nature; eventually, the TV-NAIRU would return to its long-run value, determined entirely by supply-side factors (the labour market rigidities outlined by OECD researchers). One counterargument to this, often made by New Keynesians,[1] has been that such a return would take a long time to occur. In the meantime, expansionary Keynesian policies would be effective and useful, reducing the rates of unemployment. This is called the "persistence hypothesis." The other counterargument, made by the more heterodox Keynesians, has been that realized rates of unemployment would have a *permanent* feedback effect on the NAIRU. This has been called the "hysteresis hypothesis."

Which hypothesis is more strongly supported by empirical evidence: persistence or hysteresis? Unfortunately, determining which hypothesis seems best verified by the statistical data is not a simple matter, so that neoclassical authors still cling to their belief that, in the long run, the NAIRU is determined by labour market rigidities and overly high real wage rates, and Keynesian authors keep contending that aggregate demand is the essential determinant of unemployment rates in both the short and the long run. However, meta-analysis (a method often used in medical research that involves a statistical analysis of previous empirical studies) clearly reveals that the best empirical studies—those with more information and better specifications—tend to yield support for the hysteresis hypothesis (Stanley 2004). This implies that the theoretical concept of the NAIRU, so dear to neoclassical economists, is poor science, misleading, and conducive to erroneous policy advice. Economic policy dealing with unemployment should focus instead on the issues of adequate aggregate demand and involuntary unemployment. In contrast to the TINA slogan, there are alternatives. We can have low rates of unemployment if society so desires.

NOTES

1. New Keynesian economists are neoclassical economists who adhere to some of Keynes's insights on the basis of formalized underpinnings consistent with the neoclassical tradition. They are part of what we have called the mainstream, but some of them propose policy advice that can be deemed to be "Keynesian."

DISCUSSION QUESTIONS

1. Why would lower rates of unemployment generate higher rates of inflation, as suggested by the so-called Phillips curve?
2. Following the recession induced by the financial crisis of 2007–8, should the Canadian government reduce unemployment benefits to induce Canadians to go back to work, or should it make the benefits more generous instead? Give reasons for your answer.
3. In view of the recession that began toward the end of 2008, should Canadians spend more or spend less? Why? What would be the likely impact on unemployment?

SUGGESTED READINGS AND ONLINE RESOURCES

Howells, David R., ed. 2005. *Fighting unemployment: The limits to free market orthodoxy*. Oxford: Oxford University Press.

Mitchell, William, and Joan Muysken. 2008. *Full employment abandoned: Shifting sands and policy failures*. Cheltenham: Edward Elgar.

Nell, Edward J., and Mathew Forstater, eds. 2003. *Reinventing functional finance: Transformational growth and full employment*. Cheltenham: Edward Elgar.

Piore, Michael J., ed. 1979. *Unemployment and inflation: Institutionalist and structuralist views*. White Plains, NY: M.E. Sharpe.

Statistics Canada. 2009. Labour force information. http://www.statcan.gc.ca/bsolc/olc-cel/olc-cel?catno=71-001-XWE&lang=eng.

REFERENCES

Howell, David R., Dean Baker, Andrew Glyn, and John Schmitt. 2006. Are protective labor market institutions really at the root of unemployment? A critical review of the evidence. Bernard Schwartz Center for Economic Policy Analysis. http://www.newschool.edu/cepa/publications/workingpapers/Howell%20et%20al_Institutions%20and%20Unemployment_march15.07.pdf.

Mitchell, William, and Joan Muysken. 2008. *Full employment abandoned: Shifting sands and policy failures*. Cheltenham: Edward Elgar.

Stanley, T.D. 2004. Does unemployment hysteresis falsify the natural rate of unemployment? A meta-regression analysis. *Journal of Economic Surveys* 18 (4): 589–612.

Statistics Canada. 1998. Permanent layoffs, quits and hirings in the Canadian economy, 1978–1995. http://www.statcan.gc.ca/bsolc/olc-cel/olc-cel?catno=71-539-X&CHROPG=1&lang=eng.

PART III

Macroeconomic Policies

What Is Fiscal Policy? Is Government Spending a Source of Stability or Instability?

COMPETING VIEWS

Niels Veldhuis, "The Optimal Size of Government"

Hassan Bougrine, "The Stabilizing Role of Public Spending"

Editors' Introduction

Fiscal policy pertains to any government measure that affects government expenditures, including transfer payments and/or government revenues. Hence, it refers to any government decision that could affect the budgetary balance of the public sector. In particular, when the government sector spends more than it receives in revenues, it is engaged in deficit spending; when its revenues exceed its expenditures, it is in a budgetary surplus position.

The financial crisis that began in 2008 seems to have placed fiscal policy at the centre stage of public policy, with a broad consensus existing internationally in favour of deficit spending and fiscal stimulus, especially in the area of public investment. This is a sharp reversal of a policy view that, since the 1980s, had opposed deficit spending and promoted the virtues of sound finance and budgetary surpluses. With public sector expenditures hovering around one-quarter of GDP in the industrialized world, any single percentage point change in public spending can be presumed to have major consequences for the economy. However, economists disagree on what exactly those consequences are.

The most established policy view, which was widely held at least until the recent financial crisis, was that government deficit spending limited private sector growth. In essence, it was widely believed that government net spending and net growth of the public sector would occur largely at the expense of the private sector. This could be the case for one of two reasons: government deficits would either put upward pressure on interest rates, thereby restraining private productive investment, or they

149

could be inflationary, in which case private consumption and perhaps even net exports would decline, in the latter case because of lower international competitiveness.

The competing perspective, which was put forth primarily by Keynesian economists, argues in favour of "functional finance"—that is, the pursuit of a stabilization policy that would run budgetary deficits in times of recession and budgetary surpluses when the economy is hitting full employment. Hence, running deficits in an economy that is characterized by low rates of capacity utilization will neither prevent private investment nor generate inflation. If anything, deficit spending might encourage investment by pushing the economy toward higher rates of utilization of existing capacity. As a result of the existence of much unused human and physical resources in a recessionary environment, this would not be inflationary. Moreover, if the net government spending is primarily in the domain of public investment, its effect would be to stimulate private sector productivity, which would enhance private sector growth and competitiveness.

These two perspectives are well represented in this chapter. The mainstream position, which stands in opposition to fiscal interventionism and which has been commonly accepted by most policy analysts and politicians in Canada over the last two decades, is put forth in the contribution by Niels Veldhuis. The heterodox position, in defence of active fiscal policy along Keynesian lines, is discussed in the contribution by Hassan Bougrine.

The Optimal Size of Government

Niels Veldhuis

Introduction

"Fiscal policy" is the use of government spending and taxation to provide important goods and services to society. Canadian governments at all levels—federal, provincial, and local—provide essential goods and services: policing services protect people and their property, the courts enforce laws, and the military provides national defence. These are basic services that nearly all people agree should be financed and provided by government.

In Canada, governments provide many additional goods and services, including education, health care, postal services, and television and radio stations, among others. Canadian governments also redistribute incomes through programs such as welfare, employment insurance, and public pensions. There is much less agreement on the issue of whether or not government should be heavily involved in delivering these goods and services.

In addition to providing goods and services, governments use fiscal policy to attempt to influence the economy during troubled economic times. That is, when the economy is in decline (called a recession) and unemployment is increasing, governments may change spending and tax levels in an attempt to stabilize and boost the economy.

But can the government really help stabilize and kick-start the economy by simply changing spending or tax levels? Does the level of government spending actually affect economic performance? By the end of this essay, you should find yourself able to answer these questions. While you will learn that the level of taxation and government spending does have a significant impact on the economy, this is more likely to be the case in the long run rather than in the short run.

The Size of Government in Canada

Before examining whether the level of government taxation and spending influences economic growth, it is important to have some perspective on how much money governments in Canada actually raise and spend.

In 2007 Canadian governments (federal, provincial, and local) extracted $591 billion from Canadians in taxes and other revenues. This figure represents

FIGURE 1   Sources of Government Revenue, 2007–8

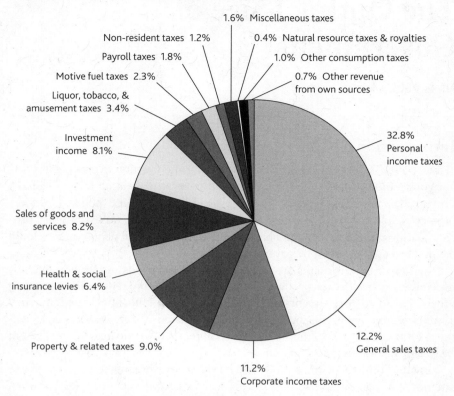

1.6% Miscellaneous taxes

Non-resident taxes 1.2%

0.4% Natural resource taxes & royalties

Payroll taxes 1.8%

1.0% Other consumption taxes

Motive fuel taxes 2.3%

0.7% Other revenue from own sources

Liquor, tobacco, & amusement taxes 3.4%

Investment income 8.1%

32.8% Personal income taxes

Sales of goods and services 8.2%

Health & social insurance levies 6.4%

Property & related taxes 9.0%

12.2% General sales taxes

11.2% Corporate income taxes

Source: Statistics Canada, CANSIM table 385-0001. Calculations by author.

38.5 percent of the income generated in the economy (the best measure of the size of government), as measured by gross domestic product (GDP). Figure 1 shows the composition of total federal, provincial, and local government revenue. Personal income taxes are the most significant source of revenue for Canadian governments (at 32.8 percent of total revenue), followed by sales taxes (12.2 percent) and corporate income taxes (11.2 percent).

During the same year, Canadian governments spent a total of $574 billion, representing 37.4 percent of the economy (GDP). Figure 2 shows the breakdown of spending by all levels of government. Health care is the government's largest expense, at 20.1 percent of total government spending, followed by education (elementary, secondary, and postsecondary) at 15.9 percent and social assistance (welfare) at 14.1 percent.

Although government spending now accounts for nearly 40 percent of all economic activity, it once accounted for a much smaller proportion. Figure 3

FIGURE 2   Government Spending, Percent of Total, 2007–8

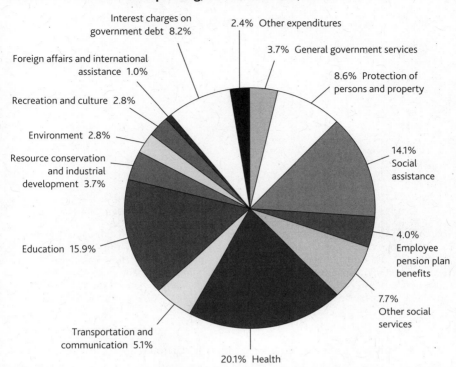

Interest charges on government debt 8.2%

2.4% Other expenditures

3.7% General government services

Foreign affairs and international assistance 1.0%

8.6% Protection of persons and property

Recreation and culture 2.8%

Environment 2.8%

14.1% Social assistance

Resource conservation and industrial development 3.7%

Education 15.9%

4.0% Employee pension plan benefits

7.7% Other social services

Transportation and communication 5.1%

20.1% Health

Source: Statistics Canada. 2008. *Canadian Economic Observer: Historical statistical supplement 2007/2008*. Catalogue no. 11-210-XWB. Calculations by author.

shows the percentage of government spending in GDP from 1929 to 2007. Until 1939, government spending was less than 27.0 percent of GDP; from 1939 to 1944, spending increased significantly as a result of the Second World War. After the war, the size of Canadian governments grew steadily, from 21.9 percent in 1948 to 53.1 percent in 1992. Throughout the 1990s, the size of the Canadian government decreased significantly, reaching 39.6 percent in 2008.

As noted above, in 2007 Canadian governments extracted $591 billion in revenue and spent $574 billion. This means that Canadian governments ran a budget surplus, as their revenues exceeded spending. Had government spending exceeded its revenues, a budget deficit would have resulted. Figure 4 shows Canadian governments' deficit or surplus relative to the size of the economy. From 1929 to 1997, Canadian government spending consistently exceeded revenues—in fact, during that time, Canadian governments ran budget surpluses in only 9 of the 68 years. Since 1997, Canadian governments have been more successful in ensuring that revenues and spending are in line.

FIGURE 3   Government Spending in Canada, Percent of GDP

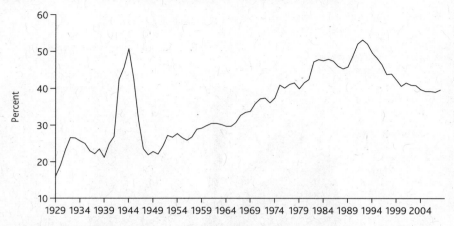

Sources: OECD. 2008. *OECD Economic Outlook* 84, annex tables; Statistics Canada. 1996. *Canadian Economic Observer: Historical Statistical Supplement 1995/1996*. Catalogue no. 11-210-XWB; Statistics Canada. 2008. *Canadian Economic Observer: Historical Statistical Supplement 2007/2008*. Catalogue no. 11-210-XWB; Statistics Canada. 2009. *Canadian Economic Observer* 22 (3); Statistics Canada. 2009. *National Income and Expenditure Accounts: Data Tables* 1 (4), fourth quarter 2008. Catalogue no. 13-019-XWE. Calculations by author.

As a result of significant deficits, Canadian governments were forced to borrow. In 2006–7, the most recent year for which data are available, Canadian government debt (accumulated deficits) stood at $1,214 billion, making large interest payments necessary. In 2007 interest payments on existing government debt amounted to 8.2 percent of total government spending (see Figure 2).

Canadian governments play an important role in the economy. The following two sections will cover how government taxation and spending affects the economy. We will first examine whether the aggregate level of taxation and spending influences the economy, and then explore whether changes in government spending and tax levels can stabilize and boost the economy in the short run.

The Economic Impact of Government Spending and Taxation

The aggregate levels of government spending and taxation have a major impact on economic performance and on Canadians' standard of living. Changes in the overall level of spending and taxation also affect economic growth, although more so in the long run. Short-run impacts of fiscal policy are examined in the following section.[1] Here, we consider the impacts of aggregate spending and taxation on the well-being of Canadians.

FIGURE 4   Government Deficit or Surplus, Percent of GDP

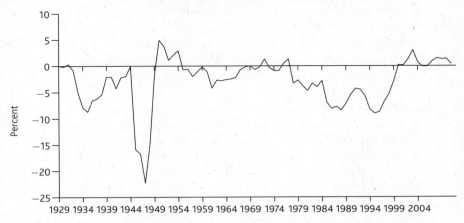

Sources: OECD. 2008. *OECD Economic Outlook* 84, annex tables; Statistics Canada. 1996. *Canadian Economic Observer: Historical Statistical Supplement 1995/1996*. Catalogue no. 11-210-XWB; Statistics Canada. 2008. *Canadian Economic Observer: Historical Statistical Supplement 2007/2008*. Catalogue no. 11-210-XWB; Statistics Canada. 2009. *Canadian Economic Observer* 22 (3); Statistics Canada. 2009. *National Income and Expenditure Accounts: Data Tables* 1 (4), fourth quarter 2008. Catalogue no. 13-019-XWE. Calculations by author.

Government Spending

Most Canadians correctly view government spending as a positive force in an economy, and very few would argue for zero government involvement. As mentioned above, governments are involved in providing services—such as police, courts, and infrastructure—that are critical to a well-functioning economy.

However, most Canadians would agree that governments can become too big and spend too much. Some types of spending—such as regional development subsidies and corporate bailouts, agricultural supports, and broadcast subsidies—reduce competition and ultimately slow the rates of innovation, productivity, and economic growth. The extreme case—an economy that is controlled entirely by the government—has proven not to be conducive to maximizing economic and social well-being. Somewhere between the two extremes of zero government intervention in the private economy and a completely government-controlled economy exists a point at which economic growth and prosperity are maximized. This is what economists refer to as the "optimal size" of government.

A growing body of academic research supports the idea that the size of government matters with respect to economic performance. Although only a limited number of studies have focused on Canada, those that have been done indicate that the growth-maximizing size of government in Canada is roughly 30 percent of GDP. This should alarm anyone interested in improving Canada's economy, since, as discussed above, government spending currently amounts to almost 40 percent of the economy.[2]

A series of studies by economists Vito Tanzi and Ludger Schuknecht (1998, 70) of the International Monetary Fund (IMF) regarding the size of government and social progress concluded that

> countries with "small" governments [spending less than 40 percent of GDP] generally do not show worse indicators of social and economic well-being than countries with "big" governments [spending greater than 50 percent of GDP]; and often they achieve an even better standard. Countries with "small" governments can provide essential services and minimum social safety nets while avoiding the disincentive effects caused by high taxes and large-scale redistribution on growth, employment, and welfare.

Given the data from Figure 3, Canadians would therefore benefit from a reduction in both government spending and associated taxes.

Taxation

Although economists differ in their opinions on many issues (as you see throughout this book), there are a few basic concepts about which virtually all would agree. One of the most important of these concepts is that people respond to incentives. People make decisions by comparing the costs and benefits of a particular action. When either the costs or benefits change, people's behaviour may also change.

Taxes distort the benefits that people and businesses receive from their hard work, savings, and investments. That is, since taxes reduce the benefits, they change people's behaviour as far as how hard or how long they work, how much they save, and how much they invest.[3] Put differently, taxes impose significant costs on the economy.

In addition, because they influence incentives and behaviour in different ways, different types of taxes have different economic effects. For example, taxes on investment (interest, dividends, and capital gains) lead to lower savings by decreasing the returns to this activity. The decrease in savings results in lower investment, which is critical to the growth of the economy and incomes.

On the other hand, taxing consumption (through sales taxes, such as the GST) increases the cost of consumption and thus discourages it in favour of saving. Economic research has quantified these incentives and behavioural effects, and has consistently found that personal and corporate income taxes impose much higher costs on the economy than other taxes, such as sales taxes. Reducing the level of government spending in Canada would allow for similar reductions in the associated tax burden, which imposes significant economic costs.

The Use of Fiscal Policy to Stabilize and Boost the Economy

Government spending and taxation have also been used to help stabilize the economy during economic downturns, when the level of economic activity declines and unemployment increases. Short-term increases in government spending and temporary tax relief are thought to increase total spending in the economy (called "aggregate demand") and help the economy grow again. This section will examine whether or not fiscal policy can actually alleviate the negative impact of economic recessions.

The notion that fiscal policy can stimulate the economy during a recession was championed by economist John Maynard Keynes in the 1930s. Indeed, the idea that government should increase spending and temporarily decrease taxes during an economic downturn has become known as "Keynesian economics." Keynesians believe that governments should use expansionary fiscal policy during recessions—that is, they should accumulate deficits as a result of increased spending and/or reduced taxes. When the economy begins to grow again, Keynesians suggest that governments should raise taxes, decrease spending, and pay back the debt accumulated during the recession (called "contractionary" fiscal policy). Put simply, Keynesians believe that the government can and should play an active role in balancing economic booms and busts.

During a recession, total spending in an economy decreases, as people demand fewer goods and services. Individuals and businesses also tend to postpone purchases of capital goods (property, machinery, and equipment), which results in decreased investment. As businesses experience declining sales, inventories increase, production levels decrease, and workers are laid off. As a result, the incomes of individuals and families typically fall in a recession; unemployment rates increase; and machinery, equipment, and other capital tend to be underutilized. To counteract the recession and provide the economy with a boost, Keynesian economists believe that fiscal policy can be used to increase the total level of spending (aggregate demand). That is, governments must take measures to offset the decline in aggregate demand.

There are two channels through which governments can attempt to increase aggregate demand. First, they can increase government spending on goods and services while keeping taxes constant. Second, governments can put more money into the pockets of consumers through tax reductions and/or increased government transfer payments to individuals and families (through welfare, employment insurance, pensions, and so on). As they spend this additional money, these consumers will increase the demand for goods and services.

Keynesian theory asserts that expansionary fiscal policy will increase the demand for goods and services and lead to increased production. Businesses will

157

increase employment and will require more capital. Ultimately, the increase in total spending will help stimulate the economy and help it return to growth.

Can Governments Help the Economy out of Recession?

Although the notion that government can stimulate the economy during a recession may seem intuitive and appealing, the reality is much different. There are several reasons why Canadians should be skeptical about the government's ability to stimulate economic activity through short-term increases in government spending and/or temporary decreases in taxes. Let us consider each channel in more detail.

INCREASED SPENDING

Keynesians and others who believe that increased spending will stimulate the economy only look at one side of the equation. That is, they only think about the impact of spending on the demand for goods and services without asking where the money will come from. During recessions, government revenues decline as a result of reduced economic activity. Increases in government spending will therefore lead to budget deficits that must be financed through borrowing.

But from whom does the government borrow? One option is for the government to borrow from the Bank of Canada by selling government bonds. In this case, the Bank of Canada would buy government bonds and credit the Canadian government's account.[4] The government would then spend the borrowed money on goods and services or transfer it to individuals and families. In either case, the money becomes someone's income or a business' profit and ultimately makes its way into the bank accounts of individuals or businesses.

While a full explanation of changes in the money supply is beyond the scope of this chapter (see Chapter 2), the increase in the money supply does have an impact on the effectiveness of government spending when the government borrows from the Bank of Canada. When deposits at Canadian banks increase (as a result of the spending), the amount of outstanding loans of these banks will also increase. The outcome is an increase in the money supply and is akin to the Bank of Canada simply printing money in exchange for government bonds.

Unfortunately, an increase in the money supply leads to increased inflation, which reduces the value of existing money (and the value of people's savings accounts). In other words, more money circulates in the economy, but the value of each dollar is worth less. Increased inflation also undermines people's ability to use prices as a useful source of information in their economic decision making. For example, unexpected increases in inflation make it difficult to estimate the future value of assets and increase uncertainty about future inflation, and for these reasons may discourage longer-term investment.[5]

Another option is for the government to finance the deficit by selling bonds directly in the private market. In this case, governments would compete with other borrowers (individuals and businesses) for investors' savings. When governments compete with individuals and businesses for credit, this creates a greater demand for credit, which in turn increases the interest rate (the cost of borrowing). Since government bonds are thought to be "risk free" (because governments rarely go broke), investors channel their savings into government bonds and "crowd out" or displace private borrowers.

In addition, a higher interest rate means that the price of borrowing for all types of investments goes up. For instance, a higher interest rate corresponds to a higher mortgage rate, which drives up the cost of home purchases. A higher interest rate also increases the cost of borrowing (through loans and lines of credit) for businesses wanting to invest in machines and equipment. These increases in borrowing costs ultimately reduce the number and value of investments made by individuals and businesses.

When governments are in direct competition with and supplant borrowers in the private sector, private investment projects—which require borrowing and are crucial to a sustained economic recovery—are displaced.[6] Since governments must borrow to finance increased spending during a recession, they will end up taking money from some Canadians (those buying government bonds), who will in turn have less to spend on goods and services or invest in the private market. In the end, the increase in government spending is offset by an equal decrease in private sector spending and investment. Total spending (aggregate demand) therefore does not change when governments engage in expansionary fiscal policy.

Furthermore, in an open economy like Canada's, increases in the interest rate caused by an increase in the demand for credit also affect the country's trade balance (exports minus imports). A higher Canadian interest rate makes Canadian assets more attractive to foreign investors. In order to invest in Canada, the latter exchange their currency for Canadian dollars and drive up the value of the Canadian dollar. An appreciation in the Canadian dollar makes Canadian goods more expensive and foreign goods cheaper. As a result, Canadian exports decrease and imports increase. A decline in net exports will have a negative effect on the Canadian economy (aggregate demand). The same would hold true if Canadian government bonds were sold directly to foreign investors in order to finance the deficit. These investors would increase the demand for Canadian dollars and drive up the value of the currency. An appreciated dollar makes Canadian goods more expensive and decreases net exports.

Although the notion that governments can stimulate the economy during a recession is appealing, the reality is that increased government spending is offset by a reduction in private sector consumption, investments, and net exports. The end result is that resources are redistributed around the economy but total economic activity does not actually increase.

TEMPORARY TAX RELIEF

Would the impact of fiscal policy be any different if the government were to cut taxes instead of increase spending? Like increases in government spending, reductions in taxes will lead to budget deficits that must be financed through increased borrowing. The money to finance the deficits would still come from Canadians who buy government bonds and who will therefore have less to spend on goods and services or to invest in the private market.

However, some consumers will have more money to spend or invest as a result of the tax relief. In spite of this, evidence shows that individuals tend to save most of the money they receive from temporary tax relief or use it to pay down outstanding debts. The end result remains the same: resources are redistributed around the economy, but total spending (aggregate demand) does not change.

The above section on government spending and taxation highlighted the impact that taxes have on people's incentives to engage in productive activities such as investing, working hard, and taking entrepreneurial risks. If reducing taxes provides improved economic incentives, wouldn't expansionary fiscal policy in the form of temporary decreases in damaging personal and corporate income taxes boost the economy? It is critical to remember that tax reductions under Keynesian fiscal policy are temporary and inevitably increase when economic growth resumes. Since the improved incentives from tax relief typically take time to change behaviour, temporary tax cuts are unlikely to change behaviour to any meaningful degree.

DEFICITS TODAY, TAXES TOMORROW

It is also important to note that today's deficits are tomorrow's taxes. When governments run deficits, the level of government debt naturally increases. In the future, Canadians will have to pay the interest costs associated with government debt and at some point pay back the debt. Put differently, running a deficit today as a result of increased spending and/or temporary tax relief implies higher taxes or lower spending sometime in the future. As a result, people and families tend to save the majority of a stimulus-induced windfall (tax relief or government transfer) or use it to pay down outstanding debts in order to brace themselves for higher taxes or lower government spending in the future. Since budget deficits are simply future taxes, deficits do not change people's total tax liability (present and future), and the timing of the taxes and deficits therefore has little impact on aggregate demand.[8]

CAN GOVERNMENTS GET THE TIMING RIGHT?

Suppose for a moment that expansionary fiscal policy—whether in the form of increases in government spending or temporary tax relief—could actually boost the economy during a recession. Even under this assumption, the government will likely not be a stabilizing force in the economy.

First, consider that it takes time (even for professional economists!) to recognize that an economy is in recession. Since recessions are typically defined as two consecutive quarters of negative real GDP growth, the economy will likely already have been shrinking for six months before economists wave their Keynesian flags and come to the conclusion that expansionary fiscal policy is needed.

More importantly, however, in order for the expansionary fiscal policy to have a stabilizing effect, we would need to forecast the direction in which the economy is heading. After all, expansionary fiscal policy will be unnecessary and costly if the economy is already starting to rebound. In addition, expansionary fiscal policy might actually be destabilizing if the economy is growing (assuming, of course, that it works). The problem, however, is that economists have a rather embarrassing record where predicting the future is concerned. There are simply too many variables and too many independent market actors (individuals, families, businesses) to predict accurately the direction of the overall economy.[9]

And it gets worse. In addition to the time lags associated with gathering data and determining that the economy is in recession, and our inability to forecast the future, it takes time to actually implement expansionary fiscal policy. Legislation must be created to increase spending or reduce taxes; typically, this legislation comes in the form of a government budget bill. To produce the budget, governments consult with the private sector, other levels of government, and the government bureaucracy. The budget must then be prepared, delivered, and voted on in the House of Commons, and finally approved by the Senate. All told, the budget process typically takes months to complete.

Once the government has finalized its expansionary fiscal policy plan (the budget) and it has been approved, it takes time for the policies to be implemented and to have an impact on the economy. Even if we assume that expansionary fiscal policy has a positive impact on the economy, the reality is that governments will not be able to get the timing right. Time lags will mean that expansionary fiscal policy will be implemented too late to have any impact on a recession. Instead, there is a significant risk that expansionary fiscal policy will be implemented as the economy is naturally moving out of recession on its own, and will be destabilizing rather than stabilizing.

BENEVOLENT GOVERNMENTS

Lastly, another deep flaw in Keynesian economic theory is the assumption that governments are benevolent and diligently seek to maximize the public interest or greater economic good. Unfortunately, this assumption is wildly optimistic. Politicians and government bureaucrats are just like you and me—self-interested human beings. As a result, they often do not act in the public interest when proposing and enacting policies.

161

If politicians did diligently pursue the public interest, spending increases and temporary tax relief would be enacted with the goal of producing the largest possible positive impact on the economy. The reality is that politicians tend to focus on specific groups, regions, and industries when proposing spending and tax relief. These targeted groups and preferred industries are often the beneficiaries of government policies not because they will deliver good economic bang for the buck but rather because they maximize the government's (and individual politicians') chances of re-election.

Conclusion

As we have discussed, fiscal policy is the use of government spending and taxation to provide important goods and services to society. In addition, governments change spending and tax levels in an attempt to influence the economy during troubled economic times. That is, when the economy is in decline and unemployment is increasing, governments may change spending and tax levels in an attempt to stabilize and boost the economy.

In summary, while aggregate levels of government spending and taxation have been shown to have a significant impact on economic performance, the government's ability to impact the economy through expansionary fiscal policy is ineffective—and perhaps even harmful—in practice. Those who claim that stimulus spending creates jobs and increases economic activity only look at the spending side of the equation. They do not ask where the money comes from.

A realistic assessment shows that increased government spending is ultimately offset by a reduction in private sector consumption, investments, and net exports. The end result is that resources are redistributed around the economy but economic activity does not actually increase. In addition, it is nearly impossible for governments to get the timing right with respect to expansionary fiscal policy, with the result that the latter will likely be implemented as the economy is naturally moving out of recession. Fiscal policy will therefore be destabilizing rather than stabilizing. The idea that governments can "stimulate" the economy is an unfortunate fallacy.

NOTES

1. The degree to which government spending and taxation positively influences the economy in the short run depends on the nature of the policies. For example, permanent incentive-based tax relief (personal income taxes) will change people's incentives and influence the economy; the long-term impacts are significantly greater than those in the short run.
2. The 30 percent historical mark may well be an overestimate given the rapid advances in technology and information over the course of the last half-century.

3. For a detailed review of these and other important issues regarding the costs of taxation, see Clemens (2008).
4. One of the central roles of the Bank of Canada is to act as the banker to the Government of Canada. The Government of Canada holds demand deposits at the Bank of Canada.
5. See White (2008).
6. For Keynesian fiscal policy to work, governments and private borrowers cannot compete for resources and bid up the interest rate. That is, there must be idle funds (money) in the economy. Without competition for the money held by Canadians, government borrowing would not impact the interest rate and would not "crowd out" or displace private sector investment projects. However, this scenario is extremely unlikely and is thought to occur only during depressions, such as the Depression of the 1930s.
8. See Law and Clemens (1998) for a detailed analysis of this phenomenon known as the Ricardian equivalence theorem.
9. See Hayek (1945).

DISCUSSION QUESTIONS

1. Explain how a large government deficit affects the interest rate. How does the change in interest rate impact the Canadian economy? Can the government borrow and not affect the interest rate? Explain.
2. Nobel Prize winner Milton Friedman suggested that if the long-term goal is to reduce the level of government spending to a more optimal level, we should prefer tax relief to increased spending when governments are determined to use expansionary fiscal policy. Why might this be the case?
3. Provide and explain three reasons why expansionary fiscal policy might not stabilize and boost the economy in practice. If expansionary fiscal policy does not work, why do governments continue to use it?

SUGGESTED READINGS

Friedman, Milton. 1962. *Capitalism and freedom.* Chicago: University of Chicago Press.
Henderson, David R., ed. 2008. *The concise encyclopedia of economics.* Indianapolis, IN: Liberty Fund.
Heyne, Paul, Peter J. Boettke, and David L. Prychitko. 2005. *The economic way of thinking.* 11th ed. Upper Saddle River, NJ: Prentice Hall.
Mankiw, N. Gregory, Ronald D. Kneebone, Kenneth J. McKenzie, and Nicholas Rowe. 2007. *Principles of macroeconomics.* 4th Canadian ed. Toronto: Nelson.

ONLINE RESOURCES

The Fraser Institute: http://www.fraserinstitute.org.
The Library of Economics and Liberty: http://www.econlib.org.
Statistics Canada: http://www.statcan.gc.ca.

REFERENCES

Clemens, Jason. 2008. *The impact and cost of taxation in Canada: The case for a flat tax reform.* Vancouver: Fraser Institute.

Hayek, F.A. 1945. The use of knowledge in society. *American Economic Review* 35 (4): 519–530. http://www.econlib.org/library/Essays/hykKnw1.html.

Law, Marc, and Jason Clemens. 1998. The Ricardian equivalence theorem: Back to the future? *Fraser Forum* (February): 35–37.

Tanzi, Vito, and Ludger Schuknecht. 1998. Can small governments secure economic and social well-being? In *How to use the fiscal surplus: What is the optimal size of government?*, ed. Herbert Grubel, 69–92. Vancouver: Fraser Institute.

White, Lawrence H. 2008. Inflation. In *The concise encyclopedia of economics*, ed. David R. Henderson. 2nd ed. http://www.econlib.org/library/Enc/Inflation.html.

The Stabilizing Role of Public Spending

Hassan Bougrine

Introduction

A salient feature of modern capitalist economies is that they are characterized by successive periods of expansions and recessions. The cause of these fluctuations in economic activity is the source of a major disagreement among economists. While some argue that the cause originates in the supply side (for instance, with technological change), others emphasize the role of demand as the driving force of the economy, which expands and shrinks following fluctuations in aggregate demand (total spending by households, firms, the government, and the foreign sectors). The supply-side and, more generally, *orthodox* economists believe that market economies are dynamic by nature and that any recessions will be short lived; recovery will rapidly move the economy toward its full employment level. From this perspective, there is no need for government stabilization policies. Proponents of this view advocate an economic system driven largely by private initiative, with minimal government intervention. This view became known as the laissez-faire approach, but we shall refer to it here as the "orthodox" approach.

The Great Depression shook the belief of many economists, who began to question the wisdom of the "automatic adjustment process" that was supposed to bring the economy back to full employment. As the crisis persisted, it was clear that the social costs of unemployment had become too high; as a consequence, many economists came to the conclusion that the traditional thinking about the economy was simply wrong. Instead, they concluded that market economies are not—and cannot be—self-correcting, and that government intervention is necessary in order to escape such prolonged stagnation. But what can governments do?

It was John Maynard Keynes (1936) who eloquently formulated the basic premises of what can be called a "mixed economy"—that is, one in which the government plays a major role in stimulating aggregate demand and helping regenerate the dynamism of the economy as a whole. In fact, this was Keynes's major contribution to macroeconomics, and these ideas helped save the capitalist system from collapse. Later, it was recognized that the government can indeed play this role, through public investment as well as through various forms of (public) transfers to the private sector in the form of subsidies, unemployment benefits or social security, and so on. These transfer payments are known as "automatic stabilizers"

165

because they operate quickly to compensate for any reduction in private incomes, thus offsetting the fall in private expenditures and, consequently, dampening fluctuations in demand. Stabilization policies, then, became widely used after the Second World War and governments relied on them to lessen the amplitude and the length of the downturn as well as the severity of its impact (costs in terms of profit loss, unemployment, and so on).

Still, advocates of the orthodox approach continue to argue even today that the best prescription for prosperity is a free market economy in which recessions are viewed as playing a positive role in the sense that they eliminate any inefficiencies and contribute to a more solid system. Economic freedom ensures the success of capitalism. In this context, government decisions are considered to be inherently inefficient, because market players—not government officials—know best how the market really works. The financial crisis that began in 2007 proves exactly the opposite; at the time of writing (early 2009), governments around the world are being called upon to come to the rescue of private banks (even nationalizing some of them) and corporations in other sectors, such as automakers.

Supporters of greater government involvement in the economy maintain that historical evidence shows that market failures are too widespread and recursive to be dismissed as accidental or transitory. Government regulation is considered necessary in order to create a more stable, equitable, and prosperous economy. Many scholars agree that government policies (fiscal and monetary) are indeed powerful tools that can promote the performance of the economy. James K. Galbraith (2008) has referred to the "inadequacy of making markets work" and has suggested that governments consider *planning* as a way of dealing with the problems of unemployment, deterioration of the environment, lack of universal health care and education, and so on, which are a byproduct of unfettered markets. The problem is that, even if everyone (or almost everyone) agrees that—by necessity—only the government can take care of the provision of such things as universal health care, public education and infrastructure, and full employment programs, most would oppose these "grand schemes" on the grounds of financing issues. The usual argument is that these activities require the use of public funds, but the government has only limited budgetary revenues and these cannot be stretched (in other words, the government faces a binding "budget constraint").

What Is the Budget and How Is Government Spending Financed?

The budget is a statement prepared every year by the government that includes details about the various activities the government intends to carry out and information about how it will obtain the money to finance them. A standard budget usually distinguishes between the resources (sources of money) and the uses (how that money is spent). So just where does the money come from? It is not an exaggeration if we say that this is *the* most controversial subject in economics. The traditional (orthodox) theory states that there are three possible ways for the government to raise money: (1) levying taxes, (2) borrowing (by selling bonds), and (3) printing money. According to this view, the basic principle in budgeting is that governments—like any other economic agent—should not spend more than their revenues, of which their only "legitimate" ones are taxes. Exceeding tax revenues would force the government to either borrow or print money, or both. In this situation, the government is said to be running a "deficit." If the scenario is repeated from one year to the next, the accumulated deficits result in what is called the "public debt," which—if not reimbursed—can become explosive and threaten the government's solvency, thus jeopardizing the entire financial/economic system. Public debt is considered a sign of bad economic management. Now, you might ask: But how does the orthodox view justify these conclusions? Before we answer that question, here is a summary of what was said above (let G denote government spending, t the tax rate, i the interest rate, D the public debt, Y the national income, and M money):

$$G + (1 - t)iD = tY + \Delta D + \Delta M$$

It is important to note that total government spending includes several payments lumped under G in addition to (net of tax) interest payments on the debt $(1 - t)iD$. This term is composed of several items, primarily: spending on various types of public infrastructure (including health care, education, and so on—something we will refer to as "public investment"), transfer payments (such as unemployment benefits, welfare and social security payments, and so on—something we will refer to as "automatic stabilizers"), and purchases of goods and services (which also include wages and salaries of public employees). According to the mainstream view, all this spending must be paid for by taxes. If that is not enough, the government has a problem; in this case, orthodox economists advise that a "fiscally responsible" government must avoid "borrowing its way out" of the problem and adding to the debt (ΔD) or "printing money" (ΔM).

The Orthodox Approach

The conventional view, which can be traced back to classical economists such as Adam Smith and David Ricardo, is that financing of economic activity (private or public) is necessarily constrained by the existence of *previously accumulated* savings. By definition, the total amount of savings is limited. Consequently, when the government runs a deficit, it must compete with the private sector for the limited available funds, which leads to an increase in interest rates. Higher interest rates discourage private investment but attract foreign capital (international money lenders), which results in an appreciation of the exchange rate. This, in turn, discourages exports and encourages imports, thus causing a trade deficit in addition to the budget deficit (hence, the "twin deficits" argument). This is the famous crowding-out hypothesis according to which increased government spending results in a fall in GDP because of the decline in private investment and exports.[1] Furthermore, it is argued that when budget deficits are financed by "printing money," the result is often higher inflation, which makes domestic products even more expensive and further increases the (now cheaper) imports, resulting in a loss of national competitiveness. The conclusion is that budget deficits must be avoided, both for these reasons and because they result in a higher public debt, which will have to be paid by future generations in the form of higher taxes. Future generations will also inherit a smaller productive capital (because of the reduced private investment), which will reduce the future productive potential. The end result (of higher taxes and lower productive potential) is that the standards of living of future generations will have been unfairly jeopardized.

In this context, public spending, regardless of its nature (for instance, whether on public infrastructure or welfare payments), is considered a mistake whenever it exceeds the government's revenue from taxes. Moreover, since persistent deficits lead to an explosive debt, they are regarded as a source of financial instability and slow growth, and even as being (at least partly) responsible for economic crises. Such views are not just academic arguments among intellectuals. They have taken shape in economic policies being implemented in the form of "structural adjustment programs" in developing countries (as recommended by the International Monetary Fund, the World Bank, and other international organizations) or in the form of sensible rules of "sound finance" elsewhere.

The Heterodox Approach

The above interpretation is based on a serious misunderstanding of the concept of money in modern capitalist economies in general and of public finance in particular. Since the subject of money is dealt with in Chapter 2, we will focus here on the financing of public expenditures. Several studies have demonstrated that the conclusions of the orthodox view regarding deficits and debts are misleading. For instance, Seccareccia and Sood (2000) have shown that there is no obvious link between budget deficits and inflation, while Blecker (1992) has argued that trade deficits are not a consequence of budget deficits. Others have documented the fact that periods of budget deficits actually tend to coincide with *lower*, not higher, interest rates (Wray 1998). Still others have insisted that, because investments have long-lasting beneficial effects, we must distinguish between a capital expenditure and more simple purchases, such as a purchase of pens and paper (Seccareccia

1995). It is also important to note that equating the government with an individual or a firm is highly misleading, and that the rule of "not spending more than one's revenue" is invalidated in practice; everyone agrees that households must *borrow* in order to buy a house "to hold" and that the existence of financial markets is justified by the fact that firms issue *debt* to finance their investment projects. Although these alternative explanations clearly discredit the orthodox approach, the most damaging criticism is the one attacking the central premise in orthodox thinking according to which any investment project (private or public) can only be undertaken if there already exists an accumulated stock of savings.

As mentioned above, classical economists believed that societies that value thrift and that save more will grow faster, because higher savings will translate into greater capital accumulation, which will foster more growth. The same ideas are currently being sold to poor and developing countries by international organizations under the guise of "technical assistance and policy recommendations." From a Keynesian perspective, however, higher saving rates simply mean that less will be spent on consumption of goods and services. This translates into low sales volumes, which means that realized profits will be low and that firms will have to lower their production, laying off workers in the process. The ensuing unemployment and loss of income will exacerbate the situation (less sales and less profits) and force firms to cut down on their investment plans, hampering growth. Therefore, investment opportunities clearly depend on the existence of an effective demand that can sustain firms' current and expected profits. *Spending*, not saving, is what spurs investment. It is through investment that incomes are generated, and it is only after these incomes have been realized that people can spend and save. Investment precedes saving, not the other way around. Still, the question remains: where do we get the money to pay for investment expenditures, whether private or public?

The answer is that, in modern capitalist economies, money is created by banks *in the form of credit* whenever they agree to give loans to investors. The credits received by investors will be transferred to the workers, the suppliers of raw materials and equipment, and the providers of other services related to production. These are the incomes that will be spent or saved. Investors in the private sector engage in this sort of activity because they are motivated by profits. Investors in the public sector—and the government in particular—do not necessarily seek profits, because the benefits from their investments will be enjoyed by the whole population. Their investment expenditures, however, are also financed via bank credit advances. In most cases, the bank that advances these credits to the government has traditionally been the *central bank*.[2]

So, how does the government pay for its purchases of goods and services? And how does it pay for the wages and salaries of the people it employs? A sovereign (national) government, such as Canada's, can pay for any expenditure—whether it is related to building a new hospital, a school, or a highway, or to the hiring of teachers, nurses, engineers, or street sweepers—simply by crediting their bank accounts (at commercial banks) and debiting its own account at the central bank. In this way, the government becomes a debtor to its own bank. Depending on the banking system, the government can carry out this operation by sending cheques to those it must pay, who will then deposit the cheques in their bank accounts; when the banks receive the cheques, they credit their customers' accounts, as they routinely do. In a more developed banking system, the government can directly credit its employees or suppliers' bank accounts by electronically "depositing" the amounts due.[3]

In either case, it is important to note that at this stage the balance sheets of commercial banks are increased by an equal amount on the liabilities side (due to the increase in deposits) and the assets side (since banks now have a claim on the government). Banks' claims on the government in this form are called "reserves." Banks can claim these reserves through the central bank, which keeps accounts for both the government and commercial banks. In a setting where the central bank is the banking arm of the government, the central bank executes the operation simply by *crediting* commercial banks' accounts (that is, by adding to their reserves, which in Canada are called "settlement balances") and *debiting* the government's account by an equal amount. Government spending results in a net injection of liquidity (money) into the private sector; the government is now running a *deficit*, but the private sector has a *surplus*. We conclude that government spending increases the private sector's incomes and, therefore, that the accumulated deficits (the "public debt") add to the private sector's wealth.

The relevance of this accounting principle is supported by empirical evidence, as many have shown (see, among others, Godley and Lavoie 2007). Figure 1 shows the net lending or borrowing by the consolidated government sector in Canada (the public sector), as well as the net lending or borrowing by the private sector (represented by households and non-financial corporations), both as a percentage of GDP for the period from 1961 to 2008 (using quarterly data). As can be seen, whenever the public sector is running a deficit (is "in the red"), the private sector as a whole will be running a surplus, and vice versa. Therefore, the public budget really does reflect—almost like a mirror—the private sector's net accumulation of savings.

It should be obvious that levying taxes would lead to the exact opposite of the above operation. That is because, when we pay taxes, our accounts are *debited* and the government's account at the central bank is *credited*. In the process, the balance sheet of commercial banks will have been reduced on both sides by the same amount, since deposits went down and (consequently) banks lost reserves (meaning that their claims on the government decreased). The central bank shows this by debiting commercial banks' accounts and crediting the government's account. One can say that the accumulated credits in the government's account at the central

FIGURE 1   Public Sector and Private Sector Balances, 1961–2008

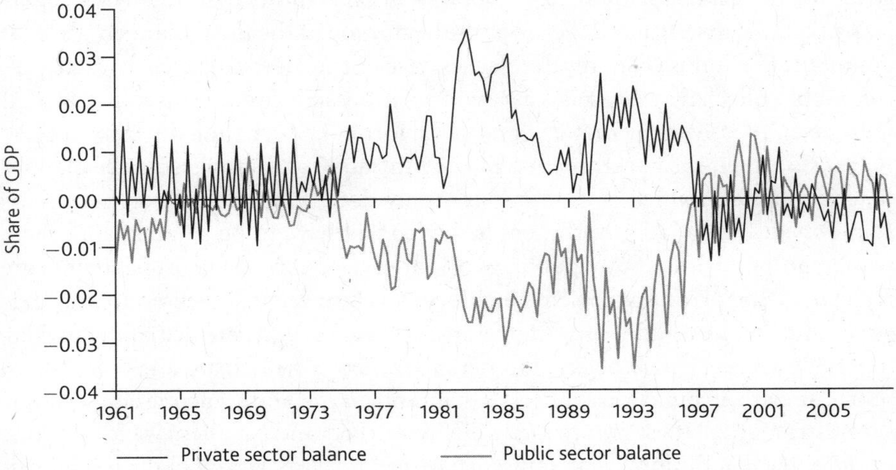

Source: Statistics Canada, CANSIM series nos. V31751, V31786, V33360, V498086.

bank will now be tallied against the government's debts, which will be reduced or eliminated; however, this has nothing to do with the *financing* of public spending, since this has already been paid for. If the government collects more taxes than it spends, its account at the central bank will have a *surplus*, but the private sector as a whole will be in *deficit*.

Moreover, since any new government expenditure increases commercial banks' reserves, the increased amount of available liquidity will put downward pressure on the interbank lending (overnight) rate and other rates, thus lowering the cost of borrowing and encouraging private investment. The fall in interest rates will continue as long as there are net government injections of liquidity into the system; the downward pressure will be stopped only if the government reverses its policy and starts withdrawing more liquidity than it injects. It can do this by levying more taxes, selling more government securities (for instance, bonds), increasing required contributions to social security and unemployment funds, or through various other means (for more details on this, see Bougrine and Seccareccia 2002). In fact, as this net withdrawal continues, interest rates will begin to increase. The central bank, acting on behalf of the government, can allow interest rates to go up until they reach a given target and then intervene again to stop that increase by injecting more liquidity. Government spending and taxing (that is, "fiscal policy") is really about controlling interest rates, since, as we have seen, it has a lot to do with *manipulating reserves* in order to achieve the *target* rate of interest and nothing to do with raising revenue to pay for government spending or balancing the public budget.

To clarify this point further, let us look at some examples. Suppose that the government decides to build a new airport—an expenditure that would be categorized as "public investment." We are at the beginning of the fiscal year (say, the first year in the life of this economy), and taxes have not yet been collected. In fact, taxes cannot be collected at this stage, as it will be impossible for citizens to pay taxes if they haven't received the money first (in the form of either bank deposits or bank notes). So, unless the government pays the contractor and suppliers in the manner described above (which is what is commonly done), the project will have to be abandoned. In fact, all government activities will have to be stopped, and there will be no provision of any public goods or services. However, as payments are made to all the private agents, the incomes thus received will be used to purchase goods and services, and we say there is an increase in aggregate demand. Furthermore, when the airport begins to operate, someone will create a taxi company, someone else will build a hotel and a restaurant nearby, and someone else will start a travel agency. All these companies will hire workers and pay them wages. Anyone would agree that the local economy will have improved as a result of the building of the airport. Government spending in general—and public investment in particular—does not crowd out private investment; on the contrary, it stimulates it. This was the idea behind the stimulus packages that governments around the world used in an attempt to escape from the financial crisis of 2008–9. When the crisis worsened in 2009, some governments were forced to take even bolder actions, such as nationalizing some private companies to prevent additional closures and layoffs.

This is in sharp contrast to the orthodox view, which claimed that government spending was a source of instability. In this regard, it is important to emphasize that the mainstream analysis of the long-term stability of the debt-to-GDP ratio and the question of sustainability of fiscal policy is carried out without taking into consideration the actual circumstances of the economy or distinguishing between the various types of government spending. For instance, when aggregate demand is low, the appropriate policy would be to lower real interest rates, which, in addition to stimulating investment, would also prevent *interest payments* on the debt from taking a larger share of public spending. However, if inflation is already low and nominal interest rates have reached the bottom—a situation that prevails today (at least in North America)—this policy will not be very helpful, and the government *must* run a deficit in order to stimulate the economy. Similarly, during a recession, it makes sense that the government extend its *transfer payments* to the unemployed in order to keep total spending at a high level and prevent further business closures and layoffs. This may lead to a higher debt-to-GDP ratio, but it cannot be considered a long-term destabilizing factor, since the policy was put in place specifically to deal with the downturn of the business cycle and attenuate the severity of the crisis. In a booming economy, there will be less unemployment and the government will not need to spend all that much on unemployment benefits. In fact, during an expansionary period the need to increase general government expenditures will be less pressing.

However, if the government instead implemented a policy based on austerity and decided to cut back on its spending (in the process, perhaps forcing the closure of an airport or not repairing a broken bridge), we would expect the local economy to suffer as a consequence. An austerity policy that seeks to balance the budget or achieve a surplus will necessarily leave the infrastructure underdeveloped or *un*developed. It is well known that countries compete for foreign direct investment by offering highly developed infrastructure and that a shabby infrastructure does not attract private investors. In fact, this is one of the main reasons why foreign investors (transnational corporations) shun poorly equipped countries, even though these may have huge pools of docile and cheap labour. In addition to discouraging private investment through this channel, a surplus policy leads to higher interest rates, thus making the cost of borrowing higher for firms and households. This is why austerity programs (fiscal and monetary restraints) are associated with slow growth and recessions (Wray 1998). Balancing budgets and reaching surpluses is a major component of the policy recommendations package given to poor countries by the IMF, the World Bank, and other international organizations. Policy-makers in these countries naively believe that these are the basic rules of "good economic management"—but nothing could be further from the truth. A policy based on budget surplus has detrimental consequences to the national economy because it hampers growth and forces millions of people into unemployment and poverty.

NOTES

1. In 2009, proponents of this view expressed the same opinion regarding the planned stimulus package proposed by the Obama administration to deal with the crisis. This view is widely held by many orthodox economists. See, for instance, Cochrane (2009), who argues that "If the government borrows a dollar from you, that is a dollar that you do not spend, or that you do not lend to a company to spend on new investment. Every dollar of increased government spending must correspond to one less dollar of private spending. Jobs created by stimulus spending are offset by jobs lost from the decline in private spending. We can build roads instead of factories, but fiscal stimulus can't help us to build more of both."

2. In the early 1990s, however, legislation was enacted in the European Monetary Union that prevented the central bank from granting credit to governments in this manner. This forced governments to rely on taxation and to resort to commercial banks—and even sell securities—to finance their expenditures.

3. This is money creation. It is important to emphasize that the creation of new money actually has very little to do with the printing of bank notes and the

minting of coins. Bills are printed and coins minted only because some transactions still require the use of "cash." But bank deposits are money par excellence, even though they are nothing more than a scripture on the "books" of the bank (in fact, it is more accurate to say, "digital symbols on the banks' computers disks"). That is why modern theory defines money as "some bills and coins" but essentially as bank deposits.

DISCUSSION QUESTIONS

1. What are bank deposits composed of? If all the bank notes and coins are destroyed, how much money will be left in the economy? Explain.
2. If the government does not need taxes and bonds to finance its expenditures, then why does it levy taxes and sell bonds?
3. Why should interest rates go down when the government is running a deficit?
4. Which would you prefer: a high interest rate or a low interest rate policy? Why?

SUGGESTED READINGS

Bell, Stephanie. 2000. Can taxes and bonds finance government spending? *Journal of Economic Issues* 34 (3): 603–620.

Graziani, Augusto. 1990. The theory of the monetary circuit. *Economies et Sociétés* 24 (6): 7–36.

Howard, Donna. 1998. A primer on the implementation of monetary policy in the LVTS environment. *Bank of Canada Review* (Autumn): 57–66.

Lerner, Abba. 1947. Money as a creature of the state. *American Economic Review, Papers and Proceedings* 37 (2): 312–317.

Wray, L. Randall. 1998. *Understanding modern money.* Cheltenham: Edward Elgar.

ONLINE RESOURCES

Bank of Canada: http://www.bankofcanada.ca/en/index.html.

Center for Full Employment and Price Stability: http://www.cfeps.org.

Post Keynesian Economic Study Group: http://www.postkeynesian.net.

The Levy Economics Institute of Bard College: http://www.levy.org.

REFERENCES

Blecker, R.A. 1992. *Beyond the twin deficits: A trade strategy for the 1990s.* Armonk, NY: M.E. Sharpe.

Bougrine, H., and M. Seccareccia. 2002. Money, taxes, public spending, and the state within a circuitist perspective. *International Journal of Political Economy* 32 (3): 58–80.

Cochrane, John H. 2009. Fiscal stimulus, fiscal inflation, or fiscal fallacies? http://faculty.chicagobooth.edu/john.cochrane/research/Papers/fiscal2.htm.

Galbraith, James K. 2008. *The predator state: How conservatives abandoned the free market and why liberals should too.* Toronto: Free Press.

Godley, W., and M. Lavoie. 2007. Fiscal policy in a stock-flow consistent (SFC) model. *Journal of Post Keynesian Economics* 30 (1): 79–100.

Keynes, John Maynard. 1936. *The general theory of employment, interest and money.* London: Macmillan.

Seccareccia, M. 1995. Keynesianism and public investment: A left-Keynesian perspective on the role of government expenditure and debt. *Studies in Political Economy* 46 (Spring): 43–78.

Seccareccia, M., and A. Sood. 2000. Government debt monetization and inflation: A somewhat jaundiced view. In *The economics of public spending: Debts, deficits and economic performance,* ed. H. Bougrine, 122–134. Cheltenham: Edward Elgar.

What Is Monetary Policy? Should Central Banks Be Targeting Inflation?

COMPETINGVIEWS

Nicholas Rowe, "Money, Central Banks, and Monetary Policy: The Path to Inflation Targeting"

Louis-Philippe Rochon, "Inflation Targeting: From Misconception to Misguided Policies"

Editors' Introduction

Monetary policy usually refers to the actions of the central bank as far as setting interest rates or influencing the amount of liquidity (including the stock of money) available in the economy is concerned. Orthodox theory emphasizes the idea that the central bank controls the stock of money and that it can exogenously set the amount of money that ought to circulate in the economic system depending on whether it wants to pursue an easy or a tight monetary policy. The basic thinking in the orthodox approach is that, since money is supplied by the central bank, the latter ought to be able to control it. However, if the central bank does not exercise caution and prudence, its actions may result in an excess supply of money relative to available output, which will lead to inflation. In this context, targeting low inflation simply means that, by using various instruments, the central bank ensures that the growth of the money stock is under tight control.

The practice of central banking has demonstrated that it is not really possible for central banks to control the quantity of money. This is due largely to the fact that the quantity of money is determined by the demand emanating from economic agents—namely, households, firms, and the government. The creation and supply of money becomes an endogenous process in which commercial banks play an essential role. Following the monetarist era of the late 1970s and early 1980s, some orthodox economists began to acknowledge the fact that central banks are not in a position to control the supply of money directly. Instead, these economists suggested that the control of central banks is only partial or indirect, and occurs via changes in interest rates. To achieve low inflation targets in this setting, the central bank needs to control its leading interest rate. Hence, whenever the inflation rate is above target, the monetary authorities should raise interest rates; when it is below target, they should lower them. Nicholas Rowe defends this view in his contribution.

On the other hand, the heterodox approach, defended by Louis-Philippe Rochon, maintains that attempts by the central bank to target inflation are misguided because they are based on the assumption that inflation is the result of a rapid growth in demand for goods and services, which is fuelled by a rapid growth of money. Since heterodox economists argue that inflation is mainly caused by increases in the costs of production, they do not believe that higher interest rates are an efficient way to achieve inflation targets. A high interest rate policy depresses the economy by changing the distribution of income in favour of the money lenders and against all borrowers (firms and households). At the same time, while they inflate the incomes of interest earners, high interest rates reduce overall demand and increase unemployment, thereby deflating the incomes of some of the most vulnerable people in society—the unemployed. For this reason, many heterodox economists consider central banks inefficient in the fight against inflation.

Money, Central Banks, and Monetary Policy: The Path to Inflation Targeting

Nicholas Rowe

Introduction

Only the very simplest economies use barter; all modern economies use monetary exchange. An apple producer who wants some bananas first sells his apples for the medium of exchange (money), and then uses the money to buy bananas. Money is the medium of exchange. Money also serves as a unit of account (we measure prices in terms of money) and as a store of wealth. While almost any good could be used as money, in practice almost all economies have evolved into using moneys with no intrinsic value, like paper money. The apple producer accepts paper money in exchange for his apples only because he expects that the banana producer will accept it in exchange for her bananas. Money's function as a medium of exchange creates a demand for it, and, provided that the producer of the money restricts supply, paper money has a value in exchange for goods that far exceeds its nearly worthless intrinsic value.

Although most countries are willing to leave the production of apples and bananas to private, profit-maximizing firms, paper money is now almost always produced by government-owned banks, called central banks, which control the supply of money. Because central banks are public institutions, their policy becomes a question for public policy debate. Since they control the supply of the money they produce, we face the following questions of monetary policy: how *should* central banks control the supply of money (that is, if they approached the question from a moral perspective—the normative question), and how *do* they (the positive question)? This chapter will focus mainly on the normative question—in particular, whether or not central banks ought to control the supply of money to target inflation.

Inflation Targeting

Inflation is defined as the percentage rate of change (per year) in the price level. The price level is defined as the price, in terms of money, of some average or representative basket of goods and services. "Inflation targeting" describes a monetary policy in which the central bank announces a fixed target for the rate of inflation (say, 2 percent per year) and adjusts the supply of money to try to keep inflation at that target level. We need to ask two questions about the monetary policy of inflation targeting: first, whether it is feasible (can central banks actually keep inflation on target, and if so, how?), and second, whether it is the best monetary policy (might some other monetary policy be better?).

How Central Banks Target Inflation

A central bank that produces money controls the supply of money it produces. That sounds simple enough, but there are many ways in which we can think about the supply of money and how the central bank can exercise that control. We can define money narrowly, as the notes and coins (and other liabilities) produced by the central bank, or more broadly, to include liabilities of the commercial banks that are close substitutes to notes and coins. We can think of monetary policy as the quantity or dollar value of the stock of money that the central bank is willing to have in circulation, or as the rate of interest at which the central bank is willing to lend or borrow money to and from the commercial banking system. We can also think of monetary policy as the price at which the central bank is willing to buy or sell money for foreign exchange, gold, or some other good.

For this discussion, it is best to think of monetary policy as a reaction function of the central bank in which it temporarily sets a rate of interest at which it borrows or lends money to the banking system. The central bank sets that rate of interest as a function of various indicators of future inflationary pressure, like output growth, current inflation, and exchange rate depreciation. This is how most inflation-targeting central banks currently operate, and how they themselves describe what they are doing.

With that view of monetary policy in mind, here is how a central bank targets inflation. Suppose a central bank has previously announced a 2 percent inflation target for the next several years. The central bank closely watches all the macroeconomic indicators that it believes are useful to try to forecast future inflation. If the central bank believes that inflationary pressures are rising and that inflation will soon rise above the 2 percent target unless it does something, the central bank will raise the interest rate. The interest rate that the central bank directly controls is typically a very short-term interest rate (on overnight loans between banks), but changes in that rate—especially if they are expected to persist—influence all other interest rates in the economy in the same direction. Higher interest rates reduce asset prices (that is, the prices of bonds and stocks, and of real assets like houses and capital goods). Higher interest rates and lower asset prices reduce investment and consumption demand (the combination reduces the incentive to invest and increases the incentive to save). Investment and consumption demand are a major part of aggregate demand for goods and services ($C + I + G + NX$), and the fall in aggregate demand relative to aggregate supply reduces the pressure on inflation, thus bringing future inflation back to the central bank's 2 percent target.

In an open economy, these investment and consumption channels are supplemented by an additional effect on net exports. The higher interest rate on domestic currency loans creates an incentive for anyone anywhere in the world to buy domestic currency on the foreign exchange market so they can lend it at higher interest rates. This causes an appreciation of the exchange rate of the domestic currency, which in turn makes our exports more expensive relative to imports, so net export demand falls. This fall in net export demand causes an additional fall in aggregate demand, further reducing inflationary pressure.

If inflationary pressures continue to rise despite the central bank's decision to raise interest rates, the bank will raise interest rates even more. If inflationary pressures fall and the central bank forecasts that future inflation might fall below the 2 percent target, it will cut interest rates in order to stimulate aggregate demand and increase inflationary pressure.

From theory and experience, we know that, while central banks are able to keep inflation close to their target, they cannot control it perfectly. It is not uncommon for actual inflation to be 1 percent or so above or below target in any given year, even if on average inflation stays very close to target. The main reason for this is clear. The decisions of the central bank are only one of the many factors that affect aggregate demand, aggregate supply, and inflation. In order to keep inflation exactly on target, the central bank would have to anticipate all those other shocks perfectly and respond with just the right adjustments at just the right time. There are lags in monetary policy, both in the time it takes for the central bank to observe and respond to indicators of inflationary pressure and in the response of the economy to the central bank's response to the indicators. In reality, the ability of central banks to forecast shocks is imperfect, as is their knowledge of how inflation will respond to those shocks and to the banks' response to them.

Is Inflation Targeting the Best Monetary Policy?

It might be nice to think that inflation targeting began as the brainchild of monetary economists who, after careful research and after comparing it with all the other monetary policies, decided it was the best policy for central banks to follow and then convinced the world's central banks and governments—along with public opinion—to adopt this superior monetary policy. Unfortunately (for monetary economists), this is not how inflation targeting began. It sort of just happened. The first central bank to adopt inflation targeting was the Reserve Bank of New Zealand, in 1990. The government of New Zealand wanted to impose strict numerical targets on all branches of government, which would be publicly announced and which each branch would be responsible for meeting. The only obvious target when it came to the Reserve Bank of New Zealand was the rate of inflation. In other words, inflation targeting arose from a policy in favour of explicit targets for public sector agencies in general, not from any theory of monetary policy.

Nevertheless, we can point to some general themes in the theory and experience of monetary policy that made the ground fertile for the quick spread of inflation targeting to other central banks around the world in the 1990s.

One such theme is the long-running debate over rules versus discretion in monetary policy. Proponents of rules argued that central banks could achieve better outcomes (like a more stable economy with a better allocation of resources) if they could influence people's expectations of inflation by making a commitment to a rule regarding future monetary policy. Moreover, changes in monetary policy can cause arbitrary changes in the distribution of wealth (for example, unanticipated inflation will transfer wealth from creditors to debtors), and people need a stable framework for long-term investment decisions; the rule of law that prevents arbitrary transfers should be applied to monetary policy just as it is to other policies. Proponents of discretion, on the other hand, argued that monetary policy was too complex and economic shocks too unpredictable for central banks to be expected to stick to some simple rule. Inflation targeting seems to give us the best of both rules and discretion. The rate of inflation is fixed by a pre-announced rule, so people can make long-term contracts without having to worry about the arbitrary whims of central bankers. The means of achieving that target rate of inflation, however, are left to the discretion of the central bankers, who can respond as they judge best to changing circumstances.

A second theme that made the ground fertile for inflation targeting was monetarism, and the writings of American economist Milton Friedman in particular. Friedman argued that "inflation is always and everywhere a monetary phenomenon." Now this can mean many things, but one persistent meaning is that monetary policy can be used to control inflation, and that central banks should be held responsible for any inflation (or deflation) they cause. Friedman also argued for the "natural rate hypothesis," according to which there exists some long-run equilibrium rate of unemployment independent of monetary policy, and any attempt to use monetary policy to try to keep unemployment below the natural rate will cause ever-accelerating inflation. The experience of many countries in the 1960s and 1970s, during which time an attempt to keep unemployment low through loose monetary policy caused rising inflation, gave support to Friedman's perspective.

Friedman proposed that central banks keep the money supply growing at a constant low rate in order to ensure a low and roughly constant rate of inflation. But in the late 1970s and 1980s central banks discovered that the connection between the growth rate of the money supply and the rate of inflation was too loose for Friedman's particular policy proposal to work. Inflation targeting—in which the central bank alone is responsible for inflation, and inflation is the sole target of monetary policy—was consistent with Friedman's monetarist perspective while rejecting his particular failed policy proposal.

A third theme that contributed to the adoption of inflation targeting was simply the failure of alternative monetary policies. As noted above, the attempt to target a low unemployment rate failed. The target of a low constant growth rate of money supply also failed. Balance-of-payments crises caused central banks to abandon attempts to fix exchange rates (or fix the price of gold under the gold standard). So far—though it is too soon to judge—inflation targeting seems to have survived where many other monetary policies have had to be abandoned.

When a central bank targets inflation, this does not mean that the central bank believes that inflation is the ultimate objective of monetary policy. Instead, central banks target inflation because they believe that doing so is the best way for monetary policy to contribute to economic welfare. By making a public commitment to keeping inflation low and stable, the central bank makes it easier for people to make good economic decisions when saving, investing, buying, selling, or setting prices and wages in a monetary exchange economy, because people can be more certain about the value of money. Also, since fluctuations in inflation are usually correlated with short-run fluctuations in real economic activity (output and employment) and both are caused by monetary instability, using monetary policy to keep inflation stable should also help reduce fluctuations in real activity (the business cycle).

As with any economic policy, with inflation targeting we can see what happens when a central bank targets inflation but not what would have happened if some alternative monetary policy had been tried instead (we call this "the counterfactual"). Comparing countries with different policies—or comparing the same country at different times, when it had different policies—may help us see which policy appears to be the most effective. However, we can never be sure that "other things are equal." Was it the policy itself that caused a better or worse economic performance, or a change in something else?

Modifications and Alternatives to Inflation Targeting

It is much too early to pronounce that inflation targeting has ended the debate over monetary policy. Many changes can be considered, ranging from minor modifications to existing inflation targeting to increasingly radical alternatives.

What Rate *of Inflation?*

Most inflation-targeting central banks choose a low positive rate of inflation, like 2 percent. Some economists argue that, since any inflation is bad, it would be better to reduce the target down to zero inflation. There are two main arguments against targeting a lower rate of inflation. The first is that some prices or wages are downwardly rigid (meaning that they won't fall); relative price shocks mean that some wages and prices might need to fall, even where average prices are constant or rising slowly. If some prices or wages in such cases refused to fall in absolute terms, the result would be excess supply or unemployment. The second argument against targeting a lower rate of inflation is that, although nominal interest rates can't fall below zero, in deep recessions the central bank might need to push real interest rates (nominal interest rates minus inflation) below zero to stimulate demand. With 2 percent inflation, the central bank could push real interest rates down to −2 percent, but with an inflation target of zero the central bank would be unable to push real interest rates below zero.

Which *Measure of Inflation?*

There are many different ways to measure inflation in practice, depending on what goods are included in the basket and how they are weighted. The consumer price index (CPI) is the most common inflation target, probably because it is the most widely reported measure of inflation. Still, perhaps a different index might be better.

What Time Horizon?

If inflation rises above target, the central bank could bring inflation back to target quickly by raising interest rates sharply, or more slowly by raising them to a smaller degree. The danger of trying to bring inflation back to target too quickly is that it might cause big fluctuations in interest rates, and possibly fluctuations in output and employment as well. Therefore, most central banks target inflation at a one- or two-year horizon.

Should Inflation Be the Only Target?

According to Milton Friedman's natural rate hypothesis, central banks cannot target unemployment, since attempting to keep unemployment permanently below the natural rate will only cause accelerating inflation. But perhaps they should have a dual objective: trying to reduce fluctuations in unemployment around the natural rate as well as reducing fluctuations of inflation around the target. In the case of demand shocks, there is no obvious conflict between these two objectives, because an increase in demand will cause higher inflation and lower unemployment and an increase in interest rates will bring both back toward the target. In the case of supply shocks, which increase both inflation and unemployment, the two objectives do conflict in the short run. However, since the deviations of unemployment from the natural rate caused by supply shocks only occur in the short run, central banks that target inflation at a longer horizon may not see much conflict between these two objectives in practice.

An alternative dual objective would be for the central bank to keep one eye on the inflation target while at the same time trying to prevent asset price bubbles. For example, if house prices or shares in tech stocks seem to be rising too high because of irrational exuberance, the central bank might raise interest rates to "prick the bubble"—even if this causes inflation to fall below target—to prevent the damage of a bigger bubble bursting at a later time. Arguments against this response include the fact that it is not easy for central banks to identify bubbles in advance; that interest rates high enough to burst a bubble might do worse damage elsewhere in the economy; and that there might be other tools that the government could use to burst a particular bubble that would not cause as much damage elsewhere.

Price-Level Targeting Versus Inflation Targeting

At first glance, there seems to be no difference between targeting a path for the price level that grows at, say, 2 percent per year and targeting 2 percent inflation. And if the central bank hits its target exactly, there *is* no difference. But suppose the central bank misses its target one year, and inflation is 3 percent. Advocates of inflation targeting say the central bank should still aim for 2 percent inflation in all subsequent years regardless of that mistake. Advocates of price-level targeting, on the other hand, say the central bank should try to keep inflation *below* 2 percent in the following years until the price level returns to its original path. One clear advantage of price-level targeting is that the price level remains predictable into the future because past mistakes are reversed, whereas inflation targeting could allow past mistakes to accumulate, making the price level in the distant future hard to predict.

Fixed Exchange Rates Versus Inflation Targeting

If a central bank is setting the interest rate to keep inflation on target, it cannot at the same time set the interest rate to keep the exchange rate fixed. If inflation falls below target and the exchange rate depreciates at the same time, the central bank can either cut interest rates to target inflation or raise interest rates to target the exchange rate, but it cannot do both (unless it uses a second policy lever, such as rationing foreign exchange, which creates difficulties for foreign trade and finance). It is common for one country to fix the exchange rate of its currency to another country's currency, but historically these fixed-exchange-rate regimes have tended to be unstable; sooner or later, a currency crisis breaks the fixed exchange rate. In the typical currency crisis, expectations of devaluation become self-fulfilling: people rush to sell the currency they expect to devalue, which causes the central bank to either run out of foreign currency reserves or raise interest rates to ruinous levels to protect the exchange rate. Without rationing foreign exchange—which creates problems for foreign trade and investment and encourages a black market with its own flexible exchange rate—the only sure way to fix an exchange rate permanently is for one country simply to adopt the currency of a foreign country (or for both to adopt a shared currency, such as the euro).

Common Currency Versus Inflation Targeting

No advocate of inflation targeting would say that inflation targeting is always and everywhere better than adopting a common currency. After all, if every country should have its own currency, regardless of how small it may be, then should every region, every town, or every street? The transactions costs of having to exchange currencies whenever you bought or sold something would destroy the very advantages of having a common medium of exchange; we would be better off using barter. At the other extreme, a few economists would argue that the whole world should share one common currency. But even if they are right, that still leaves open the question of what the world central bank controlling the world's currency should do, and advocates of inflation targeting would argue that a hypothetical world central bank should target world inflation.

From the perspective of any one country, the two options are to have its own currency and central bank or to join other countries in a common currency. From the perspective of the whole world, the question is: how many currencies and central banks should there be, and where should we draw the lines between currencies? In other words, what is the "optimal currency area"? For a country, joining a common currency area provides the advantages of reduced transactions costs and exchange rate uncertainty for foreign trade and finance. The advantage of a country maintaining its own currency is that it allows the central bank to choose an independent monetary policy. If two countries face different shocks to aggregate demand and supply, the best monetary policy for one country will be different from the best monetary policy for the other, and a common currency and single central bank cannot do what is best for both at once. So each country faces a trade-off between the lower transactions costs of a common currency and the benefits of a monetary policy tailor-made to its own circumstances.

From the perspective of a single country, then, adopting a common currency is an alternative to having its own central bank targeting inflation in that country. But from the perspective of the whole world, the question of whether central banks should target inflation is a separate question from how many central banks there should be. Common currency versus inflation targeting is a false dichotomy.

DISCUSSION QUESTIONS

1. Most countries leave the production of apples and bananas to private, profit-maximizing firms. Would it be a good idea to leave the production of money to such firms? Why or why not?
2. Central banks can target some things (like the long-run rate of inflation), but cannot target other things (like the long-run rate of unemployment). Why is this the case? What is the difference between the things that central banks can and cannot control?
3. Suppose that Canada targets 2 percent inflation and the United States targets 5 percent inflation. What would happen to the exchange rate between the Canadian and US dollars over the long run?
4. Would it be a good idea for the East and West of Canada to have different currencies? What about France and Germany? In each case, why or why not?
5. How long will it take the price level to double if average inflation is: 1 percent, 2 percent, 5 percent, 10 percent? (Hint: Google "the rule of 70.")
6. In your opinion, what is the best alternative to inflation targeting? Why?

SUGGESTED READINGS AND ONLINE RESOURCES

The Bank of Canada's website contains an excellent set of readings on inflation targeting at the Bank of Canada: http://www.bankofcanada.ca/en/monetary/monetary_main.html, including

- an explanation of how monetary policy works: http://www.bankofcanada.ca/en/monetary_mod/index.html,
- the decision-making process: http://www.bankofcanada.ca/en/monetary/monetary_decision.html, and
- why monetary policy matters: http://www.bankofcanada.ca/en/ragan_paper/index.html.

Buiter, W. 1999. Optimal currency areas: Why does the exchange rate regime matter? http://www.eabcn.org/research/documents/scotland.pdf (arguing that the United Kingdom should adopt the euro as a common currency).

Svensson, L. 2007. Inflation targeting. http://www.princeton.edu/svensson/papers/PalgraveIT.pdf (a short paper on inflation targeting written for the New Palgrave Dictionary of Economics).

Inflation Targeting: From Misconception to Misguided Policies

Louis-Philippe Rochon

Introduction

Mainstream monetary theory and policy can be summarized by the following three arguments, which can be found in virtually all introductory, intermediate, and advanced macroeconomics textbooks. First, monetary policy is identified with the ability of the central bank to control the money supply through open-market operations and, specifically, with its ability to exercise direct control over the monetary base. Accordingly, through either buying or selling government bonds or by changing reserve requirements, the central bank can inject or withdraw any amount of money that is consistent with its overall policy objectives. The money supply is said to be exogenous, and there is a direct and predictable relationship between the monetary base and the money supply: the money supply is a multiple of the monetary base, as depicted in the well-known money multiplier model.

Second, the money supply is merely an intermediate target; the central bank uses it as a way of achieving its other objectives. In theory, the central bank may have a number of policy objectives, such as economic growth, employment levels, exchange rates, or inflation. In practice, central banks around the world target inflation as their ultimate policy objective. According to the mainstream, at low and stable levels inflation generates a number of benefits—notably, increased consumption and investment (as the purchasing power of money is not losing any of its value over the medium and longer term), and lower nominal and real interest rates. Stable inflation is a self-reinforcing objective. Low inflation keeps inflation low.

Inflation is therefore considered "always and everywhere a monetary phenomenon." Milton Friedman, the father of modern monetarism, has forcefully defended this view. Money causes inflation. Hence, inflation is the result of some irresponsible central bank that allows the money supply to increase too fast. This is an important theoretical assumption, and one that has driven monetary policy both in the past and today, at least since the rise of monetarism. Indeed, inflation is thought to be caused by excess demand, of which money is a component: if there is too much money chasing too few goods, the price of all goods will go up. It is therefore important to give the central bank complete control over the money supply. When inflation is too high, the central bank tightens the money supply and inflation adjusts downward. The necessary causal link between money and inflation requires the money supply to be exogenous.

Finally, there is a separation between monetary analysis and real analysis. In other words, since money is expected to be neutral (that is, changes in the money supply have no effects on the real economy), there is a disassociation between monetary policy and productive activity. This allows us to discuss investment, wages, employment, output, and so on, without ever referring to money. Money is simply added later in the analysis, almost as an afterthought. The neutrality of money ensures that the impact of changes in the money supply is entirely borne out on prices, not output. This conclusion holds always in the long run, although some economists will allow for some short-term—and short-lived—disturbances resulting from changes in monetary policy.

The mainstream story detailing the causal relationship between money and inflation, however, is far from realistic—a conclusion that will be explained later in this essay. Nevertheless, it does summarize the mainstream view rather accurately, at least as this view is depicted in most economics textbooks.

Recently, however, some mainstream economists and most central bankers have replaced the first hypothesis with a more realistic notion—one that is more representative of current central-bank policy and practices. Indeed, realizing the fact that central banks cannot control the money supply, the mainstream view now espouses a policy of controlling the short-term rate of interest (the overnight rate), with only an indirect control over the money supply through the impact of interest rates on credit and bank loans.

Nevertheless, irrespective of whether central banks control the money supply or interest rates, very little has changed from the overall mainstream story. As we will see, replacing money supply control with interest rate control changes little, as long as the remaining two assumptions are the same. In fact, central banks still believe that the rate of growth of the money supply contains useful information regarding future levels of inflation. In the end, whichever tool the central bank uses to implement its policy, mainstream economists fundamentally believe in the ability of the central bank to affect inflation.

Inflation Targeting and Central-Bank Policy

Milton Friedman, an influential economist, Nobel laureate, and professor at the University of Chicago, argued some time ago that it was imperative for the central bank to try to control the money supply in order to control inflation, which was considered a scourge on households and other economic agents. Yet after attempting to do so in the 1970s and 1980s, central banks quickly realized that they could not control the money supply without risking a collapse of the banking system.

From this disastrous experience a new operating system emerged, one that would rest on the control of interest rates. Indeed, in the early 1990s the Bank of Canada moved to adopt a new frame of reference within which to conduct monetary policy. It abandoned reserve requirements and officially adopted a policy of inflation targeting. Today, the central bank sets a target for inflation between 1 and 3 percent, aiming for an average inflation rate of 2 percent.

These new measures are part of a theoretical model known as the New Consensus, a simple model composed of a set of three equations that together set out the theoretical frame of reference for contemporary monetary policy. There are two key components to this model: a Taylor interest rate rule and inflation targeting. More important, it clearly sets out the three arguments described in the introduction to this essay. The model also explains the effect that changes in the rate of interest will have on output and on inflation, and finally, it lays out the "transmission mechanism" of monetary policy.

The transmission mechanism is what explains how changes in monetary policy or interest rates will ultimately affect the central bank's chosen objective. In this respect, it will explain how the central bank can change the rate of interest to impact the level of inflation. For the central bank's policy to be effective, two conditions must be met. First, changes in the rate of interest must affect the demand for goods. Second, changes in demand must affect the price level, such that a general decrease in the former must lead to a fall in the latter. If one or both of these conditions are not met, the mainstream story and its explanation of the transmission mechanism must be rejected in favour of an alternative explanation.

The first equation of the New Consensus model is an IS (investment-saving) curve, which tracks the negative relationship between interest rates and investment. To better understand this model, we must remember that mainstream economists assume that there are two interest rates: a market rate, which is set by the central bank, and a natural rate, which somehow equates investment and saving. The first equation therefore suggests that any deviations of the market rate from the natural rate will have implications for output. More specifically, if the central bank sets the rate of interest below the natural rate, this will stimulate investment, and output will grow: the output gap, which is the difference between actual output and potential output, will widen.

The second equation is essentially a Phillips curve, which establishes the relationship between the output gap and inflation. As actual output grows beyond potential output, corresponding to the long-run aggregate supply curve, this will stimulate inflation, and prices will rise. This equation is basically the second assumption described at the beginning of this essay: the output gap determines inflation. Because it clearly establishes the mainstream notion that inflation is demand-determined, this is a fundamental assumption. Indeed, mainstream theorists assign virtually no role to costs or supply conditions in explaining inflation.

The final equation is what is known today as the Taylor rule. It establishes that central banks should change interest rates in two situations: whenever actual output deviates from its potential level, and whenever actual inflation deviates from the central bank's chosen inflation target. While this is essentially clear recognition of the fact that central banks are powerless in controlling monetary base or supply, this rule is still deeply rooted in orthodox and mainstream ideology. Essentially, it establishes that the central bank should raise the market rate when inflation is higher than its target. Given the first equation, this should slow down economic activity, which, given the second equation, should lower the inflation rate until it reaches its target—at which point there is no more need for changes in monetary policy. If inflation is at its target, then the market rate should be at its natural level.

What is clear here is that the transmission mechanism runs from changes in interest rate to changes in output and demand to changes in the inflation level. It therefore assumes that these relationships are strong and predictable in such a way that the central bank can have an impact on inflation with little costs to the overall economy.

Inflation Targeting: A Critique and Alternative Policy Proposals

The ideas just discussed are flawed in many respects. As an alternative, post-Keynesians (who follow the writings of British economist John Maynard Keynes as well as those of Polish economist Michal Kalecki) offer an overall view of the economy and of the monetary policy transmission mechanism that relies on the real world and that sees the rate of interest first and foremost as a distributive variable.

The overall criticism revolves around three larger issues. First, post-Keynesians reject the existence of a natural rate of interest. Indeed, it is virtually impossible to calculate such a rate, and, while policy-makers seem to recognize this, it does not stop them from using it in policy decisions. For them, the natural rate is equal to whatever rate ensures that inflation is on target. Post-Keynesians, on the other hand, believe that relying on the supposed existence of this natural rate leads to poor monetary policy decisions.

Second, post-Keynesians do not believe that inflation is demand-determined, but rather that it is determined by costs considerations. If this view is correct, then resting monetary policy decisions on demand leads again to poor policy decisions. Even worse, it leads to even higher rates of interest. In other words, if inflation is not directly determined by demand, then it is obvious that changes in interest rates will not have the desired effects.

Finally, and importantly for post-Keynesians, the New Consensus model does not allow for fiscal policy. Indeed, discussion over the importance of fiscal policy is entirely absent in it. The model therefore promotes monetary policy dominance:

the belief that only monetary policy can regulate cycles and tame inflationary pressures.

To best describe the alternative view, consider the three assumptions of mainstream theory as described at the beginning of this essay. For each, consider also the post-Keynesian alternative.

1. *Is the money supply under the control of the central bank?*

Contrary to monetarists and other mainstream economists, post-Keynesians argue that the central bank has no choice but to allow the monetary base to adjust to the needs of the banking system rather than dictating what it should be. In this sense, the money supply is said to be "endogenous": it is created when private agents, such as firms, borrow from commercial banks to cover their needs of production. As banks extend credit, money is created and the money supply increases. Although the central bank has no control over the money supply, it does have control over the rate of interest. For reasons that are beyond the scope of this essay, post-Keynesians specifically reject the existence of the natural rate of interest. Nevertheless, the central bank will target a market rate and will ensure that the rate that is determined in the overnight (or interbank) market comes as close as possible to the target rate. In fact, if the actual market-determined rate is not on target, the central bank will take the necessary steps to ensure that it converges on the target rate. The central bank will use a number of methods, such as so-called open-market operations, or will transfer government funds back and forth between commercial banks and the central bank. In this way, the central bank always acts defensively to maintain the market rate of interest on target. In Canada, the central bank can do this with great accuracy, and in normal times it has no trouble achieving its target rate of interest. One conclusion we can draw here is that open-market operations are used not to control the monetary base but rather to control the rate of interest.

The rate of interest is therefore an administered price. And while this so far resembles the New Consensus view, post-Keynesians argue that the rate of interest is also a distributive variable: it affects the distribution of income among social groups. Any monetary policy that aims at increasing the rate of interest will favour rentier income and will lead to a decrease in the share of income accruing to the working class and/or to the entrepreneurial class. Since workers' propensity to consume is higher than that of rentiers, a monetary policy that favours rentiers will lead to a decrease in the demand for goods and will slow economic activity.

2. *Inflation is always a monetary or excess demand phenomenon.*

Post-Keynesians reject the mainstream view of inflation because it does not reflect how economies actually work. Indeed, for the mainstream story to hold, you must assume that there is a direct and stable relationship between the rate of interest and demand, on the one hand, and also between demand and inflation on the other.

For post-Keynesians, there is no relationship between money and prices, and demand plays only a small role in the overall determination of prices. Indeed, careful examination of the last two decades shows convincingly that there is no causality between changes in the money supply and the inflation level. In other words, inflation is never a monetary phenomenon. If this view is correct, then what can we say about the influence of excess demand on the overall level of prices? If money does not cause prices, do changes in demand affect inflation?

To better understand the price determination process, consider two types of goods: flex-price goods (such as agricultural products, the prices of which are determined by market forces) and fixed-price goods (such as manufactured and industrial goods, the prices of which are set according to a markup over costs of production). In contemporary economies, such as Canada's, the dominant economic activity is represented by the industrial and manufacturing sectors, where prices are generally inflexible—at least downwardly—and change only infrequently. In these sectors, demand plays a very limited role in the overall determination of prices. To be sure, fixed or inflexible prices are not considered a market failure or an imperfection, but rather a dominant feature of contemporary, advanced economies.

In the industrial and manufacturing sectors, prices are once again administered and are set directly by firms. There are two components to prices. On the one hand, there are the various costs of production—wages, for instance—but also interest costs to borrowing and costs related to the purchase of other inputs of production, such as gas and petrol. On the other hand, there is the firm's markup over these costs, which can be said to contain the firm's expected rate of profit. Indeed, large firms set their prices in this way. Yet this approach underscores the possible conflict inherent in the price determination process. Consider, for instance, the scenario where unions won general increases in their nominal wages. If wages go up, firms can either pass these costs on to consumers, leaving their markup intact, or incur these higher costs, lowering their markup in order to keep prices fixed. This exemplifies well the conflict inherent in setting prices: it pits one social class against another over the appropriate or fair distribution of income. If, following increases in wages (which benefit workers), firms increase prices, this will then lower real wages. This is why post-Keynesians adopt a conflict–inflation approach to price determination. Inflation is not demand-determined, but cost-plus or conflict-driven.

3. *There is a separation between money and economic activity.*

Recall that, for mainstream economists, money is neutral in the long run such that any changes in monetary policy stance (for instance, increases in the rate of interest) may have short-term effects but will not have long-run effects on economic activity. This is certainly one of the most contentious assumptions of monetarism.

For post-Keynesians, however, money and economic activity are interlinked. Indeed, it is impossible to discuss real activity—such as investment, production, employment, and growth—without first discussing the monetary conditions and the banking sector. Indeed, as Keynes once said, economic activity can never be slowed down by a lack of saving, but it can be considerably affected by a lack of bank lending. If banks are feeling pessimistic about the ability of firms to repay their bank loans, they will curtail lending and economic activity will slow down. At the time of writing (winter 2008–9), interest rates in the United States were at a historically low level (virtually 0 percent), yet banks did not necessarily increase their lending. Despite low levels of interest rates, banks do not consider all borrowers creditworthy.

Given these alternative assumptions, what can we say about inflation targeting? Is it a good policy for central banks to follow?

On the surface, it would appear that inflation targeting was indeed a huge success. After all, inflation is low and stable, and has been for several years now, although it increased in 2008. It would appear, therefore, that the policy of inflation targeting has brought down inflation and has kept it within the central bank's target range.

Two questions arise immediately. First, is inflation targeting really responsible for bringing down inflation in Canada and around the world? And second, is inflation targeting responsible for keeping inflation levels low and stable?

I would argue that inflation targeting is responsible for neither result. First, the policy of inflation targeting was adopted in many countries at a time when inflation levels were already (very) high; moreover, they were already on a downward trajectory. Second, from a post-Keynesian perspective, this period also corresponded to a general decrease in real wages, which would have kept production costs low and placed little pressure on business firms to raise prices. This would explain why inflation levels were kept relatively low. Indeed, in order to keep inflation low, central banks—and the Bank of Canada in particular—would have kept interest rates higher than they would have been otherwise.

This brings the issue of the transmission mechanism of monetary policy to the fore. As discussed above, mainstream theory, which dominates central-bank policy around the world, rests on the idea that changes in the rate of interest will have the desired effect on inflation at little cost. Post-Keynesians, however, believe that the opposite is true: monetary policy and inflation targeting have come at high costs in terms of growth, employment, and inequality.

For post-Keynesians, the transmission mechanism of monetary policy works through income distribution. The higher the rate of interest, the more skewed is distribution in favour of the rentier class. This is important because economic activity is determined by the demand for goods and services. The higher the income share of workers, the higher are consumption, economic activity, and growth. Post-Keynesians therefore favour a policy of low and stable interest rates, a policy that should maximize our prospects for economic growth.

So just how important are the differences between these two approaches? Quite important. Consider a period of inflation. In raising the rate of interest, the central bank believes the demand for goods will fall, bringing inflation with it. But if inflation is indeed determined by costs, an increase in the rate of interest will have little effect. So when the decrease in inflation does not materialize, the central bank will respond by increasing rates even higher. In the end, rates will increase to such a level that income distribution will be affected, and will be skewed in favour of rentiers: workers' share of income will diminish. This in turn will have an impact on demand and employment. As unemployment increases, wage demands will decrease, thereby lowering cost pressures. Inflation will diminish.

Conclusion

The conclusion should now be obvious. While central-bank policy did succeed in bringing down inflation, the relationship between the rate of interest and inflation is indirect and imprecise: to be effective, the central bank had to deflate the economy before finally bringing inflation down. Central banks should therefore not be responsible for regulating economic cycles and inflation—the costs are too high. Central banks are simply inefficient in fighting inflation. Instead, they should look after the financial health of the monetary and financial systems, and leave the task of regulating economic activity to fiscal policy.

DISCUSSION QUESTIONS

1. Do you think the central bank should fight inflation? Why or why not?
2. Do you think the central bank should keep interest rates low for a long time? Why or why not? What would be the consequences of such a policy?
3. What are the consequences of using interest rates to regulate the economic cycle?

SUGGESTED READINGS

Lavoie, M. 2007. *Introduction to post-Keynesian economics*. London: Routledge.
Meyer, L.H. 2001. Does money matter? *Review* (Federal Reserve Bank of St. Louis) 83 (4): 1–15.

Rochon, L.-P. 2009. Central bank governance, the euthanasia of the rentier and interest rate policy: A note on post-Keynesian monetary policy after Taylor. In *Monetary policy and financial stability*, ed. C. Gnos and L.-P. Rochon. Cheltenham: Edward Elgar.

ONLINE RESOURCES

Bank of Canada: http://www.bankofcanada.ca.
Center for Full Employment and Price Stability: http://www.cfeps.org.
The Levy Economics Institute of Bard College: http://levy.org.

Should Central Banks Be Independent?

COMPETING VIEWS

J.A. (Jack) Galbraith, "The Case for Independent Central Banks"

Edwin Le Héron, "Governance and Confidence Instead of Independence and Credibility"

Editors' Introduction

The question of central-bank independence is of considerable importance. Suppose, for instance, that the government considers fighting unemployment to be a high priority and decides to stimulate demand and generate new jobs by encouraging various investment projects, either through lower tax rates or higher subsidies to business enterprises. If the central bank is independent (of the government) and has its own reading of the economic indicators, it might consider that inflation is too high and decide to increase interest rates in an attempt to bring inflation down to a set target. By depressing the level of economic activity, higher interest rates will cause more unemployment and therefore could largely offset the fiscal stimulus planned by the government. In such a case, whose position would hold sway? Ought it to be that of the fiscal or the monetary authorities? Interestingly, a policy conflict almost analogous to the one just described actually took place in Canada during the late 1950s and early 1960s. As a result of this conflict, known as the "Coyne affair," then-governor of the Bank of Canada James Coyne was eventually pressured to resign.

In his essay, Jack Galbraith defends the view that an independent central bank should be able to set its interest rate policy without interference from the government. The main reason for this argument is that an independent central bank is better placed to have a long-term view of which interest rates should prevail in order to guarantee general macroeconomic stability, whereas government officials are often motivated by short-term interest and the hope of political gain. An independent central bank will give the general public confidence that the bank is credible, able to resist manipulation by political parties, and will only act in the general interest of the country.

Edwin Le Héron, on the other hand, argues in favour of good governance rather than a more independent central bank. The advantage of good governance is that the government would simply delegate monetary policy to the central bank but remain in charge of defining the overall economic objectives. Moreover, since the managers of the central bank will be accountable to the government, one would expect a better performance.

The Case for Independent Central Banks

J.A. (Jack) Galbraith

Introduction

In order to take the "pro" side in the debate over whether or not central banks should be independent, it is not necessary to accept the position that a central bank should be a for-profit, private institution under contract to conduct monetary policy on behalf of some central government—although such a position is not unknown. Instead, one can accept that, nowadays, central banks in general are creatures of governments and that the latter do not deny the former some form of independence in setting monetary policy. The central issue of the debate is whether it is the government itself or a government-established central bank that should be responsible for the monetary policy of a country.

Central-Bank Models

Debate in these terms is based on the standard model of a central bank as a public interest, not-for-profit financial institution that functions as an integral part of a country's financial system—much as the Bank of Canada, which serves as Canada's central bank, does. In this model, the central bank is not just another government department but stands apart from the government as a separate legal entity. This means that the bank has a corporate structure, generally has its own board of directors, and has a staff that is not considered part of the civil service. These things confer on the bank an appearance of being entirely independent of the government, at least as far as its day-to-day management is concerned.

The bank's legitimacy, however, depends on enabling legislation that sets out its designated activities. In this way the bank—in the same way that other government corporations, such as a government deposit insurance corporation or a government mint, are—is established for a specific purpose, namely, monetary policy. So in structure, a central bank already exists as a separate unit outside of the normal structure of government.

Nevertheless, as a creation of the government, the central bank can be instructed to conduct the monetary policy that the former desires. Thus, meaningful independence for a central bank might be said to occur only when the central bank is free to choose whatever monetary policy it decides is best for the economy. This would be an extreme form of independence, however, and is unusual for any form of management-run firm, private or public. Ownership usually dictates the firm's general course of conduct, or objective. Merely stating an overall objective for a not-for-profit, public-interest firm, however, need not impinge on the day-to-day operational freedom of the management regarding how to pursue that objective. Accordingly, a government could set a specific macroeconomic objective—such as inflation targeting, or, if its concern is also to combat deflation, price stability more generally—and then leave it to the central bank to decide how best to pursue that objective. Under today's practices, this amounts to leaving it to the judgment of the central bank when to change its goal for interest rates (usually a designated short-term interest rate used to bring about changes in financial conditions), and by how much.

Thus, establishing an overall macroeconomic objective for monetary policy, whether this is accomplished by legislation, or unilaterally by the government (although it might be done in agreement and consultation with the central bank), does not have to interfere with the bank's ability to act independently in setting the current course for monetary policy, which determines how easy or tight monetary and financial conditions will be. It is the case for this type of independence that has to be made.

The Ability to Act Independently

Independence in this sense refers to the complete freedom of the central bank to decide, in accordance with present-day central-bank practices, when to signal an alteration in monetary policy through a change in the interest rate. In doing so, the bank relies on the discretion of its governing body, which is entirely external to the government. Furthermore, the government need not be consulted on any proposed change or be expected to exercise veto powers over any policy decision by the bank. That the bank can set the interest rate policy at its own discretion means that it can change the rate by as much or as little as it thinks appropriate for the current and prospective state of the economy. In order to do this, the bank must have sufficient latitude for carrying out financial transactions involving the purchase and sale of securities in established markets, setting lending terms for banks and other major market players who deal with it, and in the general handling of its portfolio and accounts carried.

In addition to setting the interest rate, a central bank—particularly in times of stress in financial markets—also acts as a lender of last resort. In this role, it provides assistance to any of its clients who are temporarily short of funds (usually major banks and related financial institutions) through short-term loans; this allows them to meet maturing debts. If the bank did not provide this assistance, solvent borrowers (those who may possess securities that cannot be quickly turned into cash, but that in time would be available to allow them to meet all their financial commitments) would be forced unnecessarily into bankruptcy.

It may well be asked why some specialized department within the government, under some political head, cannot be assigned these responsibilities. Why use a central bank in this way? Why not let the government instruct its central bank when to change interest rates and by how much? Why not let the government decide who can access the lender-of-last-resort facilities?

In the case of setting interest rates, the time it takes for a change in interest rates to become fully effective must be taken into account. These delays, or lags, might be as long as two years. So setting an interest rate now for achieving some macroeconomic objective—such as an inflation (or deflation) target—calls for looking well ahead, beyond the current situation. Future conditions must be projected in order to determine what interest rate level is needed *now* to ensure that future prices in general remain at acceptable levels. While a central bank can look beyond the next general election, political departments are less free to do so, as their political masters are often under pressure to mandate quick fixes. Thus, an independent, monetary-setting central bank is better able to deal with policy lags than are officials in a political department. Furthermore, when the task is handled by the central bank, this leads to greater confidence among the public as far as dealing in financial markets. This is because monetary policy under an independent central bank is not likely to be manipulated for short-term political gains at the expense of the larger economic interest. Since there is always a lag in the time it takes for any change in monetary policy to take full effect (often 18 months or more), the sooner a change in monetary policy can be initiated, the better. Independent central-bank managers can start the process of change as soon as the need for action is foreseen. Unfortunately, what has to be done is not always agreed upon unanimously. If the matter concerns the government and the decision rests with the government, there could be debates that will delay action.

Furthermore, when the macroeconomic objective set for monetary policy is one that depends on the weighing of options to reach, timing becomes crucial. Thus, for an objective such as inflation targeting, there will generally be different views at any one time regarding the course that inflation is taking. Events can change quickly. For example, shocks can occur—as when the price of a key commodity, such as oil, suddenly takes off, or when an economy suddenly falls into recession—and to delay acting could have serious economic consequences. In such times, the political process is not the best way to reach a conclusion regarding the monetary action that is required. Yet a government-directed monetary policy would be subject to such delaying debate. An independent central bank, however, would allow action to be taken much more rapidly in times of great need.

In addition, when an election is looming, the political parties in power always have an interest in seeing the economy stimulated beyond what would be in the longer-run interest of the public. This leads to political pressure on the central bank, at such times, to accommodate the monetary preferences of the government. Only a truly independent central bank can withstand any such unwarranted economic moves. For example, with monetary policy entirely in the hands of the government, the government might be tempted to inappropriately delay raising interest rates in the face of a pending election; at a low point in its popularity, the government might be tempted to keep monetary conditions easier than the present and future state of the economy might warrant. Conversely, at a time when the economy is falling into a recession, the government might be under pressure to avoid inflation by refusing to allow interest rates to fall, or to fall as much as they perhaps should.

There are some instances in which having monetary policy run by an independent central bank could be advantageous to a government. One example is when monetary conditions must be tightened for the good of the macroeconomy, which is not always obvious to the public. In this case, the government could defend itself against the criticism that it caused financial hardship on the grounds that the decision was an independent decision of the central bank. The government could deflect criticism that it caused inflation by letting interest rates fall on the same grounds.

The government has recourse to the same defence where the question of access to central-bank lender-of-last-resort facilities is concerned. When the administration of these facilities lies outside of the government's hands, the government cannot be charged with showing political favouritism as far as who gets loans under the facilities and who does not. Thus in theory, a case can be made that, when monetary policy is to be implemented for pursuing some desired macroeconomic objective requiring judgment, it should not be done in a political setting. That is, the democratic voting process is not appropriate for deciding at any point in time whether, and by how much, monetary conditions should be altered. This is a technical matter that must be entrusted to managers who can be held accountable. Such accountability constraints exist for governments in the form of elections. And while governments can always be punished at the polls for poor management, such opportunities do not typically arise every year. In contrast, independent central-bank managers can be hauled before legislators several times during the course of a year to account for their conduct.

In practice, however, can a central bank be truly independent, given that its governing head is in effect at minimum a political appointee? If it chose to, a government could dictate to the central bank what stance to take on monetary policy, most likely to make it more accommodating. There would be some political risk, however, in a government taking this approach, especially if the bank had established a solid reputation as a competent implementer of monetary policy, or if for some reason the government were under attack. Thus, a well-managed central bank could be expected to withstand blatant efforts on the part of the government to force it into a short-run course of action that it does not believe is in the best interest of the economy.

Resolving Differences

Nevertheless, the most appropriate monetary policy at any given time is not always clearcut, and genuine differences of view can develop among parties. Where the government holds an opposing view, some weight must be assigned to that view. A compromise between the bank and the government in the face of uncertainty as to the best way to proceed would not be unreasonable, and this should not be taken to represent a diminution in the independence of the central bank. Even when the central bank seems to be pursuing a course of action that also suits the government, this could simply be a case where the bank arrived at its decision independently—a decision that just happens to be agreeable to the government and is in keeping with the government's short-run interest. A central bank that chose its policy according to what would please its "masters" would not be acting independently, and—given the desirability of independence—this would be a cause for censuring the central bank. More to the point, the effectiveness of monetary policy depends on the acts of its managers being *feasible* in addition to appropriate. This involves not only confidence but also what is referred to as "credibility." For example, if a central bank announces that it is tightening monetary policy but does not follow this announcement with action or changes its mind later, when doing so is not otherwise justified (say, to avoid criticism), its behaviour will upset the smooth functioning of financial markets essential for the effectiveness of monetary policy. So the argument for independence assumes that an independent central bank would have greater credibility and enjoy greater confidence than a government-run institution.

Of course, granting independence to a central bank for the day-to-day conduct of monetary policy only makes sense, or is relevant, when a country has the ability to use monetary policy for domestic macroeconomic purposes. This is not the situation when the government has decided to fix the exchange rate for its currency to some other currency or bundle of currencies. Under such a regime, the government must buy or sell foreign exchange in order to keep the value of its currency at the fixed level. These transactions affect the domestic money supply and therefore determine whether monetary conditions will be tighter or easier. In other words, monetary policy here is the outcome of foreign exchange rate transactions.

This is not unlike what used to occur under the gold standard, when, in effect, countries pegged the price of gold in terms of their own monetary unit. In this case, a central bank must act whenever the market price of gold threatens to move away from its targeted price. Although the central bank can keep the price of gold at its targeted price by selling gold from the reserve stocks it holds or by buying gold, the effect is the same as if the bank were doing open-market operations, which have the effect of altering the money supply. To lessen a fall in the money supply when the central bank is selling gold to support its price, the bank would have to raise its policy interest rate, which would lead to changes in other interest rates. In the case of higher interest rates, the effect is to induce a reduction in the demand for gold in favour of domestic money. While altering interest rates to peg a gold price or a foreign exchange rate may seem like a kind of non-discretionary rule for monetary policy, it is not a precise one. It does not predict by how much interest rates should change. A true rule would run in terms of calling for a specific change in, say, interest rates (such as 25 basis points), in pursuit of a given objective, such as a rate of inflation.

Countries can also avoid the responsibility of having a domestic monetary policy by joining a multinational currency union. For instance, a number of countries that belong to the European Union have formed a monetary union, whose members give up their national currency for a common currency—the euro. The responsibility for monetary policy for the euro area is assigned to the European Central Bank, which was formed for this purpose. Although the various European national governments have retained their central banks, they have stripped them of the ability to undertake any discretionary monetary policy actions aimed at their own macroeconomies.

Another way in which a government can forgo using monetary policy in a discretionary way for active management of the economy is to adopt a simple rule for setting monetary policy that requires no day-to-day judgments. A simple rule of this nature is one that calls for the money supply to grow at a constant rate, regardless of the state of the economy. This reduces monetary policy to a more or less automatic and mechanical process. The question of independence does not arise here. An independent central bank, of course, could choose to operate by such a simple rule, and in so doing would be giving up its freedom, under the rule, to manipulate monetary policy according to its view of the state of the economy. In short, debating whether or not a central bank should have independence as far as conducting monetary policy with the aim of influencing the macroeconomy implies that it is desirable to have monetary policy determined by judgment, not by rule. This assumes, of course, that judgment will reflect the best thinking and practice of the day, uninfluenced by ideology. Otherwise, an automatic rule for changing monetary conditions could serve better.

Conclusion

In summary, given the position that monetary policy should be actively conducted according to the state of the economy for which it is designed, responsibility for implementing that policy—through interest rates generally—should fall to an independent central bank. The highly technical operations that must be carried out (that is, monetary decisions to change interest rates) must be conducted without interference resulting from essentially political concerns, which would be bound to arise if the central bank were not free to make such important decisions on its own and which could be detrimental to the interest of the macroeconomy. Such independence also enables required action to be taken more promptly, and more decisively, than would be the case if it had to be subject to a political review. The outcome of avoiding the daily scrutiny of the politicians should be a more efficient execution of monetary policy. This execution could be further enhanced by having the government and the central bank bound by legislation and formal agreement to some acceptable, and current, overall macroeconomic objective (such as inflation targeting, or, more widely, price stability) to be pursued through monetary policy. Finally, it would be inconsistent, having set up a separate central bank outside of the general organization of the government, to then deny that bank the ability to act independently in order to achieve the purpose for which it was established.

ACKNOWLEDGMENTS

A special debt is owed to Professor J. Stephen Ferris, Co-Director of the Centre for Monetary and Financial Economics, Carleton University, for help generously supplied to the author in formulating the arguments, and especially for suggesting the references. Also, Professor T.K. Rymes, Distinguished Research Professor, Department of Economics, Carleton University, offered many insights during a discussion of an early draft of this paper.

DISCUSSION QUESTIONS

1. Why cannot the conduct of monetary policy be left to the discretion of a private, for-profit financial institution established for that purpose?
2. What do you think is the strongest argument in favour of central-bank independence? Why?
3. Should a central bank be free to dictate what the overall objective for monetary policy should be? Give reasons for your answer.
4. Why should the conduct of monetary policy not be left in the hands of a regular government department?

SUGGESTED READINGS

Aisen, A., and F.J. Veiga. 2008. Political instability and inflation volatility. *Public Choice* 135 (3–4): 207–223.

Chari, V.V., and P.J. Kehoe. 2006. Modern macroeconomics in practice: How theory is shaping policy. *Journal of Economic Perspectives* 20 (4): 3–28.

Crowe, C., and E.E. Meade. 2007. The evolution of central bank governance around the world. *Journal of Economic Perspectives* 21 (4): 69–90.

Ferris, J. Stephen. 2008. Electoral politics and monetary policy: Does the Bank of Canada contribute to a political business cycle? *Public Choice* 135 (3–4): 449–468.

Krause, S., and F. Mendez. 2008. Institutions, arrangements and preferences for inflation stability: Evidence and lessons from a panel data analysis. *Journal of Macroeconomics* 30 (1): 282–307.

ONLINE RESOURCES

Bank of Canada: http://www.bankofcanada.ca.
Bank of England: http://www.bankofengland.co.uk.
Federal Reserve Education: http://www.federalreserveeducation.org.

Governance and Confidence Instead of Independence and Credibility

Edwin Le Héron

> Fundamentally, there can be no such thing as an independent central bank. For the central bank to perform well, it needs to be backed by and backed up by an effective fiscal authority—the sovereign. In this relationship, the central bank is, inevitably, the junior partner.
>
> *Willem Buiter, Bank of England (2005, C1)*

Introduction

In a relatively short period of time, central banks have become the fundamental institutions of our economies. Most central banks were created at the beginning of the 20th century, and some became independent vis-à-vis the state during the 1990s. For instance, in 1998 the European Union (EU) created the most independent central bank in history. While monetary policy was previously a prerogative of the state, it is now delegated to a monetary policy committee composed of experts and central bankers. From a historical standpoint, determining the rationale behind this wave of independence is a challenging task, but the reasons for it seem to be primarily ideological. After undermining Keynesian economics, market fundamentalism (liberalism) sought to remove the instruments of economic policy from the state in the 1980s. Within this framework, economic policy is considered ineffective. Income distribution is merely driven by the market, while balanced public budgets are the rule and monetary policy is entrusted to the newly created independent central banks. As we shall see, this independence can assume very different institutional forms.

How Can the New Independence of Central Banks Be Justified?

The "Rule Versus Discretion" Debate

During the 1970s a debate erupted over the fundamental question of whether governments should intervene in the economy, especially with regard to the implementation of monetary policy. Keynesian economists generally favoured government intervention through discretionary monetary policy, while strong pro-market economists (referred to at the time as "monetarists") advocated policy rules that would place central-bank policy on some sort of automatic pilot. In the debate between the monetarist "rule" versus Keynesian "discretion," the issue of central-bank independence did not arise until 1985. Indeed, Keynesians argued that money operates through credit, with interest rates determining output and employment. They viewed monetary policy as one component of economic policy, along with its four objectives: price stability, full employment, balanced trade, and growth. The central bank, according to Keynesians, merely enforces monetary policy as the outcome of a discretionary government policy decision.

Rejecting Keynesian economics, during the 1970s Milton Friedman proposed a policy framework known as "monetarism," which incorporates the neoclassical general equilibrium theory of markets determined by natural laws. In sharp contrast with the Keynesian view, Friedman thought that money had no influence on this equilibrium—and, more particularly, on output and unemployment—in the long run. There is a non-accelerating inflation rate of unemployment (NAIRU), or a "natural rate of unemployment," that acts as a floor in the long term. Therefore, Keynesian policies would only be effective in the short run and would be inflationary in the long run. According to Friedman, inflation is everywhere a monetary phenomenon resulting from an excessive money supply. What is needed is an unconditional *rule* that is deduced from the long-run equilibrium properties of the economy: the money supply should grow at a constant rate equal to the natural growth rate of real production so as to ensure price stability. Monetarism assumes that market forces naturally lead to this long-term equilibrium on the basis of what is believed to be the "true model" of the economy.

The "Credibility Versus Confidence" Debate

The "rule versus discretion" debate is somewhat passé and no longer relevant. In its place, debate over "credibility versus confidence" appears to be much more pertinent and useful as far as understanding the independence of today's central banks. The credibility framework belongs to "new" classical economics (NCE), which was developed in the 1980s with the aim of dismissing Keynesian discretionary practices irreversibly. The objective of new classical economists was to go beyond monetarism, the implementation of which proved impossible after 1982 due, *inter alia*, to the instability in the measure of the money supply. While NCE continues to accept the framework of an economy wherein markets clear automatically and core inflation remains a monetary phenomenon, it also introduced the idea of short-term unanticipated inflation as a consequence of a government's discretionary policy.

Monetarists believe that if the growth of the quantity of money is consistent with the long-term potential growth of output, this will be sufficient to prevent core inflation. However, to prevent any short-term unanticipated inflation, policy needs to be credible. To ensure credibility, monetary policy must be entrusted to an independent central bank that can pursue long-term objectives—not to political authorities.

The theory of credibility was criticized by "new" Keynesian economists (NKE) and by many central bankers, both of whom shifted from this theory to the theory or question of confidence. For NKE, there is uncertainty regarding the "true" model of the economy. There are also unforeseen economic shocks, and for these reasons it is impossible to apply an inviolable rule. Therefore, instead of rejecting the possibility of central-bank independence completely, NKE propose to amend the concept in order to develop a mode of governance that would reconcile the central bank with the political authorities. The aim is an enhanced cooperation between these two powers and an improved management of conflicts between long-term and short-term objectives. From the question of credibility, based on strict compliance with a rule, we will move to the issue of confidence among agents, for whom the flexibility of monetary policy becomes a key issue. Ben Bernanke (the governor of the US Federal Reserve at the time of writing, in 2009) calls it "constraint discretion." Confidence helps anchor inflation expectations on the inflation target of the central bank and hence avoid short-term unanticipated inflation. This process justifies the independence of central banks in the 1990s, and explains the different types of independence.

THE THEORETICAL FOUNDATIONS OF INDEPENDENCE: THE THEORY OF CREDIBILITY

The credibility literature usually starts with a model of the economy that was originally proposed in the 1970s. This model argues that politicians are encouraged to use monetary policy to reduce unemployment in order to increase their chances of re-election, even if they are later compelled to adopt a restrictive or recessionary policy. Policy-makers are seeking a trade-off between inflation and unemployment in order to satisfy their political interests. This *time inconsistency* of economic policies leads to an *inflationary bias*, or an average inflation rate that is higher than its long-term trend. Because firms and households are perfectly rational and cannot be permanently making expectations errors—and therefore cannot be made to increase their activity—they modify their price expectations, thereby cancelling out the effects on production. However, the anticipated inflation is nevertheless generated. Inflation expectations explain current inflation, and the credibility of central banks depends on their ability to enforce a rule for fighting inflation.

In the 1980s some economists believed that politicians could compel the central bank to change the rule. They introduced the idea of *reputation* into monetary policy, a notion that was supposed to be capable of anchoring inflation expectations better than a rule. Monetary policy must always be defined with a fixed long-term perspective and must avoid surprise effects in order to suppress short-term inflation. Because it prevents politicians from using discretionary monetary policy, central-bank independence is presented as the best institutional design for credible commitment to price stability. To achieve this, it is suggested that the government should delegate monetary policy to a conservative central banker who attaches more importance to price stability than to public opinion. Credibility should act on inflation expectations, which adjust immediately to lower inflation produced by independence. Disinflation would thus come as a "free lunch."

Let us summarize the credibility strategy. There is a natural model of the economy, which determines a single long-term equilibrium. Compliance with this model follows a monetary policy rule that is clearly announced by the central bank, which commits to enforcing it at any cost. A strong institutional independence is entrusted to the central bank to ensure credibility in the long-term commitment to price stability. The bank must demonstrate full transparency, showing its respect for the long-term equilibrium. A central bank is credible if people believe that it will do what it says. Economic agents believe that the central bank will follow the same rule regardless of economic conditions, thus eliminating short-term unanticipated inflation.

CRITICAL APPRAISALS OF THE CREDIBILITY FRAMEWORK: CONFIDENCE

The first criticism of this established view pertains to the highly questionable assumptions of the mainstream theory of credibility. For one thing, no inflation bias has ever been found. Moreover, if agents are rational, why do they vote for policies that they know are wrong? How can one explain that politicians want to adopt expansionary monetary policy for economic growth when NCE assumes it has no effects? Would central bankers be better economists than any finance minister? Why do politicians accept the independence of central banks if they needed to control them in order to get re-elected? If politicians are convinced by the arguments of inflation bias, it is simpler and as credible if they change their behaviour. What would guarantee the competence of central bankers?

The second criticism has to do with independence, which implies a democratic deficit. The less theorists are inclined to believe in some natural economic equilibrium, the more they tend to link "credibility" to the institutional design of the central bank. But the drawback of the proposed solution of a *conservative central banker* is that it suffers from a problem of transparency and a lack of democratic legitimacy. In whose name could a conservative central banker express preferences that differ from those of society? Moreover, with the independence of central banks, monetary and fiscal policies are separated and the increasingly difficult coordination implies some macroeconomic costs. In the credibility literature, a central bank dominates and imposes its viewpoint on the treasury (the

Department of Finance), claiming fiscal orthodoxy (balanced budgets), as in the EU with the Stability and Growth Pact. In the real world, however, the treasury always makes the final decision.

If there is no transmission channel from monetary policy to output growth but only to inflation, then monetary policy, it is argued, may be entrusted to "technicians" and removed from the control of the political authorities without any democratic gap. But this is not the case. Who can seriously argue today that monetary policy should focus only on inflation and not on financial supervision and economic stimulus? Since money affects the real economy, it must remain under the ultimate control of the government. Studies show that there is a cost in terms of growth when inflation is the sole target. In reality, all central banks are concerned with growth, even when they focus on price stability. Popular central-bank reaction functions that seek to model the behaviour of central banks—such as the Taylor rule—use inflation as well as output as key determinants. There exists a large gap between the pragmatism of central banks and the theories that have been used to justify the need for their independence. A government of judges cannot decide on such an important policy for citizens—rather, the decision must be made through representative democracy. Ironically, even Friedman (1992, back cover) was often quoted as saying that "money is much too serious a matter to be left to central bankers." He believed that independence gives too much importance to the personality of the governor, whose view is exaggerated, particularly by financial markets.

The third criticism relates to uncertainty, which is *the* fundamental problem of monetary policy. This criticism focuses on uncertainty in four areas: future events, the proper theory, the behaviour of agents, and the right decision.

1. Future events are unknown, and cannot be inferred from past events. In a constantly changing world, monetary policy should always be forward-looking in order to anticipate potential shocks.

2. There is no "true" model of the economy in the long run because conditions are always changing and our expectations determine what will happen in the future. We must always be willing to adopt a different model as necessary. Flexibility is more important than credibility. How can the "long-run equilibrium" position of an economy be known or determined? Keynesians do not believe that the long run is predetermined, but that it is rather a succession of temporally connected, short-period positions—and is therefore not independent of the actual time path that an economy follows. When agents make decisions during each period based on optimistic expectations, long-term growth is higher than it would be if these decisions were made with pessimistic expectations. John Maynard Keynes pointed

to the importance of self-fulfilling prophecies. Variables corresponding to long-run equilibrium cannot be determined *a priori*, regardless of how economic agents formulate their expectations. Since these variables cannot be known, it is impossible to stabilize the economy with rules formulated on the basis of these "natural" trends.

3. Without a "true" model, we must build a common understanding so that the agents can perceive reality through the "eyes" of the central bank. It is indeed a learning process. If agents adopt the central-bank view, the latter will prevail. As former chief economist of the European Central Bank Otmar Issing argued (2000, 338): "Credibility is literally defined as the ability to have one's statements accepted as factual or one's motives as the true ones." Without the confidence of the population, the central bank is ill defined. It must take into account the concerns of the economic agents.

4. The same rules do not always apply over time. Rules can be found *ex post* rather than be established for all occasions *ex ante*.

Given the above, a high accountability of the central bank must be the counterpart of its independence. The government should define the mandate whereby it assesses the central bank. Authorities must be able to question the bank's assessment of a particular situation, its strategy, and its results, and be able to apply penalties in case of failure. Accountability is a prerequisite for confidence and for the democratic legitimacy of monetary policy. Although the definition of the mandate and the possible sanctions entailed by accountability may be strong limitations as far as the independence of the central bank, they are essential in a democracy.

The ideas of economists per se are seldom decisive, but they usually justify a popular ideology or serve specific historical circumstances. The independence of central banks fits well into this analysis. Its basic theoretical assumptions are not confirmed by facts, and are now being questioned. However, since the 1980s, the new liberal ideology wished to withdraw the instruments of state policy in order to neutralize the economic policies of the government. Independence is now an integral part of the political culture; the search for a rationale for it has disappeared.

The Main Oppositions

The *credibility strategy* can be depicted in simplified form as follows:

"True" model of general equilibrium → Rule → Independence → Commitment → Transparency → Credibility

Critics of credibility show that it is better to develop a *confidence strategy*, which can be depicted thus:

Communication → Common understanding → Governance → Accountability → Confidence

According to the confidence strategy, rather than *independence,* good *governance* is needed; rather than *responsibility* for inflation, there should be *accountability* for government objectives; rather than the *common knowledge* of the "true" model, we need a *common understanding* of expectations of the different agents; and rather than full independence, the central bank must demonstrate its openness, as well as a sophisticated policy strategy.

The Different Types of Independence

Four characteristics define independence in institutional terms: the mandate, the monetary policy committee (MPC), the coordination of economic policies, and accountability. At least two models emerge: "full independence" and "instrumental independence," which emphasizes governance.

In the full independence model, the MPC determines and implements monetary policy without any real coordination with the government and without any control from the political authorities. With governance, the political authority merely delegates monetary policy and its instruments to the central bank while continuing to define and monitor the objectives; it also maintains the ability to resume authority under exceptional circumstances or to sanction the central banker. While the European Central Bank (ECB) is an example of the first model, most other central banks represent the second one and seek to live up to the challenge of being democratic and independent institutions.

The Federal Reserve Bank (the central bank of the United States, known as the "Fed") has not undergone any evolution since 1990. Although the Fed was largely more independent than average in the previous era, at the time of writing (2009) it is one of the least independent central banks while retaining its effectiveness and reputation. Whereas the ECB is a creature of central bankers, the Fed is a creature of Congress. The mandate of the ECB is enshrined in statutes that are very difficult to change. Indeed, modifying them requires a vote by the Council of Europe and a unanimous ratification of the 27 parliaments of the EU. This is a long and complex procedure.

In the United States, a vote by Congress can affect the mandate and replace the governor "overnight." While the ECB's mandate requires it to pursue price stability as a primary objective, the ECB itself was free to set the target, which it set at 2 percent in 1998. In the United States, the Fed's mandate is determined by Congress. Its current mandate (Humphrey-Hawkins 1978) is a dual mandate: it seeks to achieve both price stability and full employment. In Canada, the target of inflation is decided by the government for a period of five years after an extensive debate, thereby granting a democratic legitimacy. In 2006, the last debate fixed the target of 2 percent (2006–2011).

In the European Economic and Monetary Union (EMU), the MPC sets the monetary policy strategy. It seeks to reduce uncertainty about the economy by consulting various experts. The central bankers (who account for 15 of the 21 committee members) control the MPC of the ECB. In the case of the Bank of England, the economic reports are communicated in advance and are subject to critical analysis before the meeting of the MPC. The governor must answer to any criticisms explicitly in the official statement. Almost all independent central banks follow the US model, in which, among members, the number of outsiders (those appointed by the government) exceeds the number of insiders (those from the central bank).

The president of the United States appoints the governor of the Fed for a renewable, four-year term. Congress can revoke the appointment. However, the governor of the ECB is appointed for a non-renewable, eight-year term, and his appointment cannot be revoked. The ECB governor clearly enjoys more independence. In Canada, even though the mandate is long (seven years) and the governor is eligible for reappointment, the prime minister may exceptionally revoke the governor's appointment (article 14 of the statutes of the Bank of Canada).

The isolation of European monetary policy facing the member states of the EMU makes it difficult to coordinate the different economic policies (fiscal, income, and exchange rate). In the United States, Congress provides this coordination. With the ECB, monetary policy dominates economic policy in general. Strong accountability is necessary in order to ensure the democratic legitimacy of independent central banks, but this is something that the ECB has refused. It is not accountable to the European Parliament, to the Commission, or to the European Council. Accountability without effective sanction is neither credible nor desirable for successful democratic control. As Buiter (1999, 205) has said, we need "a European Parliament with teeth."

When central banks are accountable, governments cannot elude any problems that may arise, since the latter define the goals, manage the implementation, provide policy coordination, and may sanction central bankers. In exceptional circumstances, article 14 of the statutes of the Bank of Canada allows the government to ignore the independence of the central bank and assert control of monetary policy. The governor of the Bank of New Zealand has annual hearings at the Parliament and the appointment may be revoked if the inflation target is not reached. Congress might change the Fed mandate and ask the governor to explain his policy choice; in exceptional circumstances, Congress can revoke the governor's appointment. Rather than of independence, we must speak of governance. Independence and public accountability are not conflicting, but complementary. Accountability legitimizes independence.

Conclusion: Good Governance for Democratic Legitimacy

Independent central banks appear to be new centres of power. Many have developed a governance and coordination with the other government policies that ensures confidence and legitimacy. The Fed, the Bank of Canada, and the Bank of England are good examples. They have become political actors, maintaining a constantly evolving balance of power. In this context, the ECB seems to be stuck on the theory of credibility by insisting upon full independence.

The independence of central banks was not a necessary development, but it was consistent with ideological, historical, and economic developments of the 1980s and 1990s. However, there is a strong heterogeneity in the degree of independence and its institutional design. The devil is in the details. There is room for improvement so that confidence (which can only rest on strong accountability to political authorities) can be strengthened.

DISCUSSION QUESTIONS

1. Why has independence been requested in the name of credibility?
2. Why is confidence better than credibility for an independent central bank?
3. What features must a central bank have in order for it to be accountable?
4. What are the dangers of a fully independent central bank during an economic crisis?
5. What are the differences between the Fed and the ECB?

SUGGESTED READINGS

Le Héron, E., and P. Moutot. 2008. *Les banques centrales doivent-elles être indépendantes?* Bordeaux: Prométhée.

Mishkin, F.S. 2007. *The Economics of money, banking, and financial markets.* 7th ed. Boston: Pearson.

Siklos, P.L. 2004. *Money, banking, and financial institutions: Canada in the global environment.* 4th ed. Toronto: McGraw-Hill Ryerson.

ONLINE RESOURCES

Bank of Canada: http://www.bank-banque-canada.ca.
Bank of England: http://www.bankofengland.co.uk.
Bank for International Settlements: http://www.bis.org.
European Central Bank: http://www.ecb.int/home/html/index.en.html.
Board of Governors of the Federal Reserve System: http://www.federalreserve.gov.

REFERENCES

Buiter, W. 1999. Alice in Euroland. *Journal of Common Market Studies* 37 (2): 181–209.

Buiter, W. 2005. New developments in monetary economics: Two ghosts, two eccentricities, a fallacy, a mirage and a mythos. *Economic Journal* 115 (502): C1–C31.

Friedman, M. 1992. *Money mischief: Episodes in monetary history.* New York: Harcourt Brace Jovanovich.

Issing, O. 2000. The ECB's monetary policy: Experience after the first year. *Journal of Policy Modeling* 22 (3): 325–343.

Should Full Employment Be a Policy Objective? What Are the Implications for Growth and Development?

COMPETINGVIEWS

L. Randall Wray, "The Social and Economic Importance of Full Employment"

David Gray, "A Critique of the 'Government as the Employer of Last Resort' Policy Proposal"

Editors' Introduction

During the 1950s and 1960s, full employment, high economic growth, and reasonable price stability were all official policy goals in most Western countries. Indeed, during this so-called golden age, most industrialized countries achieved high levels of both employment and economic growth. Canada was no exception, and by the mid-1960s it was generally believed that unemployment had been largely reduced to its "frictional" level—that is, the number of individuals who are unemployed because they are temporarily "between jobs."

By the 1970s, the early postwar Keynesian concept of full employment slowly gave way to the notion of the "natural rate of unemployment" or the "non-accelerating inflation rate of unemployment" (NAIRU)—the level of unemployment that would prevent the rate of inflation from accelerating. Hence, the NAIRU became the target level of unemployment for central banks that would keep a lid on inflation. During the 1980s and 1990s, instead of the 3–4 percent unemployment rates that were consistent with full employment objectives during the 1960s, the target rate of unemployment that was consistent with a stable rate of inflation doubled, to between 6 and 8 percent. As discussed in Chapter 5, this NAIRU, however, was not a fixed anchor. It was somewhat of a wandering rate that frequently tracked the actual rate.

Heterodox economists reject the NAIRU concept, and most would argue that the older full employment goal is achievable, by means of expansionary fiscal policy and without the accompanying accelerating inflation that the NAIRU supporters fear. The contribution by L. Randall Wray articulates this policy position in support of full

217

employment, sometimes described as a fiscal policy proposal in favour of "government as the employer of last resort" (or simply "ELR").

The mainstream position maintains that an activist fiscal policy of the type promoted by the supporters of ELR would be highly destabilizing, since it would interfere directly with the operation of labour markets by altering wages and employment levels, thus undermining the efficiency of free markets and generating inflationary pressures. As David Gray argues in his contribution, the implementation of an ELR or similar program would also impose a fiscal cost on society—that is, its financing cost through taxes. Because of what is deemed to be the make-work nature of ELR jobs, this cost would have to be paid in the absence of any accompanying benefit.

Editors' note: Throughout this book, the orthodox perspective appears first in each chapter, followed by the heterodox viewpoint. However, in this chapter, because David Gray's essay is a response to the non-mainstream policies expressed by L. Randall Wray, it appears second.

The Social and Economic Importance of Full Employment

L. Randall Wray

Keynesian Theory and Full Employment Policy

Since the publication of John Maynard Keynes's *General Theory of Employment, Interest and Money* in 1936, it has been recognized that not only is unemployment a persistent feature of the capitalist economy but, what's worse, there are no endogenous market processes that would eliminate unemployment (Keynes 1964). To be sure, the classical economists had always recognized the importance of the "reserve army of the unemployed" to discipline labour, and had avoided promulgating any theory of labour market clearing. Furthermore, David Ricardo famously worried that labour-saving capital might cause ubiquitous labour redundancy, Thomas Malthus developed a (somewhat illegitimate) theory to explain the tendency of markets to face insufficient demand, and Karl Marx offered a variety of reasons to suspect that capitalism would not generate full employment with his "two departments" approach. Still, it was Keynes who provided the clearest explanation of the problem, namely, that firms produce only the quantity of output they expect to sell, and it is highly unlikely that this quantity would require full employment.

According to Keynes, even if unemployed labour bids down wages (by offering to work at lower wages), this will not induce firms to hire more labour than they need to meet expected demand for their output. It is even worse than that, however, because the existence of a preference for highly liquid assets (like money) tends to force the economy to achieve equilibrium—defined as the level of employment at which expected sales revenue is just sufficient to induce that level of production—before reaching full employment. The exact reason for this is complex and beyond the scope of this essay. What is most important to understand, for our purposes, is Keynes's main point: unemployment is *not* caused by faulty operation of the labour market (such as sticky wages, lazy workers, generous welfare benefits, or low levels of training and education). In other words, Keynes (like the classical economists Ricardo and Marx) did not see unemployment as a simple "market failure." Instead, unemployment results from insufficient effective demand, and can only be resolved by creating more jobs—which in turn requires higher demand for the output that would be generated by the additional workers. In other words,

219

unemployment is "normal"—the result of the operation of market forces—and can be resolved only through purposive social policy that is well targeted to raise aggregate demand and provide jobs for the unemployed.

In addition to unemployment, Keynes singled out excessive inequality as one of the principal faults of capitalism. Obviously, there is some link between these two faults. Since most people living in capitalist economies must work for wages as a major source of their income, the inability to obtain a job means lower income. Keynes also worried about excessive income at the top of the income distribution, which he attributed to high unearned income (what he called "rentier" income), accruing primarily to owners of financial assets. This essay will not address that issue, but instead will look in detail at unemployment and its consequences. If jobs can be provided to the unemployed, this will go a long way toward reducing inequality and poverty, although such policy will not directly address the problem of excessive income at the top of the distribution.

Many followers of Keynes have seen the solution to unemployment as various demand-stimulating policies: more government spending, lower taxes, or lower interest rates to encourage private spending (most prominently, investment). Clearly, when aggregate output is far below potential—as it was in the 1930s—raising aggregate demand is called for. The global economic downturn in 2008 caused most economists to return to Keynes's theory, as almost everyone supported fiscal stimulus policies in stagnating nations around the world. However, as an economy moves closer to full employment, it becomes far less clear that policy to raise aggregate demand should be adopted. The main objection to such policies is that, if unemployment becomes too low, inflation will result because firms will start bidding up wages to attract the more desirable workers (who will be in short supply, because most skilled workers will have already obtained jobs—although those with fewer skills and less work experience might remain unemployed). Since 1960, this fear—represented by the supposed Phillips curve trade-off, namely, that lower unemployment can only be purchased through higher inflation—has been perhaps the major barrier to achieving full employment. In fact, it has caused economists and policy-makers to resist policy that would actually achieve full employment.

Keynes was well aware of this problem. While he argued that "true inflation" occurs only when aggregate demand rises beyond the full employment level, he also argued that prices and wages could rise long before that point is reached. Indeed, he believed that a measured unemployment rate of about 5 percent might be the practical lower limit that could be achieved through aggregate demand stimulus alone. This is because bottlenecks would result in the supply of specialized labour and in the supply of some intermediate goods. Trying to push unemployment even lower would then cause inflation of the wages of skilled labour and of some output, causing overall inflation to increase. For this reason, Keynes rejected general "pump priming" (that is, general policies aimed at raising aggregate demand through a combination of tax cuts, government spending increases, and/or lower interest rates) in favour of "targeted" spending programs (Tcherneva 2008). Unfortunately, many of Keynes's followers neglected this warning, misinterpreting his ideas and believing that Keynesian policy relies solely on "pump priming."

While it is beyond the scope of this essay to go into greater detail, Keynesian policy fell out of favour during the 1970s, when stagflation (a combination of high unemployment and high inflation) afflicted many developed nations. The reason for this was simple: given the current circumstances, it appeared that Keynesian policy was no longer useful. Keynesian policy seemed to suggest that governments ought to reduce aggregate demand to fight inflation and increase it to fight unemployment. The real problem, however, was that Keynes's followers had failed to follow his theory closely enough: he neither recommended general demand pumping as the one-size-fits-all solution to unemployment, nor believed that price hikes result solely from excessive demand.

During the Great Depression of the 1930s, Keynes famously remarked that if the government could find nothing better to do, it could hire one group of workers to dig holes to bury money and then hire another group to excavate the money, which would be used to pay their wages. This might seem like a rather silly policy proposal, and Keynes meant it to be just that. What he was saying was that first, given the low levels of effective demand and the high levels of unemployment in the 1930s, virtually any paid work would be an improvement—it would provide jobs and incomes to the unemployed, raising aggregate demand and stimulating the economy. Thus, even something as seemingly useless as digging holes would be beneficial. Second, he was using such a ridiculous example to spur policy-makers to come up with more useful projects—surely even the dumbest politicians or economists could come up with something better than digging holes!

Finally, what is often overlooked is that Keynes's comments were predicated on the conditions that existed during the Great Depression, namely, massive unemployment and idled factories. Those workers burying or uncovering money would be able to earn wages and thus increase their consumption, and the factories would easily increase output to meet that extra demand. Thus, it really wasn't necessary for those newly employed workers to produce anything useful—all they needed was income to stimulate producers to use idle capacity. But such conditions do not usually exist, even in highly developed economies—and certainly not in developing economies, where unemployment can exist even with productive facilities operating with little excess capacity. In other words, outside of depressions and deep recessions, it usually would not be good policy to employ people in useless activities, because their labour would instead be needed to help provide a portion of the extra output they would buy with their new incomes. Simply paying them to do useless tasks would likely cause inflation, as their consumption would compete with that of the workers producing the goods everyone wanted.

221

Thus, what Keynes *really* advocated was targeted spending: focusing government spending on areas that are operating well below capacity, as well as directing spending toward increasing the capacity to meet social goals. Most importantly, he wanted to put unemployed labour to work—not digging holes, but in socially productive ways. This would help ensure that the additional effective demand created by government spending would not simply be exhausted in higher prices as it ran up against bottlenecks or other supply constraints. Furthermore, it would help maintain public support for the government's programs by providing useful output. Finally, it would generate respect for, and feelings of self-worth in, the workers employed in the projects (no worker would want to spend his or her days digging holes that serve no useful purpose). President Roosevelt's New Deal jobs programs (such as the Works Progress Administration and the Civilian Conservation Corps) are good examples of such targeted job-creating programs. These provided income and employment for workers; helped increase the nation's productivity; and left us with public buildings, dams, trails, and music that we still enjoy today.

Employer-of-Last-Resort or Job Guarantee Programs

Some economists, in addition to experts in other fields, have long called for a more comprehensive and sustained approach to dealing with the perennial problem of unemployment. In the "job guarantee" or "employer-of-last-resort" proposal, the government agrees to hire any workers not needed in the private sector or by existing government operations.

In a job guarantee program, the government promises to make a job available to any qualifying individual who is ready and willing to work. Requirements might include a certain age range, gender, family status, family income, educational attainment, residency, and so on. The most general program would provide a universal job guarantee, with the government promising to provide a job to anyone legally entitled to work.

Many job guarantee supporters see employment not only as an economic condition but also as a human right. Wray and Forstater (2004) justify the right to work as a fundamental prerequisite for social justice in any society in which income from work is an important determinant of access to resources. Harvey (1989) and Mitchell and Muysken (2008) argue for the right to work on the basis that it is a fundamental human (or natural) right. Such treatments find support in modern legal proclamations and statutes, such as the United Nations Universal Declaration of Human Rights or the United States *Employment Act* of 1946 and its *Full Employment and Balanced Growth Act* of 1978; other developed nations have similar laws that commit their governments to achieving full employment. Amartya Sen (1999) supports the right to work on the basis that the economic and social costs of unemployment are staggering, with far-reaching consequences beyond the single dimension of a loss of income (see also Rawls 1971).

A key proposition cited by these advocates is that no capitalist society has ever managed to operate at anything approaching true, full employment on a consistent basis. Furthermore, the burden of joblessness is borne unequally, as it is always far greater among groups that already face other disadvantages: racial and ethnic minorities, immigrants, younger and older individuals, women, people with disabilities, and those with lower educational attainment. Since markets do not operate to achieve full employment, and because they tend to leave the least advantaged members of society behind, government should—and *must*—play a role in providing jobs in an effort to achieve social justice. Proponents of a universal job guarantee program operated by the federal government argue that no other means exists to ensure that everyone who wants to work will be able to obtain a job.

There are different versions of the employer-of-last-resort (ELR) method of guaranteeing jobs. Harvey (1989) would have the government provide a public sector job to anyone unable to find work, with the pay approximating a "market wage" and more highly skilled workers receiving higher pay. In Hyman Minsky's proposal (1965)—developed further at the Center for Full Employment and Price Stability, University of Missouri at Kansas City and independently at the Centre of Full Employment and Equity, University of Newcastle, Australia—the federal government provides funding for a job creation program that would offer a uniform hourly wage with a package of benefits (Wray 1998; Mitchell and Muysken 2008). The program could provide for part-time and seasonal work, as well as for other flexible working conditions as desired by the workers. The package of benefits could include health care, child care, payment of social security taxes, and vacation time and sick leave. The wage would be set by Congress or Parliament, and a rate increase would be approved—much as the minimum wage is currently legislated in the United States.

The perceived advantage of the uniform basic wage is that it would limit competition with other employers, as workers could be attracted out of the ELR program by employers who offer to pay them a wage above the minimum wage. The most highly skilled workers would be most appealing to the private sector, and would therefore be recruited first. Since the uniform wage paid in the ELR program would be well below the market's pay for skilled workers, the latter would have a major incentive to get out of the ELR program as quickly as possible. For this reason, the ELR program would not be in competition with the private sector for any workers except those with the fewest skills and the least work experience.

Benefits of ELR programs include poverty reduction, amelioration of many social ills associated with chronic unemployment (for instance, health problems, spousal abuse and family breakup, drug abuse, and crime), and enhanced skills in the general pool of workers as a result of workers gaining on-the-job experience.

Forstater (1999) has emphasized how ELR can be used to increase economic flexibility and enhance the environment (for instance, if workers take part in cleanup and other activities, such as retrofitting buildings to make them more energy efficient). The program would improve working conditions in the private sector—since employees would have the option of moving into the ELR program, private sector employers would have to offer a wage and benefit package at least as good as that offered by the ELR program. The informal sector would shrink as workers became integrated into formal employment, thereby gaining access to protection provided by labour laws. In addition, there would be some reduction in racial and gender discrimination, because unfairly treated workers would have the ELR option; while ELR by itself cannot end discrimination, it has long been recognized that full employment is an important tool in the fight for equality (Darity 1999).

Finally, some supporters emphasize that an ELR program with a uniform basic wage also helps promote economic and price stability. ELR will act as an automatic stabilizer, as employment in the program will grow in times of recession and shrink in times of economic expansion, counteracting private sector employment fluctuations. The federal government budget will become more counter-cyclical, because its spending on the ELR program will likewise grow in recession and fall in expansion. Furthermore, the uniform basic wage will reduce both inflationary pressure in a boom and deflationary pressure in a bust. In a boom, private employers can recruit from the ELR pool of workers, paying a markup over the ELR wage. The ELR pool acts like a "reserve army" of the employed, dampening wage pressures as private employment grows. In recession, workers downsized by private employers can work at the ELR wage, which puts a floor to how low wages and income can go.

Critics argue that a job guarantee would be inflationary, using some version of a Phillips curve argument—according to which lower unemployment necessarily means higher inflation—to support their theory (Sawyer 2003). Some argue that ELR would reduce the incentive to work and would raise private sector costs because of increased shirking, since workers would no longer fear job loss. Workers would also be emboldened to ask for greater wage increases. Other arguments against ELR programs include the belief that an ELR program would be so big that it would be impossible to manage, that it would be impossible to find useful things for ELR workers to do, and that it would be difficult to discipline ELR workers; still others fear corruption. In addition, it has been argued that a national job guarantee would be too expensive, causing the budget deficit to grow on an unsustainable path (Aspromourgos 2000; King 2001).

Proponents of ELR programs have argued that these critics do not understand the proposal. (See Mitchell and Wray 2005 for responses to these critiques.) First, the critics do not see the difference between general demand pumping (which can be inflationary even before full employment is reached) and targeted spending (that is, hiring only the unemployed that the private sector does not want to hire). Second, they do not understand that putting in place a wage floor (the ELR wage) only prevents wages from falling, but cannot cause private sector wages to rise. Third, they do not recognize the counter-cyclical nature of the government's spending on the program, which automatically stabilizes the economy (as ELR spending rises in recession and falls in expansion). Finally, they do not understand that a sovereign government can always financially afford to buy anything offered for sale—a topic we will explore later in this essay.

There have been many job creation programs implemented around the world, some narrowly targeted and others more broadly based. The American New Deal included several moderately inclusive programs, including the Civilian Conservation Corps and the Works Progress Administration. The New Deal employment programs created jobs for 3.6 million workers, helping to reverse the Great Depression and stimulating some private job creation (however, even these programs were too small given the severity of the depression; full recovery did not occur until spending during the Second World War brought the US economy to—and beyond—full employment). Sweden developed broad-based employment programs that virtually guaranteed access to jobs, until government began to retrench somewhat in the 1970s. Still, Sweden operates its economy very close to full employment today by providing a variety of job-creating programs at relatively high wages (Ginsburg 1983). In the aftermath of its economic crisis that came with the collapse of its currency board in 2000, Argentina created Plan Jefes y Jefas, which guaranteed a job for heads of poor households (Tcherneva and Wray 2005). The program not only successfully created 2 million new jobs that provided employment and income for poor families, but also provided needed services and free goods to poor neighbourhoods. More recently, India passed the *National Rural Employment Guarantee Act* (2005), which commits the government to providing employment in a public works project to any adult living in a rural area. The job must be provided within 15 days of registration, and must provide employment for a minimum of 100 days per year (Hirway 2006). Supporters of ELR will be closely following India's implementation of this new job guarantee program.

Is Full Employment Affordable?

One of the most vexing issues in the full employment debate surrounds the belief that, while government job creation programs might be desirable, government cannot afford them. Given the examples that exist to the contrary, this belief appears somewhat strange. Sweden, for instance, has long maintained that, because it is a small nation, it cannot afford unemployment—it needs to have its entire adult population contributing to production in order to be able to maintain high living standards. Unemployment is very costly, not only in terms of lost output but also in terms of the social ills that accompany it, including crime, family breakup, and physical and psychological health problems. Critics of government employment programs would probably agree with these observations, but would ask where the government will get the money to pay for job creation.

In this section we will briefly examine whether a sovereign government can pay for an ELR program. Here, we define a "sovereign government" as one that issues its own currency (the Canadian dollar in the case of Canada; the US dollar in the case of the United States) and that operates without a pegged exchange rate (that is, its currency is not fixed to gold or to foreign currencies). Although many people believe that a government's spending is constrained by its ability to collect taxes and sell bonds ("borrow"), this is actually not correct in the case of a sovereign government.

Supporters of ELR argue that a sovereign nation operating with its own currency in a floating-exchange-rate regime can always financially afford an ELR program (Wray 1998). As long as there are workers who are ready and willing to work at the program wage, the government can "afford" to hire them; it pays wages by issuing cheques or by directly crediting workers' bank accounts. By doing so, it simultaneously credits the reserves of the workers' banks. A sovereign government taxes by debiting taxpayers' bank accounts (either directly, when taxes are paid "online," or after receiving bank cheques written by taxpayers) and by debiting reserves of the taxpayers' banks. If government credits more accounts than it debits through tax payments, a deficit results—meaning that workers and taxpayers have net credits to their deposit accounts. Similarly, there will be net credits to the banking system, held as bank reserves. If the reserve holdings are excessive, banks bid the overnight rate down. The government can then choose either to let the overnight rate fall to its support rate or to sell interest-paying bonds at the desired support rate; this will drain excess reserves. In no sense, then, is the government spending on ELR constrained by tax revenues or the demand for its bonds.

Spending on the ELR program will not grow without limit, either. As discussed above, the size of the ELR pool of workers will fluctuate with the cycle, automatically shrinking when the private sector grows. In recession, workers shed by the private sector will find ELR jobs, increasing government spending and thereby stimulating the private sector so that it will begin to hire out of the ELR pool. Estimates by Harvey (1989) and Wray (1998) put net spending by the government on a universal ELR program at well under 1 percent of GDP for the United States; Argentina's Jefes program peaked with gross spending at 1 percent of GDP—a figure that undoubtedly overstates net spending because, in the absence of the Jefes program, government would have had to provide more spending on other anti-poverty programs.

One of the fundamental flaws of capitalism is that it is unable to generate enough jobs for everyone who wants to work. For this reason, it is the government's responsibility to supplement private job creation with direct employment programs. The employer-of-last-resort proposal provides a novel approach to ensure that there is always a job available for anyone who wants to work but is unable to find employment in the private sector.

DISCUSSION QUESTIONS

1. According to Keynes, why don't capitalist economies generate full employment?
2. According to Keynes, why won't flexible wages eliminate unemployment?
3. What is the difference between general "demand pumping" and targeted spending programs?
4. Is the use of unemployment to fight inflation consistent with the United Nations Universal Declaration of Human Rights? Explain.
5. According to proponents, what are the advantages of paying uniform wages in an ELR program?
6. How can an ELR program provide for full employment with stable wages and prices?
7. What kinds of tasks would ELR workers perform?
8. What are the private and social costs of unemployment? What are the private and social benefits of work?
9. Explain the impacts of an ELR program on a government's budget. Can governments afford ELR programs? Explain.

SUGGESTED READINGS

Harvey, P. 1989. *Securing the right to employment: Social welfare policy and the unemployed in the United States.* Princeton, NJ: Princeton University Press.

Mitchell, William, and Joan Muysken. 2008. *Full employment abandoned: Shifting sands and policy failures.* Cheltenham: Edward Elgar.

Wray, L.R. 1998. *Understanding modern money: The key to full employment and price stability.* Cheltenham: Edward Elgar.

Wray, L.R., and Forstater, M. 2004. Full employment and economic justice. In *The institutionalist tradition in labor economics,* ed. D. Champlin and J. Knoedler, 253–272. Armonk, NY: M.E. Sharpe.

ONLINE RESOURCES

Center for Full Employment and Price Stability (a non-partisan, non-profit policy institute at the University of Missouri at Kansas City): http://www.cfeps.org.

Centre of Full Employment and Equity (a non-partisan public policy research institution that promotes full employment and equity): http://e1.newcastle.edu.au/coffee.

Economists for Full Employment (a group of economists working toward building a global network to promote full employment policy): http://www.economistsforfullemployment.org.

The Levy Economics Institute of Bard College (a non-profit, non-partisan public policy research institution): http://www.levy.org.

REFERENCES

Aspromourgos, T. 2000. Is an employer-of-last-resort policy sustainable? A review article. *Review of Political Economy* 12 (2): 141–155.

Darity, William Jr. 1999. Who loses from unemployment? *Journal of Economic Issues* 33 (2): 491–496.

Forstater, Mathew. 1999. Full employment and economic flexibility. *Economic and Labour Relations Review* 11: 69–88.

Ginsburg, Helen. 1983. *Full employment and public policy: The United States and Sweden.* Lexington, MA: Lexington Books.

Harvey, P. 1989. *Securing the right to employment: Social welfare policy and the unemployed in the United States.* Princeton, NJ: Princeton University Press.

Hirway, Indira. 2006. Enhancing livelihood security through the *National Employment Guarantee Act*: Toward effective implementation of the Act. Levy Economics Institute Working Paper 437.

Keynes, J.M. 1964. *The general theory of employment, interest, and money.* New York and London: Harcourt Brace. First published 1936 by Macmillan.

King, J.E. 2001. The last resort? Some critical reflections on ELR. *Journal of Economic and Social Policy* 5 (2): 72–76.

Minsky, H.P. 1965. The role of employment policy. In *Poverty in America*, ed. M.S. Gordon, 175–200. San Francisco: Chandler.

Mitchell, William, and Joan Muysken. 2008. *Full employment abandoned: Shifting sands and policy failures.* Cheltenham: Edward Elgar.

Mitchell, W.F., and L.R. Wray. 2005. In defense of employer of last resort: A response to Malcolm Sawyer. *Journal of Economic Issues* 39 (1): 235–245.

Rawls, J. 1971. *Theory of justice.* Cambridge, MA: Harvard University Press.

Sawyer, M. 2003. Employer of last resort: Could it deliver full employment and price stability? *Journal of Economic Issues* 37 (4): 881–908.

Sen, A. 1999. *Development as freedom.* New York: Alfred A. Knopf.

Tcherneva, Pavlina. 2008. Keynes's approach to full employment: Aggregate or targeted demand? Levy Economics Institute Working Paper 542.

Tcherneva, Pavlina, and L. Randall Wray. 2005. Gender and the job guarantee: The impact of Argentina's *Jefes* program on female heads of poor households. Center for Full Employment and Price Stability Working Paper 50. http://www.cfeps.org/pubs/wp-pdf/WP50-Tcherneva-Wray.pdf.

Wray, L.R. 1998. *Understanding modern money: The key to full employment and price stability.* Cheltenham: Edward Elgar.

Wray, L.R., and M. Forstater. 2004. Full employment and economic justice. In *The institutionalist tradition in labor economics*, ed. D. Champlin and J. Knoedler, 253–272. Armonk, NY: M.E. Sharpe.

A Critique of the "Government as the Employer of Last Resort" Policy Proposal

David Gray

Introduction

As stated by Mario Seccareccia (2004, 15–16), an editor of and contributor to this volume:

> A group of economists of post-Keynesian persuasion have quite boldly reaffirmed their commitment to full employment and have argued that full employment is not only socially desirable as a policy goal but also technically achievable via public spending without the accompanying runaway inflation that mainstream economists normally assume with this state … [T]his view has come to be described as "government as the employer of last resort" policy proposal. And, as the name suggests, it commits the state to hiring anyone able and willing to work at a given money wage, thereby effectively eradicating involuntary unemployment.

In this essay, I rely on my perspective as one of the "mainstream economists" to outline the economic case against the employer-of-last-resort (ELR) policy proposal, which has not been implemented in very many (if any) developed economies in recent decades. Nonetheless, I certainly do not hold a rigid monetarist view that all but minimal inflation must be purged from the economy even at the cost of high unemployment. Indeed, I share not only the view that full employment—which, albeit a somewhat subjective figure—is socially and economically desirable, but also the view that it can be achieved by other policy approaches without igniting an inflationary spiral. I do not dwell here on the conventional critique that is directed toward stimulative macroeconomic policies, namely, the non-accelerating inflation rate of unemployment (NAIRU) or the natural-rate-of-unemployment school. According to that perspective, it is a useless and counterproductive exercise to attempt to reduce unemployment below a certain level—the so-called natural rate (which is indeed a subjective, unknown quantity)—as the macroeconomy then encounters insurmountable supply-side constraints and consequently overheats.

I argue that the implementation of an ELR policy apparatus is unnecessary and unwarranted during the expansion phase of the business cycle. In that macroeconomic climate, the most appropriate labour market policies involve measures aimed at improving the flexibility and the efficiency of labour markets—that is, measures that address structural unemployment. In contrast to that scenario, when the nature of unemployment is cyclical or aggregate demand-deficient in nature, conventional, Keynesian, stimulative fiscal and monetary policies can and should be implemented to boost employment and reduce unemployment. In that particular climate, this type of intervention—which is sometimes labelled "stabilization policy"—should have the same impact as the ELR but would be invoked only during times of severe labour market weakness, as occurred in 2009.

The first part of this essay summarizes the recent history of the labour market in Canada, with a focus on the relationship between the business cycle and the aggregate unemployment rate. Following economic downturns in the form of contracting GDP, the official unemployment rate is stubbornly and persistently high, and takes years to return to its pre-recession level. Although on the face of it, this phenomenon does indeed strengthen the case for some kind of labour market intervention to restore labour market conditions to their peak levels more quickly, there does not appear to have been a secular trend toward higher unemployment since the mid-1970s. I also argue that there have been times, in the absence of ELR, when full employment has been reached in the Canadian labour market. In the second part of this essay, I explain in more detail why ELR policies are unsuitable in my view. These arguments hinge in part on the point of moral hazard, which has the effect of undermining the functionality and the efficiency of labour markets. In the third part of this essay, I outline my views on the appropriate mix and application of structural reforms of the labour market (which operate at the microfoundations of the global labour market) coupled with suggested monetary and fiscal policies (which operate at the macroeconomic level).

Recent Patterns of Unemployment in Canada

This survey of recent macroeconomic history commences in 1976, just as the economies of Canada and the United States were emerging from a brief but sharp decline in economic activity in 1975. It runs through 2008, which corresponds to the advent of the recession (at least as it is understood at the time of writing, in early 2009). Figure 1 shows the path of real GDP expressed as levels (in constant 2002 dollars), which is the most widely used indicator for economic activity. This variable (real GDP) has been adjusted for inflation, so it reflects the volume of aggregate output. I have fitted a trend line through the real GDP series, which shows a strong upward trend over the period. This is indicative of an economy whose potential—as well as actual—GDP levels are growing. During the recessions of the early 1980s and early 1990s, we see that actual GDP dips well below trend, but during most of this period the deviations from the trend line are not remarkable. It does appear that the level of real GDP was slightly above trend from

FIGURE 1 Level of Real GDP and Trend

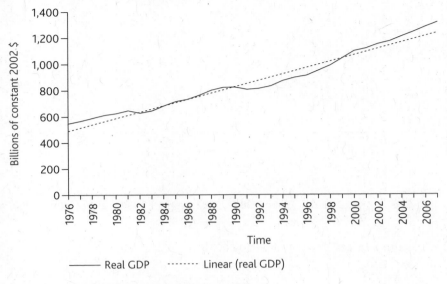

Source: Statistics Canada, CANSIM table 380-0002.

2000 to 2006. According to standard macroeconomic theory, one might expect such an outcome to be associated with rising inflation, as the economy might "overheat," but overall inflation was low during this period. It is now apparent that, although overall price inflation was well under control during this period, very economically dangerous bubbles were emerging for real estate prices in the United States and elsewhere. This type of "economic overheating" was a major cause of the harsh recession in 2008 and 2009.

As far as unemployment and the relationship between unemployment and real GDP are concerned, it is far more instructive to examine the path of the *change* in real GDP as opposed to the *level* of GDP. The former is displayed in Figure 2, which shows annual rates of growth of real GDP at a quarterly frequency. Geometrically this is interpreted as the slope of the real GDP series. It is apparent that the growth in economic output is nearly always positive, yet fluctuates greatly. Pay no attention to the slope of this series; what is significant is whether it lies above or below the horizontal axis. When the series dips below the horizontal axis into negative territory, as in 1982 and 1991, the economy is in a recession. As we will see, it is during these periods that unemployment skyrockets. The typical value for growth in real GDP from 1976 to 2007, as shown in Figure 2, is about 2.5 percent per year, which is considered moderate economic growth. Around 1985, 1994, and 2000, the economy was booming, with annual growth rates reaching 6 percent

FIGURE 2   Changes in Real GDP in Canada

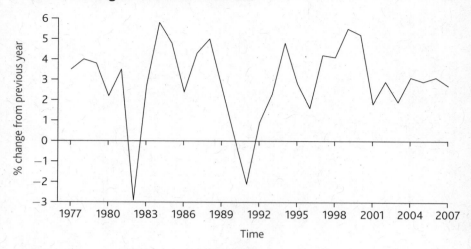

Source: Statistics Canada, CANSIM table 380-0002.

during certain quarters. According to conventional macroeconomic theory, it is in these conditions that one might expect inflation to rise, but that only occurred in the mid-1980s.

Figure 3 illustrates the unemployment rate in the years from 1976 to 2008. A huge spike in unemployment is apparent during the recession of the early 1980s and during that of the early 1990s. Although there was also a slight uptick following a slowdown in real GDP growth in 2001, unemployment subsequently declined to 5.8 percent in early 2008—the lowest unemployment rate since the early 1970s. There is also an encouraging, marked downward trend in the unemployment rate over this 32-year period, which in my view is reflective of a substantial improvement in the efficiency of the labour market.

As observed by Pierre Fortin in his essay in this volume (see Chapter 5), after a long climb in the years following the Second World War, there is a fairly marked, secular trend toward lower unemployment rates between 1976 and 2008. Secondly, there is a relatively tight, inverse relationship between economic growth in the output market and the unemployment rate. Indeed, when recessions commence and economic growth turns negative, unemployment spikes drastically. Thirdly, the relation between the unemployment rate and the growth rate of real GDP is quite asymmetrical. While unemployment is very sensitive to changes in real GDP when the economy is contracting, it is much less sensitive (working in the opposite direction) when the economy is expanding. For instance, a harsh recession began late in 1981. The level of real GDP recovered by late 1983, but the unemployment rate did not return to pre-recession levels until 1989! Another deep recession began

FIGURE 3   Unemployment Rate in Canada, 1976–2008

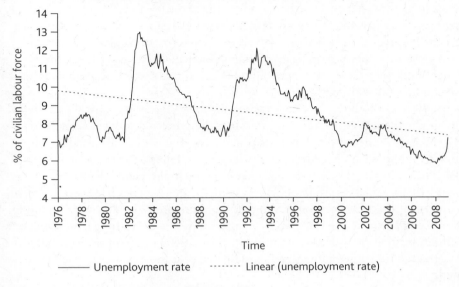

Source: Statistics Canada, CANSIM table 282-0001.

in late 1990. The level of real GDP recovered by late 1993, but the unemployment rate did not reach pre-recession levels until 1999! Unemployment generated by a recession is remarkably persistent and resilient.

Possible Explanations for the Persistence of Unemployment in the Face of Recovery in the Output Market

In the previous section, one observes a strong pattern of asymmetry that poses a challenge for policy-makers: unemployment rises sharply at the slightest provocation in the form of a downturn in real GDP, but is extremely reluctant to decline in response to an upturn in real GDP. The rate of unemployment does eventually reach its pre-recession peak, but the adjustment period required to close what is sometimes called a "recessionary gap" is very long. One would expect cyclical unemployment induced by a recession to dissipate in conjunction with a rebound in the output market, but such is not the historical experience. One view that was somewhat prevalent in the 1990s was that unemployment was subject to a "hysteresis" effect: once the labour market is hit by a recession in the market and cyclical unemployment emerges, there is also an increase in the structural rate of unemployment such that it becomes more difficult to reduce the actual rate of unemployment without triggering a substantial increase in inflation. A hysteresis pattern is sometimes likened to a "ratchet effect," whereby every tug at the lever on the way up (caused by a rise in cyclical unemployment) only partially reverses itself on the way down. An analogy would be only one step backward (in terms of employment gains) for every two steps forward (in terms of unemployment). Essentially, the natural rate of unemployment rises in the medium term, but this rise is not permanent (see Benjamin et al. 2007, 579–583).

Although the hysteresis story is consistent with the asymmetrical pattern for unemployment over the business cycle, most labour economists in Canada today (2009) believe that the level of structural unemployment in the Canadian labour market is approaching historically low levels—and may be as low as it was in the late 1960s. This implies that the natural rate of unemployment is lower than it was in the 1980s, which in turn implies that unemployment can reach low levels relative to those of the 1980s without setting off high inflation. The downward trend in the unemployment rate is shown in Figure 3; the extremely strong labour market conditions that prevailed in the mid-2000s in an environment of price stability suggest that low unemployment is sustainable over most phases of the business cycle.

There are other reasons to believe that structural unemployment in the Canadian labour market is lower now than it has been in recent decades (the 1980s and 1990s). The usual suspects believed to contribute to persistently high unemployment (even during the expansion phase of the business cycle) in much of continental Europe are not part of the landscape of the Canadian labour market—with one exception. The following factors are alleged to be associated with high unemployment in European labour markets: (a) employment protection regulations that strictly regulate the firing and the laying off of workers, (b) unduly high minimum wages, (c) rigid, monopolized, and highly regulated product markets, (d) rigid pay structures that make it difficult to adjust wages in response to market pressures, (e) very high payroll taxes, and (f) social insurance programs, most notably unemployment insurance (OECD 1994). All of these institutional features of European labour markets share a common theme: they serve to render the labour market inflexible and rigid, or "ossified," in the words of some. The allegation is that these rigidities gum up labour markets, making them less efficient and slow to adjust to changes in market conditions and to shocks emanating from numerous sources. As a result, the unemployment rate is higher than it would otherwise be, in good times as well as in bad times.

The precise mechanisms through which these rigidities have deleterious effects on the labour market are not the focus of this essay. What is relevant is that the Canadian labour market is a highly dynamic, flexible one that is not much affected by any of the factors that are alleged to worsen unemployment in continental

Europe, save for one—Canada's unique unemployment insurance regime, called employment insurance (EI). The majority view of Canadian labour economists is that EI serves to raise the rate of unemployment by perhaps 1 percentage point above the counterfactual level (that is, above what it would otherwise be). This adverse effect stems primarily from a provision of the program that allows for the payment of benefits to part-year, seasonal workers on an annual—and sometimes even semi-annual—basis. The unemployment insurance regimes of most countries are designed to cover the earnings losses of workers who are either temporarily or permanently laid off from their jobs on an unpredictable, unplanned, and infrequent basis. Unlike the Canadian program, these programs do not indemnify seasonal workers for predictable (almost planned), regular earnings losses during the off-season when they are unemployed. As a result of this provision in Canada's program, the incidence rate of frequent use or dependency on the unemployment insurance regime in Canada is among the highest in the world. By providing what are generally considered to be generous benefits to seasonal workers, the system provides a heavy subsidy to seasonal employment patterns, and hence generates a higher degree of seasonal unemployment than would be the case in the absence of the provision for seasonal unemployment. It is thought that a small but still significant number of workers are caught in the "EI trap," meaning that they have little ability and/or incentive either to move to a region that provides year-round employment or to take up an occupation that entails such employment. This applies despite the cut-backs in EI that were implemented in the mid-1990s. According to this view of the functioning of the Canadian EI system, geographical and occupational mobility is dampened by the EI system, which undermines the efficiency of the labour market and exacerbates overall unemployment, albeit to a small degree. Proponents of this view cite as evidence the fact that those regions of Canada with a high incidence of seasonal employment and a high generosity of EI benefits are perpetually the highest unemployment regions in Canada (Benjamin et al. 2007, 573–579).

For the most part, the Canadian labour market functions much like the "Anglo-Saxon model" that is associated with the United Kingdom, the United States, and Australia. This model is characterized by flexible wages, a high degree of labour mobility (across occupations as well as across regions), few restrictions on hiring and layoffs, and relatively low minimum wages. As mentioned above, the Canadian labour market performed quite well between 1997 and 2008, both by historical standards and by international standards. During this period, all of the indicators for the state of the labour market—the unemployment rate, the employment-to-working-age-population ratio, the labour force participation rate, and the average wage—have indicated a healthy situation, which in my view is attributable to sound fiscal and monetary policies operating at the aggregate level and to a lack of excessive regulation and intervention in the functioning of labour markets.

Possible Policy Measures to Reduce Unemployment

One policy measure that I do not favour as a remedy for unemployment is the ELR. To my knowledge, no such program exists on a large scale in any country at this time. While I do favour a very activist and often stimulative macroeconomic policy in the form of expansionary fiscal and monetary policies when the economy is operating well below its physical capacity (potential GDP), I am opposed to most interventions that will interfere directly with the operation of labour markets by altering wages and employment levels. In my view, the implementation of an ELR policy would likely occasion many undesirable, unintended, and unforeseen effects. The ELR essentially confers upon all working-age adults a universal right to *a* job. But what would the *actual* job look like? The characteristics of this job must be specified.

I turn first to the most conspicuous aspect of a job, namely, its wage. What would the wage level for ELR jobs be? The answer to this critical question has enormous consequences for both the fiscal cost of the program and its impact on the labour market. Presumably, the wage level would be "a living wage" that "the workers deserve." A "living wage," however, is a subjective concept; different individuals have different ideas regarding how much workers must earn to obtain a decent standard of living. The government would be under great political pressure to set this wage at levels that might even exceed the average going market wage for a given region or occupation. There would likely be an impetus for the jobs created within the ELR framework to serve as the norm or the standard for all jobs within a certain segment of the labour force. This would likely place upward pressure on the wages of all existing jobs that pay anywhere near the wage that is paid by the government through the ELR policy. The resultant major boost to wages would contravene any policy designed to lower unemployment.

Another important facet of the newly created job would be its geographical location. Is it incumbent upon the government to provide these jobs within a certain distance of the worker's home? In other words, does the worker have the right to demand that the job come to him or her (at a wage that he or she finds acceptable) rather than the other way around? How does the program deal with workers who reside in remote areas? Does the ELR stipulate that jobs paying "decent wages" be provided in sparsely populated areas, or would jobs be provided within a distance of x kilometres from workers? In a similar vein, one must consider the occupation and its skill and/or educational requirements. Assuming that it is feasible for jobs to be provided within the worker's geographical area, is it incumbent on the government to provide jobs that require a certain level of skill and education? Again the same question arises: is it the worker who should adapt to the job or the other way around? If a worker is overqualified for the ELR job on offer, does he or she have the right to refuse it? Is it the government's responsibility to find this worker a job that is more suitable within the same geographic area? If a worker is under-qualified for the ELR job on offer, does the government have a right to dismiss or to reclassify the worker? In summary, what are the expectations on the part of workers and on the part of the government as the employer as far as geographical, occupational, and skill-level suitability are concerned?

For major segments of the labour force—in particular, those in less attractive positions that pay less than average wages—the employer-of-last-resort policy would risk metamorphosing into an employer-of-first-resort mechanism. Some workers who do in fact have employment opportunities outside of the ELR framework might shun them and queue up for positions within the ELR framework as they open up. One might argue normatively that low-paying jobs in the private as well as the public sector ought not to exist in the first place, and that therefore it is most appropriate that workers shun them in favour of the ELR jobs paying "decent, living wages." Nonetheless, in my view the policy goal is not to eliminate jobs or to have publicly funded jobs displacing jobs in the private sector.

One way to improve the economic well-being of workers in low-wage, unenviable jobs is to reduce their tax burden. This is the objective of the earned income tax credit (EITC) program in the United States and its Canadian counterpart, the working income tax benefit (WITB). The former initiative has been deemed to be highly successful, while the Canadian program is still fairly new. Another intervention that is targeted at disadvantaged workers is the provision of training services designed to upgrade these workers' skills and improve their labour market opportunities.

Finally, there is the issue of the fiscal cost. Some of the jobs within the ELR framework will be of the make-work variety, meaning that they will be of dubious value. These jobs must be financed by tax dollars, and all taxes involve a certain degree of dead-weight loss. In less technical jargon, this means that the jobs that are created are not free; resources must be allocated and consumed in order to raise the required revenue. (As a numerical illustration, the act of raising $100 in revenues to be spent by the government requires a loss of perhaps $115 in income in the private sector.) If the fiscal cost of the ELR program exceeds projections—which is highly likely in my view—taxes would have to be raised by more than they would otherwise have to be, which would dampen employment growth. Furthermore, the costs of administering such an ambitious, sweeping, and complex program would be very high as well. These costs would be in addition to the salaries that the beneficiaries are receiving. An extensive bureaucracy would have to be developed and organized in order to govern such a program. Jobs would be created in order to ensure the administration of the program, but no net jobs would be created, as some jobs that would otherwise exist in the private sector would be displaced.

Conclusion

In summary, in my view it is not clear that the ELR intervention would lead in the long term to net job creation. One cannot simply take the stock of existing jobs for granted, thereby assuming that any job created through the ELR policy would be incremental. The labour market is not a static entity, and thus its dynamics would likely be affected by feedback effects. Like most interventions in markets that involve raising the transactions price and/or the transactions quantity beyond equilibrium levels, an ELR policy would amount to a major distortion in Canadian labour markets. The efficiency and functionality of existing labour markets would be considerably undermined. Those issues abstract from another major challenge of the ELR policy—its fiscal cost. The best strategy for maximizing employment is to avoid overregulation of the labour market; the latter has performed strongly when left to its own devices for much of the past 12 years or so (from 1997 to 2008). In the event of cyclical downturns, the conventional tools—stimulative fiscal and monetary policy—can be deployed in order to fight unemployment.

DISCUSSION QUESTIONS

1. Outline the case that a non-orthodox economist might make in favour of an ELR policy. What arguments might he or she raise?
2. Once you have made the case above, briefly discuss the essence of that economist's underlying philosophy and ideology as far as the labour market is concerned. In other words, how does the labour market tick? What is its true nature?
3. Outline the case that a neo-classical, quasi-mainstream economist might make in opposition to an ELR policy. What arguments might he or she raise?
4. Once you have made the case above, briefly discuss the essence of that economist's underlying philosophy and ideology as far as the labour market is concerned. (How does the labour market tick? What is its true nature?)
5. Discuss the types of economic policy that the neo-classical, quasi-mainstream economist might recommend to combat unemployment.
6. Assuming that one believes in the validity of the natural-rate-of-unemployment hypothesis, what are the implications as far as macroeconomic policy is concerned?

SUGGESTED READINGS AND ONLINE RESOURCES

Bowlby, Geoff. 2005. Divergence in the Canadian and US labour markets. *Canadian Public Policy* 31 (1): 83–92.

Macklem, Tiff, and Francisco Barillas. 2005. Recent developments in the Canada–US unemployment rate gap: Changing patterns in unemployment incidence and duration. *Canadian Public Policy* 31 (1): 101–108.

Organisation for Economic Co-operation and Development (OECD). 2006. *OECD employment outlook: Boosting jobs and incomes.* Paris: OECD.

Organisation for Economic Co-operation and Development (OECD). 2008. *OECD employment outlook.* Paris: OECD. http://www.oecd.org/document/46/ 0,3343,en_2649_33927_40401454_1_1_1_1,00.html (published annually; for very in-depth, cross-national, comparative studies on the recent performance of labour markets, see the introductory chapter).

Riddell, W. Craig. 2005. Why is Canada's unemployment rate persistently higher than in the United States? *Canadian Public Policy* 31 (1): 93–100.

Sharpe, Andrew. 2005. Revisiting the Canada–US unemployment rate gap: Introduction. *Canadian Public Policy* 31 (1): 79–82.

Sharpe, A., and T. Sargent. 2000. Structural aspects of unemployment in Canada: Introduction and overview. *Canadian Public Policy* 26. Suppl. no. 1. http:// qed.econ.queensu.ca/pub/cpp/July2000/Sharpe&Sargent.pdf (a discussion of structural unemployment in Canada).

Stanford, Jim. 2005. Revisiting the "flexibility hypothesis." *Canadian Public Policy* 31 (1): 109–116.

Statistics Canada. 2009. Latest release from the Labour Force Survey. http://www.statcan.gc.ca/subjects-sujets/labour-travail/lfs-epa/lfs-epa-eng.pdf.

REFERENCES

Benjamin, D., M. Gunderson, T. Lemieux, and W. Riddell. 2007. *Labour market economics.* 6th ed. Toronto: McGraw-Hill Ryerson.

Organisation for Economic Co-operation and Development (OECD). 1994. *The OECD jobs study: Evidence and explanations.* Part I: Labour market trends and underlying forces of change. Paris: OECD.

Seccareccia, M. 2004. What type of full employment? A critical evaluation of government as the employer of last resort policy proposal. *Investigación Económica* 63 (247): 15–43.

PART IV

International Economic Relations

Is Trade Liberalization Good or Bad for the Economy?

10

COMPETING VIEWS

Eugene Beaulieu, "The Economics of Trade Liberalization"
Ricardo Grinspun, "Trade Liberalization: The Good, the Bad, and the Ugly"

Editors' Introduction

If we focus only on recent history, we can say that from the end of the Second World War until the 1970s, policy-makers have been putting much effort into trying to find the most desirable, or "optimal," trade policy for their countries. During that era, such policies often meant using tariffs or other measures to discourage imports and subsidies to encourage exports. Under the rules of international organizations of the time (for example, the General Agreement on Tariffs and Trade, or GATT), protectionist measures were still considered to be acceptable policy responses. However, toward the end of the 1970s and during the 1980s, a new approach—sometimes labelled the neo-liberal model—became more fashionable. As a result, policy-makers began to promote less government intervention and a full liberalization of the economy. There was indeed a shift in policy in many countries, which culminated in the 1995 replacement of the GATT by the World Trade Organization (WTO).

The birth of the WTO, which immediately followed the signing of the North American Free Trade Agreement (NAFTA) in 1994, triggered a major debate about the costs and benefits of trade liberalization. Although the WTO was a mere extension of the GATT, its emergence on the world stage slowly galvanized waves of worldwide protests against the liberalization of not only trade but also finance. From Seattle to London, from Davos to Porto Alegre, wherever there has been a summit of world leaders there has usually also been a protest by the anti-globalization movement. Policy-makers, apparently acting on the advice of many established economists and international organizations such as the International Monetary Fund (IMF) and the WTO—according to which free trade is generally assumed to be beneficial to all parties—have typically been puzzled by the ferocity of the opposition.

While the advocates of trade liberalization point to the gains from trade in the form of lower prices and higher real incomes, the main argument of the opponents of trade liberalization is that, by increasing the powers of transnational corporations and financial capital, liberalization has done more harm than good to the world economy—and to developing countries in particular. Since free trade has not always been the practice in developed countries and since to this day trade is more administered than free, shouldn't developing countries also have a say in the formulation of the rules governing trade—and consequently have their own strategic trade and industrial policy? Or should they passively agree to the rules as written by the powerful players? These and similar questions are answered in the next two essays.

The Economics of Trade Liberalization

Eugene Beaulieu

Introduction

In 2008 an economic downturn began in the United States and spread rapidly to other countries. At the time of writing (early 2009), the downturn continues to grow more serious, and it seems likely that it will be deeper and more prolonged than any economic downturn since the 1930s. Historically, countries have responded to economic downturns by looking inward and adopting protectionist trade policies. Therefore, it is important to understand how protectionism—and its flip side, trade liberalization—affects the well-being of individuals and countries around the world. Understanding the impact of trade policy at this time is particularly urgent because the wrong direction in trade policy could lead to a global depression, as occurred in the 1930s.

The United States included a protectionist trade policy element (the "buy American" clause) as part of its 2009 stimulus package. Several other countries—such as Russia, India, and France—have already adopted protectionist trade policies in response to the global recession. The "buy American" clause was watered down somewhat in response to the reactions of foreign governments to the protectionist policy. It is likely that any overt US protectionist policy will lead to retaliation by other countries and to a spiralling wave of protectionism around the world. (We do not need to wait to see how a worldwide wave of protectionism will affect the world economy; we saw how this unfolded in the 1930s. The financial crisis of 1929 touched off a wave of protectionism, led by the United States, which resulted in a dramatic decline in international trade and helped turn the financial crisis into the Great Depression.)

This essay will carefully examine the costs and benefits of trade liberalization. We will explore the intellectual arguments for trade liberalization, as well as the theoretical and empirical evidence regarding the impact of international trade on economic growth and development.

The Intellectual Argument for Free Trade

The intellectual argument for liberalized trade came from the classical economists of the late 18th and early 19th centuries. These early political economists, or "classical economists," were led by David Hume, Adam Smith, and David Ricardo.

Classical economists attacked the prevailing wisdom of the day, mercantilism, which assumed that international trade is a zero-sum game in which it is not possible for all countries to benefit from trade. Mercantilists believed that the key to a nation's wealth was the accumulation of gold and silver. According to this view, exports increase wealth because exported goods bring gold and silver in payment into the exporting country. Imports, on the other hand, have a negative impact on a nation's wealth because importing goods requires payment in the form of gold or silver. This results in a decline in the precious metals held by the importing country and, therefore, in a decline of its wealth. As you can see, on the assumption that the stock of precious metals in the world is fixed, international trade is a zero-sum game where the benefits to one country must be completely offset by the losses of another country. The policy advice from mercantilists, therefore, is one of protectionism: restrict imports and (possibly) encourage exports.

David Hume, writing in 1752, challenged the mercantilist view of the world by pointing out two problems. First, individuals—and therefore nations—derive satisfaction from consuming goods, not from holding gold and silver. Second, Hume pointed out that, because a country cannot accumulate gold and silver forever, the mercantilist notion of restricting trade could allow gold and silver to accumulate in the short run but in the long run this policy could not be effective.[1]

Adam Smith confronted the notion that international trade is a zero-sum game and proved that this assumption is simply wrong. In his 1776 book *An Inquiry into the Nature and Causes of the Wealth of Nations*, Smith showed that each country can benefit from international trade through an improved allocation of labour. His argument was based on the notion of absolute advantage, whereby all countries benefit from international trade if each specializes in the production of the good that it can produce at the lowest cost and exports that good in exchange for goods that other countries produce at the lowest cost. Smith's argument requires that each country have an absolute advantage in the production of one good. Trade in this view is not zero-sum. All countries benefit from a lower cost supply of goods—and thereby gain from international trade.

Writing in 1817, David Ricardo refined Adam Smith's argument and pointed out that both countries can gain from trade by specializing in the production of goods based on comparative—rather than absolute—advantage. Taking the example of England, which was less productive than Portugal in producing both wine and cloth, Ricardo showed that both countries would benefit from trade if each specialized in the production of the good in which it had a comparative advantage. Portugal held an absolute advantage in the production of both goods, but the productivity difference was greater in the production of wine, meaning that Portugal had a comparative advantage in wine and England in cloth. Both countries would gain by specializing production in their comparative advantage good and trading it for the other good.

A simple numerical example based on Ricardo's 1817 *Principles of Political Economy and Taxation* illustrates the concepts of absolute advantage and comparative advantage and shows how international trade can improve the well-being of all nations and their citizens.[2] Suppose that labour is the only input into the production of wine and cloth, meaning that labour costs are the only production costs. Suppose also that, in England (as summarized in the table below), three hours of labour are required to produce one bottle of wine and six are required to produce one bolt of cloth. In Portugal, it takes one labour hour to produce one bottle of wine and five to produce one bolt of cloth.

Labour requirements (in hours) for producing one bottle of wine and one bolt of cloth in England and Portugal

	Wine	Cloth
England	3	6
Portugal	1	5

Notice that the labour requirements for both goods are lower in Portugal, and that Portugal therefore has an absolute advantage in the production of both goods. Given this, it is very tempting to conclude that Portugal could not possibly gain from trading with the higher-cost, less-productive England.

Ricardo's key insight was to point out that the relative costs (and therefore prices) are different, and that this difference provides the opportunity for mutually beneficial gains from trade. When countries are isolated and do not trade, the relative costs of producing wine and cloth determine the relative prices of wine and cloth, or what economists call the "opportunity costs." The opportunity cost of wine is the amount of cloth that a country must give up in order to produce one more bottle of wine. The relative cost differences determine comparative advantage and yield the gains from trade. In Portugal, the opportunity cost of wine is 1/5—that is, one bottle of wine could be produced instead of five bolts of cloth. In England, the opportunity cost of wine in terms of cloth is 3/6 (or 1/2). Based on these opportunity costs, Portugal has a comparative advantage in wine and England has a comparative advantage in cloth.

It is easy to see that both countries would gain by specializing production in their comparative advantage good. If Portugal produced one fewer bolt of cloth, this would free up five hours of labour to produce wine; by specializing, Portugal would produce five more bottles of wine. Given the differences in opportunity costs, Portugal could export three bottles of wine to England in exchange for one bolt of cloth.[3] England could produce this extra bolt of cloth (for export) by producing two fewer bottles of wine. Overall, Portugal and England consume the same amount of cloth and are both able to consume more wine.[4]

Ricardo's ideas of comparative advantage and his simple theoretical model illustrating the concept have had a profound effect on economic thought and policy up to this day. The logic of the classical argument for free trade is sound, and the case for free trade is irrefutable based on the gains from trade through comparative advantage. What do economists and non-economists think about comparative advantage?

A 19th-Century Idea in a Modern World

Some people contend that economists agree on very little. In fact, an old joke about economists goes that if all of the world's economists were laid end to end, they wouldn't reach a conclusion. However, economists *do* come to agreement on some issues.[5]

Comparative advantage is one economic principle that economists agree with almost unanimously. But how does agreement on the intellectual argument for free trade translate into the area of policy? In the more than 200 years since Ricardo, there have been many important advances in the theoretical and empirical understanding of how international trade affects the economic well-being of individuals and countries. Based on the body of this evidence, economists overwhelmingly support trade liberalization. Survey evidence reveals that over 90 percent of professional economists are in favour of free international trade.[6] But despite economists' support for policies of liberal international trade, many non-economists oppose free trade. Some oppose liberalized trade because they are philosophically opposed to international trade and refuse to accept the notion of comparative advantage. To paraphrase Nobel laureate Paul Samuelson (1969, 9), comparative advantage is an economic principle that is undeniably true, yet not obvious to intelligent people. Another Nobel laureate, Paul Krugman (1996), provides an excellent account of the opposition that some intellectuals have to Ricardo's "not-so-simple idea" of comparative advantage. According to Krugman:

> The idea of comparative advantage—with its implication that trade between two nations normally raises the real incomes of both—is, like evolution via natural selection, a concept that seems simple and compelling to those who understand it. Yet anyone who becomes involved in discussions of international trade beyond the narrow circle of academic economists quickly realizes that it must be, in some sense, a very difficult concept indeed. I am not talking here about the problem of communicating the case for free trade to crudely anti-intellectual opponents, people who simply dislike the idea of ideas. The persistence of that sort of opposition, like the persistence of creationism, is a different sort of question, and requires a different sort of discussion. What I am concerned with here are the views of intellectuals, people who do value ideas, but somehow find this particular idea impossible to grasp.

Rather than dwelling on intellectual misunderstandings about comparative advantage, let us consider the concerns of economists and the general public about liberalized trade. According to Poole (2004), survey data provide evidence that the general public understands the benefits of free trade in principle but has strong reservations about adopting free trade as a policy. There are several concerns about free international trade that appear to be particularly salient among both the general public and policy-makers. The main concerns are that trade: (1) has distributional effects and hurts domestic workers,[7] (2) hurts foreign workers, and (3) adversely affects the environment.

It is important to point out that economists share these concerns and have carefully examined the impact of international trade within the context of these concerns. Also, it is important to recognize that the public is generally concerned about all three of these issues *independent of* international trade, and that views on trade are often bundled in a negative way with these concerns. Indeed, one of the biggest challenges facing a policy of free trade stems from the fact that many policy-makers and the general public give international trade far too much credit. For example, some opponents of free trade believe that international trade causes poverty and environmental degradation. On the other hand, proponents of free trade often oversell its virtues as a panacea for all that ails an economy. These views on trade policy led Paul Krugman to characterize the debate over the North American Free Trade Agreement (NAFTA) as a debate in which "[a]nti-NAFTA people are telling malicious whoppers [and the] [p]ro-NAFTA side is telling little white lies."[8]

There is a vast literature examining the impact of trade, and one conclusion that can be gleaned is that, while international trade facilitates economic growth, it is a necessary—not a sufficient—condition for such growth. International trade has consequences for poverty and the environment, but it is not the key determinant of these things and is an extremely blunt instrument for addressing either of them.

The Distributional Effects of Free Trade

Economists understand that international trade policy has distributional consequences within a country. For example, a tariff or other trade restriction on automobiles increases the cost of automobiles in the country, and this directly benefits automobile producers. The cost of this type of policy is the higher price that consumers pay for automobiles. A "buy American" clause in a stimulus package that directs funds to domestic steel producers will directly benefit domestic steelworkers and producers, but will increase the costs and reduce the benefits of the stimulus package to other Americans.

There is a considerable body of research examining the impact of protectionist trade policy on wages and jobs in the domestic economy (for a survey of this literature, see Beaulieu 2007). The key result from this research is that, although the economy benefits from free trade overall, some groups gain from free trade while others lose. The gains from free trade, however, outweigh the losses, and can be used to compensate the losers. A good example of this is the US Trade Adjustment Assistance program, which is designed to aid workers who have lost their jobs due to international trade. Most other countries, including Canada, recognize that unemployment is a macroeconomic phenomenon and do not have a program designed specifically for workers affected by trade. Instead, they have general unemployment insurance programs that cover all unemployed workers.

In 1930, as President Hoover pondered whether or not to veto a protectionist trade bill that was passed by Congress, 1,028 economists joined together and argued against such a policy in an open letter to President Hoover. The objective of the bill, which would dramatically increase tariffs across a broad range of goods and services, was to protect American jobs in the face of a financial crisis and a looming economic recession. The evidence is clear, however, that trade policy will relocate jobs from one sector to another but will generally not affect the overall number of jobs. The overall level of employment is based on the macroeconomic conditions. A good illustration of this is the fact that both the Canada–US Free Trade Agreement (CUSFTA) and NAFTA contributed to a decline in manufacturing employment in Canada and the United States, as workers shifted from less competitive to more competitive sectors. Through all of this employment churning in these economies, the overall unemployment rate did not increase due to free trade.

When a country restricts international trade in an attempt to deal with an economic downturn, this typically leads to retaliatory measures from other countries. As seen in the 1930s, a policy of protectionism can be contagious, causing dramatic effects on international trade and significant damage to all economies.

The Impact of Trade on Foreign Workers

As we discuss trade and foreign workers, we can examine the impact of international trade on both the incomes of foreign workers in poor countries and labour standards in these countries. First, with respect to workers' incomes in poor countries, there is strong evidence that international trade contributes importantly to economic growth and that economic growth is an important factor in alleviating poverty.

The most important aspect of the relationship between international trade and economic growth is that liberalized international trade (trade openness) is *necessary*, but not *sufficient*, for economic growth. There is an extensive literature examining the relationship between international trade and economic growth, and a clear positive relationship between the two (that is, countries that grow faster tend to be more open to international trade). However, it is difficult to identify the causality of this relationship with certainty, because the causality runs in both directions: economic growth causes increased trade, and increased trade causes economic growth. There is a considerable literature on the relationship between international trade and economic growth, and the consensus is that international trade *does* contribute to economic growth, but in a necessary (not a sufficient) way. It is very rare for a country to grow without international trade; however, a poorly governed country that opens its borders to trade will not benefit from trade liberalization. Two very important and influential papers in this literature, by Sachs and Warner (1995) and Dollar (1992), present empirical evidence that international openness is correlated with economic growth. Rodriguez and Rodrik (1999) are very critical of this evidence, but their critique is technical in nature and they do not offer any evidence that trade does not increase economic growth. Moreover, in the end they recognize that restricting trade is inimical to economic growth.

One of the most thorough papers examining trade and economic growth is a paper by Arvind Panagariya (2004), which summarizes the evidence on the connection between international trade, economic growth, and poverty reduction. Panagariya examines the miracle growth episodes of countries across the world throughout the 20th century, and finds that those countries which grew rapidly were almost universally open economies, while those that experienced negative or low growth were almost all closed economies. After carefully analyzing the theoretical and empirical evidence, Panagariya concludes that liberalized international trade, economic growth, and poverty reduction are complementary.

There are several fundamental points that, based on a preponderance of evidence established in the paper, are important to understand. Panagariya presents evidence that agrees with the conclusion (already stated) that free trade is necessary, but not sufficient, for growth. He points out that, while trade need not be the main catalyst of growth, it is necessary, and that even skeptics (like Rodriguez and Rodrik) agree that turning inward is a mistake because it destroys growth.

Panagariya goes beyond examining the impact of international trade on economic growth, examining its impact on poverty. He points out that economic growth is the single most important factor in reducing poverty, and presents compelling empirical evidence that trade and growth are positively associated with poverty reduction. He also provides a conceptual link between openness and poverty reduction: poor countries tend to export labour-intensive goods, and this increases the wages of unskilled workers. Moreover, he correctly points out that protectionist policies typically discriminate against agriculture, which employs most of the poor people in poor countries. There are also indirect effects of trade on poverty. These are what Panagariya calls the "pull-up" effect of growth: rapid growth generates fiscal resources that can be spent on social programs. International trade generates economic growth, and growth increases income—which increases access to primary education and other services.

With respect to the impact of international trade on labour standards, Flanagan (2006) examines whether globalization worsens the conditions of labour, spurring a "race to the bottom." Based on analyses of 30 years of data from many countries, Flanagan concludes that, to the contrary, the three economic dimensions of globalization—greater foreign trade, foreign direct investment, and international migration—are associated with improved working conditions (such as higher wages, fewer hours of work, and fewer accidents at work) and improved workers' rights (including a reduction in child and forced labour, and greater freedom of association). Open economies have significantly better working conditions than more closed economies.

Trade and the Environment

Is international trade good or bad for the environment? This is a very complicated question, and one that has generated a vast literature. The best and most comprehensive source regarding this issue is a remarkable book by Copeland and Taylor (2003). The authors focus their analysis on two channels through which international trade affects the environment. First, if international trade increases economic growth, then the income-generating effects of trade may hurt the environment. Second, as discussed above, it is well known that international trade affects the mix of economic activity that countries engage in, and this change in the composition of economic activity could affect the environment.

A brief summary of Copeland and Taylor's findings is that, to the extent that international trade increases economic growth (what the authors call "economic activity"), there is an increase in pollution. They call this a "scale effect" of trade; international trade increases economic activity or scale, and this increases pollution. The increase in pollution is offset by the effect of higher incomes (if international trade increases economic growth and activity, it also increases real incomes). Higher real incomes generate a greater willingness and ability to implement environmental regulations. Copeland and Taylor call this the "technique effect": international trade increases incomes, and higher incomes lead to more environmentally friendly techniques. They find that the increase in environmental regulations associated with the higher growth from international trade (the technique effect) reduces pollution, and that the reduction in pollution is larger than the increase in pollution from the scale effect.

The second channel through which trade may affect the environment has to do with the concern that polluting industries will move from countries with greater environmental regulations to countries with weaker ones. On this question, Copeland and Taylor find that international trade creates only a small change in pollution, through the composition effect. There is little evidence of a pollution-haven effect with respect to dirty industries migrating to unregulated countries. In fact, the authors find that rich, developed countries have a comparative advantage in polluting industries. Overall, the net impact of the three effects of trade on the environment (the scale, technique, and composition) leads the authors to conclude that international trade is good for the environment.

Conclusions

This essay began by exploring the intellectual arguments for how countries benefit from international trade. We reviewed the concepts of absolute and comparative advantage, and discussed the costs and benefits of international trade. We argued that every economic policy, including trade policy, produces "winners" and "losers." The appropriate response is to take targeted action aimed at compensating those who are adversely affected by a policy—not to deny the benefits to the larger majority.

NOTES

1. For more on the writings of David Hume and an excellent history of thought on free trade, see Irwin (1997).
2. The Ricardian model and the concept of comparative advantage are presented in most introductory economics textbooks and international trade textbooks. A very fun and excellent novel on free trade and protectionism by Russell Roberts illustrates these concepts in a modern setting (see the list of suggested readings).
3. These terms of trade benefit both countries. *Without* trade, it would cost five bottles of wine for one bolt of cloth in Portugal, while, in England, three bolts of cloth would cost one-and-a-half bottles of wine.
4. You can work through this example and show that both countries would be able to increase consumption of cloth while keeping wine consumption constant. You can also show that both countries can consume more of each good.
5. According to Robert Whaples (2006), economists agree on a number of key economic issues. It should be noted that economics is a social science and there is debate within the profession on many policy issues. This is healthy and is not a critique of the profession. Moreover, as Whaples shows, there are several key points of consensus.
6. See Whaples (2006).
7. A related concern is that there may be disruptive effects of job loss, even if trade creates more jobs than it destroys.
8. Statement to the *New York Times*, September 17, 1993.

DISCUSSION QUESTIONS

1. Compare and contrast the mercantilist and classical views on international trade.
2. Explain the concepts of absolute and comparative advantage.

3. Explain the impact of international trade on economic growth and poverty.
4. Explain the two channels through which international trade affects the environment. What are the different effects of each channel, and the overall (or net) effect of international trade on the environment?

SUGGESTED READINGS

Beaulieu, Eugene. 2007. Trade and wages. In *Handbook on international trade policy*, ed. William A. Kerr and James D. Gaisford, 150–162. Cheltenham: Edward Elgar.

Flanagan, Robert J. 2006. *Globalization and labor conditions: Working conditions and worker rights in a global economy.* New York: Oxford University Press.

Irwin, Douglas A. 2003. *Free trade under fire.* Princeton, NJ: Princeton University Press.

Roberts, Russell. 2007. *The choice: A fable of free trade and protectionism.* 3rd ed. Upper Saddle River, NJ: Prentice Hall.

Rodriguez, Francisco, and Dani Rodrik. 1999. Trade policy and economic growth: A skeptic's guide to cross-national evidence. NBER Working Paper w7081.

ONLINE RESOURCES

Deardorff, Alan V. Alan Deardorff's homepage. http://www-personal.umich.edu/~alandear (website of Economics and Public Policy Professor Alan Deardorff, University of Michigan; the site contains links to a very useful glossary of terms and to the "family tree of trade economists").

Krugman, Paul. The official Paul Krugman web page. http://web.mit.edu/krugman/www (includes a link to Krugman's "unofficial" page).

National Bureau of Economic Research: http://www.nber.org.

Public Citizen Global Trade Watch: http://www.citizen.org/trade.

World Economic Forum: http://www.weforum.org/en/index.htm.

World Trade Organization: http://www.wto.org.

REFERENCES

Copeland, Brian R., and M. Scott Taylor. 2003. *Trade and the environment: Theory and evidence.* Princeton, NJ: Princeton University Press.

Dollar, D. 1992. Outward-oriented developing countries really do grow more rapidly: Evidence from 95 LDCs, 1976–1985. *Economic Development and Cultural Change* 40 (3): 523–544.

Irwin, Douglas A. 1997. *Against the tide: An intellectual history of free trade.* Princeton, NJ: Princeton University Press.

Krugman, Paul. 1996. Ricardo's difficult idea. http://web.mit.edu/krugman/www/ricardo.htm.

Panagariya, Arvind. 2004. Miracles and debacles: In defence of trade openness. *World Economy* 27 (8): 1149–1171.

Poole, William. 2004. Free trade: Why are economists and noneconomists so far apart? Speech at the Trade, Globalization and Outsourcing Conference, Reuters America Inc., New York City, June 15. http://www.stlouisfed.org/news/speeches/2004/06_15_04.html.

Sachs, Jeffrey, and Andrew Warner. 1995. Economic reform and the process of global integration. *Brookings Papers on Economic Activity* 1995 (1): 1–118.

Samuelson, P.A. 1969. The way of an economist. In *International economic relations: Proceedings of the third congress of the International Economic Association*, ed. P.A. Samuelson, 1–11. London: Macmillan.

Whaples, Robert. 2006. Do economists agree on anything? Yes! *Economists' Voice* 3 (9): Article 1.

Trade Liberalization: The Good, the Bad, and the Ugly

Ricardo Grinspun*

Introduction

What is international trade? Although the question sounds simple enough, the answer is less so, as the concept of "trade" is an evolving one. The term "international trade," or simply "trade," was historically first applied to the exchange of merchandise goods (such as spices or textiles) across international boundaries. Even today, a typical model of international trade used as an illustration in an economics textbook may include two countries trading in two tangible commodities, such as food and cars. Such a simplified illustration abstracts from the growing cross-border exchange of services, or intangible goods such as tourism or telecommunications. Thus, a current definition of international trade encompasses both goods and services.

In recent decades the term "international trade" has gained even newer connotations, as it is applied to a broader set of international economic relationships that transcend commerce in goods and services. This is the case with "trade agreements"—formal treaties signed by two or more countries willing to tighten their economic interdependence. A typical trade agreement signed during the last three decades includes not only chapters dealing with trade in goods and services, but others that address such issues as finance, investment, intellectual property, dispute settlement, public services, government purchases, energy, and the environment.

Trade agreements also detail the terms for "regulation" of international trade, or the rules and processes that determine *how* international trade happens. The difficulty with such regulation is that it is nearly impossible to separate the regulation of international trade from the regulation of other ambits of public policy, such as social services, culture, natural resources, or the environment. This causes such agreements to intrude into areas of social and economic management that traditionally had little or nothing to do with international trade (Shrybman 2001).

The newer controversies over trade liberalization, or the lowering of trade barriers, generally revolve around these broader meanings of trade and their implications for democracy, human rights, economic development, social justice,

* I wish to thank the editors Hassan Bougrine and Mario Seccareccia for their helpful comments and suggestions on an earlier version of this essay.

and environmental sustainability (Wallach and Woodall 2004). Although one can still find many examples of old-fashioned "protectionism," or opposition to trade liberalization from affected interest groups, this is not the most controversial aspect of trade liberalization. Indeed, there is no controversy over the desirability of an international division of labour whereby countries obtain their basket of goods and services partly through domestic production and partly through international commerce.

The real debates revolve around the timing and process of trade liberalization, as well as who makes the decisions, what kind of criteria are applied, how such liberalization affects "regulation" and the role of government, and what influence it has on the "model of development."[1] Unfortunately, traditional microeconomic analysis is of limited use in addressing such questions. A broader analysis of the complex role of trade in a modern economy, incorporating elements from neo-classical economics as well as from political economy, public policy, economic development, gender, ecology, and ethics, would be more useful.

Trade liberalization is indeed a fascinating policy endeavour. Like most public policy debates, it is not one that can be resolved by exclusive reliance on technical analysis; it also requires consideration of societal values and preferences.

The Debate on Trade Liberalization

Mainstream trade theory generally starts addressing this debate with an argument about the gains from trade. In the basic examples provided in textbooks, these gains arise from countries' comparative advantage, or differences in relative costs. Each country specializes in and exports those goods that it produces at a relatively lower cost, thus bringing about a worldwide increase in outputs without any change in the overall level of inputs. Through specialization and exchange, each country can end up benefiting from a higher consumption of all goods.

Economists identify other gains from trade, including the ability to exploit economies of scale, and lower average costs of production when serving a larger international market. There are also benefits resulting from the exposure of domestic firms to international competition: increased competitive behaviour, exposure to new ideas and methods, and a reduction in monopoly power. Finally, consumers benefit by being able to access a wider variety of goods and services at lower prices.

These gains from trade are non-controversial if—and this is a large "if"—all the necessary assumptions that economists introduce in their models actually exist in reality. Controversies regarding the impacts of trade liberalization revolve around the critical assumptions that feed into the analysis (Todaro and Smith 2009, 606–613). For instance, simple examples of comparative advantage assume that goods can move across borders but that factors of production (such as labour and capital) cannot. We live in a world where such movements, particularly of capital, play a determining role in shaping trade flows. This means that not only can comparative advantage (relative costs) influence patterns of trade, but absolute advantage (absolute costs of production) can, too.

Absolute advantage also plays a role when another crucial assumption is violated, which typically occurs in the context of developing countries. The assumption of full employment is a necessary condition for the principle of comparative advantage to hold, since, in a context of unemployment and underemployment—where increasing the production of one good does not require diminishing the production of another—it is appropriate to shift resources to the country with the lowest absolute cost. Thus, as Anwar Shaikh reminds us (2007), when unemployment is the norm, it is absolute advantage that guides decisions. We conclude, therefore, that the maintenance of full employment and macroeconomic stability is a prerequisite for the standard arguments for free trade, and thus their applicability to the reality of most developing countries remains in doubt. In short, although trade models may still provide useful insights, the simple and straightforward lessons arising from them need to be critically examined to see if they hold under more realistic conditions.

"Trade policy" deals with measures and policies that affect a country's international trade. There is a large gap in this case between model representations of trade policy, such as the typical microeconomic analysis of an import tariff in a single market, and the complex reality of trade policy, where assumptions such as perfect competition do not hold. Mainstream analyses focus on efficiency effects related to overall consumer and producer surplus while glossing over other effects, such as impacts on the environment.

Such analyses also downplay crucial redistributive effects: the displacement of employment between industries or regions, and the redistribution of benefits from importers to exporters, from shrinking industries or sectors toward expanding ones, and from low-skill workers with few opportunities for retraining and reincorporation in new jobs to highly trained and highly mobile workers. International trade theory textbooks argue that a test for whether or not a certain trade policy is beneficial is to see if the gains from trade outweigh the losses. Since this kind of direct measurement is impossible to do, it calls for a hypothetical exercise whereby the winners can *potentially* compensate the losers. So if it is possible *in theory* to redistribute income so that everyone is better off than before trade liberalization, then that proves there are net gains from trade (Krugman and Obstfeld 2009, 72–73). This kind of intellectual exercise, however, is of little consolation to those who have to bear the losses from trade in their *real* lives.

Economic analysis emphasizes the distorting effects of trade policy and uses that as an argument for free trade. A distortion is any measure that changes the market price of a product, as in the case of an import tariff. Students of economics are taught that when the market price is anything other than what it would be in a free market, it creates an inefficiency because it sends the "wrong" signals to producers and consumers. In this view, there is less emphasis on the fact that such analysis is correct only if the initial situation is efficient to start with. If the markets in question are riddled with market failures, such as labour market imperfections, then such arguments for free trade do not hold.

As environmental concerns have come to the fore in recent years, economists are recognizing the pervasive negative environmental externalities resulting from virtually any production or trading process; these may take the form of pollution, contamination, congestion, destruction of habitats, land erosion, release of greenhouse gases, and so on. Once we recognize that the real world of trade policy is one where market failures abound, economic theory falls silent regarding what type of trade policy is optimal. The most that economics textbooks can do is to make a *political* argument for free trade: in a world of uncertainty about optimal policies, it is easy for trade policy to become dominated by special-interest politics, and thus the safe path is to avoid all market intervention (Krugman and Obstfeld 2009, 222). I consider this a weak argument for a laissez-faire policy, when there are other strong reasons that justify an active public policy.

A thorny question in trade policy relates to governmental actions that directly or indirectly subsidize or promote domestic production or exports. If these subsidies are considered illegal or inappropriate, then they may be considered "unfair trading practices" in trade parlance and may lead to a trade dispute. Which measures are legal and appropriate is of significance for broad public policy objectives that have little to do with international trade, such as regional development and environmental stewardship. This is the case with the Western grain transportation subsidies, in place to promote regional development in Western Canada by lessening the competitive disadvantage resulting from huge shipping distances. This program was discontinued in 1993, partly because it contravened the terms of the trilateral North American Free Trade Agreement (NAFTA) (Regehr and Norrie 2009).

The Broader Context of Trade Liberalization

As emphasized throughout this essay, the broader impacts of trade liberalization—those that do *not* relate directly to the industrial and labour market restructuring resulting from particular trade flows—are the most controversial. The question of *domestic regulation*, one of the most complex aspects of international trade, is a prime example.

Domestic Regulation

Governments establish domestic regulatory mechanisms for markets in the form of laws, regulatory directives, technical and safety standards, public programs, and so on, to make sure that market participants behave in desired ways. Regulations are controversial. Although they can be seen as necessary tools for advancing desirable goals (such as social equity, economic development, health and safety, and environmental sustainability), they can also be seen as non-tariff barriers (NTBs) that obstruct international trade, or as illegal subsidies that constitute unfair trade practices—both of which arise when governments want to benefit particular social groups. Regulations can therefore be associated with "rent-seeking behaviour," or even corruption.

Beneficial types of regulation abound in developed societies. Much regulation addresses the proper domestic management of cross-border trade, such as customs, transportation, provision of warranty services for imported goods, and so on. Other regulations are not specific to traded goods and services but have an impact on them. They may address allowable levels of pesticides and toxic chemicals in the food chain, or safety features required in cars. These are health and safety regulations. Some countries have strong protections for labour rights and do not allow selling products produced with prison labour or exploitive children's labour. There are also many rules related to consumer information and protection, such as labelling requirements.

The controversy is particularly heated over health and safety, environmental, and labour rights regulations, since these can sometimes serve as thinly veiled forms of rich-country protectionism (Srinivasan 2000). When an imported product doesn't meet a particular standard, the effect is the same as if a prohibitive tariff were applied to that good—it cannot enter the country. For advocates of free trade, such regulation can be seen as a protectionist measure that effectively obstructs trade and diminishes economic efficiency. For consumer advocates, it may be an essential requirement for life in a safe and healthy society.

This disagreement, which is splashed over the headlines every time there is a major protest against a new trade agreement, suggests that the real debate is about something bigger than trade. What is really at stake is the role of governments and the kind of social arrangements we desire as a society. This is a point that trade economists do not readily emphasize, their focus being instead on the protectionist impact of domestic regulation.

Trade Agreements

In contrast to *domestic* regulation and law, the *international* regulation of international trade is embedded in a host of international trade agreements signed between two or more countries. These can take the form of bilateral, trilateral, and subregional free trade agreements (FTAs), or of the multilateral trading system incorporating more than 150 countries, institutionalized in the World Trade Organization (WTO) in 1995. The recent proliferation of FTAs has raised many questions, including whether they are contributing to an increase in trade liberalization worldwide or restricting it instead to its signatories.

Trade agreements, whose purpose is to bring about reciprocal trade liberalization among the "parties" to the agreement, are always controversial. They create winners (internationally competitive sectors able to expand their exports), and losers (domestic sectors unable to compete with inexpensive imports). Economic theory suggests that in most cases there will be net gains when countries enter into such agreements, meaning that the winners would be able—if the redistributive mechanisms existed—to fully compensate the losers and still come out ahead. As mentioned, however, in most cases such mechanisms to compensate the losers (such as unemployment insurance, or retraining and relocating assistance) are weak or non-existent. The losers remain losers.

The redistributive effects among countries, not just within countries, are contested. The terms of a particular agreement dictate how the benefits will be spread among the parties. Mexican critics of NAFTA, for instance, argue that the terms of the agreement—influenced by the larger power of the United States and its business lobbies—are harmful to Mexican interests. They point to a host of elements in NAFTA that, in their view, cause negative impacts on economic development, rural poverty, environmental sustainability, and labour rights (Espinosa et al. 2002).

Deregulatory Bias

Critics argue that international trade rules intrude into areas of domestic regulation and promote downward harmonization of health, safety, labour, or environmental standards. Such rules tend to be embedded with deregulatory bias, which views any interference with trade as eminently negative. One case in point is the sanitary and phytosanitary measures (SPS) agreement in the WTO, which regulates the health and safety of animals and the food chain. The argument regarding this agreement is that it places an effective ceiling—but no floor—on standards by placing onerous "scientific proof" requirements on countries that want to set higher standards (Shrybman 2001). According to the rules, a country can be challenged at the WTO for having standards that are too high, but never for having them too low. This creates an inherent bias toward lower health and safety standards, or, as some have argued, encourages a "race to the bottom."

Investors' Rights Versus Human Rights

Some trade agreements, such as NAFTA, incorporate strong "investors' rights." These provisions extend rules originally designed for trade in goods and services, such as "national treatment," to investment. They imply that domestic policies cannot discriminate in favour of domestic investors, ruling out well-established policies aimed at promoting local and regional development. Such policies go against the grain of investment clauses. Investment clauses also hinder the abilities of local and national governments to regulate investment and make sure it meets certain criteria. This difficulty arises frequently in cases of developing countries' mining operations, where investors' profits may clash with objectives of protecting the environment or upholding labour rights. That's why enshrining "investors' rights" in trade agreements may conflict with legally recognized *human* rights.

Transnational Corporations

Controversies over trade agreements and trade liberalization become heated when transnational corporations (TNCs) are brought into the discussion. Free trade advocates argue that trade liberalization opens up competition, as protected domestic monopolies face off with foreign competition, thus lowering prices and providing more choice to consumers. Critics argue that what happens instead is that TNCs, with a presence both within and outside the country, gain political and economic power. The political process driving the negotiations of trade agreements is such that the views of corporate actors receive privileged attention. The provisions on intellectual property rights in the WTO are one example of corporate influence, driven by lobbies such as Big Pharma. Rather than promoting freer flow of information, ideas, and technology, the purpose of these rules is to place restrictions on the use of such information, ideas, and so on, and to increase the royalties and profits for rich-country holders of patents, copyrights, and trademarks. Similarly, the provisions on foreign investment and investor rights mentioned earlier provide enormous benefits to the largest corporations active in the country. In poor countries, the restructuring that accompanies trade liberalization may accelerate foreign takeover of key resource sectors (such as in oil, mining, forestry, and fishing), leading to more—not less—market concentration.

Export-Led Growth and Model of Development

For developing countries, the question of how trade liberalization will affect economic development is a crucial one. The World Bank believes that promoting trade and competitiveness in developing countries facilitates their integration into the global economy and spurs economic growth (World Bank 2009). That integration is driven by dynamic, export-led sectors such as resource industries, agriculture, manufacturing, and—more recently—service industries (for instance, call centres in India). There's little doubt that these activities contribute to economic growth, but there has been less emphasis on some of their undesirable social, economic, and ecological consequences. Polluted tailings from mining operations, collapsed fish stocks, depleted water aquifers, devastated coastal mangroves, deforestation and desertification, contaminated lakes and rivers—this is a sampling of the eco-logical destruction resulting from some export operations.

Despite the economic growth, trade-led restructuring can also have negative economic impacts, such as shrinking high-employment sectors that cannot with-stand import competition. During Mexico's trade liberalization in the late 1980s—which included the country joining GATT (predecessor of the WTO) in 1986—the relative shares of employment in agriculture, mining, and manufacturing dimin-ished as imports surged. Much employment was shifted to the "informal" sector, and some observed that "the generation of employment in Mexico during 1987–1992 [was] associated with inferior jobs in terms of quality, productivity and real wages" (Dussel Peters 1996, 102).

Such trade liberalization is part of broader changes in the development model involving a policy shift away from import-substituting policies and toward export-oriented growth strategies, which entails bringing down trade barriers and opening capital markets. But the results of this policy shift have been mixed, with one study concluding that "[e]conomic opening in Argentina, Brazil and Mexico did not lead to export dynamism and had a disappointing impact on employment, even though ... [there was] a strong increase in trade" (Ernst 2005, i). Other countries pursuing export orientation, but with a different policy mix, have been hailed as success stories, particularly some countries in East Asia. Trade liberalization and openness are certainly not panaceas for all that ails development.

Impact on Rural Development

How does trade liberalization affect poor people, the majority of whom live in rural areas in developing countries? A main strategy advanced by the World Bank has been to encourage export-oriented agricultural sectors that produce goods that are in demand in richer countries. In addition to the continued export of tradi-tional tropical cash crops (such as coffee, cacao, bananas, sugar cane, and cotton), newer agricultural exports in fruits and vegetables from countries such as Chile and Mexico have enjoyed enormous growth. Standardized, export-oriented agri-culture tends to be highly capitalized and technologically advanced, as well as high in chemical inputs such as fertilizers and pesticides. As it expands, it crowds out subsistence forms of agriculture, which use traditional farming methods and are oriented to the local market, more labour intensive, and less capitalized and chem-ically intensive. This is significant because the poorest populations in the world derive their livelihoods from subsistence agriculture. Such is the case in Mexico, where the expansion of horticultural exports and the NAFTA-induced liberaliza-tion of imports of maize (a traditional subsistence crop) brought about enormous displacement of poor peasants from the rural areas to the fringes of large urban sectors in both Mexico and the United States.

North–South Relations

In short, the current trade regime, which enshrines unequal and dependent relations, has not favoured developing countries. Much can be added to the points raised above. One long-standing concern has been the instability—and in some cases, the long-term decline—in the terms of trade with respect to developing countries, which contributes to worsening global inequality. When commodity prices plummet, as they did in the global economic downturn that began in 2008, primary-export dependent countries are hit the worst. The proliferation of labour-intensive manufacturing in developing countries further weakens terms of trade, as competition drives down the prices of the goods that are produced. Wealthy countries make things worse by establishing rigid intellectual property laws to protect their economic rents arising from control over commodity chain segments such as research, design, and branding.

Protectionist policies in industrialized countries tilt the balance of benefits even more in one direction, with the help of restrictions imposed by WTO rules on imports from the developing world. This fits a pattern whereby developed-country policies promote intra-industry trade among developed countries (which import and export similar products) while discouraging inter-industry trade between developed and developing countries (where the latter have a comparative advantage), with the purpose of minimizing adjustment costs in the richer countries (Bougrine 2004). Canada, for instance, has promoted both the exportation and importation of automobiles while moving slowly—assisted by the protectionist WTO Agreement on Textiles and Clothing—to liberalize the importation of fibre and textiles, products produced primarily by poor, developing countries but also domestically, which means that such liberalization would also affect domestic low-skill workers.

Conclusion: The Past and the Future of Trade

In this essay I have argued that the case for trade liberalization is more nuanced and multi-sided than the simple arguments on gains from trade presented in introductory economics textbooks might suggest. Harvard professor Dani Rodrik (2001) has persuasively argued that, from a developmental perspective, there is no one single policy approach that is universally appropriate. He questions the centrality of trade and trade policy and emphasizes instead the critical role of domestic institutions and conditions. Rodrik concludes that trade policy should be part of a broader set of policies focused on development priorities, and that countries should be able to restrict trade or suspend WTO obligations for reasons that include social and distributional goals as well as development priorities.

A similar argument can be made regarding the industrialized countries, where the overriding purpose of economic policy should not be GDP growth but finding more effective ways of sharing existing wealth and reconverting the economy toward a sustainable and less environmentally destructive path. Here again, trade expansion cannot be seen as a goal in itself, but rather should be tailored to achieve positive economic, social, and ecological goals.

These conclusions are supported by historical experience. Ha-Joon Chang (2007) examined the mythical notion that the rich countries of the world climbed to the top of the economic ladder pursuing laissez-faire policies. He shows that the real history is very different. The giants of international trade—such as the European countries (historically), the United States and Canada, and (in more recent times) the "Asian tigers" and now China—did not industrialize and develop into world traders by following the precepts of free trade. Instead, they used interventionist trade and industrial policies to promote and protect their own interests. They only "discovered" free trade after they became internationally competitive, at a relatively late stage in their development. Chang concludes that successful development requires today's developing countries to fashion similar protective policies, with even higher tariff barriers given that the playing field is even more unequal than it was in the past.

Latin America provides a contrasting historical experience, where the aggressive pursuit of free trade and market-friendly policies since the 1980s—with encouragement of the World Bank and the International Monetary Fund—has had mixed results at best. There has been a major expansion of trade, but the spurts of economic growth have been uneven over time and across countries, with growing inequality, entrenched poverty, increasing informality in labour markets, and severe environmental damage (Shamsie and Grinspun 2007). In contrast, countries such as South Korea and Taiwan have managed to achieve much better results by pursuing an unorthodox set of policies within a context of outward-oriented development. They have not pursued across-the-board trade liberalization, but instead have protected the home market to raise profits, implemented export subsidies, encouraged their firms to reverse-engineer foreign patented products, and imposed restrictions on foreign investors. All of these policies are now severely restricted under the WTO agreements (Rodrik 2001).

The international trading system needs to change in order for it to become an engine of human sustainable development in both poor and rich countries. Not only do policy approaches have to shift, but so do existing trade rules and institutions. For the WTO to become a more open and transparent institution that does not cater primarily to the industrialized countries and powerful business lobbies within it, deep reforms are required. Free trade agreements need to focus more on the direct regulation of trade flows and less on shaping the broader role of governments and markets. Investment rules in particular should be excluded from trade agreements. The multilateral trading system must be compatible with a wide variety of models of development and policy approaches, rather than serving as an instrument to impose a one-size-fits-all policy approach.

New and incipient alternatives to the existing relations of trade and invest-ment are flourishing everywhere. Such is the case with "fair trade," a set of trade arrangements that provides benefits to consumers in the North as well as to poor producers in the South. A flourishing fair trade market in coffee originating from Latin America and other regions has already improved the lives of thousands. Fair trade organizations work with communities in the South organized as co-operatives, encouraging their economic empowerment and assuring them of fair and stable prices for their products, equitable and long-term relationships, and assistance in promoting sustainable and organic production methods. Consumers in the North not only enjoy a high-quality product, but also benefit from knowing that their consumption is bringing about social transformation and improved opportunities for poor subsistence farmers.

NOTES

1. The "model" or style of development refers to the defining characteristics of a development process. For example, in countries well endowed with natural resources, trade liberalization may encourage an increasing reliance on the exploitation of primary products—which is usually accompanied by severe environmental damage—instead of a shift toward a more diversified economy.

DISCUSSION QUESTIONS

1. Discuss two contrasting views of the WTO and the multilateral trading system. Do these contribute to creating shared prosperity in a shrinking global village, or to greater inequality and more protection for the interests of rich countries and privileged elites? Provide reasons for your answer.
2. There is growing public recognition of a variety of environmental threats and the need to take action. What contribution can international trade make to solving these problems, and what changes may be required in trade policies, rules, and institutions?

SUGGESTED READINGS

French, Hilary F. 2000. *Vanishing borders: Protecting the planet in the age of globaliz-ation.* New York: Norton (emphasizing the environmental impacts of trade).

Grinspun, Ricardo, and Yasmine Shamsie, eds. 2007. *Whose Canada? Continental integration, fortress North America, and the corporate agenda.* Montreal and Kingston: McGill-Queen's University Press (a comprehensive analysis of NAFTA from a Canadian perspective).

Rodrik, Dani. 2001. *The global governance of trade: As if development really mattered.* New York: United Nations Development Programme (a useful critique of the trading system from a developmental perspective).

Shrybman, Steven. 2001. *World Trade Organization.* 2nd ed. Toronto: Lorimer (a short, critical introduction to the WTO and its shortcomings).

Stiglitz, Joseph E. 2006. *Making globalization work.* 1st ed. New York: Norton (a readable and critical analysis of globalization, including a chapter on "making trade fair").

Wallach, Lori, and Patrick Woodall. 2004. *Whose trade organization? The comprehensive guide to the WTO.* Rev. ed. New York: New Press (a detailed treatise emphasizing the health, safety, and environmental impacts of trade).

Waridel, Laure. 2002. *Coffee with pleasure: Just java and world trade.* Montreal: Black Rose Books (a fascinating introduction to the topic of fair trade).

ONLINE RESOURCES

Council of Canadians: http://www.canadians.org.

International Centre for Trade and Sustainable Development: http://ictsd.net.

Public Citizen. Global trade watch. http://www.citizen.org/trade.

Third World Network. Trade issues. http://www.twnside.org.sg/trade.htm.

World Bank. Trade and competitiveness. http://go.worldbank.org/WKDKGZVPO0.

REFERENCES

Bougrine, Hassan. 2004. The World Trade Organization, free trade areas, and the distribution of wealth. In *Global political economy and the wealth of nations: Performance, institutions, problems and policies,* ed. P.A. O'Hara, 171–187. London: Routledge.

Chang, Ha-Joon. 2007. Kicking away the ladder: The "real" history of free trade. In *Globalization and the myths of free trade: History, theory and empirical evidence,* ed. A. Shaikh, 23–49. London: Routledge.

Dussel Peters, Enrique. 1996. Structural change in Mexico's employment and the impact of NAFTA. *Revista de Economia Politica* 16 (4): 87–114.

Ernst, Christoph. 2005. *Trade liberalization, export orientation and employment in Argentina, Brazil and Mexico.* Geneva: International Labour Organization. http://www.ilo.org/public/english/employment/strat/download/esp2005-15.pdf.

Espinosa, J. Enrique, Jaime Serra, John Cavanagh, and Sarah Anderson. 2002. Happily ever NAFTA? *Foreign Policy* (September/October): 58–65.

Krugman, Paul R., and Maurice Obstfeld. 2009. *International economics: Theory and policy.* 8th ed. Boston: Pearson Addison-Wesley.

Regehr, T.D., and Ken Norrie. 2009. Crow's Nest Pass Agreement. In *The Canadian encyclopedia.* http://www.thecanadianencyclopedia.com.

Rodrik, Dani. 2001. *The global governance of trade: As if development really mattered.* New York: United Nations Development Programme.

Shaikh, Anwar, ed. 2007. *Globalization and the myths of free trade: History, theory and empirical evidence.* London: Routledge.

Shamsie, Yasmine, and Ricardo Grinspun. 2007. Rethinking Canada's approach to Latin America and the Caribbean. Paper presented at the XXVII International

Congress of the Latin American Studies Association, September 5–8, Montreal.

Shrybman, Steven. 2001. *World Trade Organization.* 2nd ed. Toronto: Lorimer.

Srinivasan, T.N. 2000. *Developing countries and the multilateral trading system: From the GATT to the Uruguay Round and the future.* Boulder, CO: Westview Press.

Todaro, Michael P., and Stephen C. Smith. 2009. *Economic development.* 10th ed. Boston: Pearson Addison-Wesley.

Wallach, Lori, and Patrick Woodall. 2004. *Whose trade organization? The comprehensive guide to the WTO.* Rev. ed. New York: New Press.

World Bank. 2009. Global dialogue on trade and development. http://go.worldbank .org/DFKAADHXX0.

Should Financial Flows Be Regulated?

11

COMPETING VIEWS

Eric Santor and Lawrence L. Schembri, "The Case for Financial Liberalization"

Gerald Epstein, "Financial Flows Must Be Regulated"

Editors' Introduction

The business of buying and selling commodities internationally consists of relatively simple transactions: the buyer gets the good or service and the seller gets the money. Financial transactions, however, are much more complex, and their effects on the domestic economy can be quite serious. These transactions generally entail the buying and selling of financial assets (such as bonds, stocks, and so on) and real assets (such as factories, buildings, and so on), but also involve lending and borrowing. International money lenders (acting as individuals or through financial institutions that they own) are obviously motivated by profits, and for this reason they are constantly monitoring the global financial markets, looking for sectors and areas offering the highest returns. Consequently, they are often ready to move huge sums of money very quickly from one country to another, in the process causing appreciation and depreciation of the currencies involved. Currency and banking crises are often linked to the disruptive behaviour of international financiers. It is for this reason that many countries historically have sought to regulate the movements and types of international capital. The objective behind such regulations is to create a more stable financial environment and to eliminate the volatility and erratic behaviour that are usually associated with speculation and excessive risk-taking.

In this context, it is understandable that countries would prefer and encourage long-term international flows related to the financing of production activities (foreign direct investment) and discourage or put restrictions on short-term flows seeking immediate gains. Gerald Epstein, who defends the view that financial flows must be regulated, gives a fairly thorough analysis of the different types of controls and measures that have been—or can be—put in place to achieve, among other things, the goal of a more stable international financial system.

269

Reflecting largely the established position taken by governments since the breakdown of the Bretton Woods system in the early 1970s, Eric Santor and Lawrence Schembri argue for the liberalization of financial flows (both within and between countries) and recommend regulation only under special circumstances. Their view follows from the general belief that government intervention will hinder the normal development of free financial markets—where the latter are considered the best way to achieve an optimal allocation of resources, more efficient investments, and higher economic growth. In this context, government regulation is thought to thwart investment and prevent the deepening of financial markets, in terms of greater provision of financial services, in many countries of the developing world.

The Case for Financial Liberalization

Eric Santor and Lawrence L. Schembri*

Introduction

The global financial crisis that began in August 2007 with the collapse of the US subprime mortgage market has sparked a comprehensive re-examination of the regulation, supervision, and structure of domestic financial systems—and of the international financial system as a whole. The proximate cause of the crisis was the inadequate regulation and supervision of financial institutions, primarily in the United States, the United Kingdom, and Europe. Moreover, the financial turmoil that began in these countries was transmitted to emerging market economies (EMEs) through financial channels—in particular, portfolio capital flows and bank lending. As a result of the crisis, there have been widespread calls for a massive re-regulation of financial institutions, financial markets, and financial transactions (Barroso 2009). Although such an approach may be superficially appealing, we instead argue that, although additional regulation may be required, it should be done in a targeted and nuanced manner.

At the same time, it is important to keep in mind that some of the current financial problems (at the time of writing, in 2009) reflect inappropriate or overly intrusive regulation. In particular, an important contributing factor to the crisis was the lack of financial sector development in many EMEs. Put simply, there was a shortage of secure, high-quality assets into which residents of these countries could place their savings, which caused many investors to turn to US financial institutions and markets. This large capital inflow, which resulted from what Federal Reserve Chairman Ben Bernanke (2005) famously labelled a "savings glut," placed a great deal of pressure on the US financial system, exposing regulatory and supervisory weaknesses in the system and thereby accelerating the arrival of the crisis.

This essay will make the case that the current global financial crisis does not necessarily imply that the appropriate response to all of the observed problems is greater regulation. Enhanced regulation may be required to fill the cracks in the system—in particular with respect to institutions, such as large investment banks

---

* The opinions expressed in this essay are those of the authors and not those of the Bank of Canada.

271

and insurance companies, that are now seen as being "too big to fail," or those financial institutions (such as hedge funds) that fell outside of the regulatory net. Likewise, more coordinated and effective regulation of institutions that span domestic and foreign jurisdictions, such as subprime mortgage brokers and multinational financial institutions, should be considered. In other cases, however—those in which the key problem as far as precipitating the crisis was the *lack* of financial market activity rather than too much—less regulation (or greater liberalization) may be needed.

In response to the crisis, the Financial Stability Board (FSB), G20, and other international policy-makers have offered many reform proposals; while some expand the scope of regulation to include institutions in the shadow banking sector (such as hedge funds, private equity funds, non-bank mortgage providers, broker-dealers, and conduits and structured investment vehicles), most seek to address existing regulatory weaknesses. In contrast to the proposed reforms that aim to improve market-based outcomes, in response to the crisis some countries may take more direct and permanent control of their financial sectors, place more controls on international capital flows, and increase official reserve holdings, particularly by maintaining undervalued managed exchange rates. Such reforms are short sighted, as they focus on short-term, rather than long-term, gains. Over time, shutting out market forces only serves to create macroeconomic imbalances and increase instability.

The next section provides a brief overview of the benefits and costs of free financial flows and financial liberalization more generally, especially for EMEs. This is followed by an examination of the causes of the financial crisis that highlights the key failures that policy-makers must now address. We then examine the reform proposals at the national and international levels, and conclude with some brief remarks about ongoing policy processes aimed at achieving future reforms.

Benefits and Costs of Financial Liberalization and Unregulated Financial Flows

The period since the early 1990s has been characterized by both ongoing and intense financial liberalization and financial globalization. At the domestic level, developed countries—and, to a lesser extent, developing ones—have sought to liberalize financial market activity and encourage ongoing financial innovation. Actions that illustrate this include the repeal of the *Glass-Steagall Act* (which removed restrictions on the activities of commercial and investment banks in the United States), the relaxation of cross-border banking restrictions in the euro area, the liberalization of capital flows, and the development of developing-country local bond markets. Most policy-makers have, to a considerable extent, embraced the notion that financial liberalization is ultimately beneficial to the economy, because financial markets and institutions will allocate savings where the returns are highest. This efficient intermediation of savings between lenders and borrowers not only benefits these two groups; because the country's capital stock is more productive, it benefits society at large. The impact of capital account liberalization and financial innovation on economic outcomes has been enormous. For instance, international capital flows have expanded dramatically in recent years, especially to EMEs (see Figure 1).[1] At the same time, however, a persistent characteristic of financial systems in the era of financial deregulation and globalization has been their tendency to experience crises—since 1975 there have been more than 190 currency crises and 100 banking crises in developed as well as developing economies.

The Role of the Financial System in the Real Economy

From a theoretical perspective, finance matters for real economic decisions when there are missing or incomplete markets due to transaction costs and asymmetric information (that is, moral hazard and adverse selection).[2] The development of the formal financial system—of financial intermediaries and markets—contributes to economic efficiency by addressing frictions in these markets, through better screening and monitoring of borrowers' investment projects, better methods for the transfer of corporate control, increased competition and risk diversification, a reduction in the market price of risk, and reduced dependence on informal financial markets. Likewise, capital account liberalization should theoretically also lead to better economic outcomes, especially for EMEs. In countries where savings are too low, capital flows should help increase investment, and thus economic growth. But low-income and emerging market countries are generally not savings-constrained (and in fact, savings are often viewed as being too high). Instead, the benefits of capital account liberalization are more indirect (Prasad and Rajan 2008; Demirguc-Kunt and Levine 2008). First, capital flows can serve to spark domestic financial sector development, through greater competition (Claessens, Demirguc-Kunt, and Huizinga 2001), increased stock market liquidity, and enhanced supervision and regulation (Mishkin 2006). Second, capital account liberalization forces countries to adopt better corporate governance structures and support institutional development (especially if the source country for the capital has better-developed institutions). Third, financial openness serves to discipline macroeconomic policy, as the recipient country wants to avoid pushing investors toward the exit.

As noted above, financial and capital account liberalization can contribute to a better allocation of savings, more efficient investment, and—ultimately—higher long-run growth. On the other hand, the recent crisis (and many of those that preceded it) highlights the fact that financial and capital liberalization, if not matched with appropriate regulation and supervision, can lead to poor economic outcomes. For instance, financial innovation with respect to subprime lending

FIGURE 1 International Capital Flows to EMEs

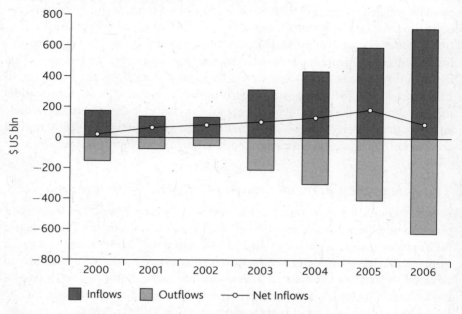

Source: International Monetary Fund, Bank for International Settlements.

and securitization, while initially beneficial, clearly contributed to the current crisis in the absence of sufficient regulatory oversight.[3] Likewise, while many countries have benefited from financial globalization in the past decade, EMEs that were initially thought to be relatively immune to the subprime crisis were nonetheless negatively affected by contagion and capital flight once the crisis intensified in the fall of 2008. Given these conflicting effects, the question remains: Do the benefits of financial and capital account liberalization outweigh the costs?

Benefits and Costs

There are two empirical questions related to the primary question posed above: (1) whether financial liberalization (and hence financial development) leads to higher growth, and (2) whether capital account liberalization positively affects economic outcomes.[4] Empirically, more financial development generally leads to higher growth. Specifically, countries with large, privately owned banks that direct credit to the private sector and whose stock exchanges are more liquid grow faster than those countries without these characteristics (Demirguc-Kunt and Levine 2008). While there are many caveats associated with the estimation of the effects of financial development on growth (for instance, which way does the causality run?), there is nevertheless a consensus that financial development is beneficial over the longer run. More controversial is whether capital account liberalization—that is, the free flow of funds—leads to better economic outcomes.

Numerous cross-country studies have sought to quantify the impact of capital account liberalization on economic growth, but there appears to be only a weak relationship at best (Eichengreen 2001; Prasad et al. 2003). The lack of evidence, however, can be attributed to a number of issues, including the fact that capital account liberalization is typically crudely measured (Prasad and Rajan 2008) and that it may only help those countries that are above a certain threshold of financial development (Klein 2005). Moreover, opening the capital account too early or in the presence of a fixed exchange rate can result in negative economic outcomes (Demirguc-Kunt and Levine 2008; Edwards 2007).

The ongoing crisis has also sparked renewed interest in capital controls—but do such actions improve economic growth? Many countries imposed capital controls beginning in the 1980s, with varying degrees of effectiveness. For instance, Malaysia imposed capital controls in 1998 (and refused IMF assistance) in the aftermath of the Asian crisis, an action that some argue led to positive macroeconomic outcomes when compared to the experience of Korea or Thailand (Prasad and Rajan 2008; Kaplan and Rodrik 2001). Likewise, Chile's imposition of controls on capital inflows in 1991 has been cited as a similarly successful intervention. However, close inspection of both episodes suggests that the benefits are often overstated, and that in practice capital controls are often evaded over time. More recent attempts to impose capital controls, as in the case of India or Thailand, were largely unsuccessful.

Although the literature has yet to provide conclusive results, there is emerging evidence that, if conducted in the proper sequence, capital account liberalization can be beneficial. And there is a growing consensus that financial liberalization—and hence financial development—is a key determinant of long-run economic growth. With this in mind, we proceed to discuss the causes of the financial crisis and the appropriate policy response.

Causes of the Financial Crisis

At the time of writing, the financial and economic crisis that began in August 2007 is the most severe since the Great Depression. Global banks may ultimately recognize losses of $US 2–3 trillion—roughly 5 percent of world GDP—and the value of stock markets and housing will have declined by almost 50 percent in some countries by the time the crisis comes to an end (IMF 2009). Countries all around the world have been hit. Because of the intensity and geographic breadth of the crisis, there is no single cause, but rather a host of related policy and market failures. Among these, the most important is clearly the chain of regulatory failures that permitted:

1. the issuance, often fraudulently, of subprime mortgages totalling hundreds of billions of dollars to households that had insufficient incomes, and that borrowed on the mistaken expectation that house prices would continue to increase;
2. the combining of these mortgages into extremely complicated and opaque financial instruments (for example, collateralized debt obligations); and
3. the holding of large numbers of these highly leveraged instruments by the biggest global banks in the United States and Europe.

Consequently, when house prices began to fall, subprime mortgages began to go into delinquency in 2007; the value of these instruments plummeted and the market for them immediately dried up; and banks incurred huge losses, forcing them to "deleverage"—that is, to call in other loans in order to hoard cash, minimize their losses, and rebuild capital. This deleveraging process was the main channel through which the financial shock was transmitted to the real economy, as many legitimate borrowers could not gain access to credit for a wide variety of household and corporate requirements (in particular, auto and student loans, credit cards, mortgages, and trade and investment financing). Likewise, global banks reduced their exposure to EMEs as part of this deleveraging process, causing capital outflows and financial instability.

There were two other important and related contributing factors: historically low interest rates and global current account imbalances. First, in many countries interest rates were very low and credit was easily accessible at modest terms. Interest rates were low due to a number of factors: low and stable inflation and reduced risk premia (due to the relatively stable macroeconomic environment), and relatively easy monetary policy (primarily in the United States, where policy interest rates had been too low for too long). Second, there was an excess of world savings that also served to lower interest rates. Since interest rates were so low, investors were looking for alternative financial instruments that would allow them to earn higher returns. Pools of mortgages—consisting of both subprime and prime mortgages—appeared very attractive, as they promised relatively high returns while being rated as relatively safe by credit rating agencies. These agencies believed that large pools of such mortgages adequately diversified credit risk; that is, it was seen as very unlikely that all of the mortgages would go into default at the same time.[5] Unfortunately, the risk surrounding these financial assets was not only credit risk, but liquidity risk. Once mortgage defaults began, the markets and funding for these instruments dried up immediately. This realization of liquidity risk was completely unanticipated by the issuing banks, rating agencies, and investors.

Finally, there were important global macroeconomic imbalances, consisting primarily of large current account surpluses (China, Japan, and OPEC), and huge deficits (the United States; see Figure 2).

FIGURE 2   Deficit Countries, 2008

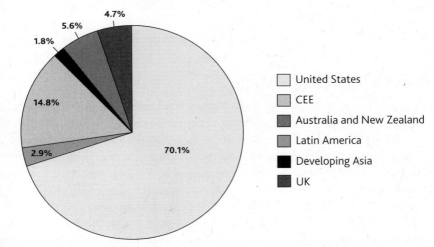

Source: UN Comtrade.

These imbalances resulted in hundreds of billions of dollars flowing into US capital markets. Although these flows were, in theory, good for the US financial sector, they also created considerable pressure on US financial institutions to produce assets that were relatively safe and yet promised high returns. Thus, these pressures accelerated the market and regulatory failures associated with the subprime mortgage crisis. Among other factors, the root causes of these imbalances included US fiscal deficits, undervalued and heavily managed Asian exchange rates, and underdeveloped financial sectors in many EMEs that caused savings to flow outside those countries. It is important to note that these latter two factors were largely the result of too much government intervention and regulation. The undervalued and heavily managed exchange rates were the consequence of the governments' desires to promote exports and to accumulate official reserves for precautionary purposes. China alone accumulated reserves of almost US $2 trillion over the 2002–2009 period. Moreover, to achieve the exchange rate level necessary for rapid export growth, the Chinese government imposed various controls on capital flows to constrain price and exchange rate adjustment. These measures also served to hinder the development of the financial sector, with the result that the latter was unable to provide sufficiently attractive investment instruments to keep residents' high savings at home. Instead, these eventually found their way to US capital markets.

In summary, inadequate financial sector regulation and supervision in the United States and Europe, low global interest rates, and global imbalances all were contributing factors to the crisis. To address the first problem requires more effective and comprehensive regulation, while to address the latter two requires better monetary and fiscal policies—but also less government intervention and regulation, to allow financial institutions and markets to develop and work efficiently.

Reforms: Right and Wrong

Given the severity of the financial crisis, there have been loud and frequent calls for wholesale reforms to the regulation and supervision of all aspects of the financial sector, including limiting financial flows. Although the financial crisis has highlighted numerous weaknesses in the regulation and supervision of the financial sector at both the national and international levels, it is important that these reforms be considered carefully and be targeted to address key gaps or weaknesses. A careful balance must be struck between stability and efficiency. Simply, the financial sector should be driven largely by economic incentives and market forces. But some regulation is necessary, because financial institutions and markets can transform savings into investment at low cost only when there is trust that institutions and market participants will honour their obligations. This trust can be fragile, since financial information is not evenly distributed across all market participants; inside information exists, and the behaviour of institutions and market participants is difficult to monitor perfectly. Therefore, regulation should attempt to preserve the integrity of competitive market forces and economic incentives in order to achieve efficient outcomes, while at the same time maintaining the stability of the system by ensuring excessive risk is not taken (this will preserve the trust of investors).

The numerous reform proposals can be grouped into three key areas: (1) systemic and macroprudential financial sector regulation at the national level; (2) international cooperation and coordination among national regulatory and supervisory organizations, especially with respect to large multinational financial institutions; and (3) effective financial surveillance at the global level, to maintain global stability by preventing crises. While some of these proposals expand the depth and scope of regulation—for example, to include institutions such as hedge funds—most address regulatory weaknesses.

One of the main weaknesses identified by the crisis is that the existing regulation of the financial sector is focused almost exclusively at the level of the individual institution, rather than at the financial system as a whole. That is, existing regulation tries to ensure that each financial institution has sufficient capital to absorb potential losses. This approach, which is largely centred on credit risk, ignores systemic liquidity or market risk, and thus can create the wrong incentives for the stability of the system as a whole. For example, during a period of slower economic activity, it may make sense for an individual institution to be more prudent and limit lending to preserve the required ratio of capital to assets. But if all institutions behave in the same manner, the behaviour will become self-fulfilling and the economy will suffer. New macroprudential regulation that considers the financial system as a whole and leans against this inherent procyclicality must be put in place.

Another important reform is to increase the amount, distribution, and transparency of financial information by requiring that financial instruments be standardized and exchange-traded, or traded through centralized market-makers. This reform would improve the liquidity and resilience of financial markets, especially in times of stress. At the domestic level, particularly in the United States, there is a need to consolidate the existing fragmented system of regulation and supervision of financial institutions into a system that is comprehensive, coherent, and dynamic. The financial sector is highly innovative; new instruments and markets are constantly being developed. And while these innovations generally improve market outcomes, regulatory oversight must keep pace with such developments to ensure that perverse incentives, in which the innovation is driven by the opportunity to exploit regulatory gaps, are not created.

Since financial markets are global and large financial institutions operate in many jurisdictions, it is important that the regulation of these institutions be coordinated at the global level to prevent regulatory arbitrage. The FSB and the Basel Committee on Banking Supervision have put forward proposals to develop best-practice standards and codes for financial regulation and to oversee the largest global institutions. Part of this effort aims to expand the scope of regulation to cover all systemically important financial institutions, including hedge funds. Given the severity of the current crisis, it may seem prudent to extend regulation to a much broader set of financial activities to prevent similar crises in the future. Such a regulatory expansion, however, could come at a considerable cost, as the efficiency and innovative dynamism of the financial system could be compromised. Moreover, in some cases, extensive regulation may not be as effective as planned, as in the case of hedge funds.[6]

In contrast to these well-reasoned reforms that seek to improve market-based outcomes, concerns have been raised that in response to the crisis, some countries may become more heavy handed in their interventions in the financial sector. In particular, emerging market countries that have been hurt by the recent reversal of capital inflows may react by placing more controls on international capital flows, increasing their official reserve holdings, and maintaining undervalued managed exchange rates. Such potential reforms suffer from the fallacy of composition: while they may seem to improve outcomes in the short run, the country will be worse off in the long run, because a well-developed financial sector is critical to achieving an efficient allocation of capital and the resulting higher standards of living. Moreover, the global economy will be less stable, because shutting out market forces will only serve to create (or exacerbate) macroeconomic imbalances and increase instability. Instead, EMEs should accelerate domestic financial sector development in order to increase the likelihood that domestic savings will remain at home and be intermediated by an efficient domestic financial sector, thus supporting domestic consumption and investment.

Lastly, there is a clear need to address the problem of global imbalances, and more generally, to ensure a well-functioning and stable market-based international financial system. To this end, the International Monetary Fund (IMF) is well-positioned to provide candid, even-handed, and objective surveillance—both at the individual country and global levels—in order to ensure that countries are pursuing policies that are not detrimental to the global economy. But it is not just up to the IMF: countries must live up to their obligations under the IMF articles and submit themselves to the surveillance process, taking into due consideration the IMF's advice and ensuring that they pursue policies that contribute to the stability of the international monetary system (Lavigne, Maier, and Santor 2009).

Conclusion

The current financial crisis has exposed many weaknesses in the global financial system. In response to these concerns, policy-makers, regulators, and supervisors have commenced ambitious plans to overhaul the regulation and supervision of domestic financial systems as well as the international system. These include broadening the scope of regulation, introducing macroprudential supervision, enhancing international cooperation, and ensuring that market participants (and their compensation schemes) have the proper incentives.

Although many of these initiatives seek to address weaknesses within the current system, some observers have advocated for a slowdown—if not a reversal—with respect to financial and capital account liberalization. In their view, the current crisis highlights the flaws of such policy choices, and as such, market-based reforms should be avoided. The difficulty with this approach is that it ignores the considerable benefits that financial liberalization—and, for that matter, globalization—has provided since the mid-1990s (for EMEs in particular). Given that, on average, the benefits of financial liberalization outweigh the costs, it is important that the weaknesses in the current system be addressed appropriately—lest more onerous regulations critically undermine the efficiency of the international financial system.

NOTES

1. Capital flows slowed sharply in 2008, and estimates for 2009 are for net outflows.
2. "Adverse selection" arises when lenders cannot perfectly observe the true characteristics of borrowers: if borrowers have private information regarding

the riskiness of their projects, then risky borrowers have an incentive to pose as safe borrowers. "Moral hazard" implies that the borrower may deviate from the terms of the contract or actually use the loan for purposes other than those sanctioned by the lender.

3. Subprime lending allowed borrowers who were previously excluded from home ownership to obtain mortgages, while securitization allowed for a greater diversification of risk within and across financial markets.

4. An extensive literature has examined the influence of financial development on growth. The determinants of financial development are varied, and include legal origin and political structure, macroeconomic policies, investors' rights and enforcement, regulation and supervision, and the degree of financial liberalization (Demirguc-Kunt and Levine 2008).

5. The ratings agencies themselves had a serious conflict of interest because they were being paid by the issuers of these instruments to design and rate these instruments in order to meet certain guidelines.

6. King and Maier (2009) argue that regulating hedge funds would be ineffective and could impair market efficiency.

DISCUSSION QUESTIONS

1. What are the main benefits of financial market liberalization?
2. Explain the factors that were responsible for the current financial crisis.
3. Which proposed reforms to the financial sector are necessary to prevent future financial crises?

SUGGESTED READINGS

Carney, M. 2009. What are banks really for? Remarks to the University of Alberta School of Business, Edmonton, Alberta, March 30. http://www.bankofcanada.ca/en/speeches/2009/sp300309.pdf.

Edwards, S. 2007. *Capital flows and capital controls in emerging economies: Policies, practices, and consequences.* Chicago: University of Chicago Press.

Eichengreen, B. 2004. *Capital flows and crises.* Cambridge, MA: MIT Press.

Ocampo, J., and J. Stiglitz. 2008. *Capital market liberalization and development.* New York: Oxford University Press.

ONLINE RESOURCES

Bank for International Settlement: http://www.bis.org (includes information on the bank's various committees under the "Monetary and financial stability" tab).

Financial Stability Forum: http://www.fsforum.org.

G20: http://www.g20.org.

International Monetary Fund: http://www.imf.org.

World Bank: http://www.worldbank.org.

REFERENCES

Barroso, J.M.D. 2009. Declaration on the preparation of the G20 summit. Speech by the President of the European Commission to the European Parliament, March 24.

Bernanke, B. 2005. The global saving glut and the U.S. current account deficit. Remarks at the Sandridge Lecture, Virginia Association of Economics, Richmond, Virginia, March 10.

Claessens, S., A. Demirguc-Kunt, and H. Huizinga. 2001. How does foreign entry affect domestic banking markets? *Journal of Banking and Finance* 25 (5): 891–911.

Demirguc-Kunt, A., and R. Levine. 2008. Finance, financial sector policies, and long-run growth. Commission on Growth and Development Working Paper 11. Washington, DC: World Bank.

Edwards, S. 2007. Capital flows, capital flow contractions and macroeconomic vulnerability. NBER Working Paper 11170. Cambridge, MA: National Bureau of Economic Research.

Eichengreen, B. 2001. Capital account liberalization: What do cross-country studies tell us? *World Bank Economic Review* 15 (3): 341–365.

International Monetary Fund (IMF). 2009. *Global financial stability report: Responding to the financial crisis and measuring systemic risks.* Washington, DC: IMF. http://www.imf.org/external/pubs/ft/gfsr/2009/01/pdf/text.pdf.

Kaplan, E., and D. Rodrik. 2001. Did the Malaysian capital controls work? NBER Working Paper 8142. Cambridge, MA: National Bureau of Economic Research.

King, M.R., and P. Maier. 2009. Hedge funds and financial stability: The state of the debate. *Journal of Financial Stability* (forthcoming).

Klein, M. 2005. Capital account liberalization, institutional quality and economic growth: Theory and evidence. NBER Working Paper 11112. Cambridge, MA: National Bureau of Economic Research.

Lavigne, R., P. Maier, and E. Santor. 2009. Renewing IMF surveillance: Transparency, accountability, and independence. *Review of International Organizations* 4 (1): 29–46.

Mishkin, F. 2006. *The next great globalization: How disadvantaged nations can harness their financial systems to get rich.* Princeton, NJ: Princeton University Press.

Prasad, E., and R. Rajan. 2008. A pragmatic approach to capital account liberalization. *Journal of Economic Perspectives* 22 (3): 149–172.

Prasad, E., K. Rogoff, S.-J. Wei, and M. Kose. 2003. Effects of financial globalization on developing countries: Some empirical evidence. IMF Occasional Paper 220. Washington, DC: IMF.

Financial Flows Must Be Regulated

Gerald Epstein*

I. Introduction and Historical Context

Prior to the First World War—in the late 19th and early 20th centuries—the industrialized economies of Europe and the United States were characterized by a high degree of global financial integration, a relatively large role for markets, and a philosophy based on limited government regulation (laissez-faire). Capital could flow freely with very light regulation both within and between countries, and there were relatively low barriers to trade in goods and services. Many countries' monetary systems were based on a gold standard, which fixed countries' exchange rates relative to one another. The Bank of England "orchestrated" the system with help from central banks in France and elsewhere on the European continent. This system helped bring great wealth to bankers and industrial capitalists in the richer countries, and spread investments in infrastructure and other projects to the colonial and semi-colonial countries of the New World, enriching some elites in those countries as well.

However, in the 1930s, this system of free capital mobility collapsed, as did most of the world economy. Figure 1 shows the rise of capital flows in the late 19th and early 20th century, and then their dramatic collapse in the 1930s. Among the key causes of the collapse were the excesses allowed by the laissez-faire approach to financial markets, which led to excessive accumulations of debt and highly speculative investments—a significant number of which failed spectacularly. Equally important was the role of international capital flows in worsening the crisis as it broke out, with capital fleeing those countries perceived to be in trouble and flooding into those seen as safe havens (Block 1977; Kindleberger 1986; Eichengreen 1992). Figure 1 also shows that international capital flows tend to precede banking crises.

In the aftermath of the collapse and the ensuing, catastrophic Second World War, governments in most of the world—with the reluctant blessing of the newly

---

* The author thanks his co-authors and colleagues James Crotty, Ilene Grabel, Arjun Jayadev, and Jomo K.S. for their contributions to his understanding of capital management techniques and for their work, on which he draws liberally here. Of course, they are not responsible for any errors.

FIGURE 1   Capital Mobility and the Incidence of Banking Crisis: All Countries, 1800–2008

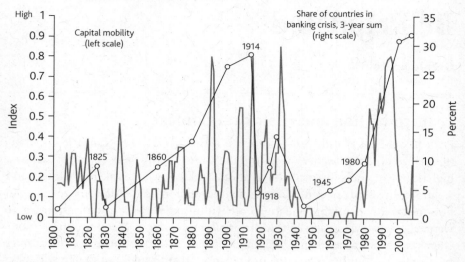

Source: Reinhart and Rogoff (2008, 23).

created International Monetary Fund (IMF)—adopted government controls (exchange and capital controls) to manage the international flows of money and capital. This policy had been strongly advocated by John Maynard Keynes, the most important economist of the 20th century and co-architect of the Bretton Woods agreements that, in 1944, had established the IMF and the World Bank as well as a global system of fixed exchange rates (Crotty 1983). For at least the first three decades following the Second World War, controls over the international flow of capital became the norm in most of the world.

Over time, as the world economy recovered and much of the developed world flourished in the so-called golden age of economic growth in the 1950s and 1960s, memories of the financial crises of the Great Depression faded and governments began to relax restrictions on the international flow of capital and money (Helleiner 1984). From 1971 to 1973, the postwar Bretton Woods system of fixed exchange rates broke down and exchange rates became more flexible. A general shift in economic fashion occurred, from an approach (prevalent from the 1940s to the 1960s) based on financial regulation of the market aimed at maintaining stability and achieving social goals to a return to a more laissez-faire approach in which the market dominates. This movement back toward laissez-faire accelerated with the oil crises and stagflation of the 1970s and the coming to power of Margaret Thatcher in the United Kingdom and Ronald Reagan in the United States—both very strong advocates of smaller government, less regulation, and more promotion of market dominance and the interests of business as the best approach for economic development (Diaz-Alejandro 1985; Glyn 1986). Naturally, these policies were strongly supported by banking and business interests, as well as by some workers and members of the middle class who had suffered during the stagflationary period of the 1970s.

The next 20 years witnessed a secular move toward more financial deregulation and the reduction of controls over financial flows in the United States, Canada, and Europe, as well as in many developing countries. Figure 2 shows the reductions in capital regulations and the corresponding increases in capital mobility, which rose in most types of countries in the 1980s. Note that Figure 2 is based on capital flow (account) *regulations* (de jure capital controls), whereas Figure 1 is based on *actual* flows of capital (de facto capital flows). At the same time, the frequency and severity of banking and financial crises accelerated, especially in developing countries (Figure 1). Still, the majority of economists and the IMF continued to press for financial liberalization and the elimination of capital controls in the developing world.

Then, in 1997, the so-called Asian financial crisis hit, creating havoc in many highly successful Asian countries including Thailand, South Korea, and Malaysia. This crisis was soon followed by the Russian financial crisis. Figure 1 reflects these crises and illustrates a general rule. Prior to crises, international financial flows accelerate. Then, when the crisis hits, international capital flows tend to drop precipitously (so-called sudden stops), the inflows exacerbating the buildup to the crisis and then the outflows worsening its severity.

With the Russian and Asian crises, continued pressure for financial liberalization by bankers and economists collided head-on with the reality of unstable financial flows, which were clearly contributing to—and even causing—financial crises with alarming frequency. This clash was perhaps most apparent in the debate over a proposed amendment to the IMF bylaws that would have made capital account liberalization a requirement of membership; the proposal was made just as the Asian financial crisis was hitting. In a symposium held by Princeton University to debate this amendment, Harvard Professor Dani Rodrik presented a paper critical of full capital account liberalization, which included the following analogy (1998, 55):

> Imagine landing on a planet that runs on widgets.[1] You are told that international trade in widgets is highly unpredictable and volatile on this planet, for reasons that are poorly understood. A small number of nations have access to imported widgets, while many others are completely shut out even when they impose no apparent obstacles to trade. With some regularity, those countries that have access to widgets get too much of a good thing, and their markets are flooded with imported widgets. This allows them to go on a widget binge, which makes everyone pretty happy for a while. However, such binges are often interrupted

FIGURE 2   Capital Account Liberalization, 1973–1995

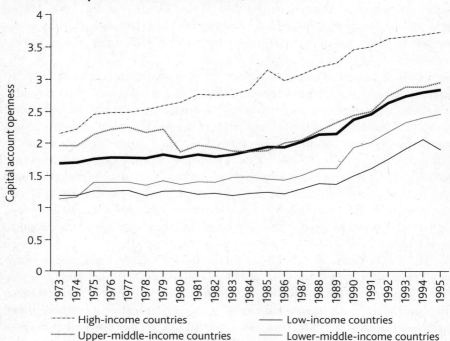

Source: Lee and Jayadev (2005, 26).

by a sudden cutoff in supply, unrelated to any change in circumstances. The turnaround causes the affected economies to experience painful economic adjustments. For reasons equally poorly understood, when one country is hit by a supply cutback in this fashion, many other countries experience similar shocks in quick succession. Some years thereafter, a widget boom starts anew. Your hosts beg you for guidance: how should they deal with their widget problem? Ponder this question for a while and then ponder under what circumstances your central recommendation would be that all extant controls on international trade in widgets be eliminated. Substitute "international capital flows" for "widgets" above and the description fits today's world economy quite well.

Indeed, during the Asian financial crisis, countries that had strong controls over international financial flows (for example, China and India) were much less negatively affected by the financial crisis than were countries that had few controls (see the discussion below). This observation led some economists in academia, the IMF, and other policy circles to question the conventional wisdom that free flows of international capital will lead to the best outcomes.

More than a decade after it was written, Rodrik's analogy is still highly relevant—perhaps even more so than in 1998. The financial crisis, which spread in 2008 from the "subprime" housing markets of the United States to many other financial markets via international capital (and trade) flows, has placed in focus once again the instability and difficulties that can be created across national borders by the unregulated flow of finance. Once again, then, the question is raised: Should financial flows be regulated? This essay answers the question with a "yes."

The remainder of this essay is organized as follows. The next section, section II, includes a brief discussion of the arguments for unregulated ("free") capital mobility and a comparison of these with the empirical evidence. Section III discusses the goals of regulating international capital flows and the types of controls that governments can use to manage these flows. Section IV presents evidence regarding the costs, benefits, and effectiveness of different types of controls. Section V presents my conclusions.

II. Arguments for Unrestricted International Capital Flows

Economists' arguments in favour of minimal government restrictions on the international flows of money and capital stem from their basic faith in the efficiency of the market and the inefficiency and/or inefficacy of government regulation. While this faith is quite general, it is usually applied more specifically in specific contexts. In the case of financial markets, the arguments are rooted in the following perceived "functions" of money, finance, and financial markets: (1) to provide a medium of exchange, means of payment, and unit of account; (2) to allocate credit to its most productive uses; (3) to serve as an efficient intermediary between savers and investors; (4) to allow savers to reduce the risks associated with making investments; and (5) to provide an efficient means to save for the future (what economists refer to as "smoothing the consumption stream over time"). In effect, these economists argue that financial markets "free from government regulation" can achieve these aims better than regulated markets can (Neely 1999).

Economists make a leap when they apply these arguments for the efficiency of the free flows of capital, taken from an analysis of a national economy, and apply them to international flows of finance between countries, because in fact there are big differences between purely domestic financial transactions and international ones. Moreover, these arguments are based on a *microeconomic* logic and do not take into account many key *macroeconomic* concerns, such as the impact on unemployment, and financial instability.

In any event, the upshot of these claims is that free capital mobility should be associated with the following, all relative to contexts in which there are more regulations and controls over capital flows: (1) higher levels of output and investment;

(2) more rapid productivity growth and economic growth overall; (3) an allocation of financial resources away from those who need them less (rich countries) and toward those who need them more (poor countries); (4) less risk; and (5) an improved ability to smooth consumption over time.

What does the evidence show? There is now a large body of empirical literature that investigates these claims over time and across countries (see Lee and Jayadev 2005; Reinhart and Rogoff 2008; Rodrik and Subramanian 2008; and Kose et al. 2009).[2] A number of studies have attempted to examine the link between free capital mobility and growth. Overall, this literature shows a lack of any compelling evidence for a positive link between capital account liberalization and growth. Perhaps the most careful and detailed summary of this literature is provided by Kose and others, who conclude that, taken as a whole, "the vast empirical literature provides little robust evidence of a causal relationship between financial integration and growth" (2009, 10).

As Figure 1 shows, there is a strong correlation between capital mobility and financial crisis. Moreover, there is strong evidence that financial crises result in permanent losses of output (Cerra and Saxena 2008).

In short, capital account liberalization and integration do not appear to increase economic growth or investment; instead, they contribute to financial crises that can have devastating short-term effects as well as costly long-term effects on output. Furthermore, capital account liberalization and crisis can increase inequality (Lee and Jayadev 2005). There is very little to no evidence that free capital mobility delivers the benefits suggested by advocates. Still, it is possible that controlling flows with government regulation could make the situation even worse, or, at best, is unnecessary. Moreover, there are many different ways to manage flows and many different types of flows to manage.

In light of these findings, it is not surprising that many countries use capital controls to manage the flows of finance across borders. What are the main goals of these policies? What types of policies work best, and under what circumstances?

III. Goals and Mechanisms for Controlling International Financial Flows[3]

Types of Controls

First, it is important to be aware of the techniques that are available for controlling and managing the quantity, type, and impact of international financial flows. Table 1 presents a list and typology of controls. Controls, first of all, are simply government regulations or taxes that affect inflows or outflows of capital. Capital flows into a country when foreign residents buy domestic assets or when foreigners lend money to domestic residents, and flows out of a country when domestic residents lend money abroad or buy foreign assets. These assets are usually financial assets—stocks, bonds and securities of various types, currency, and bank deposits—but they can also refer to real assets, such as land. These securities and assets can be short term and highly liquid, such as bank deposits and short-term government bonds, or they can be longer term and less liquid, such as significant ownership of businesses (foreign direct investment), long-term government bonds, or real estate. Currency itself (dollars, euros, pesos, and so on) is the most short term and liquid. Increasingly, complex financial assets and liabilities (debts) called derivatives are involved in the flows of capital in and out of countries; these are hard to control, mostly because they are almost completely unregulated and relatively little is known about the roles of these securities in many financial transactions (Dodd 2002; Garber 1998).

Typologies for understanding controls usually distinguish between controls on *outflows* (domestic buying of foreign assets, including foreign currency) and those on *inflows* (the buying by foreign residents of domestic assets, including domestic currency). Another key distinction is between controls that work mainly through price measures, such as taxing inflows or outflows, and those that work primarily through quantitative measures, such as placing a quota on buying or selling assets, restricting the types of assets that can be bought or sold, or placing an absolute ban on the buying or selling of particular assets. This distinction is similar to the distinction in international trade, where economists distinguish between restrictive measures that rely on tariffs (price-based measures) and those that rely on quotas (quantity-based measures) (see Neely 1999).[4]

Finally, regulations that affect the inflows or outflows of capital directly can be distinguished from those that affect them and their impacts indirectly, by implementing *prudential regulations* on financial institutions. These prudential regulations can be capital regulations, regulations concerning maturity mismatches between short- and long-term assets and liabilities, regulations concerning derivative contracts, regulations concerning the borrowing of domestic currency from offshore banks, and so on. While such regulations might not affect the flows of foreign assets and liabilities directly, they will often affect them indirectly. In many countries, derivative contracts are often entered into with foreign counterparties, maturity mismatches often involve foreign flows, dealing with offshore banks often involves buying and selling foreign assets and liabilities, and so on.

The term "capital management techniques" is used to refer to the combination of capital and exchange controls plus the financial prudential regulations that indirectly affect these flows and their impacts. In the discussion that follows, we will move interchangeably between the terms "capital controls" and "capital management techniques" for ease of exposition.

Examples of controls that involve taxes are direct taxes on the buying or selling of foreign exchange. An example of this is the "Tobin" tax, named after Nobel prize-winning economist James Tobin, who proposed such a tax in the 1970s (see Tobin 1978). The Tobin tax would place a small tax on all foreign exchange transactions,

TABLE 1   Objectives and Types of Capital Management Techniques

	Objectives	Price-based	Quantity-based	Prudential
Inflows	• Keep a stable and competitive real exchange rate • Limit excessive debt and maturity or locational mismatch to prevent financial instability • Alter the composition of inflows to attract desired inflows • Limit foreign ownership of assets for sovereign purposes or to protect domestic industries	• Tobin tax (tax on foreign exchange transactions) • Reserve requirements on inflows of capital (e.g., URR, unremunerated reserve requirements) • Taxation of capital inflows	• Quantitative limits on foreign ownership of domestic companies' assets • Reporting requirements and quantitative limits on borrowing from abroad • Limits on ability to borrow from offshore entities	• Keynes tax (tax on domestic financial transactions) • Reporting requirements and limitations on maturity structure of liabilities and assets • Reserve requirements on deposits • Capital requirements on assets and restrictions on off-balance-sheet activities and derivatives contracts

(Table 1 is continued on the next page.)

290

TABLE 1 Continued

	Objectives	Price-based	Quantity-based	Prudential
Outflows	• Protect tax base by reducing capital flight • Maintain stability of exchange rate • Preserve savings to finance investment • Enhance credit allocation mechanisms to support "industrial policy" and investments for social objectives • Enhance the autonomy of monetary policy in order to reduce inflation or expand employment and economic growth	• Tobin tax • Multiple exchange rates	• Exchange controls • Restrictions on purchase of foreign assets including foreign deposits • Limits on currency convertibility	• Limits on asset acquisition • Asset-backed reserve requirements
Inflows and outflows	• All of the above	• "Trip wire and speed bump" approach (Grabel 2004): identify a set of early warning signals and implement these various qualitative and quantitative policies gradually and dynamically, with an emphasis on controls on inflows.		

thereby discouraging the buying and selling of foreign exchange for very short-term purposes, which some economists argue tends to be for speculative purposes. The tax could raise significant amounts of revenue if implemented on an international scale. If that were to happen, some economists and policy-makers have urged that any revenues generated be used for a variety of purposes, including aid for economic development (Chang and Grabel 2004). A "Keynes" tax would implement a small tax on all domestic transactions and would serve similar purposes to the Tobin tax but on a domestic scale (Pollin 2005).

Another example of a tax-based control is the "unremunerated reserve requirement" (URR), or *encaje*, used in Chile and Colombia. In Chile, this policy required foreign investors who wanted to invest in the country to place some of the funds in a bank account for a period of time; they received no interest on the funds. This policy works like a tax, since the investors lose out on the interest they could have received if they were able to invest in interest-bearing securities or bank accounts.

Quantitative regulations include quotas on buying foreign exchange, limits on buying equity in certain industries, limits on ownership shares of firms, and an inability to borrow money from offshore banks unless the funds are used for particular purposes.

Another important distinction is whether countries utilize controls in a rigid or flexible way. Importantly, countries often use controls in a *dynamic* fashion, tightening or loosening them as circumstances demand rather than keeping them in place in a fixed—and therefore *static*—way. For example, when a crisis hits, countries may tighten controls; when the crisis eases, they may loosen them again.

Objectives of Capital Management Techniques

There are many ways to categorize the goals of capital management techniques (see Table 1 for a detailed list of goals). More generally, capital management techniques are used to achieve the following four objectives: to promote financial stability; to encourage desirable investment and financing arrangements; to enhance policy autonomy, including the maintenance of stable and competitive exchange rates; and to enhance national sovereignty and democracy. The more specific goals in Table 1 can be seen as particular means of achieving these objectives.

In order to understand the goals, challenges, and trade-offs associated with capital management techniques, we first need to understand the "trilemma" problem of international finance.

THE "TRILEMMA"

Capital mobility creates challenges for countries that want to set interest rates for domestic purposes. For example, central banks may want to lower interest rates to reduce the cost of borrowing in order to increase investment, employment, and economic growth. At other times, governments and central banks may want to raise interest rates to slow down an "overheated" economy and reduce inflation. International capital mobility can undermine these policies because, in integrated, global financial markets, domestic interest rates are strongly affected by foreign interest rates. Domestic and foreign investors will move capital from countries that have lower interest rates—adjusted for political and exchange rate risks—to countries that have higher interest rates. So if a central bank lowers its interest rate to try to encourage domestic investment, capital might leave the country in search of higher interest rates abroad, counteracting the policy. Similarly, if central banks try to raise interest rates to fight inflation, then investors might send capital flowing into the country, thereby driving down interest rates and undermining the policy.

Capital mobility also causes problems for countries wishing to fix or smooth their exchange rates. If investors think that risk has increased in a country, then they might sell their investments and take their money out of the country. When they do this, they sell their domestic currency assets and buy foreign exchange, thereby lowering the value (depreciating or putting pressure for a devaluation) of the domestic currency. If the country does not want its currency value to go down, then it will have to raise its interest rates to try to keep domestic assets more attractive and prevent the capital from leaving. But what if the country does not want to raise interest rates, because, say, it is facing a recession and wants lower interest rates to promote domestic investment?

Here, we see the "trilemma." Countries have a very difficult time maintaining all three of these goals—free capital mobility, autonomous monetary policy directed to domestic concerns, and fixed (or highly managed) exchange rates—at once. In general, they can have at most two out of the three. For example, they can choose free capital mobility and autonomous monetary policy, but then they must let the market determine the exchange rate. Or they can have free capital mobility and a fixed exchange rate, but then they must give up the autonomous monetary policy and use it to keep the exchange rate fixed in the face of market-determined capital flows.

This problem can also be explained by the "interest parity relation," which says that in a financially integrated international economy, domestic interest rates are tied to foreign interest rates (adjusted for expected changes in exchange rates and risks associated with default or political instability).

If a country wants to have domestically oriented monetary policy and a fixed or highly managed exchange rate, then it must control capital mobility. That is where capital controls or capital management techniques come in.

1. CAPITAL MANAGEMENT TECHNIQUES CAN PROMOTE FINANCIAL STABILITY

Capital management techniques can promote financial stability through their ability to reduce currency, flight, fragility, and/or contagion risks. Capital management can thereby reduce the potential for financial crisis and attendant economic and social devastation (Grabel 2003; Epstein, Grabel, and Jomo 2005). "Currency risk" refers to the risk that a currency will appreciate or depreciate significantly over a short period of time. "Investor flight risk" refers to the likelihood that holders of liquid financial assets will sell their holdings en masse in the face of perceived difficulty. "Lender flight risk" refers to the likelihood that lenders will terminate lending programs or will only extend loans on prohibitive terms. "Fragility risk" refers to the vulnerability of an economy's private and public borrowers to internal or external shocks that would jeopardize their ability to meet current obligations. Fragility risk arises in a number of ways: borrowers might employ financing strategies that involve maturity or locational mismatch; agents might finance private investment with capital that is prone to flight risk; or investors (domestic and foreign) might overinvest in certain sectors, thereby creating overcapacity and fuelling unsustainable speculative bubbles. Finally, "contagion risk" refers to the threat that a country will fall victim to financial and macroeconomic instability that originates elsewhere. Capital management techniques can reduce contagion risk by managing the degree of financial integration and by reducing the vulnerability of individual countries to currency, flight, and fragility risks.

2. CAPITAL MANAGEMENT TECHNIQUES CAN PROMOTE DESIRABLE TYPES OF INVESTMENT AND FINANCING ARRANGEMENTS AND DISCOURAGE LESS DESIRABLE ONES

Capital management techniques can influence the composition of the economy's aggregate investment portfolio and the financing arrangements that underpin these investments. Capital management techniques—particularly those that involve inflow controls—can promote desirable types of investment and financing strategies by rewarding investors and borrowers who engage in them. Desirable types of investment are those that create employment; improve living standards; and promote greater income equality, technology transfer, learning by doing, and/or long-term growth. Desirable types of financing are those that are long term, stable, and sustainable. Capital management can discourage less desirable types of investment and financing strategies by increasing their cost or precluding them altogether (Nembhard 1996).

3. CAPITAL MANAGEMENT TECHNIQUES CAN ENHANCE THE AUTONOMY OF ECONOMIC AND SOCIAL POLICY

Capital management techniques can enhance policy autonomy in a number of ways. They can reduce the severity of currency risk, thereby allowing authorities to protect a currency peg. They can also keep exchange rates at competitive and stable levels. Capital management can create space for the government and/or the central bank to pursue growth-promoting and/or reflationary macroeconomic policies by neutralizing the threat of capital flight (via restrictions on capital inflows or outflows). Moreover, by reducing the risk of financial crisis in the first place, capital management can reduce the likelihood that governments will be compelled to use contractionary macro- and microeconomic policies, as well as social policy, as a signal to attract foreign investment back to the country or as a precondition for financial assistance from the IMF. Finally, capital management techniques can reduce the spectre of excessive foreign control or ownership of domestic resources.

4. Capital Management Techniques Can Enhance National Autonomy and Even Democracy

It follows from the third point that capital management can enhance democracy by reducing the potential for speculators and external actors to exercise undue influence over domestic decision making either directly or indirectly (via the threat of capital flight). Capital management techniques can reduce the veto power of the financial community and the IMF and create space for the interests of other groups (such as advocates for the poor) to play a role in the design of economic and social policy. Capital management techniques can thus be said to enhance democracy because they create the opportunity for pluralism in policy design.

Costs of Capital Management Techniques

Critics of capital management techniques argue that they impose four types of costs: they reduce growth; reduce efficiency and policy discipline; promote corruption and waste; and aggravate credit scarcity and uncertainty. Critics argue that the benefits that derive from capital management (such as financial stability) come at an unacceptably high price.

In sum, many critics argue that there are significant costs associated with capital management techniques. However, there is little consensus in the empirical literature on the size—or even the existence—of these costs. More important, researchers have largely failed to investigate the relative weight of costs and benefits.

IV. Evidence on the Costs, Benefits, and Effectiveness of Capital Management Techniques

There have been many studies of the impact, effectiveness, and costs and benefits of capital controls and capital management techniques (for recent surveys, see Epstein, Grabel, and Jomo 2005; Magud, Reinhart, and Rogoff 2005). Some of these offer a statistical/econometric analysis, while others rely on case studies.

Case Study Evidence[5]

I first present case study evidence compiled by Epstein, Grabel, and Jomo (2005). (See Tables 2 and 3.) The researchers undertook case studies of capital management techniques in seven countries: Chile, Colombia, China, Taiwan, India, Malaysia,

TABLE 2 Summary: Types and Objectives of Capital Management Techniques Employed During the 1990s

Country	Types of capital management techniques	Objectives of capital management techniques
Chile	**Inflows:** • Foreign Direct Investments (FDI) and Portfolio Investments (PI): One year residence requirement • 30% URR • tax on foreign loans: 1.2% per year **Outflows:** • no significant restrictions **Domestic financial regulations:** • strong regulatory measures	• Lengthen maturity structures and stabilize inflows • Help manage exchange rates to maintain export competitiveness • Protect economy from financial instability
Colombia	Similar to Chile	Similar to Chile
Taiwan	**Inflows:** *Non-residents* • Bank accounts can only be used for domestic spending, not financial speculation • Foreign participation in stock market regulated • FDI tightly regulated *Residents* • Regulation of foreign borrowing **Outflows:** • Exchange controls **Domestic financial regulations:** • Restrictions on lending for real estate and other speculative purposes	• Promote industrialization • Help manage exchange rates to maintain export competitiveness • Maintain financial stability and insulate itself from foreign financial crises

(Table 2 is continued on the next page.)

TABLE 2 Continued

Country	Types of capital management techniques	Objectives of capital management techniques
Singapore	**Inflows:** • "Non-internationalization" of the Singapore currency (S$) **Outflows:** *Non-residents* • financial institutions can't extend S$ credit to non-residents if they are likely to use for speculation • if they borrow for use abroad, must swap first into foreign currency **Domestic financial regulations:** • restrictions on creation of swaps, and other derivatives that could be used for speculation against S$	• prevent speculation against S$ • support "soft peg" of S$ • help maintain export competitiveness • help insulate itself from foreign financial crises
Malaysia (1998)	**Inflows:** • Restrictions on foreign borrowing **Outflows:** *Non-residents* • 12-month repatriation waiting period • Graduated exit levies inversely proportional to length of stay *Residents* • Exchange controls **Domestic financial regulations:** *Non-residents* • Restricted access to Malaysian currency *Residents* • Encouraged to borrow and invest domestically	• Maintain political and economic sovereignty • Kill the offshore ringgit market • Shut down offshore share market • Help reflate the economy • Help create financial stability and insulate the economy from contagion

(Table 2 is continued on the next page.)

TABLE 2   Continued

Country	Types of capital management techniques	Objectives of capital management techniques
India	**Inflows:** *Non-residents* • Strict regulation of FDI and PI **Outflows:** *Non-residents* • None *Residents* • Exchange controls **Domestic financial regulations:** • Strict limitations on development of domestic financial markets	• Support industrial policy • Pursue capital account liberalization in an incremental and controlled fashion • Insulate domestic economy from financial contagion • Preserve domestic savings and foreign exchange reserves • Help stabilize exchange rate
China	**Inflows:** *Non-residents* • Strict regulation on sectoral FDI investment • Regulation of equity investments by segmenting stock markets **Outflows:** *Non-residents* • No restrictions on repatriation of funds • Strict limitations on borrowing Chinese renminbi for speculative purposes *Residents* • Exchange controls **Domestic financial regulations:** • Strict limitations on residents and non-residents	• Support industrial policy • Pursue capital account liberalization in incremental and controlled fashion • Insulate domestic economy from financial contagion • Increase political sovereignty • Preserve domestic savings and foreign exchange reserves • Help keep exchange rates at competitive levels

Source: Epstein, Grabel, and Jomo (2005, 304–305).

and Singapore. As Table 2 shows, these countries used quite specific combinations of the types of controls listed in Table 1 for a variety of purposes (mostly those listed in Table 1).

First, consider four commonly held—and mistaken—ideas about capital management techniques. One is that these techniques can only work in the short run, not the long run. However, with the exception of Malaysia, all of the cases show that management *can* achieve important objectives over a significant period of time. Taking China and Singapore as two cases at different ends of the spectrum in terms of types of controls, we see that both countries effectively employed capital management techniques for more than a decade in the service of important policy objectives.

A second common view is that, for capital management to work over a long period of time, measures have to be consistently strengthened. In fact, the reality is much more complex than this. In Malaysia, Chile, and China, during times of stress it proved necessary to strengthen controls to address leakages that were being exploited by the private sector. However, as these same cases demonstrate, controls can be loosened when a crisis subsides or when the international environment changes, and then reinstated or strengthened as necessary. In short, dynamic capital management techniques have been successfully utilized across a range of countries.

A third common (but misleading) view is that, for capital management to work, there must be an experienced bureaucracy in place. It is certainly true that having experience helps; China, India, and Singapore are all examples of countries that have long-term experience with government direction of the economy. Malaysia, however, is an important counterexample. The country was able to successfully implement capital management even without having had a great deal of experience in doing so. In the case of Chile, to take another example, the central bank had no previous experience implementing the reserve requirement scheme, though it had had some negative experiences trying to implement capital controls in the 1970s. What is more important than experience is *state capacity* and *administrative capacity* more generally.

A fourth view, which has recently become popular, is that controls on capital inflows work but those on outflows do not. However, in our sample we have seen examples of policy success in both dimensions. For example, Chile and Colombia maintained controls on inflows, while China, India, and Malaysia maintained controls on outflows. In addition, Singapore and Taiwan maintain controls on the ability of residents and non-residents to use domestic currency offshore for purposes of "speculating" against the home currency. This is a control on outflows that has successfully insulated these countries from crises and helped their governments manage their exchange rates.

We now turn to the lessons to be drawn from the case studies, which are summarized in Tables 2 and 3. First and most generally, capital management techniques

TABLE 3 Summary: Assessment of the Capital Management Techniques Employed During the 1990s

Country	Achievements	Supporting factors	Costs
Chile	• Altered composition and maturity of inflows • Currency stability • Reduced vulnerability to contagion	• Well-designed policies and sound fundamentals • Neo-liberal economic policy in many domains • Good returns offered to foreign investors • State and administrative capacity • Dynamic capital management	• Limited evidence of higher capital costs for small- and medium-sized enterprises
Colombia	• Similar to Chile, but less successful in several respects	• Less state and administrative capacity than in Chile, meaning that blunter policies were employed • Economic reforms in the direction of neo-liberalism	• No evidence available
Taiwan	• Competitive exchange rate and stable currency • Insulated from financial crises • Enhanced economic sovereignty • Debt burdens and financial fragility are insignificant	• High levels of state and administrative capacity • Policy independence of the central bank • Dynamic capital management	• Limited evidence of concentration of lending to large firms, conservatism of banks, inadequate auditing of books, and risk and project assessment capabilities • Large informal financial sector • Limited evidence of inadequate liquidity in financial system

(Table 3 is continued on the next page.)

TABLE 3 Continued

Country	Achievements	Supporting factors	Costs
Singapore	• Insulated from disruptive speculation • Protection of soft peg • Financial stability	• Strong state capacity and ability to use moral suasion • Strong economic fundamentals	• Possibly undermined financial sector development • Loss of seigniorage
Malaysia (1998)	• Facilitated macroeconomic reflation • Helped maintain domestic economic sovereignty	• Public support for policies • Strong state and administrative capacity • Dynamic capital management	• Possibly contributed to cronyism and corruption
India	• Facilitated incremental liberalization of capital flows • Insulated from financial contagion • Helped preserve domestic saving • Helped maintain economic sovereignty	• Strong state and administrative capacity • Strong public support for policies • Experience with state governance of the economy • Success of broader economic policy regime • Gradual economic liberalization	• Possibly hindered development of financial sector • Possibly facilitated corruption
China	• Facilitated industrial policy • Insulated economy from financial contagion • Helped preserve savings • Helped manage exchange rate and facilitate export-led growth • Helped maintain expansionary macro-policy • Helped maintain economic sovereignty	• Strong state and administrative capacity • Strong economic fundamentals • Experience with state governance of the economy • Gradual economic liberalization • Dynamic capital management	• Possibly constrained the development of the financial sector • Possibly encouraged non-performing loans • Possibly facilitated corruption

Source: Epstein, Grabel, and Jomo (2005, 328–329).

can contribute to currency and financial stability, macro- and microeconomic policy autonomy, stable long-term investment, and sound current account performance. There may also be some costs associated with capital management techniques, such as the fact that they can create space for public corruption.

Second, successful implementation of controls over a significant period of time depends on the presence of a sound policy environment and strong fundamentals. These include a relatively low debt ratio, moderate rates of inflation, sustainable current account and fiscal balances, consistent exchange rate policies, public sectors that function well enough to be able to implement coherent policies (administrative capacity), and governments that are sufficiently independent of narrow political interests to be able to maintain some degree of control over the financial sector (state capacity).

Third, we can see that causation works both ways: from good fundamentals to successful capital management techniques, and from successful capital management techniques to good fundamentals. Good fundamentals are important to the long-run success of capital management techniques because they reduce the stress on these controls and thereby enhance the chance that they will be successful. On the other hand, capital management techniques also improve fundamentals. Thus, there is a synergy between capital management techniques and fundamentals.

Fourth, the dynamic aspects of capital management techniques are perhaps their most important feature. Policy-makers need to retain the ability to implement a variety of management techniques and alter them as circumstances warrant.

Fifth, capital management techniques work best when they are coherent and consistent with the overall aims of the economic policy regime, or—better yet—when they are an integral part of a national economic vision. To be clear, this vision does not have to be one of widespread state control over economic activity. Singapore is a good example of an economy that is highly liberalized in some ways, but where capital management techniques are an integral part of an overall vision of economic policy and development.

Sixth, there is not one type of capital management technique that works best for all countries; in other words, there is no single "best practice" when it comes to capital management techniques.

As I suggested earlier, despite the economic crisis, there is still pressure on developing countries to liberalize their capital accounts more than they already have. Epstein, Grabel, and Jomo (2005) suggest that, in many cases, it is not in the interests of developing countries to seek full capital account liberalization. The lesson of dynamic capital management is that countries need to have the flexibility to both tighten *and* loosen controls. Thus, if countries completely liberalize their capital accounts, they might find it very difficult to re-establish any degree of control when the situation warrants or even demands it. This is because market actors might see the attempt to re-establish capital management as *abandonment* of a liberalized capital account, and might then react rather radically to this perceived change. By contrast, if investors understand that a country is maintaining a system of dynamic capital management, they will expect management to tighten and loosen over time. It is therefore less likely that investors will overreact if management techniques are tightened in these circumstances.

Statistical Analysis of Capital Controls

Magud, Reinhart, and Rogoff (2005) summarized and synthesized more than 30 statistical studies of the impact of capital controls. Their results are instructive, though subject to further scrutiny. They distinguish between controls on inflows and outflows, and find that while capital controls on inflows appear to "make monetary policy more independent; alter the composition of capital flows [to make them longer term]; [and] reduce real exchange rate pressures," they "seem not to reduce the volume of net flows" (21). As for outflows, the authors find that "there is Malaysia and there is everybody else. In Malaysia, controls reduced outflows, and may have given room for more independent monetary policy" (2). However, "[t]here is little evidence of 'success' in other countries attempting to control flows, either in terms of altering the volume or regaining monetary independence" (21).

Hence, there is a great deal of evidence in support of the ability of inflow controls to help achieve important goals; the evidence on the impacts of outflow controls is more mixed. One lesson from this is that capital management techniques that control the quantity—and especially the quality—of inflows are likely to reduce the necessity of countries engaging in outflow controls for lengthy periods of time if problems arise.

V. Conclusions

As the instability and difficulties associated with uncontrolled international financial flows have become more apparent (in the crises of 1997 and 2007–2009), interest in capital management techniques has been revived. Studies reveal that there are many different types of capital management techniques that can be custom fit to different countries' needs and circumstances. Of course, capital management techniques are no panacea for economic problems, and they will not work well unless they are part of an overall, appropriate framework of economic management. For countries navigating the treacherous waters of international finance, however, they can be useful components of the macroeconomic toolkit.

NOTES

1. At the time this article was written, "widgets" simply meant "things"; this was before the current use of the term for cool programs connected to your desktop, blog, or cellphone.
2. Thanks to Arjun Jayadev for sharing some of his unpublished work in this area, which I have drawn on here.
3. This section draws heavily on my joint work with Ilene Grabel and Jomo K.S. (2005) and on the separate work of Grabel (2003, 2004).
4. Another distinction concerns measures that affect only the flows of capital (the so-called capital account) and those that affect trade and inflows and outflows of returns from holding investments (the so-called current account). Since we will not discuss this distinction further, it is not reflected in Table 1.
5. This section draws heavily on Epstein, Grabel, and Jomo (2005).

DISCUSSION QUESTIONS

1. How can capital management techniques contribute to more financial stability? To more domestic policy autonomy? To democracy?
2. What are some of the potential problems and costs of capital management techniques? What does the evidence show as far as the importance of these factors?
3. What are the arguments for free capital mobility? What are the pros and cons and evidence in support of these arguments?

SUGGESTED READINGS

Crotty, James. 1983. Review: Keynes and capital flight. *Journal of Economic Literature* 21 (1): 56–65.

Epstein, Gerald, Ilene Grabel, and Jomo K.S. 2005. Capital management techniques in developing countries. In *Capital flight and capital controls in developing countries*, ed. Gerald Epstein, 301–333. Northampton, MA: Edward Elgar.

Helleiner, Eric. 1984. *States and the reemergence of global finance: From Bretton Woods to the 1990s.* Ithaca, NY: Cornell University Press.

Kaplan, E., and D. Rodrik. 2002. Did the Malaysian capital controls work? In *Preventing currency crises in emerging markets*, ed. Sebastian Edwards and Jeffrey A. Frankel, 393–441. Chicago: University of Chicago Press.

Neely, Christopher J. 1999. An introduction to capital controls. *Review* (Federal Reserve Bank of St. Louis) 81 (6): 13–30.

ONLINE RESOURCES

Bretton Woods Project: http://www.brettonwoodsproject.org/index.shtml.
International Monetary Fund: http://www.imf.org.
New Rules for Global Finance: http://www.new-rules.org.
Political Economy Research Institute (PERI): http://www.peri.umass.edu.

REFERENCES

Block, Fred L. 1977. *The origins of the international economic disorder: A study of international monetary policy.* Berkeley: University of California Press.

Cerra, Valerie, and Sweta Chaman Saxena. 2008. Growth dynamics: The myth of economic recovery. *American Economic Review* 98 (1): 439–457.

Chang, Ha-Joon, and Ilene Grabel. 2004. *Reclaiming development: An alternative economic policy manual.* London: Zed Press.

Crotty, James. 1983. Review: Keynes and capital flight. *Journal of Economic Literature* 21 (1): 56–65.

Diaz-Alejandro, Carlos F. 1985. Good-bye financial repression, hello financial crash. *Journal of Development Economics* 19 (1–2): 1–24.

Dodd, Randall. 2002. Derivatives, the shape of international capital flows and virtues of prudential regulation. UNU WIDER Discussion Paper 2002/93. http://www.financialpolicy.org/dscwider2002.pdf.

Eichengreen, Barry J. 1992. *Golden fetters: The gold standard and the Great Depression, 1919–1939.* New York: Oxford University Press.

Epstein, Gerald, Ilene Grabel, and Jomo K.S. 2005. Capital management techniques in developing countries. In *Capital flight and capital controls in developing countries,* ed. Gerald Epstein, 301–333. Northampton, MA: Edward Elgar.

Garber, Peter M. 1998. Derivatives in international capital flows. NBER Working Paper W6623. Cambridge, MA: National Bureau of Economic Research.

Glyn, Andrew. 1986. Capital flight and exchange controls. *New Left Review* I/155 (January–February): 37–49.

Grabel, Ilene. 2003. Averting crisis: Assessing measures to manage financial integration in developing countries. *Cambridge Journal of Economics* 27 (3): 317–336.

Grabel, Ilene. 2004. Trip wires and speed bumps: Managing financial risks and reducing the potential for financial crises in developing economies. G-24 Discussion Paper 33. http://www.unctad.org/en/docs/gdsmdpbg2420049_en.pdf.

Helleiner, Eric. 1984. *States and the reemergence of global finance: From Bretton Woods to the 1990s.* Ithaca, NY: Cornell University Press.

Kindleberger, Charles P. 1986. *The world in depression, 1929–1939.* Rev. and enlarged ed. Berkeley: University of California Press.

Kose, M. Ayhan, Eswar Prasad, Kenneth Rogoff, and Shang-Jin Wei. 2009. Financial globalization: A reappraisal. *IMF Staff Papers* 56 (1): 8–62. http://prasad.aem.cornell.edu/doc/research/imfsp200836a.pdf.

Lee, Kang-Kook, and Arjun Jayadev. 2005. Capital account liberalization, growth and the labor share of income: Reviewing and extending the cross-country evidence. In *Capital flight and capital controls in developing countries,* ed. Gerald Epstein, 15–57. Northampton, MA: Edward Elgar.

Magud, Nicolas E., Carmen Reinhart, and Kenneth Rogoff. 2005. Capital controls: Myth and reality; A portfolio balance approach to capital controls. http://www.webmeets.com/files/papers/LACEA-LAMES/2006/168/ Magud-Reinhart-Rogoff%20(May-09-06).pdf.

Neely, Christopher J. 1999. An introduction to capital controls. *Review* (Federal Reserve Bank of St. Louis) 81 (6): 13–30.

Nembhard, Jessica. 1996. *Capital control, financial policy and industrial policy in South Korea and Brazil.* New York: Praeger Press.

Pollin, Robert. 2005. Applying a securities transactions tax to the US: Design issues, market impact and revenue estimates. In *Financialization and the world economy*, ed. Gerald A. Epstein, 409–425. Northampton, MA: Edward Elgar.

Reinhart, Carmen, and Kenneth Rogoff. 2008. Banking crises: An equal opportunity menace. NBER Paper 14587. Cambridge, MA: National Bureau of Economic Research.

Rodrik, Dani. 1998. Who needs capital account convertibility? *Essays in International Finance* (Princeton University) 207: 55–65.

Rodrik, Dani, and Arvind Subramaniam. 2008. Why did financial globalization disappoint? Mimeo, Harvard University. http://ksghome.harvard.edu/~drodrik/Why_Did_FG_Disappoint_March_24_2008.pdf.

Tobin, James. 1978. A proposal for monetary reform. *Eastern Economic Journal* IV (3–4): 153–159.

Should Countries Float, Fix, or Dollarize?

COMPETING VIEWS

Thomas J. Courchene, "Canada's Floating Rate Needs Fixing"

Matías Vernengo and Carlos Schönerwald da Silva, "Beyond the Bipolar Consensus: An Intermediary Solution"

Editors' Introduction

For trade to take place in the contemporary world, individuals must ultimately be able to convert one currency into another. The foreign exchange rate is therefore a key economic variable in any economy that is "open" to the rest of the world. An exchange rate is merely the relative price ratio of any one pair of currencies internationally. To conduct international transactions, an individual economic agent— whether it is a consumer or a firm—must have the ability to acquire foreign currency on the foreign exchange markets.

Countries seek to adopt the foreign-exchange-rate regime that they believe can best fit their trade and financial needs. There exist quite a variety of exchange rate arrangements internationally. On one end of the spectrum is the freely floating exchange rate system, as exemplified by the Canadian dollar, which fluctuates because of supply/demand conditions internationally. On the other end, there are monetary unions, in which countries agree to give up their national currency and share a single one, as many European countries have done since 1999 when the euro was introduced. Between these two polar opposites there are many other arrangements. These include a fixed-exchange-rate system, which allows fluctuations in the international price of a currency but only within a fairly narrow band. There is a "peg" or hard fix, in which case the monetary authorities stand always ready to intervene in the foreign exchange market to sustain the country's pegged exchange rate. Additional restrictions exist under a currency board arrangement, in which case the board maintains a hard fix vis-à-vis a key foreign currency, such as the US dollar, while the country simultaneously ties its domestic currency emission to the amount of reserves of this key foreign currency. Finally, there are "dollarized" (or even "euroized") monetary systems, which

307

have altogether given up—either officially or in practice—their domestic currency in favour of a dominant foreign currency.

During the early 1990s, many countries (especially in the developing world) were encouraged to integrate monetarily with the objective of better achieving monetary "discipline" and a low inflation environment domestically. This took many forms: fixed exchange rates (as in East Asia), currency boards (as in Argentina), and official dollarization (as in Ecuador). By the late 1990s and during the early 2000s a number of these exchange arrangements—the most spectacular cases in this hemisphere being Brazil and Argentina—unravelled and reverted to floating-rate regimes.

Canada itself was under great pressure to integrate as our dollar started to depreciate significantly after 1992 and reached bottom at the beginning of 2002. In response, the Canadian monetary authorities consistently argued that the benefits of a floating exchange rate, particularly in terms of preserving monetary policy independence and achieving their inflation targets, outweigh the costs of exchange rate volatility. However, in recent years, as the Canadian dollar has shown signs of becoming a petro-currency (a currency that appreciates or depreciates in tandem with the international price of oil), some have argued that it is time to seek new monetary arrangements that will insulate the Canadian dollar from those upward and downward pressures. The contribution from Thomas Courchene in this chapter takes the view that it would be advantageous for Canadians if we abandoned the current floating-rate system (which has been in place since 1970) and replaced it with some form of fixed-exchange-rate arrangement. The contribution by Matías Vernengo and Carlos Schönerwald da Silva argues instead for a more eclectic position that rejects the polar extremes of a pure float and a hard fix, especially for the developing world.

Canada's Floating Rate Needs Fixing

Thomas J. Courchene

The Canada–US exchange rate is the most important price in our economy. Yet volatile energy prices are generating exchange rate swings that are rendering some sectors uncompetitive. The underlying problem is that our currency area is too small to accommodate a dynamic energy sector and a world-class manufacturing/services sector. We need to immerse the Canadian economy into a larger currency area via a fixed-exchange-rate regime with the US in the near term and to work toward a North American version of the euro in the longer term.

Canada's civil servants are more than hard-working and dedicated. They are highly motivated and very talented, easily the match of civil servants anywhere and everywhere. Intriguingly, this poses an awkward problem for students of public policy: namely, that policy approaches that are analytically or structurally flawed can, in the guiding hands of our capable civil servants, be made to perform more than tolerably well. Hence, the policy reform process becomes more difficult because the pressures for reform have been contained or overcome by adept implementation and/or internal program restructuring.

This situation is doubly awkward for those who toil in the area of monetary policy reform. Here, the Bank of Canada's pursuit of inflation targeting under the leadership of governors Crow and Thiessen and Dodge has been exceptional and has been recognized as such not only in Canada but in central banking circles internationally. In addition, the bank's inflation-targeting model is widely viewed by the vast majority of Canada's policy community as "state of the art" in terms of a monetary strategy for a small open economy. And the evidence speaks for itself: the bank has been impressively successful in keeping Canada's inflation rate well within the announced target range. As a result, the Bank of Canada has gained enormous credibility, and deservedly so on this count, among the Canadian policy community and more generally among Canadians at large. One might even go so far as to suggest that inflation targeting has made the leap from being the preferred monetary policy instrument to donning the mantle of a policy goal.

This, then, is the environment within which any criticism of Canadian monetary policy must of necessity proceed. In the critique of monetary policy that follows, my disagreements are not related to how our successive governors implemented inflation targeting. Indeed, as the above comments suggest, I would join

309

the Canadian policy community in awarding them top marks. Rather, my questioning of Canadian monetary policy goes deeper: namely, that the underlying philosophy is faulty. Not only is floating-rate inflation targeting not a policy goal, it is the wrong policy instrument. What Canada needs, the analysis will maintain, is some version of exchange rate fixity, initially a fixed exchange rate with the US but, hopefully, evolving in the direction of a common currency (for example, a Canada–US or North American version of the euro). Since the choice of exchange rate regimes rests with the government, the ensuing critique is probably best viewed as being directed to the government (and particularly Finance Canada) rather than to the Bank of Canada.

The fundamental issue is straightforward: in the face of highly volatile energy prices, the Canadian currency area is way too small to accommodate at the same time one of the world's most diversified and dynamic energy sectors and a world-class manufacturing and services sector. This is abundantly clear from Figure 1, which plots the movements in the Canada–US exchange rate (expressed as the number of US cents per Canadian dollar) and the movements in the per-barrel price of oil. The correlation between the two is so high that "petro-loonie" is now an apt title for our currency. This of course is the Dutch disease in action, so named because Holland's North Sea energy exports so appreciated its currency that the result was to clobber the Dutch manufacturing sector.

That the petro-loonie is serving to clobber Canada's manufacturing is clear (see Figure 2). Canada's unit labour costs in manufacturing have increased dramatically relative to those in the US—by roughly 50 percent, as seen in Figure 2. Note that this does not capture the full competitiveness deterioration since it only goes to the end of 2005.

Two qualifications are needed in interpreting these charts. The first is that the deterioration in competitiveness triggered by the appreciating loonie relates to Canadian value added, not to the full value of the product in question. Specifically, products that are heavily dependent on imported inputs, which are then converted into Canadian exports, are more or less unaffected since the high dollar reduces the costs of these foreign inputs. The second caveat is that while most of the discussion of the Dutch disease focuses on manufacturing, the Dutch disease is far more general. Essentially, it affects any sector whose product prices have not risen in line with the exchange rate increase. This can even have a major impact on aspects of the resource sector. Forestry is an excellent example here, one that illustrates both of these clarifications. Thanks to the mortgage-related financial debacle and the associated collapse in new housing starts on both sides of the border, some prices in the forestry sector are presumably falling, which means that the risk to these forestry firms is even worse than the predicament captured by Figure 2. Secondly, a high percentage of the price of forest products would come from Canadian value added. That this sector is reeling under the influence of the petro-loonie should hardly be surprising.

There is another way to come at this underlying issue, one mentioned in a *Policy Options* article in October 2007. This relates to my claim that Canada has become less a single east–west economy and more an east–west series of north–south, cross-border economies. To see the implications of this for the Dutch disease, let us assume that the two sides of each of these north–south economies are in rough equilibrium: BC is competitive with the Pacific northwest, Alberta is in line with the Texas Gulf, central Canada has accommodated itself to the New York/Chicago trading area, the Maritimes are in sync with Boston and New England, and so on. Now assume that fossil energy prices spike upward. Initially, this energy price increase affects both sides of each cross-border region in the same way—hence Vancouver would continue to be onside with Seattle, Winnipeg with Minneapolis, Windsor with Detroit, Halifax with Boston, and so on. What has changed is that the energy regions (Alberta and the Texas Gulf) have changed relative to other areas of their respective countries. But now let us further assume that the Canadian dollar appreciates or "buffers" the energy price spike. Suppose that this is in the order of 60 percent, roughly in line with what occurred as shown in Figure 1. Now every Canadian region is thrown off side vis-à-vis its US counterpart.

Note what has happened here. It is the exchange rate appreciation—not the original energy price spike—that is driving a wedge between the Canadian and US partners in each of the regions. While Canada has diversified its exports (away from the US) in recent years, something like two-thirds of our exports are still destined for US markets, so that this is a very questionable policy. Canadians would hit the roof, as it were, if the US put a 60 percent import tariff on the Canadian value added of our exports. Yet we do not seem to mind when our chosen monetary policy strategy is effectively levying a 60 percent export tax on the Canadian value-added component of our shipments to the US.

Along similar lines, we spend a great deal of time and effort attempting to ensure that, in the wake of 9/11 and concerns for homeland security, the border policies are such that we still have timely physical access to the US market whereas we make no similar effort when it comes to "economic" access.

It is important to emphasize that the challenge here is not so much the fact that the exchange rate is at, say, US$1.05, but rather the speed at which we arrived there. For much of the 1990s the Canadian dollar was in the low 70-cent range, then falling to the low 60-cent range from 1998 to 2002 in the wake of the Asian currency crisis. During this period the purchasing power parity (PPP) value of the exchange rate was probably in the mid to high 80-cent range, so that Canadian producers became accustomed and adjusted to an undervalued dollar. This certainly exacerbated the difficulties of grappling with the impacts of a very rapid rise in the dollar to parity and beyond. Had we been appreciating at a few cents

FIGURE 1   Canada-US Exchange Rate and Crude Oil Prices (US $)

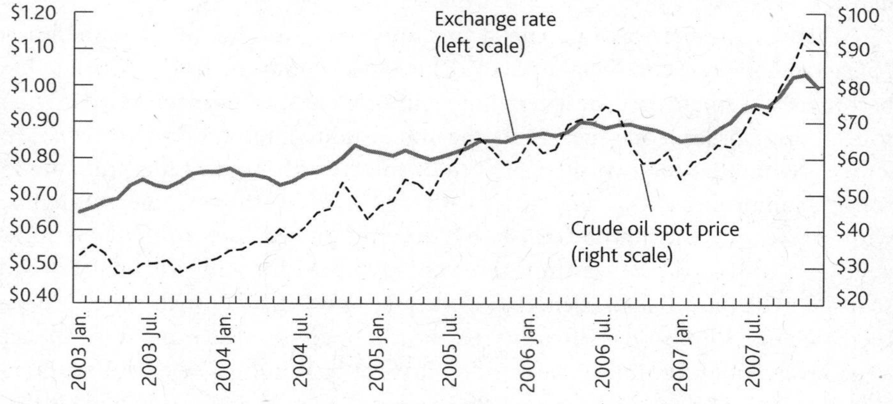

Source: Bank of Canada (xrate); US Energy Information Administration (Oil).

per year over a long period, we could much more readily handle a dollar at parity or at US $1.05.

This substantial undervaluation of the dollar during the 1992–2002 period is arguably the author of another of Canada's economic challenges: namely, productivity growth lower than that experienced by the Americans. Specifically, the fall in the dollar (from 89 cents to 62 cents over the 1990s) meant that the price of any machinery and equipment rose apace (assuming that it is priced in US dollars) so that Canada underinvested in machinery and equipment, with the result that our capital-labour rate fell and so did productivity (both relative to the US).

To be sure, this should be rectified now that the loonie is overvalued. Finance Canada thinks that it will be, and Finance Minister Jim Flaherty has cut corporate tax rates and introduced accelerated depreciation to speed along the process of capital deepening. The problem here is that the appreciation has been so rapid that some firms are engaging in downsizing, outsourcing, and offshoring, so any recapitalization will likely be on a reduced domestic base. Moreover, with the US now super-competitive vis-à-vis Canada (at the new exchange rates) and with some reputable market analysts calling for much higher energy prices (and a potential worsening of the picture contained in Figure 2), capital investments in some industries will likely remain low, or at least delayed.

I conclude this section with a further puzzle. I understand why we are allowing markets to buffer energy prices via currency appreciation (because of macro/inflationary implications, which I address below), but nonetheless it is passing strange to do so. This is because no matter where the exchange rate ends up, the

FIGURE 2   Index of US Dollar Manufacturing Unit Labour Costs, Canada and the US, 1980–2005 (1992 = 100)

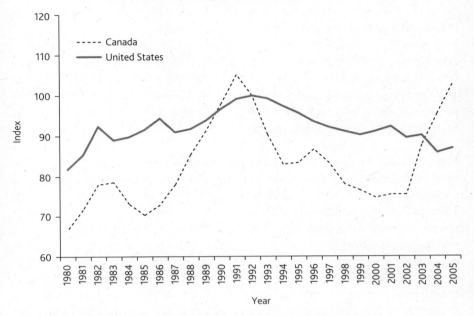

Source: Calculations by the author based on US Bureau of Labor Statistics data.

oil is still in Alberta. However, one can easily pick an exchange rate where plant X or Y will move south or otherwise disappear. Hence, to buffer the price increases of immobile assets will end up making footloose or mobile firms even more footloose and mobile.

Relatedly, Canada has great "national assets" or trump cards—a sharing community, a quality labour force, a good public education system, safe neighbourhoods, medicare, and the like. But it is hard to play these trump cards when we cannot guarantee cost certainty for access to NAFTA's economic space. Perhaps this is why Canada's share of North American inward foreign direct investment has continued to fall in spite of the FTA and NAFTA.

One answer to all this is: "Why worry?" The economy is doing quite well [as of February 2008, when this essay was first published], our fiscal position is rosy, unemployment is at a 30-year low, and economic activity is appropriately shifting toward the resource sectors—something it will continue to do as India and China continue their economic ascent. Moreover, Canadians are much better off in that the higher value of the dollar has substantially increased their purchasing power. Most important of all, however, advocates of inflation targeting would point out

313

that the above critique misses the entire point of inflation targeting. As David Laidler put it in the *National Post* in January 2008: "Canada's current choice is between the status quo—stable domestic inflation supported by a floating exchange rate—and a pegged rate accompanied by greater domestic instability that would itself tend to undermine the very regime producing it." In other words, without a floating rate the Bank of Canada's response to rising energy prices would have to be to create Canadian dollars to hold down the rate. This would lead to upward wage and price pressures and may eventually make the fixed rate difficult to hold, so that the dollar may well appreciate in any event. So why not let it float right away and temper the domestic impact?

Now one cannot rule out this scenario, but there are some important caveats that need mentioning. By far the most important of these is that Canada has had a successful experience with fixed exchange rates (1962–1970), which included the 1963–1968 Lester Pearson era. This is the period when we Canadians created or reworked much of our social envelope (Canada–Quebec Pension Plans, medicare, making equalization comprehensive, enriching the funding for postsecondary education and the Canada Assistance Plan). On the economic front, our productivity growth increased relative to that in the US. Hence, the fixed-rate regime and, therefore, our reliance on US monetary policy did not affect our performance on the economic front and certainly did not prevent us from creating our own social vision for the upper half of North America. Moreover, we did not follow the US into Vietnam, so it did not affect our ability to conduct our own foreign policy.

Among other counterpoints, one would note that wages and prices have become much more flexible across Canada's regions, so that some of the aggregate demand pressures will be taken out regionally rather than nationally. Second, labour is also much more mobile across regions than we anticipated it to be. Moreover, booming provinces like Alberta are also actively accessing temporary foreign workers on a significant scale. Third, under fixed exchange rates, similar firms on different sides of the border will be facing similar cost and price structures. This will temper some of the pressure for wages to rise. Relatedly, given that outsourcing and offshoring have become real options, they, too, will temper wage increases. Fourth, prices of traded goods are being held in check by China and India and other low-wage exporting countries. And above and beyond all of this there still remains the old chestnut—fiscal policy or stabilization policy. Canada has the tools and the financial flexibility to bring fiscal policy to the task of ensuring that the overall macro environment is consistent with holding the exchange rate. Overall, therefore, I am convinced that we are significantly underplaying the role and stabilizing influence that fixed rates can play in the current environment.

In a different vein, it should be noted that Norway handles the Dutch disease in part by placing some of its foreign exchange inflows back into international capital markets. Provincial ownership of energy makes this more difficult in Canada, but it remains an option that may be worth pursuing. For example, were Alberta to do some of this, it would lessen the appreciation of the loonie, thereby increasing the Canadian-dollar value of any energy exports. The final counterpoint is that floating rates, as noted, have a demonstrated tendency to overshoot their purchasing power parity (PPP) equilibrium and to remain there for considerable periods of time. Hence, one may obtain an exaggerated view of the aggregate demand pressures under fixed rates from looking at the pressures arising under flexible rates. For example, the cost deterioration shown in Figure 2 is a result of exchange rate overshooting or "over-appreciation." One notes in this context that both Holland and Austria maintained their fixed exchange rates with Germany, even throughout the unification of the two Germanys, which was a major macro shock by any standards.

Nonetheless, if energy prices spike to $150 per barrel, then we are in trouble under either exchange rate regime. My preference would be to tolerate a bit more inflation rather than tolerating a bit more industrial hollowing out, especially if the energy spike turns out to be temporary. Others will clearly choose differently.

I now turn to alternative versions of exchange rate fixing. One obvious approach is a "currency board" (CB), anchored on the US dollar, where the exchange rate is precisely fixed and the CB stands ready to buy and sell US dollars at this rate. There is little or no scope for domestic monetary policy because a CB is not a central bank. Received wisdom points to Argentina as a case study of why currency boards do not work. This too has to be put in perspective on two counts. The first is that during Argentina's economic troubles, the CB continued to hold so well that Argentina had to legislate it out of existence. Second, Argentina anchored its CB to the US dollar, but the US was not one of its major trading partners. During the 1990s high-tech boom in the US, the American dollar appreciated against many currencies and certainly against the Brazilian real. Beyond this, Brazil actually devalued its currency. For both reasons, Argentina's currency (effectively the US dollar) became way offside vis-à-vis that of Brazil, its major trading partner, with admittedly devastating results. The key point here is that if we were to have a CB, we would be anchoring it against the currency of our dominant trading partner.

One can imagine mechanisms that would strengthen a fixed rate without going the full route to a CB. For example, were the US Fed to agree to support one side of the exchange rate (that is, agree to buy Canadian dollars in the foreign exchange market when the Canadian dollar is tending to fall), then the fixed-rate regime would become much more robust.

The longer-term goal of a fixed-rate regime would be a common currency or a North American monetary union (NAMU). Quoting Laidler again, "A full North American monetary union supported by a high degree of goods and labour market integration would mitigate many of these problems" (problems that he associates with fixed exchange rates but that I would not). The features of a NAMU might be as follows. It would be modelled along euro lines, with a supranational central bank—say, the International Reserve Bank of North America (IRBNA)—composed of the 12 existing Federal Reserve banks and the Bank of Canada. Acceptability on Canada's part would probably require that we be on any executive committee of the board. The US would maintain its currency (why unwind what is still the world's foremost currency?). Canada would issue a new currency that would trade one for one with the US dollar. Suppose the chosen conversion rate was Cdn $1.10 for each US dollar, or roughly US 90 cents per Canadian dollar. Then 100 of the new Canadian dollars would exchange for 110 of the old Canadian dollars and items that used to cost 110 old dollars would now cost 100 new dollars. Thus we maintain the existing purchasing power differences between the two currencies. And, as noted, the new Canadian dollars will be perfect substitutes for US dollars. While this may seem complicated, it is identical to the process that all European countries went through en route to the euro.

Obviously the process would be much easier and much more transparent if the conversion rate was one for one (parity). Indeed, the concept of a NAMU may well become much more acceptable to Canadians now [February 2008] that parity is in the choice set for the conversion rate.

One side of the new Canadian currency (say, the $5 bill) would say (bilingually) that this is a North American $5 bill, issued by the IRBNA, and identical to US $5, or some comparable message. The other side could have a picture of the Rockies, for example. Hence, Canadian symbolism could remain.

The Bank of Canada would issue the new currency, in the same way that the 12 Federal Reserve banks used to issue US currency, and would do so under the overall surveillance of the IRBNA to ensure inflation control. Thus we would keep the seigniorage. Among other issues, we would want to maintain control over financial regulation, and bank clearings would occur within Canada before settling with the US. Finally—and this is the whole point of the exercise—there would be no exchange rate.

I agree with Laidler that NAMU is not on the near-term horizon, neither for the US nor for us. However, the US currency has been having a hard time of late. As it puts its fiscal house in order and rethinks/reworks its role in the community of nations, the US will probably be interested in expanding its formal currency area, especially if the euro begins to make meaningful headway in South and Central America. Stay tuned.

The final alternative is dollarization: using the US dollar for our currency. We could do this unilaterally, whereas NAMU requires US cooperation. And dollarization does eliminate the exchange rate and deliver many of the benefits of NAMU. However, we would lose seigniorage and currency symbolism. Beyond this, the nightly clearings would probably go north–south (cross-border) by region, and our financial institutions and financial regulatory system would likely be drawn into the US ambit and orbit.

There would be no rationale for the continued existence of the Bank of Canada, so that it would become difficult to withdraw from dollarization. All in all, dollarization would work well on the economic front, but would not rank high with most Canadians because it would begin a process of Americanization across a wide swath of sectors. But it does represent a way for Canadians to opt out of their current exchange rate arrangements.

By way of concluding, the Canadian currency area is too small to accommodate a world-class energy sector and a world-class manufacturing/services sector. Hence, volatile energy prices and floating exchange rates are pitting the energy sector against manufacturing. And it certainly does not help that there is a regional nature to this tug-of-war. It need not be this way: under fixed rates the recent increase in energy prices would have allowed both sectors to be better off than they currently are. The reality is that the exchange rate is the most important price in Canada. It does not need to be left to the overshooting tendencies of the inflation-targeting monetary strategy. Finally, I recognize that it was not until business supported the FTA that it came to fruition. The same will be true for fixed exchange rates. But business is not yet onside. Nonetheless, my view remains that Canada's floating exchange rate needs fixing.

A version of this essay originally appeared in *Policy Options*, February 2008, 24–28.

DISCUSSION QUESTIONS

1. Provide a list of the benefits of greater monetary integration, according to the possible scenarios of a fixed exchange rate, dollarization, and a single North American currency.
2. Why would some argue, as did Canadian-born Nobel Prize winner Robert Mundell in the early 1960s, that North America would be better off if divided monetarily along east–west lines, rather than north–south?
3. What is the Dutch disease? How would greater monetary integration between Canada and the United States solve this problem in Canada, as the latter's dollar has attained the status of a petro-currency?

SUGGESTED READINGS

Courchene, Thomas J. 2007. The loonie and the FTA. *Policy Options* (October): 56–61.

Courchene, Thomas J., and Richard G. Harris. 1999. From fixing to monetary union: Options for North American currency integration. *C.D. Howe Institute Commentary* No. 127. Toronto: C.D. Howe Institute.

Dean, James W., Dominick Salvatore, and Thomas A. Willett, eds. 2002. *The dollarization debate*. Oxford: Oxford University Press.

Grubel, Herbert G. 1999. The case for the Amero: The economics and politics of a North American monetary union. *Critical Issues Bulletin*. Vancouver: Fraser Institute.

Beyond the Bipolar Consensus: An Intermediary Solution

Matías Vernengo and Carlos Schönerwald da Silva

Introduction

The foreign exchange rate—the domestic price of foreign currencies (or conversely, the foreign price of domestic currency)—is one of the essential macroeconomic prices, the other two being the rate of interest and wages. In an increasingly interconnected world, the exchange rate is central to the economic performance of a country, and the policy options available should be adequate to the needs of promoting growth, price stability, and income equality. Exchange rate policy, however, is only one instrument, and is not sufficient to achieve all three objectives. Furthermore, different exchange rate policies may be needed at different times depending on the policy priorities, which are in constant flux. In other words, an exchange rate policy that might be adequate for dealing with a balance-of-payments deficit, for example, may not be satisfactory for dealing with an inflationary crisis.

This essay will briefly discuss the major advantages and disadvantages of alternative exchange rate regimes. The first section provides a simple taxonomy of exchange rate regimes, while those that follow explore the pros and cons of those regimes. It will be shown that no exchange rate system is devoid of problems and that no system can be efficient in all situations; to cope with changing circumstances, the exchange rate arrangement must maintain a certain degree of flexibility. Next, we discuss the role of the exchange rate as a development tool and propose the stable and competitive real exchange rate (SCRER) as an example. We conclude by explaining why most countries avoid the extremes of free float and hard pegs (including dollarization)—sometimes referred to as the "bipolar solution"—and opt instead for an intermediary regime, and why that seems to be an adequate stance at this juncture of the international financial system (early 2009).

A Concise Taxonomy of Exchange Rate Regimes

The exchange rate regime describes the main official arrangement adopted by a country with respect to the determination of the price of its currency. The classification introduced by the International Monetary Fund (IMF) in 1982 distinguishes

319

five exchange rate regimes: fixed to a single currency, fixed to a basket of currencies, limited flexibility (or quasi-pegged), managed flexibility, and independently floating. However, in practice, exchange rate regimes are difficult to categorize. In particular, since exchange rate interventions can vary from direct (buying and selling domestic currency in exchange for foreign ones) to indirect prodding of the market in one direction or another, it is far from clear what amount of interference is consistent with the category of independently floating regime.

Be that as it may, the IMF categorization might be a useful first step in clarifying the range of policy options available and in discussing the main advantages and disadvantages of alternative policy regimes. We will discuss the various arrangements, from the fixed to the flexible, using a slightly modified and more detailed classification than that of the IMF, starting with dollarization, which is an extreme version of the pegged regime.

There are several types of fixed-exchange-rate arrangements. Dollarization, the most extreme form, involves eliminating the domestic currency altogether and replacing it with a foreign currency, such as the US dollar (the reason for its name), the euro, and so on. Another, less extreme version of a pegged-exchange-rate regime is a currency board, in which the currency is permanently fixed against a foreign currency. A currency board is similar to the old "gold standard" regime, in which the value of the currency was fixed in terms of gold rather than another currency. Finally, a country may simply decide to target a particular exchange rate, in which case its central bank must be capable of protecting that rate by selling and buying domestic currency at that price in all circumstances.

The main advantage of a hard peg is that it reduces uncertainty about a particular and important price in the economy. As a result, the economic calculus is more predictable and speculation becomes less attractive. For this reason, some heterodox economists have favoured fixed exchange rates, in particular when these are accompanied by capital controls to further curb speculative behaviour. A fixed exchange rate may also serve as an anchor for domestic prices and, consequently, as an important instrument in the fight against inflation—the main reason why orthodox economists too have advocated fixed exchange rates.

On the other hand, fixed exchange rates may reduce the ability of policy-makers to deal with balance-of-payments problems. Faced with the impossibility of devaluing the currency, a country with a trade and/or current account deficit is left only with the option of reducing imports, usually by reducing the pace of economic activity. Heterodox authors generally argue against fixed pegs for this reason, while orthodox economists tend to be critical of fixed rates because they may be seen as an arbitrary government intervention that violates the sanctity of the market.

There are several intermediary regimes, sometimes referred to as BBCs (band, basket, and crawl; see Williamson 2000). Two common quasi-pegged regimes are adjustable pegs, in which the currency is fixed against a foreign currency or a basket of currencies and is not often changed, and crawling pegs, in which the currency is initially fixed but policy-makers subsequently adjust the exchange rate at regular intervals. Band regimes are slightly more complex quasi-pegged regimes involving the announcement of a central exchange rate together with a fluctuation band (which may or may not be symmetric) around that central rate. The central exchange rate is managed in some fashion—being, for instance, fixed or crawling. The implicit commitment of the central bank is to intervene actively at the margins of the band to prevent the exchange rate from moving outside of it. The implementation of a band also requires the adoption of a set of rules to guide foreign exchange market intervention, if any, within the band.

Flexible-exchange-rate regimes, in which the exchange rate is allowed to fluctuate in response to changes in the demand and supply of foreign exchange, generally presume that the central bank does not intervene in the market for foreign exchange at all. The main advantage of exchange rate flexibility is that it allows dealing with balance-of-payments disequilibria. Yet despite this advantage, flexible regimes are sometimes seen as more likely to be associated with inflation.

The adoption of the free-float regimes is quite uncommon, and countries usually adopt a managed float. Calvo and Reinhart (2002) have suggested that most countries that are officially classified as free-floaters actually manage their foreign exchange rates. The reason for this fear of floating is associated with the possibility of foreign exchange crises.

During the 1990s a consensus developed that the only way to avoid financial crises was to either let the currency float or establish a credible commitment to a hard peg, a position that was referred to as the "bipolar view" (Fischer 2001). However, in the aftermath of the Asian financial crisis of 1997—and in light of the subsequent financial crises in Russia in 1998 and Brazil and Turkey in 1999, and the crisis in Argentina in 2001—the bipolar view was discredited. Since then, it has become increasingly clear that there is no single exchange rate regime that is right for all countries at all times (Frankel 1999).

The Impossible Trinity and the Exchange Rate Regime

No exchange rate regime can completely prevent macroeconomic turbulence. Yet in particular moments, certain exchange rate arrangements are better suited to promoting the specific needs of a country. Because different exchange rate regimes can promote price stability and high economic growth, the economic institutions that determine exchange rate policies should be sufficiently flexible to adapt to new circumstances and changes in the policy priorities. Furthermore, the priorities of central or developed countries, which have achieved a significant level of material well-being, are different from those of peripheral or underdeveloped countries, which have appreciably lower levels of income per capita.

Conventional wisdom suggests that the policy trade-offs can be represented by what has sometimes been called the "impossible trinity"—that is, countries cannot achieve exchange rate stability, monetary policy independence, and free capital mobility simultaneously. A country can achieve any two of these goals, but it must pay the price by forgoing the third.

For example, policy-makers may decide to maintain monetary policy independence and determine the rate of interest according to the needs of the domestic economy, as well as to curb foreign exchange speculation in order to keep rates of interest relatively low without fear of capital flight. The ability to control domestic interest rates is one of the reasons why John Maynard Keynes defended capital controls as a necessary complement to the Bretton Woods policies that tried to curb exchange rate volatility and use interest rates to promote full employment at home (Vernengo and Rochon 2000). It must be noted that the fundamental goal for Keynes—and for most economists in the aftermath of the Great Depression and the Second World War—was to maintain full employment. Exchange rate stability and low rates of interest to curb speculation were seen as crucial to achieving that objective, and reduced capital mobility was not deemed a very high price to pay for full employment.

Critics of the Keynesian policies of the 1950s and 1960s suggested that fixed exchange rates and low rates of interest led to excessive demand stimulus and demand-pull inflation, particularly in the latter decade. Even if that argument is not correct and inflation might have had other plausible causes (for instance, cost-push factors), it is still the case that inflation became the centre of policy preoccupations. This led to alternative choices in terms of the trinitarian options.

A second possibility, which became increasingly popular after the demise of the Bretton Woods system in the early 1970s, would be to decide that free capital mobility cannot be sacrificed on the altar of full employment, and that an independent monetary policy may lead to a higher risk of inflation. In this case, a fixed-exchange-rate regime would be seen as the necessary condition for price stability. In this view, just as the main advantage of a floating exchange rate may be that it allows the monetary authorities some discretion and flexibility to use monetary policy to cope with balance-of-payments shocks, its main weakness is that it allows *too much* discretion for monetary authorities and hence may not provide a sufficiently firm nominal anchor for domestic prices. However, it must be noted that, since the late 1980s and early 1990s, most countries have been able to keep inflation under control with relatively flexible exchange rate regimes, which suggests that the evidence on whether fixed- versus floating-exchange-rate regimes are associated with lower inflation rates is not clearcut and that flexible regimes might be less prone to inflation than was previously thought (Reinhart and Rogoff 2004).

Fixed regimes that lead to the abandonment of monetary independence—as in a monetary union or dollarization—are seen as central to maintaining price stability. The various European arrangements that culminated in the adoption of the euro and the decisions of several developing nations to dollarize fall into this category. According to the advocates of fixed-exchange-rate regimes, unemployment is not a major problem because the economy will eventually return to the natural rate of unemployment, as suggested by Milton Friedman; in other words, the domestic level of activity will take care of itself. Furthermore, according to this approach, free capital mobility is essential to promoting the efficient allocation of resources. Markets, not government officials, should be trusted to promote increased welfare.

There are many troubles with regimes that opt for some form of monetary unification—that is, that choose exchange rate stability and free capital mobility at the expense of monetary independence. The two most glaring problems are the presumption that the economy will adjust to full employment more or less automatically and that the balance-of-payments adjustment will be smooth and painless.

The natural-rate-of-unemployment hypothesis has been completely undermined by the empirical evidence, and by the 1990s most authors agreed either that there is no reasonable way to determine a constant natural rate or that the concept should be abandoned (Galbraith 1997). As a result, an exchange rate regime that does not concern itself with the level of activity may lead to high levels of unemployment for a prolonged period. The experience of Argentina with the currency board from 1991 to 2000 is the most spectacular example of the failure of pegged regimes to promote full employment. The Argentinian experience should serve as a cautionary tale for those, in Canada and elsewhere, who believe in the advantages of greater monetary integration and dollarization.

It must be noted that hard pegs, monetary unions, and dollarization all eliminate the possibility of using currency devaluation as an instrument to adjust for a trade and/or current account deficit. In the case of hard pegs and dollarization, the deficit country has only one possible course of action, namely: contract the economy in order to reduce imports. In other words, these regimes promote a strong contractionary bias to macroeconomic policies. A monetary union may have other alternatives, such as fiscal transfers from other member countries to finance the trade and/or current account deficit. Also, it is possible that unemployed workers in the deficit country might find jobs in other union-member countries. However, it is still the case that a contractionary bias is imposed on the deficit countries by a monetary union and dollarization. In other words, if Canada were to promote greater monetary integration with the United States, lower rates of growth and higher unemployment should be expected.

The inability to provide non-contractionary ways for dealing with the balance-of-payments constraint is particularly problematic for developing countries, since the constant need to import intermediary and expensive capital goods by exporting commodities and manufactures produced with cheap labour exposes those countries to recurrent balance-of-payments crises. In this sense, hard pegs, currency boards, and dollarization are particularly problematic for developing countries that must grow faster than central countries to catch up.

The scenarios described above suggest preferences for stable exchange rates and, in that sense, for a relatively fixed exchange rate, accompanied in the Keynesian framework by capital controls to promote low rates of interest and full employment or supplemented in the monetarist analysis by reduced monetary independence to promote price stability. The last choice, between the three incompatible trinity options, would involve giving up exchange rate rigidity. In other words, policy-makers may decide to maintain monetary policy independence and determine the rate of interest according to the needs of the domestic economy, but with free capital mobility. This arrangement would imply that the whims of international financial markets, and the volatile capital flows, would determine the exchange rate.

There are at least two problems with violent fluctuations of the exchange rate. First, it has long been known that devaluations might be contractionary (Krugman and Taylor 1978). Devaluations make imports more expensive (reducing the purchasing power of consumers) and exports cheaper (boosting the income of the exporting corporations). Given that consumers' propensity to spend might be higher than the propensity of corporations to invest, the net effect might very well be a fall in the level of income. Eventually, the positive effect of the devaluation of exports may boost the level of income above the initial level, so that the contractionary effect may just be a short-term phenomenon. The contractionary effect of devaluations underscores the fact that a recession is part of the balance-of-payments adjustment process in both fixed- and flexible-exchange-rate regimes.

In addition to being contractionary in many instances, devaluations are clearly inflationary, since, by increasing the price of imported goods and services, they lead to higher consumer prices. This is particularly the case for peripheral economies, which traditionally are highly sensitive to devaluations because they often exhibit a high pass-through coefficient—that is, the coefficient that relates the price of imported goods and services to domestic consumer prices (Hausmann, Panizza, and Stein 2001). However, it must be noted that developing countries in the 1990s experienced a rapid downward trend in the degree of pass-through; consequently, a lower pass-through and reduced inflationary pressures are no longer a luxury exclusive to central economies (Frankel, Parsley, and Wei 2005). This means that mild depreciations might not be excessively inflationary.

In addition to the problems caused by devaluations, a flexible regime has to cope with the negative effects of overvaluation. A relatively long period of capital inflows may lead to the appreciation of the domestic currency and the buildup of trade and current account deficits. Prolonged periods of overvaluation may also have a negative impact on domestic production. Because overvaluation leads domestic consumers to prefer cheaper, imported goods to domestically produced goods, something akin to a Dutch disease may take hold. In other words, as much as the discovery of natural gas had a negative impact on the Dutch domestic industry, causing consumers in the Netherlands to buy cheap imports rather than domestically produced goods, an appreciation caused by capital inflows may lead to deindustrialization and long-term employment effects.

In sum, it must be accepted that, according to the impossible trinity, no policy option is completely devoid of difficulties. Yet under certain circumstances, the harsh trade-offs imposed by this unholy trinity might be softened. For example, it is not unimaginable that regulated (but free) capital markets, which would allow productive flows of capital but curb speculative flows, might be compatible with relative exchange rate stability and the use of the interest rates for domestic policy purposes. In other words, it is not impossible to design an international financial system in which the impossible trinity does not hold.

Arguably, that was exactly what Keynes wanted to create with his Bancor plan during the discussions that led to Bretton Woods. The Bancor plan implied the creation of an international currency (Bancor) and the provision of credit for deficit countries in that currency. Keynes believed that surplus countries had an obligation to finance deficit countries and share the burden of adjustment. Even without Keynes's particular plan, it is still possible to use exchange rate policy in a globalized world to promote a more civilized society—this would require maintaining a large degree of monetary independence and a certain degree of exchange rate flexibility. If the price for that were a little less capital mobility, this would probably not be too steep a price to pay. Monetary independence and some measure of exchange rate flexibility are particularly important for developing nations, where the gap between the harshness of reality and the desire for prosperity seems to be excessively large.

The Exchange Rate as a Development Tool

There is an extensive literature that suggests that the essential constraint to economic growth is the balance of payments (for example, McCombie and Thirlwall 1994). The idea is relatively simple. If a country exports less than it imports, it must borrow from other countries to buy goods and services. Borrowing, however, is an option only for a certain period of time. After a while, the country must be able to export not only to pay for imports but also to pay interest and principal on the accumulated debt. Therefore, countries cannot grow persistently above their trading partners without incurring an unsustainable accumulation of external debt. Not surprisingly, negative terms of trade shocks and debt crises are instrumental in explaining the end of growth accelerations, and depreciations often occur at the beginning of such episodes (Hausmann, Pritchett, and Rodrik 2005).

It must be emphasized that the evidence suggests that a competitive (that is, relatively devalued in real terms) but stable exchange rate is usually an essential component of growth accelerations; in this context, "stable" does not mean fixed, but simply that extreme volatility is controlled. Furthermore, Frenkel and Taylor (2006) argue that the macroeconomic regime focused on the preservation of a stable and competitive real exchange rate (SCRER) has been the principal factor in the rapid growth experienced in many developing countries during the last boom (2003–2007). It is clear, however, that for developing countries, other factors have been equally important (for example, the positive terms of trade shock; see Pérez Caldentey and Vernengo 2008).

A competitive exchange rate promotes domestic production by making foreign goods relatively more expensive. It also tends to lead to trade and current account surpluses and reduce the risks of foreign debt accumulation, guaranteeing that the country will be able to service the debt with export proceeds. In that sense, a competitive exchange rate reduces the pressures associated with the balance-of-payments constraint.

The competitive exchange rate must also be stable (which does not mean fixed, as we noted). It can fluctuate, but changes should not be sudden in any direction. In order to maintain the competitiveness of the exchange rate, a certain amount of flexibility must be allowed, so that the currency can depreciate whenever necessary. It is clear that in the current context a SCRER is possible only for countries that either have capital controls or have accumulated foreign reserves in amounts significant enough to allow them to intervene in foreign exchange markets. One of the effects of the last boom in the developing world has been the accumulation of vast stocks of foreign reserves, which suggests that a SCRER is a feasible strategy for many countries on the periphery.

Conclusion

The choice between floating, fixing the exchange rate, and dollarizing is not always clearcut. However, contrary to the now-discredited bipolar consensus, it seems that intermediary regimes are more likely to be conducive to growth and price stability. Intermediary regimes do allow for some amount of exchange rate fluctuation, but demand intervention to exclude excessive volatility. Fear of floating implies that most countries, even those that say they float, do *not* float, and in a world with recurrent financial crises that seems a reasonable course of action. Most developing countries would be subjected to wild fluctuations of their currency value and would be prisoners of the humours of volatile financial markets.

By the same token, most countries—though not all—avoid the extreme solution of completely fixing their exchange rate. Interestingly, whereas almost no country allows free floating, the number of countries that subscribe to some sort of relatively rigid peg (for instance, currency boards, monetary unions, dollarization, and so on) is considerably larger. This suggests that policy-makers view the risks of inflation associated with devaluations and a more autonomous monetary policy as larger than those of unemployment and stagnation. The financial crisis that began in the summer of 2007 in the United States may very well change that misconceived perception.

DISCUSSION QUESTIONS

1. Describe the main advantages of fixed- and flexible-exchange-rate regimes.
2. What is the bipolar view and what are its main limitations?
3. Explain the implications for exchange rate policy of the impossible trinity.
4. What are the advantages of the stable and competitive real exchange rate (SCRER) as part of a development strategy?
5. What are the benefits and the costs of dollarization or currency union?

SUGGESTED READINGS

Fischer, S. 2001. Exchange rate regimes: Is the bipolar view correct? *Journal of Economic Perspectives* 15 (2): 3–24.

Frenkel, R., and L. Taylor. 2006. Real exchange rate, monetary policy and employment. UN/DESA Working Paper 19.

Vernengo, M., and L.-P. Rochon. 2001. Parités fixes ou flexibles, une question de circonstances. *Problèmes Économiques* 2698 (31): 8–9.

ONLINE RESOURCES

Frankel, Jeffrey A. The international finance and macroeconomics program. National Bureau of Economic Research. http://www.nber.org/programs/ifm/ifm.html.

International Monetary Fund: http://www.imf.org.

REFERENCES

Calvo, G., and C. Reinhart. 2002. Fear of floating. *Quarterly Journal of Economics* 117: 379–408.

Fischer, S. 2001. Exchange rate regimes: Is the bipolar view correct? *Journal of Economic Perspectives* 15 (2): 3–24.

Frankel, J. 1999. No single currency regime is right for all countries or at all times. *Essays in International Finance* 215, Department of Economics, Princeton University. http://www.princeton.edu/~ies/IES_Essays/E215.pdf.

Frankel, J., D. Parsley, and S.-J. Wei. 2005. Slow pass-through around the world: A new import for developing countries? CID Working Paper 116. http://www.cid.harvard.edu/cidwp/pdf/116.pdf.

Frenkel, R., and L. Taylor. 2006. Real exchange rate, monetary policy and employment. UN/DESA Working Paper 19. http://www.un.org/esa/desa/papers/2006/wp19_2006.pdf.

Galbraith, J. 1997. Time to ditch the NAIRU. *Journal of Economic Perspectives* 11 (1): 93–108.

Hausmann, R., U. Panizza, and E. Stein. 2001. Why do countries float the way they float? *Journal of Development Economics* 66: 387–414.

Hausmann, R., L. Pritchett, and D. Rodrik. 2005. Growth accelerations. *Journal of Economic Growth* 10 (4): 303–329.

Krugman, P., and L. Taylor. 1978. Contractionary effects of devaluation. *Journal of International Economics* 8: 445–456.

McCombie, J., and A. Thirlwall. 1994. *Economic growth and the balance-of-payments constraint.* London: Macmillan.

Pérez Caldentey, E., and M. Vernengo. 2008. Back to the future: Latin America's current development strategy. The IDEAs Working Paper Series 07/2008.

Reinhart, C., and K. Rogoff. 2004. The modern history of exchange rate arrangements: A reinterpretation. *Quarterly Journal of Economics* 119: 1–48.

Vernengo, M., and L.-P. Rochon. 2000. Exchange rate regimes and capital controls. *Challenge* 43 (6): 76–92.

Williamson, J. 2000. *Exchange rate regimes in emerging markets: Reviving the intermediate option.* Washington, DC: Institute for International Economics.

Is Globalization Reducing Poverty?

COMPETING VIEWS

Dominick Salvatore, "Globalization, Growth, and Poverty"

Manfred Bienefeld, "Globalization and Poverty: Why There Is Reason to Be Concerned"

Editors' Introduction

Globalization is not a recent phenomenon. Trade and finance—the two major aspects of globalization—have been carried out on an international scale for centuries. Transnational corporations producing goods and services have also been operating since the colonization period, which began in the 1500s. However, the second half of the 20th century witnessed an unprecedented increase both in the volume of trade and finance and in the relocation of production facilities worldwide. These changes have brought with them waves of transformations that have deeply affected societies not only economically, but also—and perhaps more important—culturally.

One of the issues often debated is whether globalization has increased or reduced poverty and inequality both within and between countries. Proponents of globalization argue that the increased international economic integration results in net welfare gains. For instance, it is argued that foreign capital flows have a positive impact on the local economy because they contribute to employment creation, improve the quality of the labour force through training, increase efficiency, introduce new technology, and stimulate new investments through (forward and backward) linkages. In the end, globalization leads to a convergence in income levels, costs, and growth rates. Therefore, there should be less poverty and less inequality in the world. The main conclusion of the supporters of globalization is that the latter benefits countries that participate fully in the process and penalizes those that maintain restrictions on trade and capital flows. In this chapter, Dominick Salvatore defends this view.

On the other hand, critics argue that the gap between the rich and the poor at all levels (local, national, and international) has widened during the heyday of globalization, which they believe has weakened social support institutions and systems, and threatened identities and established values. The anti-globalization movement emphasizes that it is against a specific type of globalization—namely, the neo-liberal model, which seeks to increase the power of transnational corporations through privatization as well as through deregulation and liberalization of all markets. In this context, when financially and technologically powerful transnational corporations relocate to developing countries, they often operate in enclaves relying on low-skilled and non-unionized labour. They also tend to displace local firms by driving them out of business (therefore increasing unemployment) or simply by acquiring them (therefore reducing competition). The main conclusion of this view, defended by Manfred Bienefeld, is that globalization has not lowered poverty and inequality and that, instead, in some parts of the world poverty is actually rising dramatically.

Globalization, Growth, and Poverty

Dominick Salvatore

Introduction

The past two-and-a-half decades have witnessed a rapid tendency toward globalization in the world economy, which has significantly affected the rate of economic
growth and poverty around the world. A great deal of controversy, however, exists
regarding whether or not globalization has resulted in an increase or a reduction
in world inequalities and poverty. This paper begins with an analysis of the process
of globalization in production and labour markets since the early 1980s, and then
examines how globalization has affected economic growth and poverty around
the world.

Globalization in Production and in Labour Markets

There is a strong trend toward globalization in production and labour markets in
the world today. For those firms and nations that take advantage of this trend, the
results are increased efficiency, competitiveness, and growth. Global corporations
play a crucial role in the process of globalization. These are companies that are
run by an international team of managers, have research and production facilities
in many countries, use parts and components from the cheapest sources around
the world, sell their products globally, and finance their operations and are owned
by stockholders throughout the world. More and more corporations today operate
on the belief that their survival requires them to be one of a handful of global corporations in their sector. This is true in the automobile, steel, telecommunications,
and aircraft industries, and for companies that produce computers, consumer
electronics, chemicals, drugs, and many other products. Nestlé, the world's largest
food company, headquartered in small Switzerland, has production facilities in 59
countries, while America's Gillette has facilities in 22. Ford has component factories
in 26 different industrial sites around the world, assembly plants in 6 countries,
and employs more workers abroad than in the United States.

One important form of globalization in the area of production is outsourcing,
or the foreign "sourcing" of inputs. There is practically no major product today
that does not have some foreign inputs. Foreign sourcing is often not a choice made
by corporations in the hope of earning higher profits, but simply a requirement

for those that wish to remain competitive. Firms that do not look abroad for cheaper inputs risk not being able to compete in world—and even domestic—markets. This is the reason why, during the mid-1980s, US $625 of the $860 total cost of producing an IBM PC was incurred for parts and components manufactured by IBM outside of the United States or purchased from foreign producers. Such low-cost, offshore purchase of inputs is likely to continue to expand rapidly in the future and is being fostered by joint ventures, licensing arrangements, and other non-equity collaborative arrangements. Indeed, this represents one of the most dynamic aspects of the global business environment of today.

Foreign sourcing can be regarded as manufacturing's new *international* economies of scale in today's global economy. Just as companies were forced to rationalize operations within each country during the 1980s, in 2009 they face the challenge of integrating their operations for their entire system of manufacturing around the world in order to take advantage of the new international economies of scale. In order to have a distinctive production advantage, a company should focus on those components that are indispensable to its competitive position over subsequent product generations and "outsource" all the rest from outside suppliers.

Globalization in production has proceeded so far that it is now difficult to determine the "nationality" of many products. For example, should a Honda Accord produced in Ohio be considered American? What about a Chrysler minivan produced in Canada? Is a Kentucky Toyota or Mazda American if nearly 50 percent of its parts are imported from Japan? It is clearly becoming increasingly difficult to define what is "American" or "Canadian," and opinions differ widely. One could legitimately ask if this question is even *relevant* in a world that is growing more and more interdependent and globalized. Today, the ideal corporation is strongly decentralized in order to allow local units to develop products that fit into local cultures, and yet it must be very centralized at its core so that it can coordinate its activities around the globe.

Even more dramatic than globalization in production has been the globalization of labour markets. Work that was previously done in the United States and other industrial countries is now often done much more cheaply in some emerging markets. This is the case not only for low-skill, assembly-line jobs, but also for jobs requiring advanced computer and engineering skills. Most Americans have only now come to fully realize that there is a truly competitive labour force in the world that is willing and able to do their jobs at a much lower cost. If anything, this trend is likely to accelerate in the future.

Even service industries are not immune to global job competition. For example, more than 3,500 workers on the island of Jamaica are connected to the United States by satellite dishes and perform tasks including making airline reservations, processing tickets, answering calls to toll-free numbers, and data entry for US airlines—all at a much lower cost than could be done in the United States.

Highly skilled and professional people are not spared from global competition, either. Some years ago, Texas Instruments set up an impressive software programming operation in Bangalore, a city of 4 million people in southern India. Other American multinationals soon followed. Motorola, IBM, AT&T, and many other high-tech firms are now doing a great deal of basic research abroad.

Workers in advanced countries are raising strong objections to the transfer of skilled jobs abroad. Companies in all advanced countries are outsourcing more and more of their work to emerging markets in order to bring or keep costs down and remain internationally competitive. In the future, more and more work will simply be done in those emerging markets best equipped to do a particular job the most economically. If governments in advanced nations tried to restrict the flow of work abroad to protect domestic jobs, their firms would risk losing international competitiveness and they might end up having to move all of their operations abroad.

Globalization in production and labour markets is important and inevitable—important because it increases efficiency, and inevitable because international competition requires it. Besides the well-known static gains from specialization in production and trade, globalization leads to even more important dynamic gains, which result from extending the scale of operation to the entire world and the more efficient utilization of capital and technology of domestic resources at home and abroad. Globalization is inevitable because firms have no choice but to outsource parts and components from wherever in the world they are made better or more cheaply and to invest their capital and technology wherever these will be most productive. Otherwise, their competitors will do so, and the firm will lose its markets and might even be forced to shut down. For the same reason, firms must outsource labour services or employ labour offshore, where it is cheaper.

Globalization, Economic Growth, and Development

Growth is the most important economic goal of countries today. The best available measure of growth in standards of living that will also allow for comparisons across countries is in terms of purchasing power parity (PPP) per capita incomes. Since we are interested in examining the effect of globalization on growth and development, we will compare the growth of real PPP per capita incomes in various countries and regions during the period from 1980 to 2006, which is usually considered the most recent period of rapid globalization. Of course, the rate of growth and development of a nation depends not only on globalization but also on many other domestic factors, such as political stability, improvements in education and labour skills, the rate of investment and absorption of new technology, the rate of population growth, and so on. But globalization is certainly a crucial ingredient to growth.

For example, no one forced China to open up to the world economy, but had it not done so it would not have received the huge inflows of capital and technology that it did and it would not have been able to increase its exports so dramatically and thus achieve such spectacular rates of growth from 1980 to the present (2009). An apparently strong positive correlation between globalization and growth does not, of course, establish causality, but it does refute the assertion of anti-global groups that globalization has caused increased inequalities between advanced and developing countries during the past two decades.

Table 1 gives the weighted yearly average real PPP (with base 1993) per capita income in various regions and countries of the world in the 1960–1980, 1980–2000, and 2000–2006 periods. From the table, we see that East Asia and Pacific did well during the 1960–1980 period and have done spectacularly well since then. South Asia grew at an average rate only half that of East Asia and Pacific during the 1980–2000 period, but almost as fast during the period from 2000 to 2006. China and India grew about as fast as East Asia and Pacific as a whole from 1980 to 2006. The Middle East and North Africa did well during the first and third periods, but badly during the second period because of political turmoil and wars. Sub-Saharan Africa did not do well during the first period and actually became poorer during the second because of political instability, wars, droughts, and AIDS, but managed an average growth of 4.7 percent from 2000 to 2006. Latin America did reasonably well during the first and third periods, but per capita incomes were practically stagnant during the second period (thus considered to be the "lost" decades as far as economic development is concerned) because of political and economic crises.

The developing world as a whole did reasonably well during the first period, better during the second period, and best during the third period. The former communist countries of Europe and Central Asia performed poorly during the second period (no data were available for the first period) as a result of the economic collapse associated with the fall of communism and the necessary economic restructuring that followed, but grew rapidly during the third period. Overall, only Asia grew faster than industrialized countries and sharply reduced inequalities vis-à-vis industrialized countries as a group during the 1980–2006 period. Latin America, the Middle East and North Africa, and Europe and Central Asia did poorly, and so inequalities with respect to high-income countries increased during the second period, but did better during the third period. Sub-Saharan Africa actually became poorer in an absolute sense during the second period, causing it to fall further behind advanced countries, although it recovered some of the lost ground in the third period.

Table 2 shows the correlation between globalization and growth. It shows that the growth of real per capita (PPP) GDP increased sharply in each decade from 1980 to 2006 for the developing countries that globalized (that is, those for which

TABLE 1 Weighted Yearly Average Real PPP per Capita Income in Various Regions, 1960–1980, 1980–2000, and 2000–2006

Region	1960–1980	1980–2000	2000–2006
East Asia and Pacific	2.9	6.1	8.6
South Asia	0.6	3.0	6.9
China and India	1.7	5.8	8.5
Middle East and North Africa	3.2	0.2	4.1
Sub-Saharan Africa	1.3	−0.6	4.7
Latin America and Caribbean	3.1	0.1	3.1
Developing World	2.1	3.1	4.9
Europe and Central Asia	—	1.1	5.7
High-income countries	3.9	2.3	2.0
World	2.5	2.9	5.2

Source: Bhalla (2002) from World Bank (2008a).

TABLE 2 Weighted Yearly Average Real PPP per Capita Income Growth in Rich Countries, Globalizers, and Non-Globalizers in the 1960s, 1970s, 1980s, and 1990s

Group of countries	1960s	1970s	1980s	1990s	2000–2006
Rich countries.............	4.7	3.1	2.3	2.2	2.1
Globalizers	1.4	2.9	3.5	5.0	6.1
Non-globalizers	2.4	3.3	0.8	1.4	2.3

Sources: Dollar and Kraay (2001); World Bank (2008a).

the ratio of trade to GDP increased) and far exceeded the average growth of rich countries and non-globalizers. The growth of rich countries was very high—much higher than that of globalizers and non-globalizers—during the decade of the 1960s, but it declined in each subsequent decade. The growth of non-globalizers increased from the decade of the 1960s to the decade of the 1970s, but then it declined sharply during the 1980s and was very low during the 1990s; however, it increased during the 2000–2006 period, even exceeding the growth of the rich countries. It seems that growth can be rapid without liberalization and globalization at the beginning of the growth process, but as the nation develops, economic efficiency associated with liberalization and globalization becomes increasingly important.

Although there is no perfect correspondence between non-globalizers and the poorest countries in the world, most of the poorest countries in the world are non-globalizers. Thus, inequalities in per capita incomes and standards of living did increase between non-globalizers, on the one hand, and globalizers and rich countries, on the other. But the fault for this increased inequality cannot be attributed to globalization as such. Indeed, it was the globalizers that grew fast while the non-globalizers stagnated or regressed. Thus, the only criticism that can be levied against globalization as a process is that it did not permit the poorest countries in the world to participate—alongside the rich countries and the developing-country globalizers—in the tremendous benefits in terms of economic efficiency and growth in living standards that globalization makes possible. This is a far cry, however, from globalization itself being the cause of the increased inequalities between the rich and the globalizing developing countries, on the one hand, and the poorest and non-globalizing developing nations, on the other, during the last two decades of the 20th century, as the opponents of globalization claim.

Globalization and Poverty

Another important question that needs to be answered is what effect globalization has had on actual world poverty at the country level and at the individual level. Depending on how we choose to measure relative poverty, however, we get dramatically different results.

One way to measure the evolution of relative poverty is to measure the change in the number of times that the income per capita in the richest country (the United States, if we exclude the small country of Luxembourg) exceeds the income per capita in the world's poorest country, in the 10th-poorest country, or in the 20 poorest countries, as compared with the 20 richest countries in the world, over time. Based on this measure, the United Nations (2008), the World Bank (2001), and many left-leaning intellectuals—such as Pritchett (1997) and Stiglitz (2002)—have asserted that globalization caused or resulted in increased income inequalities and poverty in the poorest developing countries beginning in the 1980s.

The data presented in Table 3 shed light on this position. The second column of the table shows that the ratio of real PPP per capita income in the United States relative to the poorest country (Lesotho) was 48.3 in 1960, 47.1 (Lesotho) in 1970, 47.4 (Tanzania) in 1980, 51.6 (Tanzania) in 1990, 73.3 (Sierra Leone) in 2000, and 62.3 (Burundi) in 2006. Thus, according to this measure, world income inequalities have indeed increased significantly from 1960 to 2000, and declined somewhat only between 2000 and 2006. To avoid the problem of outliers, the third column of Table 3 shows that the ratio of real per capita PPP income in the United States relative to the 10th-poorest country (Guinea-Bissau) was 27.6 in 1960, 31.0 (Nigeria) in 1970, 31.3 (Bhutan) in 1980, 32.5 (Burundi) in 1990, 44.6 (Zambia) in 2000, and 44.3 (Zambia) in 2006. Thus, again, inequalities seem to have increased, except between 2000 and 2006, when they remained about the same. Finally, the same conclusion can be reached from the last column of Table 3 when inequalities are measured as the ratio of the top 20 countries to the bottom 20 countries.

TABLE 3 Ratio of Real PPP per Capita Income in Rich and Poor Countries, 1960–2006

Year	In US, relative to poorest country	In US, relative to 10th-poorest country	In the 20 richest countries, relative to the 20 poorest countries
1960	48.3	27.6	23.0
1970	47.1	31.0	26.2
1980	47.4	31.3	25.7
1990	51.6	32.5	30.8
2000	73.3	44.6	36.3
2006	62.3	44.3	34.3

Sources: Bhalla (2002); World Bank (2008b).

A different and more direct method of measuring changes in poverty around the world is to measure the change in the number of poor *people*. There are two ways of doing this: one utilizes national accounts data and the other uses data from national surveys. Table 4 gives the number of people and the proportion of the total population who lived on less than US $1.00 per day ($1.08 in 1993 prices, to be more precise), used by the World Bank as a measure of poverty in various regions and countries of the world in 1981, 1993, and 2005.

The top portion of Table 4 shows that the total number of poor people in all developing countries declined from 1,528 million in 1981 to 879 million in 2005. As a percentage of the total population of developing countries, the number of poor people declined from 41.7 percent in 1981 to 16.1 percent in 2005. Thus, according to these data, there was a dramatic decline in the number and in the proportion of poor people in the developing world during the most recent period of rapid globalization (1981 to 2005).

Of the 649-million reduction in the number of the world's poor between 1981 and 2005 (1,528 million minus 879 million), Table 4 shows that by far the majority of this reduction—624 million—occurred in China. There was a 37-million reduction in the number of poor people in South Asia, of which 29 million were in India. In sub-Saharan Africa, on the other hand, the number of poor people increased dramatically, from 157 million in 1981 to 299 million in 2005. Because of the increase in the population of sub-Saharan Africa, however, the percentage of poor people remained more or less constant at about 39 percent. For the most part, the countries of sub-Saharan Africa were also the countries that failed to globalize and experienced wars, political instability, droughts, and the AIDS crisis. The number of poor people in the other regions shown in Table 4 was small and did not change much between 1981 and 2005. Chen and Ravallion (2008), however, prefer to define (dismal) poverty as anyone living on less than US $1.25 per day, rather than

TABLE 4   World Poverty: Number and Percentage of People Living on Less Than $1.00 per Day, 1981–2005

	1981	1993	2005
	(in millions)		
Region/number of poor people			
East Asia (of which China)	948 (730)	600 (444)	180 (106)
South Asia (of which India)	387 (296)	341 (280)	350 (267)
Sub-Saharan Africa	157	247	299
Middle East and North Africa.......	6	5	6
Latin America and Caribbean.......	27	34	28
Eastern Europe and Central Asia	3	10	16
Developing world................	1,528	1,237	879
Region/ratio of poor people			
East Asia (of which China)	68.7 (73.5)	36.1 (37.7)	9.5 (8.1)
South Asia (of which India)	41.9 (42.1)	28.6 (31.1)	23.7 (24.3)
Sub-Saharan Africa	39.5	44.3	39.2
Middle East and North Africa.......	3.6	2.2	2.0
Latin America and Caribbean.......	7.4	7.3	5.0
Eastern Europe and Central Asia	0.7	2.1	3.4
Developing world................	41.7	27.0	16.1

Source: Chen and Ravallion (2008).

the $1.00 traditionally used by the World Bank. According to this definition, the number and percentage of poor people in the world is about 40 percent higher than at $1.00 (or $1.08) per day, but the decline in the number of poor people and as a percentage of the population of all developing countries remains very large indeed.

Conclusion

Thus, we arrive at the general conclusion that relative poverty seems to have increased around the world when measured by average national incomes across nations. Looking at individuals rather than nations as a whole, however, we find that the number of people who live in poverty (defined as those who live on less than $1.00 or $1.25 per day in terms of 1993 PPP) decreased significantly over the past two decades, but that most of this decrease occurred in China. In short, globalization can be (and has been especially for China) a force for reducing poverty in the world for those nations that take advantage of it (that is, that globalize). The challenge for the world is how to spread the gains from globalization to the poorest countries that did not globalize.

DISCUSSION QUESTIONS

1. Distinguish between the "static" and "dynamic" gains from specialization internationally.
2. What is outsourcing? Highlight some of the benefits and costs of outsourcing. Why do advocates of globalization argue that the benefits far outweigh the costs?
3. Some of the poorest countries in the world are the "non-globalizers." What factors might account for this?

SUGGESTED READINGS

Barro, Robert J., and Xavier Sala-i-Martin. 2004. *Economic growth.* 2nd ed. Cambridge, MA: MIT Press.

Bhagwati, Jagdish. 2004. *In defense of globalization.* New York: Oxford University Press.

Commission on Growth and Development. 2008. *The growth report: Strategies for sustained growth and inclusive development.* Washington, DC: World Bank.

Grilli, Enzo, and Dominick Salvatore. 1994. *Economic development.* Westport, CT: Greenwood Press.

IMF. 2008. World economic outlook and financial surveys: World economic outlook database. April 2008 ed. http://www.imf.org/external/pubs/ft/weo/2008/01/weodata/index.aspx.

Salvatore, Dominick. 1993. *Protectionism and world welfare.* New York: Cambridge University Press.

Salvatore, Dominick. 2004. International trade and economic development. *Institutions and Economic Development* (June): 543–551.

Stern, Nicholas. 2002. *A strategy for development.* Washington, DC: World Bank.

World Commission on the Social Dimension of Globalization. 2004. *A fair globalization.* Geneva: International Labour Organization.

ONLINE RESOURCES

Global Policy Forum. Globalization. http://www.globalpolicy.org/globaliz/index.htm.

International Monetary Fund (IMF). World economic crisis stalls globalization. http://www.imf.org/external/np/exr/Key/global.htm.

World Bank. 2001. Globalization. http://www1.worldbank.org/economicpolicy/globalization.

REFERENCES

Bhalla, Surjit S. 2002. *Imagine there's no country.* Washington, DC: Institute for International Economics.

Chen, Shaohua, and Martin Ravallion. 2008. The developing world is poorer than we thought, but no less successful in the fight against poverty. Policy Research Working Paper 4703, Development Research Group, World Bank.

Dollar, David, and Aron Kraay. 2001. Growth is good for the poor. Policy Research Working Paper 2587. Washington, DC: World Bank.

Pritchett, Lant. 1997. Divergence, big time. *Journal of Economic Perspectives* 3: 3–17.

Stiglitz, Joseph. 2002. *Globalization and its discontents.* New York: Norton.

United Nations. 2008. *Human development report.* New York: Oxford University Press.

World Bank. 2001. *World development report.* Washington, DC: World Bank.

World Bank. 2008a. *World development report.* New York: Oxford University Press.

World Bank. 2008b. *World development indicators.* Washington, DC: World Bank.

Globalization and Poverty: Why There Is Reason to Be Concerned

Manfred Bienefeld

Introduction and Summary

The question of how neo-liberal globalization[1] has affected global poverty and inequality has been intensely controversial and will undoubtedly remain so. The dominant view, which is closely associated with the World Bank (hereafter "the Bank") and is widely held in official development circles, claims that the evidence shows that globalization has accelerated growth and reduced global poverty on a historic scale. Others, looking at the same evidence, challenge these conclusions with varying degrees of enthusiasm, in some cases merely arguing that the evidence is not strong enough to sustain such claims, in others arguing that the evidence can lend support to the fear that globalization, in its current form, poses a serious potential threat to human and social welfare (Bello 2002; Bienefeld 2004; Chossudovsky 2005).

This essay is in two parts. The first reviews the data on global poverty trends, beginning with a critical examination of several key Bank studies that had a major impact on the debate at the beginning of the new millennium. The second shows that when the Bank turns to the problem of devising more effective policies to deal with poverty and inequality, it essentially abandons the highly unreliable, stylized facts underpinning the debate on global trends. Instead of focusing almost exclusively on individual income trends, it now recognizes that poverty and inequality must be understood not simply as economic problems but as problems of political economy.[2] And that reveals why globalization often exacerbates such problems.

Deconstructing the Evidence on Globalization, Poverty, and Inequality

The issues of poverty and inequality rose to prominence in the 1990s when the resumption of financial flows to the developing world appeared to generate renewed growth, but not development. Concern was widespread, as noted by the United Nations Conference on Trade and Development (UNCTAD) (1997b, overview 6):

341

The big story of the world economy since the early 1980s has been the unleashing of market forces. ... The "invisible hand" now operates globally and with fewer countervailing pressures from governments than for decades. ... [But] the world has been characterized by rising income inequality and slow growth. ... Polarization among countries has been accompanied by increasing income inequality within countries.

Potentially, "this poses a serious threat of political backlash against globalization, one that is as likely to come from the North as from the South" (UNCTAD 1997a, 1).

It was in this context that the Bank "rediscovered the state";[3] finally agreed to discuss debt relief;[4] shifted its priorities to focus on governance, popular participation, and poverty reduction;[5] and expanded its analytical and statistical work on poverty and income inequality.

Of course the Bank was not the ideal institution to be put in charge of this research, since it was clearly—and aggressively—committed to globalization (Wade 1994) and since it had already, together with the International Monetary Fund (IMF), published and promoted several studies endorsing neo-liberal reform and globalization based on unsuitable and problematic evidence.[6] In one such case, a study endorsing the impact of IMF reforms on poverty had admitted, in a passage buried deep in the report, that its conclusions were not based on the evidence but on "deductive reasoning" and on "the axiomatic acceptance of a J-curve in the economy's trajectory."[7] As a result, the perception that these reforms often lacked credible empirical support was widespread. Indeed, Stiglitz has argued that the IMF's enthusiasm for capital market liberalization must be understood "either as a matter of ideology or of special interests, and not on the basis of careful analysis of theory, historical experience or a wealth of econometric studies" (Stiglitz 2000, 1076), while Bhagwati famously suggested that the explanation must lie with the power of "the Wall Street–US Treasury complex" (Bhagwati 1998).

An examination of the debate on globalization and poverty must therefore recognize that on matters of such importance and complexity, interests will inevitably insert themselves into apparently scientific debates, pushing for certain methodologies, emphasizing certain results, and exercising judgments in particular ways. And this is as it should be, since, when the same evidence leads people to different conclusions, "this may not be due to a lack of understanding of the economic fundamentals so much as a different reading of the scientific evidence and, more important, a different weighting of the risks" (Stiglitz 1998, 25). And different interests will weigh risks differently.

In addition, it is worth remembering that economists tend to have a "predilection" for market-based solutions when they are reading evidence,[8] especially when deriving conclusions from the stylized world of comparative statics. And they are often reluctant to expand the boundaries of their discipline to incorporate other dimensions of reality into their analyses.

Interests and such predilections probably played a role in shaping several Bank studies (Dollar 2001; Dollar and Kraay 2001a; Dollar and Kraay 2001b; Dollar and Kraay 2002) that celebrated globalization's historic success in reducing poverty and concluded that, "This most recent wave of globalization, starting around 1980, represents the first time in history that there has been a large decline in the number of extreme poor in the world (people living on less than $1/day at PPP"[9] (Dollar 2001, 17).

In essence these studies celebrated the "integration of the world economy over the past twenty years" (Dollar and Kraay 2001b, under "Conclusion"), claiming that global integration "accelerates development" (Dollar 2001, 2), that "[b]ackward economies that integrate with the world tend to grow rapidly" (Dollar 2001, 23), and that "increased trade has strongly encouraged growth and poverty reduction" (Dollar and Kraay 2001b, first page). The studies described the "losers" as "developing countries that have not been able to seize the opportunities to participate in this process" (Dollar and Kraay 2001b, under "Conclusion") and implied that they had only themselves to blame, since "[w]eaknesses in institutions should not be an excuse to remain closed … [as] … countries can use the international market for services to improve economic governance" (Dollar 2001, 23).

Ultimately, these sweeping conclusions all rested on one observation—namely, that after 1980 the group of countries identified as "globalizers" had, on average, grown significantly faster (in per capita income, as measured at purchasing power parity (PPP) exchange rates) than non-globalizers (Figure 1). And because income inequality did not appear to have increased,[10] it was assumed that the benefits of this superior growth were shared by the poor in those countries, as also indicated by the Bank's poverty survey data.

However, the conclusions of these studies went far beyond what the evidence permitted.[11] Given the central emphasis on observed differences in average growth rates between globalizers and non-globalizers, much depended on whether the criterion used to define globalizers was analytically meaningful, relatively unambiguous, and rigorously applied. In fact, it was none of these things.

First, the criterion that was ultimately used—"growth in trade intensity"[12] between 1975 and 1979, and between 1995 and 1997—was analytically inappropriate, since it refers to a policy outcome, while the study was designed to assess a policy choice: "global integration." And when the authors used an alternative policy-based criterion to see whether trade intensity could serve as a reasonable proxy for trade policy, the alternative group of 26 globalizers included only 9 of the original group of 26.[13]

Second, the criterion was also highly ambiguous because both the proportion of countries to be included ("the top third") and the time period over which the change in trade intensity was measured (1975–1979 and 1995–1997) were quite arbitrarily selected, providing a disconcerting degree of leeway in the research

FIGURE 1   Real per Capita GDP Growth (at PPP Exchange Rates)

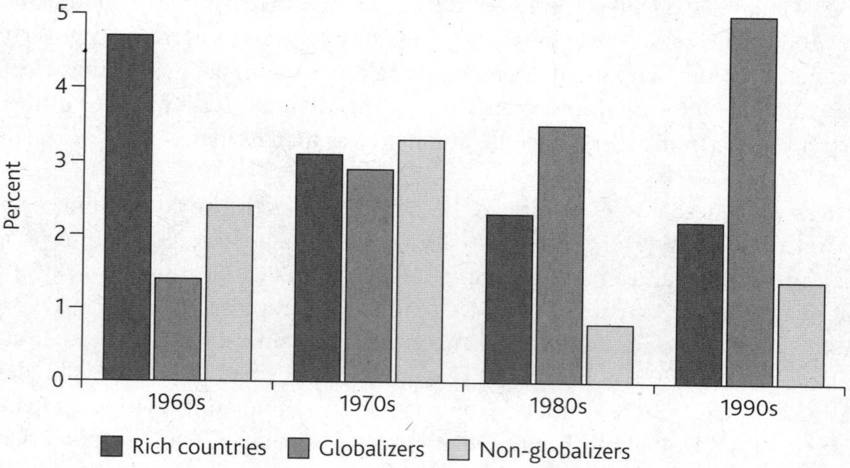

Source: Dollar and Kraay (2001a, 38, table 3).

protocol. Finally, to make matters worse, the chosen rules were not rigorously applied; when they were, the globalizers had "an undistinguished performance."[14]

The problems do not end here. Even if one takes the numbers at face value, the superior growth performance of the globalizers turns out to be a statistical illusion. The first reason for this is that the link between national policy choices and national growth rates is better reflected by unweighted than by weighted averages, and a comparison of unweighted averages shows no significant difference between the two groups. Both experienced relatively rapid growth in the 1960s and 1970s, then suffered a sharp decline in the 1980s followed by a partial recovery in the 1990s (Table 1).

In addition, even the higher (weighted) average growth rates of the globalizers cannot be ascribed to that group as a whole. The globalizers' superiority is due largely to China, whose 1990s growth rate (8.2 percent) was more than six times the average for the other globalizers (1.3 percent).[15] In fact, apart from China, there were 6 other countries experiencing rapid growth in this group,[16] and their superior performance needs to be understood. However, for the other 17 globalizers, there is no superior performance to be explained. Indeed, their average growth rate falls to just 0.1 percent, well below the 0.6 percent of the non-globalizers.[17]

Ultimately these numbers, even when they are taken at face value, provide no basis for celebrating neo-liberal globalization. What they show is that the vast majority of developing countries enjoyed relatively rapid growth in the 1960s and 1970s, followed by sharp reversals in the 1980s—the first neo-liberal decade—and then a modest, partial recovery in the 1990s. Meanwhile, the developed

TABLE 1 Average Annual per Capita GDP Growth (at PPP Exchange Rates)

	1960s	1970s	1980s	1990s
Rich countries				
Simple	4.4	3.6	2.6	2.4
Weighted	4.7	3.1	2.3	2.2
Globalizers				
Simple	2.3	3.1	0.5	2.0
Weighted	1.4	2.9	3.5	5.0
Non-globalizers				
Simple	2.5	2.4	0.1	0.6
Weighted	2.4	3.3	0.8	1.4

Source: Dollar and Kraay (2001a, 38, table 3).

countries suffered steadily declining growth rates; only China and India, together with a few other developing countries (mostly Asian), made major economic gains. Fortunately, as these countries contained a large proportion of the world's population, these gains raised many out of poverty. The main question posed by these numbers is therefore: How did those relatively successful countries manage to escape the negative trends otherwise associated with the era of accelerated globalization?[18]

Despite the initial impact of these studies, their claim that globalization is an ally and protector of the poor—let alone a guarantor of development success—has not been sustained. Indeed, today (2009) these studies remain significant mainly as a reminder that it is dangerous for research to be conducted, or financed, by interested parties. And at a time when publicly funded research is in retreat almost everywhere—with the Bank and the IMF playing an ever larger role in the field of development research—this is not an unimportant point, since the Bank continues to generate most of the numbers at the heart of this debate. In fact, a recent authoritative review of those numbers by Pogge and Reddy (2006, 1) has shown that the Bank's estimates of poverty and inequality continue to be deeply problematic:

> Estimates of the extent, distribution and trend of global income poverty [by the World Bank] are neither meaningful nor reliable. ... The systematic distortion introduced by ... three flaws[19] likely leads to a large understatement of the extent of global income poverty and to an incorrect inference that it has declined.

Of course we need to use the best numbers that we have, and we need to use them wisely. But in order to do so we must understand that internationally comparable poverty numbers are difficult and expensive to generate, highly unreliable (especially when produced by interested parties), highly sensitive to minor changes in definitions, and inevitably divorced from local policy processes. Much more emphasis should therefore be placed on generating numbers that understand poverty and inequality as policy problems within particular societies, reflecting the circumstances of those societies and using their definitions of social justice, based on their social, economic, and political priorities and their development objectives. That task will be briefly discussed in the next section. For now let us examine what the current international poverty numbers allow us to say, or to know.

The proportion of people living in extreme ("absolute income") poverty globally fell between 1980 and 2007, but solely because of the sharp decline achieved in the Asian region,[20] and especially in China. Indeed, with China excluded, the global number has increased marginally (see Table 2).

This is good news, but no cause for celebrating globalization. First because China's extraordinary success cannot be ascribed to globalization, if only because it is shared by so few others; second because absolute income poverty is a very narrow—some would say impoverished—definition of poverty, and relative poverty[21] has almost certainly increased globally (since within-country inequality has been rising—see below); and third because recent statistical revisions have wiped out many of these gains, even as the current crisis has revealed their precariousness in the real world.

The extreme precariousness of this international numbers game was dramatically highlighted recently when the application of newly revised (2005) PPP exchange rates raised the estimated number of individuals living in extreme poverty by more than 400 million, or by over 40 percent[22] (see Table 2). And although the Bank was quick to allay fears that this might call into question previously reported declines in global poverty by publishing a paper entitled "The Developing World Is Poorer Than We Thought, but No Less Successful in the Fight Against Poverty" (Chen and Ravallion 2008), this is hardly reassuring. Indeed, given the heroic assumptions that must be made when projecting these new estimates back in time, the brash confidence of the paper's title points to yet another instance of politically convenient conclusions that go well beyond what the evidence allows.

Bearing in mind the weakness of the data, it seems possible to say that the proportion of people living in extreme absolute income poverty globally has probably declined since 1980. However, even then, it is impossible to know the extent to which this represents an improvement in people's lives until we know the cost at which the implied income increases were achieved—in terms of social dislocation, insecurity, working conditions, or stress[23]—and until we can be sure that those income increases were not nullified or offset by losses suffered because of the reduced availability of goods or services from shrinking domestic or subsistence economies.[24]

Turning now to the issue of inequality, the question of how it has evolved since 1980 is even more contentious, if only because there are so many types of inequality.

TABLE 2   World Bank Estimates of Absolute Income Poverty (at PPP Exchange Rates)

	$1/day (1993 PPP)				$1.25/day (2005 PPP)			
	%		Million		%		Million	
Region	1981	2004	1981	2004	1981	2005	1981	2005
East Asia and Pacific	58	9	796	169	78	17	1,072	316
of which China	64	10	637	128	84	16	835	208
South Asia	50	31	455	446	59	40	548	596
of which India	52	34	364	371	60	42	421	456
Middle East and North Africa	5	1	9	4	8	4	14	11
Eastern Europe and Central Asia	1	1	3	4	2	4	7	17
Latin America and the Caribbean	11	9	39	47	12	8	42	46
Sub-Saharan Africa	42	41	168	298	54	51	214	391
Total	40	18	1,470	969	52	25	1,896	1,377
Total excluding China . . .	31	21	837	841	n/a	n/a	1,061	1,169

Sources: Ferreira and Ravallion (2008, tables 2 and 3, for 1993 PPP); Chen and Ravallion (2008, tables 7 and 8, for 2005 PPP).

The Bank agrees that certain types of inequality have clearly increased, including absolute inequality, unweighted intercountry inequality, within-country inequality,[25] and inequality at the extremes.[26] Meanwhile, global inequality[27] appears to have declined (see Sutcliffe 2003 for a detailed summary of various estimates)—an observation so often highlighted by advocates of globalization (Wolf 2004). However, as with the observed reductions in the incidence of extreme global income poverty, these reductions in global inequality cannot be ascribed to globalization, since they were almost entirely due to China's extraordinary success in raising the incomes of so many millions[28] (Figure 2). Moreover, recent PPP revisions have created significant uncertainty by sharply reducing the estimated national incomes of most developing countries—including 40 percent reductions for both China and India[29]—thereby sharply increasing estimates of current levels of global inequality.[30] And given the extreme difficulty of projecting the new PPP exchange rates backward through time, it may be impossible to establish the impact of these revisions on recent trends in global inequality.

In any event, those who believe that globalization may be promoting dangerous and destructive degrees of inequality and insecurity do not necessarily expect

FIGURE 2 Intercountry Inequality, 1950–2000

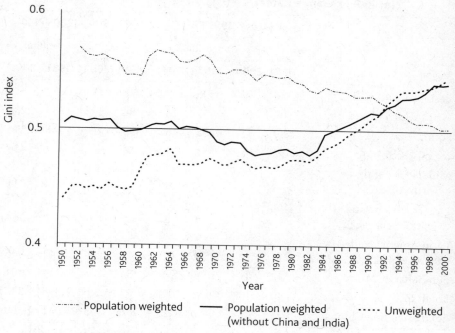

------ Population weighted   —— Population weighted   ····· Unweighted
                                           (without China and India)

Source: Ferreira and Ravallion (2008, 33).

all measures of global inequality to increase. Indeed, as incomes within the richest and poorest countries continue to polarize, one would expect an increasing overlap in national income dispersions, with quite unpredictable impacts on various measures of global inequality.[31] In such a world, even declining intercountry income inequality could turn out to be a mixed blessing if societies turned out to be converging on the conditions associated with "underdevelopment," as increasing proportions of people were excluded and marginalized in all of them.

Ultimately the most worrisome aspects of globalization include the continued growth of within-country inequality;[32] the polarization of incomes at the extremes; and the dramatic increase in corporate income and power, which is unaccountably absent from most of these discussions.

However, to assess the significance of these developments one needs to understand how the forces of globalization influence policy processes within individual societies[33]—that is, how they affect the social, institutional, ideological, and political forces that ultimately determine whether (and in what sense) poverty and inequality will be defined, and addressed, as serious policy problems. One needs, in other words, to turn to political economy.

A Political Economy Perspective on Globalization, Poverty, and Inequality

Although the Bank continues to focus attention on changes in individual absolute income poverty, it does accept that such indicators are only "useful for international benchmarking" (World Bank 2008, 1) and "not a substitute for national-level policy analysis ... for domestic policy purposes" (World Bank 2008, 2). And when it addresses those policy concerns, as it did in its 2006 *World Development Report* (World Bank 2006), it accepts the need for broader and more appropriate concepts of poverty and inequality, and the need to move the discussion squarely into the sphere of political economy.

Of course, in doing so, the Bank does not lose sight of its fundamental commitment to the empowerment of markets. And so, although it broadens the definition of poverty and inequality to include multiple forms of exclusion, it insists that public policy responses must not second-guess—or "distort"—market-determined outcomes. Hence, it suggests that "public action should focus on the distribution of assets, economic opportunities, and political voice, rather than directly on inequality of incomes" (World Bank 2006, 3). However, when addressing these fundamental questions of political economy, the Bank recognizes that disparities in income and power can create "inequality traps" in which "economic, political, and social inequalities tend to reproduce themselves over time" (World Bank 2006, 2). Hence,

> the primary focus of this report is on the instrumental relationship between equity and development, with particular emphasis on two channels: the effect of unequal opportunities when markets are imperfect, and the consequences of inequity for the quality of institutions a society develops. (World Bank 2006, 7)

Accordingly, much of the report focuses on the need to remove inequities in access to education, credit, and jobs. Consistent with the Bank's neo-liberal priorities, special emphasis is placed on the need for greater labour market flexibility to deal with the inequitable privileges enjoyed by formal sector workers over their informal sector counterparts, but with little concern for the impact of such policies on the balance of power between formal sector workers and their employers. Ultimately, the report reaches an important conclusion:

> Unequal power leads to the formation of institutions that perpetuate inequalities in power, status, and wealth—and that typically are also bad for the investment, innovation and risk-taking that underpin long-term growth. ... Basic patterns in cross-country data and historical narratives support the view that countries moving onto institutional paths that promoted sustained prosperity did so because the balance of political influence and power became more equitable. (World Bank 2006, 9)

349

Yes, indeed! In fact, slightly amended, this statement could serve as a summary of this paper's basic argument, namely:

> The massive and growing inequality of global power and wealth is leading to the emergence of integrated global institutions and structures that perpetuate and widen inequalities in power, status, and wealth—and that are typically also bad for the investment, innovation, and risk-taking that underpin long-term growth. Basic patterns in data and historical narratives support the view that the global system in the years following the Second World War (the Bretton Woods system, which was based on capital controls and managed exchange rates) promoted sustained prosperity, economic and financial stability, and social equity because it struck a more equitable and desirable balance between capital and labour, and between national and international interests.

Conclusion

The evidence, as summarized in this paper, provides reasons to be concerned about the welfare impact of globalization even though it is narrowly focused on the distribution of personal incomes and therefore ignores the main sources of increasing inequality in global power and wealth—namely, the explosive growth of global corporations[34] and of financial actors with access to previously unthinkable amounts of liquidity, whose interests increasingly dominate the global policy process. The fact that there has been some decline in the incidence of individual income poverty and in certain measures of individual global inequality does not begin to negate these concerns. Indeed, even when considering only individual incomes, the era of globalization has been associated with often significant increases in relative poverty, economic insecurity, within-country inequality, intercountry inequality, and absolute inequality, while modest improvements in the incidence and distribution of absolute income poverty turn out to be almost entirely due to China's transformation. Meanwhile, investment rates and growth have declined, and financial instability has become endemic—with potentially serious social and political implications for people and societies around the world.

Such concerns are reinforced by the fact that the main exceptions to these trends have been countries (mainly in East Asia) that have managed their global integration with great care—specifically, seeking to sustain a more reasonable balance between national and international interests, one that allowed them to protect their capacity to implement effective long-term national development strategies and to manage the distributional conflicts inevitably associated with growth and change.[35] And this includes China, whose cautious approach to financial integration continues to provide it with a significant degree of policy autonomy.

Of course history does not stand still, and the current global crisis may lead to a significant shift in the globalization process, hopefully restoring those "more equitable balances of political influence and power" that the World Bank—along with most of the rest of the world—is speaking of. Globalization will undoubtedly continue in some form. The question is how it will affect the balance of power between capital and labour, between capital and other social interests, between national and international interests, and—ultimately—between the demand for accumulation and profit and the demands for other human and social objectives, including environmental sustainability, social coherence, community harmony, and human freedom from insecurity and the tyranny of unstable, onerous, repetitive, ill-paid jobs. A different world is possible, as history has shown.

NOTES

1. In this paper "globalization" refers to *neo-liberal* globalization, defined as a process of global integration driven by "the unyielding promotion of an open global-market economy"—what *BusinessWeek* thought should be the main purpose of US military and diplomatic power following the Cold War (*BusinessWeek* 1994). "Neo-liberal" refers to instances when policy prescriptions derived from neoclassical theory are applied to the real world without adequate regard for the imperfections of the latter, as when Frank Hahn described Mrs. Thatcher and her advisers as saying "much more than even the pure theory allows them to say, and infinitely more than the applicability of that theory permits" (Hahn 1982, 20).

2. While neoclassical economics asks the static question of whether competitive markets allocate resources Pareto optimally at a given moment in time, political economy asks how real-world economies can promote human welfare. Political economy includes classical economics (once called political economy), the Austrian School (Hayek, von Mises, Schumpeter), Marxian economics, and institutional economics (Douglass North, Oliver Williamson). Williamson's definition of an institutional economist as an "economic archaeologist" studying how certain policy problems were handled in the past (Williamson 1994) makes the point that on this methodological terrain history is king, while mathematical models play only a minor role.

3. "Many have felt that a minimalist state would be the optimal solution … [but] the Report explains why this extreme view is at odds with the evidence of the world's development success stories, be it the development of the industrial economies in the nineteenth century or the post-war growth 'miracles' of East Asia. These examples show that development requires an effective state" (World Bank 1997, abstract).

4. The initial decision of international financial institutions (IFIs) to rule out debt relief in response to the Third World debt crisis was ethically indefensible (because it absolved creditors of all blame for the crisis), entailed great human costs (because it imposed enormous losses on many developing countries), and was economically unwise (because it ensured that the neo-liberal reforms subsequently attached as conditions to adjustment loans would be so relatively unsuccessful) (Bienefeld 1989).

5. In 1999 the Bank announced that its concessional lending would henceforth be based on Poverty Reduction Strategy Papers (PRSPs), which would "be formulated with government and with participatory processes" (World Bank 1999, 20). However, as these had to be based on "sound economic policies"—as defined by the Bank—this did not imply a break with earlier neo-liberal adjustment policies, and the evidence to date confirms that PRSPs have had little impact on underlying economic policy prescriptions (Piron and Evans 2004; Driscoll and Evans 2005).

6. See Bienefeld (2000) for a discussion of the problems with earlier Bank and IMF studies.

7. Deductive reasoning estimated the short-to-medium-term impact; "the axiomatic assumption of a J-curve" (that is, an initial decline followed by a steady increase) estimated the long-term impact (Heller et al. 1988, 8, 10).

8. This predilection can allow ideology to trump science, as when economists respond to evidence suggesting a need for market intervention by simply asserting that state intervention would "almost always" be worse. See Delong (2004, 6) for a telling example.

9. Purchasing power parity (PPP) exchange rates convert local currency into dollar equivalents when making welfare comparisons by estimating the amount of local currency needed to purchase goods and services equal to what US$1 can buy in the United States. Although the concept is important, the calculations are complex and highly uncertain.

10. "In a large sample of countries spanning the past four decades, we cannot reject the null hypothesis that the income share of the first quintile does not vary systematically with average incomes" (Dollar and Kraay 2002, 196).

11. Numerous critiques have been levelled at these studies, and this discussion builds on these to varying degrees (Weisbrot 2001; Rodrik 2000; Nye, Reddy, and Watkins 2002; Wade 2005; Pogge and Reddy 2006).

12. Globalizers were defined as "the top third" (of a group of 73 developing countries for which data were available beginning in the 1970s) "in terms of their growth in trade as a share of GDP in constant prices between 1975–79 and 1995–97" (Dollar and Kraay 2001a, 8).

13. The alternative group was defined as "the top one-third of tariff cutters"—unaccountably measured over a different period (Dollar and Kraay 2001a, 8). The 9 countries common to both groups were Argentina, Brazil, China, Bangladesh, India, Colombia, Uruguay, Thailand, and Nicaragua. The implication is that the link between trade policy and trade outcomes is rather weak.

14. According to Rodrik, the studies "include in their list 6 additional countries (out of 18) that do not fit the stated criteria"; when the decision rule is rigorously applied, one gets "a very different picture" (Rodrik 2000, 1–2).

15. This is an unweighted average.

16. Three geographically contiguous pairs of countries: India/Bangladesh, Malaysia/Thailand, and Argentina/Uruguay.

17. Unweighted averages (from Dollar and Kraay 2002, table 3). Weighted averages would not change the basic point being made.
18. China and India cannot be used as examples of long-term neo-liberal development. While both have liberalized their economies, India is building on a base created during a long period of state intervention and retains many key financial controls, while China remains a relatively statist economy, especially in finance and industry.
19. Namely: "The Bank uses an arbitrary international poverty line unrelated to any clear conception of what poverty is. It employs a misleading and inaccurate measure of purchasing power 'equivalence' that vitiates international and intertemporal comparisons of income poverty. It extrapolates incorrectly from limited data and thereby creates an appearance of precision that masks the high probable error of its estimates" (Pogge and Reddy 2006, abstract).
20. Including the Middle East/North Africa region.
21. Poverty is generally defined in relative terms in the developed world and in most discussions of social justice. Absolute income poverty is more appropriate as a concept of "minimum subsistence."
22. The increase would have been higher if the new equivalent poverty line had been defined in the usual way, by applying US inflation rates to the 1993 line. In this case, the new line would then have been $1.45/day and the number of poor would have risen by 782 million. Instead, the Bank chose a new line of $1.25/day based on changes in "mean poverty lines in the 15 poorest countries in the world" (Chen and Ravallion 2008, 11).
23. And there is evidence to suggest that these aspects of people's lives have deteriorated in much of the developing world as informal sectors grow, migration increases, and financial crises become endemic (ILO 2009; UNDP 2005).
24. Ironically, one reason why PPP exchange rates differ from official rates is that many goods and services continue to be produced within networks that are not fully monetized, or that operate within parallel economies.
25. "The last two decades in the twentieth century saw resumption in the upward trajectory of within-country inequality" (Ferreira and Ravallion 2008, 13–14).
26. The gap between the richest and poorest 1 percent of the world's population rose sharply between 1980 and 2000, from 216:1 to 415:1, according to one estimate, and from 214:1 to 360:1, according to another (Sutcliffe 2003, 27).
27. There are two measures of global inequality, one based on all global individual incomes (which reflects intercountry and within-country inequality) and the other based on population-weighted national average per capita incomes (which ignores within-country inequality).
28. "Once China and India are excluded from the international distribution, the post-1980 trend ... changes dramatically, and becomes much closer to the rising trend in intercountry inequality" (Ferreira and Ravallion 2008, 13).
29. China: −39 percent; India: −40 percent; Bangladesh: −37 percent; Philippines: −41 percent; South Africa: −32 percent; and Indonesia: −17 percent. But at

the same time, Nigeria: +58 percent; Mexico: +9 percent; and Russia: +7 percent (Milanovic 2007, 3).

30. It is estimated that unweighted intercountry inequality rises by 2.6 Gini points, weighted international inequality by 6.3 Gini points (3.6 points if China is excluded), and global inequality by 4.2 Gini points (Milanovic 2007).

31. Firebaugh (2008, 2) has argued that the "[f]ixation on whether global inequality is rising or falling is misplaced because it misses the singular feature of global inequality today: its changing contour. ... [T]he richer regions are no longer the growth leaders ... [and] at the same time, inequality is rising within many, but not all countries in the West and elsewhere ... [which] implies that the link between nationality and income will diminish over time." But this overstates the degree to which intercountry inequality is falling and ignores the possibility that the deeper global integration of developing countries may hamper their capacity to develop (Wade 2004, 11).

32. This includes the industrial world. From 1985 to 2005 the Gini coefficient for all OECD countries rose by 12 percent (at market incomes) and by 9 percent (after social transfers) (OECD 2008, 5). Meanwhile in the United States, real earnings for production workers have stagnated or fallen since 1974 (Collins, Leondar-Wright, and Sklar 1999).

33. In 2000, a comprehensive review of the literature on the link between inequality and growth concludes: "It seems to us far better to focus directly on policies, or combination of policies, which will generate growth without adverse distributional effects, rather than rely on the existence or nonexistence of an aggregative, reduced form relationship between per capita income and inequality" (World Bank 2006, 44).

34. Anderson and Cavanagh (2000) report that the top 200 corporations' combined sales are bigger than the combined economies of all countries minus the biggest 9; that is, they surpass the combined economies of 182 countries.

35. This is the feature identified by Rodrik as the one most consistently associated with successful development in recent decades (Rodrik 1999).

DISCUSSION QUESTIONS

1. Consider and explain how uncertainty—about the definition of poverty, the way to measure and compare incomes, the way to allow for non-monetary gains and/or losses—can be used by interested parties to their advantage.

2. Critically evaluate the following claim: "Poverty should not be considered an economic policy problem. People's rewards should be determined by the market value of their contribution to society. Deviations from this rule will impose welfare losses on society that cannot be economically justified. Of course, as people, or citizens, economists can have opinions about whether such welfare losses might be deemed acceptable for ethical, or political, reasons."

SUGGESTED READINGS AND ONLINE RESOURCES

Frank, Robert H. 2007. *Falling behind: How rising inequality harms the middle class.* Berkeley: University of California Press.

Pogge, Thomas. 2009. How world poverty is measured and tracked. Applied Statistics Papers, Columbia University. http://applied.stat.columbia.edu/papers/ThomasPogge_project.pdf.

Sutcliffe, Bob. 2003. A more or less unequal world? World income distribution in the 20th century. PERI Working Paper 54, Political Economy Research Institute, University of Massachusetts at Amherst.

Wade, Robert. 2008. Globalization, growth, poverty, inequality, resentment and imperialism. In *Global political economy*, 2nd ed., ed. John Ravenhill, 373–409. Oxford: Oxford University Press.

REFERENCES

Anderson, Sarah, and John Cavanagh. 2000. Top 200: The rise of corporate global power. http://www.corpwatch.org/article.php?id=377.

Bello, Walden. 2002. *Deglobalization: Ideas for a new world economy.* Halifax: Fernwood Books.

Bhagwati, Jagdish. 1998. The capital myth: The difference between trade in widgets and dollars. *Foreign Affairs* (May–June): 7–12.

Bienefeld, Manfred. 1989. A time of growing disparities. In *Canada among nations 1988: The Tory record*, ed. B.W. Tomlin and M. Molot, 125–148. Toronto: Lorimer.

Bienefeld, Manfred. 2000. Structural adjustment: Debt collection device or development policy? *Review* (Fernand Braudel Center) XXIII (4): 533–587.

Bienefeld, Manfred. 2004. Capitalism and the nation state in the dog days of the twentieth century. In *The globalization decade*, ed. Leo Panitch, Colin Leys, Alan Zuege, and Martijn Konings, 44–79. Halifax, NS: Fernwood Books. First published in the *Socialist Register 1994.*

BusinessWeek. 1994. Editorial. January 17: 102.

Chen, Shaohua, and Martin Ravallion. 2008. The developing world is poorer than we thought, but no less successful in the fight against poverty. Policy Research Working Paper 4703, Development Research Group, World Bank.

Chossudovsky, Michel. 2005. *The globalization of poverty and the new world order.* Ottawa: Global Research.

Collins, Chuck, Betsy Leondar-Wright, and Holly Sklar. 1999. *Shifting fortunes: The perils of the growing American wealth gap.* Boston: United for a Fair Economy.

Delong, J. Bradford. 2004. Should we still support untrammelled capital mobility? Or are capital controls less evil than we once believed? *Economists' Voice* 1 (1): article 1.

Dollar, David. 2001. Globalization, inequality, and poverty since 1980. Development Research Group, World Bank. http://www.sfu.ca/~akaraiva/e455/dollar-glob.pdf.

Dollar, David, and Aart Kraay. 2001a. Trade, growth, and poverty. Policy Research Working Paper 2615, Development Research Group, World Bank.

Dollar, David, and Aart Kraay. 2001b. Trade, growth, and poverty. *Finance and Development* 38 (3). http://www.imf.org/external/pubs/ft/fandd/2001/09/dollar.htm.

Dollar, David, and Aart Kraay. 2002. Growth is good for the poor. *Journal of Economic Growth* 7 (3): 195–225.

Driscoll, R., with A. Evans. 2005. Second-generation poverty reduction strategies: New opportunities and emerging issues. *Development Policy Review* 23 (1): 5–25.

Ferreira, F., and M. Ravallion. 2008. Global poverty and inequality: A review of the evidence. Policy Research Working Paper 4623, Development Research Group, World Bank.

Firebaugh, Glenn. 2008. Debate about global income inequality trends—Firebaugh response to Wade critique. http://ucatlas.ucsc.edu/blog/?p=55.

Hahn, Frank. 1982. Reflections on the invisible hand. *Lloyds Bank Review* 142 (April): 1–21.

Heller, P.S., A.L. Bovenberg, T. Catsambas, Ke-Young Chu, and P. Shome. 1988. The implications of fund-supported adjustment programs for poverty. IMF Occasional Paper 58.

International Labour Organization (ILO). 2009. *2008/09 Global wage report: Minimum wages and collective bargaining.* Geneva: ILO.

Milanovic, Branko. 2007. An even higher global inequality than previously thought: A note on global inequality calculations using the 2005 ICP results. Policy Research Working Paper Series, Development Research Group, World Bank.

Nye, Howard, Sanjay Reddy, and Kevin Watkins. 2002. Dollar and Kraay on "Trade, growth, and poverty": A critique. http://www.maketradefair.com/en/assets/english/finalDKcritique.pdf.

OECD. 2008. Are we growing unequal? New evidence on changes in poverty and incomes over the past 20 years. Media brief. Paris: OECD. http://www.oecd.org/dataoecd/48/56/41494435.pdf.

Piron, Laure-Hélène, with Alison Evans. 2004. Politics and the PRSP approach: Synthesis paper. Working Paper 237. London: ODI. http://www.odi.org.uk/resources/download/1363.pdf.

Pogge, Thomas, and Sanjay Reddy. 2006. Unknown: The extent, distribution and trend of global income poverty. Working Paper Series, Columbia University, Institute for Social and Economic Research and Policy.

Rodrik, Dani. 1999. The new global economy and developing countries: Making openness work. ODC Policy Essay 24. Washington, DC: Overseas Development Council.

Rodrik, Dani. 2000. Comments on "Trade, growth, and poverty," by D. Dollar and A. Kraay. http://ksghome.harvard.edu/~drodrik/Rodrik%20on%20Dollar-Kraay.PDF.

Stiglitz, Joseph. 1998. More instruments and broader goals: Moving toward the post-Washington consensus. 1998 Annual WIDER Lecture, Helsinki, January 7.

Stiglitz, Joseph. 2000. Capital market liberalization, economic growth, and instability. *World Development* 28 (6): 1075–1086. http://cas.umkc.edu/econ/AFEE/ stiglitz.pdf.

Sutcliffe, Bob. 2003. A more or less unequal world? World income distribution in the 20th century. PERI Working Paper 54, Political Economy Research Institute, University of Massachusetts at Amherst.

United Nations Conference on Trade and Development (UNCTAD). 1997a. UNCTAD sounds warning on globalization, advocates policies to counter economic polarization and growing income inequality. UNCTAD Press Release TAD/INF/PR/9712, August 25. http://www.unctad.org/Templates/ Webflyer.asp?docID=3303&intItemID=2068&lang=1.

United Nations Conference on Trade and Development (UNCTAD). 1997b. *Trade and development report, 1997*. Geneva: UNCTAD.

United Nations Development Programme (UNDP). 2005. *Human development report 2005*. Geneva: UNDP.

Wade, Robert. 1994. Japan, the World Bank, and the art of paradigm maintenance: The East Asian miracle in political perspective. *New Left Review* 217 (May– June): 3–37.

Wade, Robert. 2004. Inequality and globalization: Comment on Firebaugh and Goesling. eScholarship Repository. http://www.soc.iastate.edu/sapp/ GlobalizationOutcomes6.pdf.

Wade, Robert. 2005. Global inequalities: What is all the fuss about? For American Political Science Association Task Force on Inequality, University of Virginia, Charlottesville, April 22–23. http://www.apsanet.org/imgtest/ TaskForceDiffIneqDevWade.pdf.

Weisbrot, M., D. Baker, R. Naiman, and G. Neta. 2001. Growth may be good for the poor—But are IMF and World Bank policies good for growth? A closer look at the World Bank's recent defense of its policies. CEPR (Center for Economic and Policy Research). http://www.cepr.net/documents/publications/ econ_growth_2001_05.htm.

Williamson, Oliver. 1994. The institutions and governance of economic development and reform. In *Proceedings of the World Bank annual conference on development economics*, 171–208. Washington, DC: World Bank.

Wolf, Martin. 2004. *Why globalization works: The case for the global market economy*. New Haven, CT: Yale University Press.

World Bank. 1997. *World development report 1997: The state in a changing world*. Washington, DC: World Bank. http://publications.worldbank.org/ ecommerce/catalog/product?item_id=203593.

World Bank. 1999. Building poverty reduction strategies in developing countries. http://siteresources.worldbank.org/INTPRS1/Resources/ 383606-1092340662634/build_en.pdf.

World Bank. 2006. *World development report 2006: Equity and development.* Washington, DC: World Bank.

World Bank. 2008. Revised internationally-comparable poverty estimates for ECA countries. *Europe and Central Asia Region Poverty Team Quarterly Newsletter* 25 (October): 1–2.

Glossary

Bretton Woods
A conference was held at Bretton Woods, New Hampshire in July 1944 to set up institutions and procedures to manage international economic relations. The Bretton Woods Agreements gave birth to institutions such as the International Monetary Fund and the International Development and Reconstruction Bank, which is now part of the World Bank. It is also known for the particular exchange rate regime that was put in place, in which the price of gold was fixed in US dollars and countries tied themselves to the US dollar through a system of fixed (but adjustable) exchange rates.

Budget deficit
A situation where a government's (or company's or individual's) expenditures exceed its receipts over a specified period of time.

Capacity utilization
The extent to which a business, factory, or nation uses its productive capacity to create goods or services.

Capital control
A government policy that regulates the inflow and outflow of international capital.

Central bank
Also known as a "reserve bank," an institution that is often considered the government's bank and acts as a lender of last resort to provide liquidity to private financial institutions (for example, commercial banks). Its main task is to implement monetary policy by setting the leading rate of interest.

Chartalism
Also known as the "state theory of money," a monetary theory that claims that money is a debt–credit relationship and derives its value from the fact that tax liabilities must be discharged in the unit of account chosen by the state.

Chicago School
A school of thought associated with the names of Milton Friedman, George Stigler, and Henry Simons, all of strong neoclassical pedigree, who held strong libertarian views about private sector regulation, with the possible exception of the monetary domain, where they remained committed to a government-regulated central bank, which, they maintained, should not engage in discretionary monetary policy and should follow a set rule about money supply growth.

Circuit theory

A theoretical macroeconomic framework whose emphasis is on the importance of bank credit and the circular nature of credit creation/destruction. The first part of the circuit process (the flux, or the monetary creation stage) begins with entrepreneurs borrowing money (credit) from the banks and using it for various payments related to the production of goods and services. The second part (the reflux, or the monetary "destruction" stage) is when the entrepreneurs sell their products for money, which they use to pay back their loans. In the process, they make a profit.

Commodity money

A view that considers money to be a tangible object, whose intrinsic value and physical characteristics qualify it as a medium of exchange. The usual examples are gold and silver. The peculiarity of a commodity money system is that money appears an asset without being at the same time a liability.

Comparative advantage

The gain that a country can obtain by specializing in the production and export of those commodities that it can produce at a lower relative opportunity cost than its trading partners, and by importing all other commodities.

Convergence

An assumption often connected with the neoclassical paradigm, according to which disparities (among individuals or countries) in income or growth will be eliminated in the long run.

Credit money

Money that comes into existence whenever there is an agent who is willing to become a debtor and another one who is willing to become a creditor. For this reason, Chartalists and monetary circuit theorists argue that historically money has always been a debt–credit relationship. A credit money system is one in which money appears as both an asset and a liability.

Crowding in

Occurs when public investment (or public spending in general) stimulates private investment.

Crowding out

Occurs when public investment (or public spending in general) discourages or replaces private investment.

Currency union

Two or more countries sharing a single currency that is controlled by one central bank. For example, a number of EU countries have formed this type of monetary union and share the euro, which is controlled by the European Central Bank.

Depreciation

The decline in the value of a currency through market interactions in the foreign exchange markets.

Depression
A severe economic downturn that can last for several years and causes a drop in all economic activity. It is typically characterized by very high unemployment, excess supply of goods and services, falling or stagnant prices and wages, and undermined consumer and investor confidence.

Devaluation
A decision by the government to lower the international value of the country's currency in the foreign exchange markets.

Displacement
A situation in which one market agent (for example, a powerful transnational corporation) forces another market agent (for example, a small local company) to either move out or disappear.

Distortions
A term used to describe a situation in which the imposition of rules and regulations are seen as obstacles to the functioning of free markets.

Dollarization
The process by which a country chooses to eliminate its own currency and adopt that of another one. Usually, it is the US dollar that is adopted, but it can also be any other major currency.

Effective demand
In macroeconomics, the aggregate real expenditures of households (consumption spending), firms (investment spending), government (public spending), or foreigners (net exports), which constrains the amount of overall goods and services that can effectively be sold in an economy.

Endogenous money
A view according to which the supply of money is necessarily determined by the demand for it from private agents, namely, households and firms.

Equalization
A process by which the returns (or earnings) of factors of production (labour or capital) are made equal because of mobility and competition.

Exogenous money
A view according to which the supply of money (and therefore the amount of liquidity that the private sector shall have) can be set independently by the central bank.

Fiat money
Money that has value not because it is a valuable commodity but because the state says it must be accepted by "fiat" or law for all transactions in the country. All modern money is fiat money.

Fixed-exchange-rate system
An exchange rate system in which the international price of a currency is fixed in relation to another currency. Under a fixed-exchange-rate system, a country's central bank must always stand ready to buy or sell a country's currency in the foreign exchange markets to maintain/defend its value.

Flexible-exchange-rate system
Also called a "floating-exchange-rate system," an exchange rate system in which the value of a currency changes because of the international conditions of supply and demand for the country's currency.

Free enterprise (or free market)
An approach to business that emphasizes the freedom of private individuals or businesses to operate and maximize profits, with minimal government regulation or interference.

Free trade
Trade between countries that is not subject to government rules and regulations.

Functional finance
A system in which the fiscal balance of the government (surplus/deficit) varies so as to achieve a target (or full) employment level of output; originally proposed by the Keynesian economist Abba Lerner in the 1940s.

General Agreement on Tariffs and Trade (GATT)
An international agency that existed from 1947 to 1994, at which time it was superseded by the World Trade Organization. Its main objective was the reduction of trade barriers.

Globalization
The process of increasing economic (and social) integration among countries, usually through trade and investment, leading to the emergence of a single global market.

Gold standard
A system in which countries fix the price of a specified weight of gold in their respective currencies and stand ready to defend its domestic price, thereby establishing a fixed-exchange-rate system internationally that is tied to gold. Concurrently, at the domestic level, each country would ensure convertibility of its national currency in terms of gold upon which the domestic emission of the currency is based.

Government securities
Bonds, treasury bills, and other debt instruments that are sold by a government to private agents. They are considered the safest assets.

Gross domestic product (GDP)
The market value of all final goods and services produced by a country in a given period, usually a year. The rate of its growth is often used to measure the performance of the economy.

Horizontal (or flat) Phillips curve
Whereas the Phillips curve assumes an inverse relationship between unemployment and inflation rates, or a trade-off between unemployment and inflation, some recent empirical evidence has shown that, over a significant range, the lowering of unemployment has occurred without any change in the rate of inflation, thereby establishing an important horizontal segment.

Hot money
Volatile, short-term capital that is moved quickly by its owner from one investment to another, or from country to country, to take advantage of changing exchange rates or high short-term return rates.

Household debt
Debt that is held by households, individually or collectively, as opposed to corporate debt or public debt held by the government. Examples of household debt are mortgages, loans, and credit card debt.

Hyperinflation
Very high (or out-of-control) inflation in which prices increase rapidly, leading to serious or even catastrophic devaluation of a country's currency and severe economic dislocation, with people progressively engaging in barter.

Hysteresis
A situation in which, after a strong demand shock, the long-term rate of unemployment (or the non-accelerating inflation rate of unemployment) does not return to its initial level.

Income distribution
The sharing of the national income among the major social classes, namely, the workers, the capitalists (or entrepreneurs), and the money lenders (also referred to as the rentiers).

Inflation
A persistent increase in the price of goods and services in an economy. It is usually measured by the rate of change of the consumer price index or other related indexes, such as the GDP deflator.

Inflation targeting
A policy undertaken by the central bank of a country such as a decision to increase interest rates in an attempt to bring inflation down to a predetermined target rate or range.

Interest rate
The price charged to a borrower for a loan, usually a percentage of the amount loaned. The *nominal interest rate* is the rate of interest before adjustment for inflation.

Interest rate parity
A situation in which the return from holding an asset to maturity in one currency is equal to the return from holding a similar asset in another currency while considering exchange rate risk.

International Monetary Fund (IMF)
An institution designed to lower trade barriers between countries, stabilize currencies, and lend money to developing nations.

Involuntary unemployment
The case in which workers who are able and willing to work cannot find jobs at existing conditions of employment.

Laissez-faire
The economic doctrine that advocates limited government involvement in the economy and stresses the importance of economic freedom (free market and free enterprise) in achieving the best social outcome.

Liquidity
Of assets, the ability to convert from one asset to another with minimum losses to the holder with a ready group of willing buyers at minimal time. The most liquid of assets is money.

Market failure
A situation in which markets fail to produce the desired results. Examples include low supply of goods and services because of a monopoly, high prices because of the collusive behaviour of firms, or unemployment because of a deficiency in aggregate demand. Negative externalities such as pollution can also be regarded as market failures.

Monetarism
Also referred to as the "quantity theory of money," the view that it is movements in the money supply that have a causal influence on nominal income and that, while in the short run these could have an effect on output, in the long run they can only affect prices. Given the powerful long-run effects on inflation, monetarism argues that it is best to prevent central banks from engaging in discretionary monetary policy.

Monetization
A situation in which the central bank accepts to extend credit (money) to the government. The government uses this credit to pay for its expenditures. The government's debt toward the central bank is symbolized by bonds, which are held by the central bank.

Money supply
The total amount of money in circulation within a country's economy at a specific point in time. The most frequently referred to definition of the money supply is currency in circulation plus all chequable deposits in the banking system.

Moral hazard
A situation that arises because individual agents take decisions without assuming the full consequences of their actions and leave others with some responsibility. For example, the holding of insurance may encourage individuals to be less careful in their behaviour because the cost is incurred by their insurance company. The behaviour is associated with the existence of information asymmetry.

Natural rate of unemployment
A term originally coined by Milton Friedman, it is the unemployment rate consistent with a labour market state in which there is equilibrium of supply and demand in all labour and product markets with no tendency for wages and other costs to rise in excess of people's expectations of inflation. In practice, it is often treated synonymously with the non-accelerating inflation rate of unemployment (NAIRU).

Neo-liberalism
A policy perspective that promotes the doctrines of classical liberalism in the contemporary world. The basic principles of neo-liberalism are free (or deregulated) markets, with minimal state intervention, and free trade in goods, services, and capital.

Nominal interest rate
See *Interest rate*.

Non-accelerating inflation rate of unemployment (NAIRU)
A steady rate of unemployment that does not cause inflation to increase or accelerate.

Optimal currency area
The grouping of regions or countries in order to better absorb international demand- and supply-side shocks, through the adoption of a single currency or fixed exchange rates.

Optimality
The best possible outcome taking into account some constraints or considerations.

Perfect capital mobility
The ability of international investors to move their money freely from one country to another without any restrictions.

Phillips curve
A relationship that links inflation to unemployment, usually depicted graphically as a downward-sloping curve.

Poverty line
The minimum level of income that is seen as being required in order to provide an adequate standard of living in a country.

Profitability
A measure of the profit that an investor, company, or industry can generate through commercial activities, based on revenues as compared to all costs associated with that investment or the production of goods.

Quantitative easing
Essentially, the purchasing of securities in the financial markets to increase the volume of reserves (or positive settlement balances) in the monetary system to encourage bank lending to the public; this has occurred when central banks have reached a zero lower bound to nominal interest rates, as in Japan during the 1990s and the United States and Canada during 2008–9.

Recession
A period of general economic decline, usually defined as a decline in GDP occurring for two or more consecutive quarters; a business cycle contraction.

Regulation
A form of government intervention designed to influence the behaviour of firms and individuals in the private sector. Regulation can be aimed at narrowing choices in certain areas, including regulating prices (for example, minimum wages, telephone rates), supply (broadcasting licences, agricultural production quotas), or disclosure of information (food content labelling).

Saving rate
The share of income that is not spent.

Social cohesion
A term used primarily in sociology and political science to describe the bonds that bring and hold diverse groups of people together. It is widely accepted that economic factors such as employment, education, housing, and health care play fundamental roles in ensuring social cohesion.

Speculation
The buying and selling of all types of commodities and/or assets with the hope of making a monetary gain from the fluctuation in prices.

Structural unemployment rate

A long-term unemployment rate that comes from the mismatching between the skills that employees possess and the job vacancy characteristics. These mismatchings can also result because of industrial and geographic dispersions of unemployed people and jobs.

Subsidies

Financial assistance granted by a government in support of an enterprise, business, or economic sector, usually deemed to be in the public interest.

Tariff

A tax paid on imported goods and services.

Technology transfer

The sharing of technology, industrial expertise, and other knowledge among governments and other institutions to ensure that any scientific and technological developments are easily accessible to a wider range of people, who can then further adapt or develop the technology for new applications or products.

Tobin tax

A suggested tax on all foreign currency exchanges; proposed by economist James Tobin in the 1970s.

Unfair competition

Any action used to gain a commercial advantage through false, fraudulent, or unethical conduct or trade practice.

Voluntary unemployment

Unemployment that results when workers refuse to work for wages that are unacceptably low such as below the minimum wage; such workers are considered to be voluntarily unemployed.

World Bank

Set up at the end of the Second World War in Bretton Woods together with the International Monetary Fund, an institution that manages funds from its member countries by managing several types of funding mechanisms geared to providing loans and grants to countries mostly in the developing world that are facing debt-servicing problems. It also provides infrastructure, human development, and technical assistance to developing countries with the aim of reducing poverty.

World Trade Organization (WTO)

An international organization designed to manage mainly transactions in international trade (in commodities) but its activities also cover international financial transactions such as investment by transnational corporations.

Index

U